THE GUNSMOKE CHRONICLES

A NEW HISTORY OF TELEVISION'S GREATEST WESTERN

BY DAVID R. GREENLAND

The Gunsmoke Chronicles: A New History of Television's Greatest Western

© 2013 David R. Greenland

For information, address:

BearManor Media
P. O. Box 71426
Albany, GA 31708

bearmanormedia.com

Book design and layout by Valerie Thompson

Published in the USA by BearManor Media

ISBN—1-59393-733-4
978-1-59393-733-1

TABLE OF CONTENTS

DEDICATION

To **BARRY CRAIG** (1952–2011)

My oldest friend and the first
Gunsmoke *fan I ever met.*

ACKNOWLEDGMENTS

Since 1989 there have been at least three books devoted to *Gunsmoke*, all of them worthwhile, each with its own unique perspective. So, one might logically ask, why write another? Simply stated, there remains a wealth of interesting and important—as well as overlooked—information about this legendary series that has never been compiled in one source. Considering that *Gunsmoke* was on the air for an incredible two decades, generating a massive amount of publicity and commentary, this is understandable.

Of course a project of this magnitude cannot be accomplished alone. In addition to welcome encouragement from various friends and relatives, I was fortunate to have the active assistance of the following: Barbara Douglass, Claude Faulkner, Sandy Grabman, Paul Greenland, Jeff Kadet, Angela Mantley, Milton T. Moore, Michelle Morgan, Ben Ohmart, Richard Stanford, Valerie Thompson, Lanny Tucker, Dan Turpin, and Morgan Woodward. Special thanks to my wife, Cleo, who has always tolerated my habit of usually spending Saturday afternoon watching classic television Westerns.

Among those no longer among the living, I will always be most grateful for the cooperation of Peggy Rea, Jeremy Slate and Dennis Weaver.

For their pioneering work on the subject at hand, I offer a tip of the Stetson to fellow *Gunsmoke* scribes SuzAnne Barabas, Gabor Barabas, Ben Costello, and John Peel. This book is intended to complement, not replace, their fine work. In order to avoid redundancy and include as much neglected or fresh material as possible, I referred to the earlier books only when absolutely necessary.

Thanks also to Boyd Magers, editor and publisher of the always essential Western Clippings, which no Western enthusiast should be without.

Unless otherwise indicated, most of the photographs in this book were distributed to various media outlets by the CBS Television Network. These were obtained from private collectors or memorabilia dealers. No copyright ownership by the author is claimed or implied.

DAVID R. GREENLAND
MARCH 2013

PREFACE

This book could conceivably have been the first history of *Gunsmoke*. In 1977, two years after the final network broadcast, I began gathering all of the material relating to the series that I had collected since at least as far back as 1964 and proceeded to seek out even more. The late Dennis Weaver was kind enough to send me a publicity photo, along with his professional resume. I even spoke to a security guard at CBS Studio City who shared his impressions of the cast ("Knew 'em all!") and told me how sorry they were when the show was canceled ("They all wanted it to continue!"). However, life and other projects took precedence, always keeping the Dodge City saga on the proverbial back burner. By 2006 three books about the show had reached the marketplace, and even I conceded that the world did not need another. Yet readers who enjoyed my *Bonanza: A Viewer's Guide to the TV Legend* (and, more recently, *Rawhide: A History of Television's Longest Cattle Drive*) urged me to reconsider, so I took a second look at the several boxes of research and memorabilia that had been gathering dust in a corner of my home office. Afterward, I came to the conclusion that there was indeed more to be said about *Gunsmoke*. Happily, my publisher agreed.

Although I did not become a faithful viewer of the series until it expanded to an hour in 1961 (and CBS began rerunning the half-hour episodes as *Marshal Dillon*), it seems as if *Gunsmoke* has always been a part of my life. The example I give most often: My wife was born exactly nine months to the day after the September 10, 1955 premiere, and by the time the show ended in 1975, we had been married for almost a year. Growing up in the 1950s and early 1960s, my two younger brothers and I acquired our fair share of the merchandise that was part of the television Western stampede, the majority—Dodge City play set, Matt Dillon gun and holster, Matt Dillon figure and horse, comic books, etc.—*Gunsmoke*-related. In the summer of 1968, my family visited Dodge City, Kansas, where I had my picture taken outside the Long Branch Saloon. The next year, I purchased an original laminated brick from Front Street (#A 1712) being sold through *TV Guide*. Today, the six collector plates painted by Dick Bobnick and released by Royal Doulton in 1994 sit prominently on a shelf in my living room, and I have turned down offers for the 110 *Gunsmoke* trading cards issued by Pacific Trading Cards in 1993. One of my few truly prized possessions is an autographed copy of James Arness' 2001 autobiography, which I never loan out. The same goes for all 635 episodes of *Gunsmoke*, safely stored on both DVDs and more than 100 videotapes. (Honoring the requests of several potential readers who have not seen all of *Gunsmoke* and want to be surprised, I intentionally kept the episode summaries brief.) Matt Dillon's most familiar order was "Get outta Dodge!" I doubt I ever will.

DAVID R. GREENLAND
MARCH 2013

INTRODUCTION

*G*unsmoke was the most authentic and consistently well-written Western series produced for television, guided by nine producers with various titles, and 72 different directors. Its two-decade network run was equaled only by NBC's recently canceled *Law & Order*, which ended with no one from the original cast remaining, and would have had to continue for several more seasons to match *Gunsmoke*'s 635 episodes. Similarly, James Arness' twenty-year portrayal of Marshal Matt Dillon was eventually tied by Kelsey Grammer's Dr. Frasier Crane, although it took two different shows (*Cheers, Frasier*) to reach that goal, and with considerably less total screen time.

While *Gunsmoke*'s longevity is certainly a testament to its overall quality, it was not, in the final analysis, the most popular Western on television. (That accolade belongs to *Bonanza*, a Top 20 show for twelve of its fourteen seasons.) But popularity does not necessarily indicate excellence, and the fact that *Gunsmoke* ranked in the Top 20 for fifteen of its twenty years—is indeed impressive. It was the first series in television history to finish the season at #1 four years in a row, and one of the extremely few shows to have its cancelation reversed. Even when it was ultimately axed, *Gunsmoke* was being watched by over 20 percent of television viewers, a number that would be astronomical today, when a show with half that audience is considered a hit.

Realistic, ironic and often grim storytelling about the human condition was what made *Gunsmoke* unique. Unexpected twists and surprise endings were typical hallmarks of the show's scripts, resulting in remarkably few weak episodes and an overwhelming abundance of exceptional ones. Even an average segment of *Gunsmoke* was superior to the best of what most other series had to offer. Unlike most filmed entertainment, especially today, substance did not take a backseat to style, and character development was equally as important as plot. Nearly 100 writers wrote for the show (with another two dozen contributing story ideas), among them such outstanding talents as Ron Bishop, Jim Byrnes, Calvin Clements, Les Crutchfield, John Dunkel, Kathleen Hite, Sam Peckinpah, Paul Savage, Clyde Ware, and John Meston, who along with producer Norman Macdonnell originally created *Gunsmoke* for CBS radio. There were 413 programs broadcast from April 1952 to June 1961, most of them eventually adapted for the television version.

It is possible for a good actor to salvage a mediocre script, but a lousy actor can reduce an otherwise fine piece of writing to the importance of the classified section in a month-old newspaper. Fortunately, the *Gunsmoke* writers were able to see their work come to life in the performances of two excellent casts, first on radio:

William Conrad (familiar as the narrator of *The Fugitive* and star of the *Cannon* and *Jake and the Fatman* series) played Matt Dillon, later directed two episodes of the television series and narrated one. Parley Baer (Mayor Stoner on *The Andy Griffith Show*, to name but one of his many credits) portrayed Chester Proudfoot, the surname changed to Goode for television. Howard McNear (Mayberry barber Floyd Lawson on *The Andy Griffith Show*) was cast as Doc Adams and made five guest appearances on the television version. Finally, the part of Kitty Russell was given to Georgia Ellis, who began her career in a Hopalong Cassidy film but worked primarily on radio.

However, to generations of viewers—past, present and future— Matt, Doc, Chester, and Kitty will always be James Arness, Milburn Stone, Dennis Weaver, and Amanda Blake. Not forgetting Ken Curtis, Buck Taylor, Glenn Strange, Burt Reynolds, Roger Ewing, and more than twenty other regular or semi-regular "citizens" who made Dodge City a destination for millions of viewers for twenty years of outlaws, renegades, crooked gamblers, vigilantes, con men, claim jumpers, land grabbers, professional gunmen, hide cutters, muleskinners, horse thieves, snake oil salesmen, orphans, mountain men, soiled doves, feuding ranchers, railroad barons, bureaucrats, cavalry soldiers, army deserters, drunks, prairie fires, tornadoes, all sorts of diseases…and even an elephant.

DAVID R. GREENLAND

CHAPTER 1
THE GUNSMOKE FAMILY

JAMES ARNESS
"MATT DILLON"

(September 10, 1955–March 31, 1975)
(September 26, 1987–February 10, 1994)

"I was always restless as hell. On days when the wind was blowing, I'd almost go crazy sitting in school."
(James Arness, 1966)

Television's most famous United States marshal—and Old West detective—was born James Aurness (original family spelling) on May 26, 1923, in Minneapolis, Minnesota. Like the fictional lawman he would portray for over two decades, he became a consummate outdoorsman more at ease alone or with a few friends than in a crowd. He and his younger brother, the future actor Peter Graves, spent most of their free time hiking, hunting, fishing and swimming. Athletic but uncomfortable about his six-foot-seven height, he preferred ice skating, sailing and skiing to team sports, although he did play some baseball and football.

After graduating from high school in 1942, Arness' mother encouraged him to at least give college a try. Despite his preference for wide open spaces, he enrolled in southern Wisconsin's Beloit College for only one semester. Evidently he formed a sufficient number of lasting friendships during this brief time because some twenty years later he attended a reunion of his fraternity brothers in nearby Rockton, Illinois.

World War II was raging, and Arness saw military service as an honorable way to avoid what he considered the tedium of higher education. His hopes of becoming a Navy pilot, however, were grounded by his lack of the required two years of college. In addition, his eyesight was not sharp enough, and he was judged too tall. Instead, he was drafted by the Army, where his height was regarded as an advantage during the January 1944 invasion of Anzio: To test the depth of the water, Arness was the first soldier in his platoon ordered off the landing craft. Fortunately, the water was only waist-high. Even better, the enemy was nowhere in sight. But that was not the case on the first night of February, when Arness stumbled upon a German machine gun emplacement and was wounded in his right leg, the bullets savagely fracturing the bone. In the later seasons of *Gunsmoke*, the injury as well as related back trouble made it necessary for his stunt double to step in for the more arduous scenes. (In 2000, the Army presented him with the Bronze Star, Purple Heart, Good Conduct Medal and a Rifleman's Badge.)

Following a long period of recovery, Arness briefly attended the University of Minnesota, where a professor urged him to train as a radio announcer. He eventually found work doing on-air commercials and interviews, but just as soon as he felt he had discovered his niche in life, a friend convinced him to drive out to California in a 1938 Plymouth. There, Arness developed a lifelong passion for surfing and at first had no intention of trying to break into the movie business. He gradually changed his mind, joined a theater group, and was invited to do a few screen tests. Rather than starting out in subpar productions, he made his debut in RKO's *The Farmer's Daughter*, released in 1947 and co-starring such industry heavyweights as Joseph Cotten, Ethel Barrymore, Charles Bickford and Loretta Young, who won an Academy Award for the title role. Arness truly enjoyed the experience, saying later, "Once I got a taste of this, it was hard to go back."

For the next eight years, Arness, who had dropped the "u" from his surname, appeared in more than two dozen films of varying quality, including *Stars in My Crown* (with future co-star Amanda Blake), the science-fiction classics *The Thing* and *Them!*, John Ford's *Wagonmaster*, and, most significantly, four with John Wayne (*Big Jim McLain, Hondo, Island in the Sky* and *The Sea Chase*), with whom he signed a contract.

When CBS decided to adapt radio's *Gunsmoke* for television, Wayne suggested that Arness see producer Charles Marquis Warren (who had directed the young actor in 1952's *Hellgate*) and audition for the part of Matt Dillon. Among those vying for the role were Raymond Burr, Richard Boone, John Pickard and Denver Pyle, who almost won. Harry Ackerman, the network's head honcho on the West Coast, agreed with Wayne that Arness was a perfect choice, but there was one problem: Arness did not want the job. "I didn't want to do it. The only Western television programs were *Hopalong Cassidy, Cisco Kid*, and other children's shows," said Arness, who had done an episode of *The Lone Ranger*. "I wanted to be seen by adults, and television did not seem the way to go." Wayne and Ackerman kept up the pressure, which included a meeting between Arness and Jack Van Volkenberg, the network's new television president. It did not help matters that the actor's agent, Kurt Frings, was not eager for his client to do a television series.

Although Arness reluctantly gave in and signed the deal, he had second thoughts and decided to back out the night before he was to report for a wardrobe fitting. He said he was going to do a Western

Arness researching the true Old West

for Republic Studios instead. When his phone rang, Arness found himself talking to powerful CBS executive William Dozier. "You don't know me," said Dozier, "but I want to tell you that you are about to do something very unprofessional." The future Matt Dillon was summoned to the executive's palatial Beverly Hills estate for a meeting to discuss why breaking the contract was not a good idea. According to Arness, however, it was his friend Duke Wayne who finally persuaded him to commit to *Gunsmoke*. He was soon shooting—at being shot at—on the dusty streets of Gene Autry's

Melody Ranch, and using a saddle designed exclusively for his height and weight.

While he made numerous public appearances during the first few seasons of the show, Arness was widely thought to be reclusive and temperamental, neither charge strictly true. "Aloneness is absolutely essential to my life," he said. "I can't see how people don't need it occasionally. I'm not a loner, damn it—it's just that I don't seek out people. I need a lot of quiet time. Truth is, I don't have a social life. I just avoid social situations." For Arness, his then-wife Virginia Chapman (an actress whom he married in 1948), their three children, and the *Gunsmoke* cast and crew were just about all the companionship he needed.

And though Matt Dillon was largely stoic and reserved, the man portraying him was famous for cutting up and keeping the atmosphere light when the cameras were not rolling. In the early years of the series, Milburn Stone felt Arness did not take the job seriously enough. "I felt he did not belong in the business at all," Stone said in 1965. "I said, 'I've read my contract and there's nothing in it that says I have to put diapers on you or wait for you. And if you ever show up late again, buddy, you'll have two things to explain—not only where you were, but where I went!" Shortly before his death fifteen years later, Stone recalled, "He used to annoy me, because at rehearsals he'd sit there and whistle or make all kinds of silly noises. So one time I started in on him really screaming and yelling. Jim's got a frightening habit in such circumstances. When he gets really tense, he kinda winces and bites his front teeth together real fast."

Rather than becoming defensive, Arness agreed that his co-star was correct to chastise him, responding, "Milburn, you are absolutely right." Stone continued, "I had embarrassed the hell out of him, but Jim stood there and took it and then had the guts to say that."

Arness also took it upon himself to improve as an actor, spending weekends studying with an acting coach for about six months during *Gunsmoke*'s second season, often giving her a copy of the next week's script. Diligent viewers will note a difference in the way Matt Dillon comes across when comparing the first season to later years. Gone are the occasionally wooden movements and somewhat stilted line readings, replaced by a nearly mysterious depth of character. Giving some insight into his performance, Arness once observed,

Arness & Milburn Stone, circa 1960

"Matt Dillon was a guy who not only had to see that the laws were carried out, but had to live them himself. He had to do the right thing."

Like the rest of the regular cast, Arness developed an instinct for what did and did not work for the show, frequently paring his dialogue down to a few lines that had a greater impact than a lengthy speech, or suggesting that something he was supposed to say would sound better coming from another character. This lack of inflated ego on the star's part contributed greatly to the overall harmony of the *Gunsmoke* set.

When asked, in 1957, if he had any interest in the business side of the entertainment industry, he said, "I don't want any part of those headaches. I have a wife, three growing kids—plus a full-time job; that's enough for me." However, at the beginning of the 1959 season, Arness was listed in the credits as an associate producer, an off-camera role that continued until he sold his partial share of the series back to CBS in the fall of 1964, on the eve of the record-breaking tenth year.

Barbara Lord & Arness on the set of "The Long, Long Trail, 1961

By this time Matt Dillon was, arguably, the most instantly recognizable fictional male character on television. Fans had learned that before becoming marshal of Dodge City, he had driven cattle, wrangled horses, known mountain men and Indians, been involved with more than a few women, fought in the Civil War, and worked for a number of different lawmen in towns all over the West. Over the years, hints of his background emerged in such memorable episodes as "Cara," "20-20," "How to Cure a Friend," "Matt for Murder," "Friend's Pay-Off," "Double Entry," "Friend," "Abe Blocker," "The Cousin," "Old York," "Kimbro," "Time of the Jackals," "Stryker" and others.

During the 1960s, his workload was gradually reduced so he could spend more time with his family and enjoy the benefits of his success. He purchased a catamaran he christened Seasmoke (and later donated to the Sea Scouts) and a Cessna 206 light plane so he could fly himself to remote surfing sites as well as *Gunsmoke* locations. His success also enabled him to support environmental causes and non-profit charities, and when a crew member underwent treatment for cancer, Arness made sure the medical bills were paid.

When CBS briefly canceled *Gunsmoke* in 1967, Arness could not bring himself to attend the show's last wrap party, but there was no way he could avoid the 1973 International Broadcasting Dinner sponsored by the Hollywood Radio and Television Society, at which he was honored as Man of the Year. Joining more than one thousand broadcasting and advertising executives at the Century Plaza Hotel in Los Angeles were Milburn Stone, Amanda Blake and Ken Curtis, who told the press, "I've been on the show ten years and Jim hasn't changed one iota. I've seen many shows go down the drain because the star becomes impossible and disliked by everyone. He's terrific to work with. When the time comes to buckle down to work, he's ready."

"I don't think Jim's changed a bit," agreed Stone. "He's the most unhypocritical man I know. He's consistent. He is what he is, lives the way he does, and that's it."

"In eighteen years of working with him he's never changed," added Blake. "Jim is the mystery man. Like most men he's an over-grown twelve-year-old. He's delightful, charming, one of the funniest men I've ever known. I really don't know much about him because he's a private person. But he's fun to work with."

For the occasion, Arness bought a tuxedo that he promptly wadded into a bundle and threw into a garbage can as soon as he returned home.

Two years later, *Gunsmoke* was canceled virtually without warning. "We didn't do a final wrap-up show," the series' star reflected. "We finished the twentieth year, we all expected to go on for another season, or two or three. The network never told anybody they were thinking of canceling. But the ban imposed on violence, even when it was essential to our script, is what ruined things."

Arness was not out of work long. A few months after the final first-run *Gunsmoke* aired, he signed to star as Zeb Macahan in the

ABC television movie *The Macahans.* The network announced that if it became a series, Arness would "appear in every third episode as a frontier scout for a family moving West in Civil War times." *The Macahans* was the hit ABC expected it to be, resulting in the epic *How the West Was Won*, which ran off and on from February 1977 to April 1979.

"Zeb Macahan came from an era when men were the law unto themselves," Arness said shortly before the series ended. "He was a free spirit, made his own rules. He was used to taking everything over and not consulting anybody. Except that after the Civil War— the stage we've got him at now—it's more civilized times and he's running into a little trouble. Matt Dillon was the opposite—a guy who not only had to see that the laws were carried out, but live by them himself. He had to do the *right* thing. As a consequence, he always had to hold his own personal feelings or desires in restraint."

Although he claimed to have no desire to tackle a modern day series ("Haven't seen one contemporary role yet I'd ever want for myself, all that stuff about marriage problems and all those urban problems."), he starred next in the police drama *McClain's Law,* which NBC bought without seeing a script or a pilot. The show was somewhat unique in that it told stories from the perspective of the victim rather than the criminal, yet it ran only one season, from November 1981 to August 1982.

Arness remained out of the public eye for much of the next five years, making a rare appearance to induct CBS chairman William S. Paley into the Television Hall of Fame in 1984, at Paley's request. Arness was grateful to the head of the network for giving *Gunsmoke* a second chance in 1967 and always trying to visit the set each season to make certain everything was running smoothly on what the chairman maintained was his favorite show. "That really impressed me," Arness said. "I know that program executives are probably saying that kind of thing to all their star performers, but he seemed real genuine. I just got a feeling that he really meant it. Man to man."

In August of 1986, Arness went to San Antonio, Texas, to portray Jim Bowie in the three-hour NBC movie *The Alamo: 13 Days to Glory.* (In 1960, busy with *Gunsmoke*, he turned down an offer to play Bowie in John Wayne's production of *The Alamo*.) He was named honorary mayor for a day, toured the original Alamo, and told the press, "I only do things now that capture my interest, and believe me, this caught mine. If I could line up four or five things this good, I'd work more often."

The telefilm aired in January 1987, kicking off an active period that included five *Gunsmoke* movies, a television remake of the John Wayne classic *Red River* (1988), hosting a 1989 PBS documentary of Wayne, and even an ad for an insurance company.

In 2001, Arness published his autobiography, co-written by James E. Wise, Jr., featuring a foreword by Burt Reynolds and an impressively long list of the awards and honors he had earned. That November, he graciously autographed copies—including those ordered over the Internet—at a book signing that took place at the Autry Museum of Western Heritage in Los Angeles. "Many of the actors and writers came by to see me, which was a lot of fun," he said. "Over the years, I kept in touch with quite a few. I kept in touch with Dennis Weaver, Amanda Blake and Milburn Stone until they left us, which was a sad day for all of us."

Arness and his second wife, Janet, were very involved with their favorite charity, United Cerebral Palsy, and he regularly connected with fans via his website jamesarness.com. "I especially like the e-mails from the younger generation who watch with their parents and grandparents," he said. "Many people write to me and say they can't find anything today where they can sit down with the whole family and enjoy an evening show together. *Gunsmoke* had that quality, and people remember that and can pass it on."

In his final years, Arness enjoyed watching reruns on the cable networks TV Land and Encore's Westerns Channel, and observed, "With *Gunsmoke* we had an outstanding quality of writing. What made us different from other Westerns was the fact that *Gunsmoke* wasn't just action and a lot of shooting. They were character study shows. They're interesting to watch all these years later." Among his favorite episodes were "The Gallows," "Snow Train," "The River" and "Chato." "The episode 'Chato' is probably my all-time favorite show," he said in 2005, the same year he contributed episode introductions and commentary to a 50th anniversary collection of DVDs.

Ellen Burstyn (then McRae), Joan Marshall and Arness on the set of "Wagon Girls," 1962

Although he seemed, in the words of his friend and frequent co-star Morgan Woodward, "almost indestructible," Arness posted a farewell letter on his website shortly before his death from natural causes on June 3, 2011.

Of James Arness' passing, *The Los Angeles Times* reporter Robert Lloyd wrote: "While it may be that Arness was born to play Dillon, you do not keep a character alive and interesting across five decades without some appreciation of real art; it takes substance to keep goodness from becoming blandness, from growing tiresome with time. Could any other actor have carried that weight as long, with as much grace and as little groaning? Maybe. But this one did."

Arness, Blake, Stone in 1955

MILBURN STONE
"DOC ADAMS"

(September 10, 1955–March 31, 1975)

"Jim said, 'I guess we didn't know how lucky we were.' And I told him, 'Maybe you didn't, but I sure as hell did!'"

(Milburn Stone, 1978)

Doctor Galen Adams may not be the first character that comes to mind when recalling the most popular television physicians, but Milburn Stone received accolades not bestowed on the likes of Dr. Kildare (Richard Chamberlain), Ben Casey (Vince Edwards) or Marcus Welby (Robert Young). While viewers actually sought medical advice from all four actors, only Stone was made an honorary member of the Kansas Medical Society and the National Coroner's Association. During the period Dennis Weaver was still on the show Stone remembered fans often asking him, "Why the heck don't you fix Chester's leg?"

Stone was born in Burton, Kansas, on July 5, 1904, but grew up in Larned, some fifty miles from Dodge City. An excellent student, he won a Congressional appointment to the U.S. Naval Academy at Annapolis. But, like his cousin Fred, a star on Broadway and in vaudeville, he had the show business bug. He first joined the Helen B. Ross stock company and became an accomplished song and dance man, touring the Midwest and western states for several years. In Denver, he and a partner named Smokey Strain made the rounds and even sang and did routines on radio. It was during his vaudeville days that he married his wife, Nellie, a fellow thespian who gave him a daughter, Shirley, in 1926. Three years later, after one failed attempt, Stone finally made it to the Broadway stage. He played opposite his cousin Fred in Sinclair Lewis' *The Jayhawkers*, then *Around the Corner*, neither of which ran for more than a few weeks. Due to an illness in the family, the particulars of which have been lost in the dust of time, Stone moved his wife and daughter to California. Sadly, Nellie became ill in 1937 and two years later, died while pregnant with another child. After recovering from these losses, Stone remarried in 1940. He and his second wife, Jane, divorced a few years later, but married a second time in 1946 and stayed together until Stone's death in 1980.

In Hollywood, fortune smiled where Broadway had not, and Stone became one of the busiest character actors in town, appearing in both serials and features at nearly every major and minor studio for two decades. Between 1935 and 1955 he made so many films that he once told an interviewer he was not certain of the total. A conservative estimate is 150, including such A and B classics as *China Clipper, Crime School, Young Mr. Lincoln, Johnny Apollo, Reap the Wild Wind, Sherlock Holmes Faces Death, Cass Timberlane, Buck Privates Come Home, Flying Leathernecks, The Long Gray Line, The Private War of Major Benson,* and *Arrowhead*. The latter was a Western directed by Charles Marquis Warren, with whom Stone did not and never would get along. Nonetheless, when it came time for Warren to choose an actor for the role of Doc Adams, he had to admit that Stone, who was meticulous in choosing his wardrobe, was ideal.

Easily the most experienced and professional member of the *Gunsmoke* cast, Stone did not hesitate to confront a director or writer if he felt there was something wrong with a line of dialog or the way a scene was being played. Nor did he let his fellow performers off the hook, resenting what he considered James Arness' annoying behavior. "He'd be late or never show up—never apologize," Stone remarked to *TV Guide* after the tenth season had wrapped. "And once he was there he'd clown around." The following year he told the same magazine, "I spent the first two years on *Gunsmoke* despising Jim's lack of professionalism. Now I say his acting has reached classical proportions." Earlier that year, in an interview with *The Los Angeles Times*, he said the reason *Gunsmoke* worked was "because Jim is the star on and off the set and we never had a serious quarrel or impasse." After the rocky first two years of the series, the two men remained good friends for the rest of Stone's life.

He and Amanda Blake also grew to be close friends, and Stone commented more than once that *Gunsmoke* would be just another Western without her. "Without Amanda, it wouldn't be *Gunsmoke*," he said in a 1960 story about Blake. "And that's a fact." He was primarily responsible for convincing Miss Kitty to accompany Doc and Chester—and sing—at publicity functions.

While Stone and Ken Curtis hit it off and never lost touch with one another, he was more than a little irritated by Dennis Weaver's attempts to leave the show, only to return the following season. "We had about nine funerals over him," the typically blunt Stone famously recalled in 1965.

One cast regular Stone actively encouraged to leave *Gunsmoke* was Burt Reynolds, whom the older actor felt had potential to score in movies. During a television interview many years later, Reynolds said Stone had also reminded him that acting was "an honorable profession as long as no one catches you at it." And certainly no one ever saw the wheels turning in Stone's head as he gave Adams an assortment of trademark mannerisms—the tilt of his head, the hand swiped across his moustache, the quick tug on his ear, the hesitant step up onto the boardwalk—that seemed as natural as breathing.

The character of Doc Adams, as portrayed on television, was less shady than Parley Baer had played him on radio, though his background was never clearly discussed. Viewers learned that he had been an army surgeon during the Civil War, had been the on-board physician for a riverboat, and that was about all. Very few acquaintances from his past ever looked him up in Dodge. Stone

Dennis Weaver and Milburn Stone, circa 1961

based Adams on a Doctor Hampstead he had known as a youngster in Kansas, as well as his grandfather, Joe Stone. "He was a cantankerous old guy but he had a great sense of humor and loved to tease people." Joe Stone was likely who his grandson had in mind when needling Chester and Festus.

Once cast as Doc Adams, Stone did little work outside *Gunsmoke*. He made only one more film, 1957's *Drango*, a Western starring Jeff Chandler, and episodes of *Front Row Center* and *Climax*.

In 1968 he was awarded a long overdue Emmy for the episode "Baker's Dozen," but it was hardly the only exceptional performance Stone had given throughout the years. Other memorable "Doc" installments included "Apprentice Doc," "The Hunger," "Old York," "Doctor's Wife," "Thursday's Child," and "Sam McTavish, M.D.," for which he should have been honored with a second Emmy.

Shortly after the conclusion of the sixteenth season, Stone underwent heart surgery and missed the first eleven episodes of the next. Pat Hingle temporarily stepped in as Dr. John Chapman in six of them, beginning with "New Doctor in Town," in which Doc's friends learn he has gone back east to study advancements in medicine. Stone returned in "The Bullet," the only three-part episode of the series, just in time to extract a bullet lodged near Matt Dillon's spine—and aboard a train plagued by outlaws at that.

A few years after *Gunsmoke* was canceled, Stone confessed to a reporter that he was restless and found retirement boring. "I haven't worked since we finished shooting the series in 1974 except to take part in a Dean Martin roast of Dennis two years ago," he said. "Since then all I've done is take walks and get out to do some fishing on the Colorado River...I stopped playing golf because it was driving me crazy. I couldn't beat anyone!" He added that even though he had enjoyed being invited to participate with 120 other actors for a special celebrating the 50th anniversary of CBS, "I felt bad because Ken Curtis was not included. Amanda Blake was invited, but she couldn't make it. But Jim and Dennis and I spent the whole day talking about the good times we had together."

In 1977, Stone made one last trip to Dodge City, where he was given an honorary doctorate degree from St. Mary of the Plains College. Predictably, a large crowd attended when the mayor proclaimed the event Milburn Stone Day. The next year, Stone recorded some radio spots promoting the college, telling listeners that they might remember him "as old Doc on *Gunsmoke*."

Milburn Stone's final public appearance was with Ken Curtis on an ABC special, *When the West Was Fun*, hosted by Glenn Ford and televised in 1979. The following summer, on June 12, he died in his sleep at Scripps Memorial Hospital in La Jolla, California, less than a month from what would have been his seventy-sixth birthday. Dr. Sidney Kingdon, an Illinois dentist who had known him for fifty years, told the press that compared to other actors, Stone "was different from most. He never got a big head. I never heard him say a bad word about anybody, even other actors. He was a lot like the character Doc as far as his ways. He was well liked."

Stone was buried in La Jolla on June 16, 1980. At a memorial service held in Los Angeles, James Arness, Amanda Blake and Ken Curtis were reunited one last time.

AMANDA BLAKE
"MISS KITTY RUSSELL"

(September 10, 1955–April 1, 1974)
(September 26, 1987)

"I had to walk a very narrow line and tread between schoolmarm sweet and saloon girl tough. The guys didn't have this problem."

(Amanda Blake)

Amanda Blake was a pioneer, the first actress to star as a regular on a television Western, and the first woman—and living person—to be inducted into the Hall of Fame of Great Western Performers at the National Cowboy Hall of Fame and Western Heritage Center in Oklahoma City, Oklahoma. And, as Blake was proud of pointing out, her *Gunsmoke* character was television's first liberated woman. Indeed, Miss Katherine "Kitty" Russell progressed from saloon hostess to saloon owner while the majority of the other female roles on 1950s television were limited to housewives, secretaries, or mere window dressing. She and Matt Dillon had an "understanding," yet she relied on no one but herself unless it became absolutely necessary for the marshal to step in. She had no family, but was a matriarchal figure to Doc, Chester, Festus, Newly, and anyone else worthy of friendship, compassion, or just a free beer. When she up and sold the Long Branch after nineteen years, Dodge City was never the same.

The woman born to play Miss Kitty entered the world as Beverly Louise Neill, an only child, on February 20, 1929, in Buffalo, New York. By the time she reached the fifth grade, she knew what she wanted to do with her life, and by the age of twenty-one was working at M-G-M in Hollywood and being compared to a young Greer Garson. Her first film, 1950's *The Duchess of Idaho*, was a pedestrian romantic comedy starring Esther Williams and Van Johnson. That same year she and James Arness had small parts in the Joel McCrea feature *Stars in My Crown*. Between then and *Gunsmoke*, she made seventeen more pictures, and was not always listed in the credits. Oddly, she was given billing for the 1954 version of *A Star is Born*, but her scenes in the troubled production ended up either on the cutting room floor or were never shot at all. Her largest role came in a Bowery Boys comedy, *High Society*, released the same year *Gunsmoke* began its twenty-year run.

Blake, who had done some television work on such shows as *Schlitz Playhouse*, *Lux Video Playhouse*, *Cavalcade of America*, *Fireside Theatre* and *Four Star Playhouse*, was aware that radio's *Gunsmoke* was being adapted for television. "I knew I had to have the part of Kitty," she told a reporter in 1971, "so I hounded the producer until I got it." Her perseverance also paid off in overcoming her fear of horseback riding, which she eventually did, both sidesaddle and Western style, particularly during the first eight seasons. If she was ever nervous, it never showed.

Blake signed a five year contract with CBS for $350 a week—with yearly raises of $100—and promptly threw the network into a panic when she remarked to the press that Kitty Russell was a tramp. That was the general impression made by Georgia Ellis on the radio program, but not a characterization easily tolerated on the home screen in millions of homes. There were no repercussions, serious or otherwise, and Kitty went on to be regarded as a businesswoman no more a threat to the decency of Dodge than boardinghouse owner Ma Smalley. Over the course of the series viewers were informed that Kitty hailed from New Orleans, spent some time in St. Louis, and had a no-good gambler for a father. From time to time, a person from her past would pass through town, but her backstory would remain intriguingly vague, as would the exact nature of the relationship between her and Matt Dillon.

It was agreed early on that there would be no overt romance between Kitty and the marshal depicted, and certainly never a wedding, although several episodes—especially "The Way It Is," "The Badge" and "Kitty's Love Affair"—dealt with their complicated arrangement. "Jim and I used to play what we called our eyeball scenes," Blake recalled in 1987. "We didn't think we had to show anything more. It worked; it was that mystique." In the seventeenth season's three-part episode "The Bullet," written by Jim Byrnes, Kitty reminisced about the first time she saw Matt in a poignant monolog lasting more than three minutes:

"Seventeen years. Seventeen years ago this month, I'll never forget that day as long as I live. It was raining and I was cold and hungry and miserable. When I stepped off that stagecoach and saw those ugly buildings and all those muddy streets, I hated Dodge City. I was down to my last $40, and it couldn't have taken me much further, but you couldn't have paid me to stay in Dodge. I waded over to the café and was hurrying through breakfast so I could get back on the stage when a man came in and he sat across the room from me. He was the biggest man I'd ever seen in my life and he also ate the biggest breakfast I'd ever seen in my life. He was so busy polishing off all those eggs and ham and biscuits that he didn't even notice me, but I noticed him. I noticed him so much

Blake and Arness

that I decided to stay a while. And stay I did, in spite of the fact that I found out that the big man wore a big badge and he didn't think he had any right to get involved in any kind of permanent relationship. Oh, we really fought some battles about that! Seems to me that I left three or four times just swearing up and down that under any circumstances was I gonna see him or his damn badge again. But I always came back and once, he even came to get me. Now here we are after seventeen years and that's got to be the longest non-permanent relationship in history, but I wouldn't change one day of it, not one day."

During the first few seasons of *Gunsmoke*, Blake worried that the producers would decide not to keep her on the show, a concern that could explain why she accepted outside jobs (*Alfred Hitchcock Presents, State Trooper, Studio One in Hollywood, G.E. True Theater, Steve Canyon, Red Skelton*) while continuing as Kitty Russell. By 1959, when nominated for an Emmy, she had no qualms about her future with the series for the next fifteen years. She joined Milburn Stone and Dennis Weaver on the entertainment trail, each of them taking a turn in the spotlight. Blake insisted she could not sing, claiming she "had a voice so low it could easily pass for bass." Yet when she sang her solo numbers, "The Long Branch Blues" and "When You and I Were Young, Maggie," the fans always responded enthusiastically.

Before production began on the 1974-75 season, the network stunned fans by announcing that Blake would not be returning to *Gunsmoke*. In August she was a guest on the Mike Douglas Show and told the host she had grown tired of commuting between her home in Phoenix and Hollywood, and that she was always complaining about something. Truthfully, she and producer John Mantley did not have the best relationship, and her departure was a classic case of the employee who quits before they are fired. Mantley was relieved to have her gone, but he and Blake agreed that to spare the show and the cast any negative publicity, she would simply contend that her departure was voluntarily. Ten years later, she was still sticking to the official story, telling *The Los Angeles Times*, "I was tired and it was time to go. It was the end of the trail. The show only lasted one year without me."

That same year, 1984, President Ronald Reagan presented Blake with the American Cancer Society's annual Courage Award. In 1979 she had gone to Cheyenne, Wyoming, for a convention of the organization's state chapter, telling reporters that her two-pack-a-day cigarette habit had given her cancer on the bottom of her mouth two years before. It was necessary to remove part of her tongue, mouth and some glands in her neck. "I lisped a lot," she said, "and had to learn to talk again. I did my own therapy."

Her compromised oral ability was evident in the first *Gunsmoke* television movie, in 1987, but it did not detract from the welcome return of Miss Kitty. It was Blake, nostalgic for her days in Dodge,

Stone, Blake, Weaver

who, along with a Nebraska businessman, first attempted to put together a reunion film. Lacking support from CBS, the project died, but only temporarily. The network reconsidered, Blake and Mantley mended fences, and *Return to Dodge* aired in September 1987 to excellent ratings and generally good notices. The following spring, Blake, Arness and Mantley appeared at a *Gunsmoke* retrospective sponsored by the Los Angeles County Museum of Art, where the episodes "Matt Gets It" and "Matt's Love Story" were screened.

After leaving *Gunsmoke* in 1974, Blake worked only sporadically, guest starring on such shows as *The Quest, Hart to Hart, The Love Boat*, and the daytime drama *The Edge of Night*. The *Gunsmoke* movie did little to jump start her career, nor was her personal life the happiest. She had married for the fifth time, in 1984, but the marriage, to an Austin city councilman and real estate investor eight years her junior, lasted barely a year. Her husband, Mark Spaeth, filed for divorce, telling the court their union "has become insupportable because of discord or conflict of personalities between petitioner and respondent that destroys the legitimate ends of the marriage." By then Blake was living back in California. "I've never been a big Los Angeles fan," she told a reporter, "and it's not improving." But that was where the work was—when she could find it.

In 1988 she landed small parts in the films *B.O.R.N.* and *The Boost*, but complained to the press, "It's hard to get work when everyone thinks you're dead." At the time she was renting a small house and claimed to be nearly broke. "My wonderful, loyal fans have helped me through the tough times, even though they had no idea what I've been going through," she said. "I read every letter. A few months ago I was very depressed over my situation, then the mail came and there was a fan letter from a little girl who'd seen a *Gunsmoke* episode on cable. She told me how much she liked Miss Kitty, and closed by saying she prayed that God would bless me. It was so moving and so touching that I found new strength to keep going. With fans like that I can't lose. I may be down—but I'm not out." Her last acting job was an episode of *The New Dragnet*.

Blake, an animal rights crusader, moved to the ranch of animal trainer Pat Derby, in Galt, California. On August 18, 1989, it was announced that the 60-year-old red haired actress who had portrayed Kitty Russell for nineteen years had died two days earlier in Sacramento's Mercy General Hospital, where she had spent the past three weeks. "She was frail," said Derby, "not in great health. But she had a will of iron." The official cause of death was given as mouth and throat cancer, but almost three months later Blake's physician, Dr. Lou Nishimura, confirmed that her condition had been "complicated by a type of viral hepatitis brought on by acquired immune deficiency syndrome." Because Blake was not a user of drug needles and had not contracted the disease through a blood transfusion, it was logically assumed that her last husband had been responsible for giving her AIDS. Butterfly, her dog, was with her at the end, and friends requested that donations be made to one of her favorite charities, Performing Animals Welfare Society (PAWS).

"Amanda was one of the most beautiful and gracious ladies ever on the television screen," said James Arness. "She was a straight-ahead, strong individual, and that's what she represented on the screen. She was a large part of the overall mystique of *Gunsmoke*."

"She had a loving heart and wonderful spirit," Dennis Weaver added. "She was an extremely caring person in the way she pursued making a better place for animals that need help. She expressed an infinite love in that manner. I am fortunate to have worked with her and known her as a real friend. In person she was very much like the character of Miss Kitty. She had a heart as big as a water-melon."

"She was a great friend and I'll miss her," Burt Reynolds said. "Amanda was a gallant lady with a terrific sense of humor and the bawdiest laugh I ever heard. She was a truly beautiful woman."

Dennis Weaver, photo courtesy of Weaver

DENNIS WEAVER
"CHESTER GOODE"

(September 10, 1955–April 11, 1964)

"I wanted to grow as an actor, to create, to expand, and quitting **Gunsmoke** *was the biggest decision I had to make in my life."*

(Dennis Weaver, 1979)

In a 1987 interview, Dennis Weaver admitted that he originally thought he was auditioning for the part of Matt Dillon when the television version of *Gunsmoke* was being cast. Disabused of that notion, he read for Chester Goode, but did not feel he had done a very good job and asked for another chance. Fortunately, producer Charles Marquis Warren had recently directed Weaver in the film *Seven Angry Men* and knew the actor was capable of more. The second time through, Weaver adopted the lazy drawl of a fellow student he had known at Oklahoma University, and he became the first cast member signed to the series. Because Weaver was both tall and physically fit, Warren suggested that Chester be given some sort of disability to explain why the character did not do much more than sweep out the jail and hang around the Long Branch Saloon. At first, Weaver was against Chester being somehow handicapped, but after reconsidering came up with the idea of the famous limp. In his autobiography, Weaver wrote, "Well, had I known that I was going to be playing Chester for nine years stiff-legged, I might have thought differently about it. Have you ever tried building a campfire stiff-legged or put your boot on and not bend your knee?"

It is to the producers' everlasting credit that Chester's infirmity was never explained, leaving the circumstances to the audience's imagination. Viewers gradually learned that Chester had been orphaned and served in the military, but was he born lame? Had he been injured as a young man, or possibly wounded in the Civil War? It was anyone's guess, and as Weaver remarked, "Chester's stiff leg became an unbelievably strong identifying characteristic. I think that was part of the reason why Chester was received with such love by so many people—they sympathized with him." So convincing was the portrayal that several fans—including doctors—assumed Weaver truly did have a limp. Real or not, CBS chairman William S. Paley objected to this creative touch, but never made an issue of it. When the editing of one first season episode made it appear as if Chester was walking normally, some viewers wrote the network to say how pleased they were that he had been "cured."

Ironically, it was Arness who actually had a hitch in his step. According to Burt Reynolds, "Before each shot, Dennis would be walking along, and Dennis, you know, was a tremendous athlete—

Weaver & Arness, circa 1958

he almost went to the Olympics. And Jim had this terrible limp from catching shrapnel in his leg at Anzio during the war. So the director would say, 'Roll em! Action!' And here Jim would be walking without a limp and Dennis would be limping. It was the weirdest thing."

Weaver was born on June 4, 1924, in Joplin, Missouri, and developed an interest in sports and theater while in high school. Excelling at both football and track, he earned a scholarship to Joplin Junior College, but his education was cut short by World War II, during which he trained as a pilot and performed admirably on the Navy's track and field team. Following the war, he enrolled at Oklahoma University and continued to concentrate on dramatics and track, trying out for the Olympics after graduating with honors. Still serious about acting, he auditioned for the prestigious Actor's Studio in New York and was accepted. His stage work included *A Streetcar Named Desire*, with Shelley Winters, and *Come Back, Little Sheba*, with Shirley Booth. He later went to Hollywood and aced a screen test that resulted in a contract offer from Universal-International. Between 1952 and heading to the streets of Dodge City, he made more than a dozen features, the majority of them Westerns such as *The Lawless Breed, Column South* and *War Arrow*. It was on the first of these—*Horizons West*—that he first met his future co-star, James Arness.

Chester Goode may have been a sidekick to Marshal Dillon, but Weaver's considerable thespian skills made the character multi-dimensional. Although he spent most of his time cleaning the jail, emptying the ashes from the stove, feeding the prisoners, playing checkers—or arguing—with Doc, and did not ordinarily carry a firearm, he was the only man Matt could count on in a crisis. An eternal optimist, he never allowed a perpetual lack of funds to prevent him from enjoying the ladies, a mug of beer or a card game. And Chester remained proud of his talent for brewing a perfect pot of coffee, even if few agreed with him.

Personal appearances by Weaver, Milburn Stone, and Amanda Blake were hugely popular. According to a press release sent to venues where the trio would be performing, "Dennis Weaver is a comedian at heart. He works in the character of Chester and his gags are based around the people involved in the *Gunsmoke* TV show. In addition to his comedy routines he plays a guitar and sings parodies, which he has written himself. During the first fifteen or twenty minutes of Weaver's act, it is strictly in the character of Chester and then all of a sudden he runs out into the arena and jumps hurdles (which we set up previously) with his stiff leg. On this return trip over the hurdles, he goes like crazy without the stiff leg (we do not mention this to the public as this is a surprise to them, as most people think he really does have a stiff leg). Dennis Weaver will keep the people rolling in the aisles for a minimum of twenty minutes."

Milburn Stone and Amanda Blake were sometimes absent from the 233 half-hours but Weaver did 215 before getting a break. Before that, determined to avoid being typecast, he managed to fit in two major films (1958's *Touch of Evil* and 1960's *The Gallant Hours*), as well as guest starring on several other series (*Dragnet, Playhouse 90, Alfred Hitchcock Presents, The Twilight Zone*).

Although he was permitted to flex his creative muscles by directing four episodes, only two months into *Gunsmoke*'s seventh season, its first as an hour-long series, he told the press he had signed to host a variety show called *TV Tonight* and would not be back for the eighth year. "The time is ripe for me to leave *Gunsmoke* in terms of my having the best chance to get something worthwhile," he announced. "Seven years is a long time to play the same character and now I want to do something new and on my own. My exit, thank heaven, is a graceful one."

But his exit would be delayed. CBS offered Weaver a series of his own if he would return for the 1962-63 season, and he consented to continue as Chester for fifteen more episodes. A pilot for the proposed show—*The Giant Step*—was shot, with Weaver portraying a high school vice-principal, but the network declined to go ahead with production. Nor did *TV Tonight* get beyond the pilot stage. He turned down the lead role in *The Fugitive*, feeling the sample script "read like a soap opera." Reluctantly, Weaver said he would return to *Gunsmoke* for only a dozen episodes of the 1963-64 season, but that he had a firm deal to do *Kentucky's Kid* (renamed *Kentucky Jones*), a show for NBC.

On April 11, 1964, in "Bently," an episode revolving around him, Chester was seen in Dodge City for the last time. "I saw the character change, develop, flesh out through about five years," Weaver said in 1973, "and after that I got tired of it, felt that I had to get on to something different because I had almost exhausted all of the different areas of the character. From the standpoint of money and security it could not be beat. But money is a drag if you let it become an end instead of a means."

Weaver directing "Marry Me" episode, 1961

In later years there were discussions about bringing Chester back as a guest star, but the right script could never be developed. Even if he had been willing, Weaver may not have had the time. NBC canceled *Kentucky Jones* after one season, but unlike many actors who leave a successful series, he was never out of work. "I'm one of the few actors, if not the only one, ever to go from a gangly, second banana role to a leading man," he recalled in later years. Before landing another series, he was able to display his versatility in such shows as *Dr. Kildare, The World of Disney*, and *Combat!*, and in the films *Way...Way Out*, with Jerry Lewis, and the Western *Duel at Diablo*, co-starring James Garner and Sidney Poitier. In 1967 he starred as a wildlife ranger in the feature *Gentle Giant*, which was the basis for the two-season CBS series *Gentle Ben*. Between seasons, he made the adventure film *Mission Bantangas*.

After guest parts on *Name of the Game* and *Judd, for the Defense*, as well as an episode of *The Virginian*, Weaver created the second iconic character of his career, Deputy Marshal Sam McCloud in *McCloud*, loosely inspired by the Clint Eastwood film *Coogan's Bluff*. The show, which ran as part of an NBC anthology series from 1970 to 1977, was not on every week, giving him the opportunity to play opposite Shelley Winters, his fellow alumni from the Actor's Studio, in the 1971 film *What's the Matter with Helen?* He continued working in television on several series and telefilms, including Steven Spielberg's classic *Duel*. In 1979 he starred on the short-lived police drama *Stone*, and returned to series work in 1983 for the similarly brief *Emerald Point N.A.S.*

When the first *Gunsmoke* movie was proposed in 1986, Weaver, then in preparation for his final series (*Buck James*), claimed he was never asked to participate, though John Mantley said the actor's representatives were approached more than once. Weaver then backtracked and admitted, "there were some early discussions." Consequently, the former Chester Goode's last visits to the Hollywood prairie were on a 1994 episode of the syndicated *Lonesome Dove: The Series* and the 2000 television remake of *The Virginian* for TNT. While doing publicity for the latter, Weaver revealed that he and James Arness, with whom he had always remained in touch, had discussed reuniting for a special in which an aged Chester and Matt look back on their lives at the turn of the century. "It's just kind of a transition for these two guys into the automobile age," he said. "We are what we are. I just think it would be wonderful." The project, unfortunately, never happened.

Weaver, who was also a musician, vegetarian, passionate environmentalist, and co-founder of the charity food distribution service LIFE (Love Is Feeding Everyone), published his autobiography (*All the World's a Stage*) in 2000. Among his last jobs in front of the camera were portraying a ranch owner on ABC Family Channel's *Wildfire*, and, appropriately, hosting reruns of the rarely-seen hour-long black-and-white episodes of *Gunsmoke* for Encore's Westerns Channel. He spent his last sixteen years in a Colorado home he dubbed the Earthship, constructed of tin cans and old tires, and died of complications from cancer on February 24, 2006, at the age of 81. "He was a wonderful man and a fine actor," said Burt Reynolds, "and we will all miss him."

Reynolds with cast, 1964

BURT REYNOLDS
"QUINT ASPER"

48 Episodes
(September 29, 1962–March 20, 1965)

"When the show finally ended, I asked Jim about the set because I wanted something. God love him, he remembered me. I have the swinging doors to the saloon. They're in Florida at my ranch where I built a saloon."

(Burt Reynolds, 1995)

When Burt Reynolds signed on as Quint Asper, Dodge City's half-white/half-Comanche blacksmith for *Gunsmoke's* eighth season, he was under the impression that he would be filling the void left as soon as Chester finally limped into the sunset. In truth, producer Norman Macdonnell wanted a character who might appeal to the show's younger viewers. Dennis Weaver had agreed to stay on a limited basis—27 episodes during seasons eight and nine—and his eventual replacement, Ken Curtis as Festus, was not introduced until a little more than two months after Reynolds' first episode. Even though Curtis would not become a permanent member of the cast until the following season, Reynolds remarked later, "As soon as Ken Curtis guested as Festus, I knew that was what the show needed." Even though he felt Reynolds' face was "too fat," Macdonnell offered him the part of Dodge's resident "half breed"— unaware that the actor was, ironically, part Cherokee—for $3,000 a week.

Reynolds, born in Waycross, Georgia (as was *Bonanza's* Pernell Roberts), in 1936, grew up in Florida and had hopes of becoming a professional football player until he was seriously injured in a car crash. Instead, he turned to acting, first in college and later New York. By 1959 he was working on such television series as *Naked City, The Twilight Zone, Schlitz Playhouse of Stars, M Squad* and *The Lawless Years.* His first steady job was on NBC's *Riverboat,* co-starring Darren McGavin, with whom Reynolds did not have the greatest relationship.

Until *Gunsmoke* came along, Reynolds made his first two features— *Armored Command* and *Angel Baby*—and racked up several more television credits, including *Playhouse 90, The Aquanauts, Michael Shayne, Malibu Run, Perry Mason, Route 66,* and his first two Westerns, *Johnny Ringo* and *Zane Grey Theatre.*

If his *Riverboat* experience had made him reluctant to seek steady work on another series, Reynolds' attitude changed once he joined the *Gunsmoke* family and was immediately accepted by his co-stars. "Between takes, Jim, Amanda Blake, and Milburn Stone...sat on director's chairs on that wooden sidewalk and traded some of the best, funniest stories I'd ever heard," he recalled in his 1994 autobiography. His debut resulted in an avalanche of fan mail, so CBS chartered a plane and sent him around the country

Blake, Stone, Curtis, Reynolds

to promote the show and meet with the network's affiliate station owners.

On one of these press junkets he met actress Judy Carne, who would become his first wife. Reynolds told his co-stars what a great cook Carne was, and the couple were soon hosting dinner parties for Amanda Blake, Milburn Stone and Ken Curtis. When Reynolds and Carne were married in June of 1963, the guest included Kitty,

Doc and Festus. According to Carne, as the *Gunsmoke* stars arrived at the ceremony, "the photographers had a field day." After the wedding, the couple settled down and bought a dachshund puppy they named Festus.

Although today Reynolds remembers his years on *Gunsmoke* as the happiest of his life, he was becoming creatively frustrated, even though a story idea he and Ken Curtis suggested became the 1965 episode "Eliab's Aim." "The bottom line was the job had become boring," he confessed many years later. "Each week Quint got insulted. Then Jim, after spending six days in Hawaii, would show up on the set and beat up the guy who insulted me." Milburn Stone knew of Reynolds' restlessness and advised him to move on. "You're a movie star," Stone told him. "Get the hell out of here! Go do it!"

"Milly was like a surrogate father to me," Reynolds said. "He was an extraordinary man. He gave me the courage to leave, and I don't regret it."

The final Quint episode, "Bank Baby," aired on March 20, 1965, toward the end of the tenth season. Just as there was never any explanation of where Chester had gone, the Dodge City blacksmith simply vanished and was mentioned only in passing on two occasions ("The Goldtakers" in 1966, "The Fourth Victim" in 1974).

After *Gunsmoke*, movie stardom for Reynolds was still a few years off. With the exception of the 1965 feature *Operation C.I.A*, he made the rounds on such shows as *Branded, Flipper, The F.B.I.* and *12 O'Clock High*. In the fall of 1966 he headlined a series of his own, ABC's *Hawk*, in which he played a modern day detective who also happened to be an Iroquois Indian. Despite the novelty of being filmed on location in New York, the show lasted barely three months, and he once again hit the guest star circuit, including an episode of Dennis Weaver's *Gentle Ben*.

Hoping to duplicate Clint Eastwood's success in Italian-made "spaghetti Westerns," Reynolds went overseas to star in 1967's *Navajo Joe* under the impression that the film was being made by Eastwood's collaborator Sergio Leone. The director, however, turned out to be one Sergio Corbucci, and *Navajo Joe* would never be mentioned in the same breath as *A Fistful of Dollars*. Back home, Reynolds fared somewhat better in the Western features *Sam Whiskey* and *100*

Rifles, both in 1969. After one more respectable film, (*Impasse*) and two stinkers (*Shark!, Skullduggery*), it was back to the guest star circuit and *Dan August*, another short-lived detective series on ABC.

A major turning point in Reynolds' career was the 1972 feature *Deliverance*, which finally fulfilled Milburn Stone's prophecy. Burt Reynolds was now a movie star, but he was determined to keep his ego in check. More than three decades after his time on the series, he reflected that "*Gunsmoke* was where I learned what a set should be like. You know, the stars don't go to lunch with the day players and the day players don't eat with the extras. Jim Arness just tore that all to hell and everybody was treated very nice. And it does start with the star of the show. *Gunsmoke* was a very classy show and nobody dared act like an ass or a jerk because Jim wasn't."

Following such high profile films as *The Longest Yard, Smokey and the Bandit, Semi-Tough, The End, Starting Over* and *Sharky's Machine*, the only television appearances he made would be those he felt like making. His first regular series was *B.L. Stryker*, a 1989-90 private eye show that aired every few weeks as part of *The ABC Mystery Movie*. Much more successful was the CBS sitcom *Evening Shade*, which ran for four seasons and earned him an Emmy. The show was shot at CBS Studio City, where he had spent his last two seasons as Quint Asper. When feeling sentimental, he would wander to where the exterior set of Dodge City had stood before being dismantled in 1988. "It's all torn down," he told a reporter, "but I've walked around with great feeling for those days. I was very happy then."

Ken Curtis

KEN CURTIS
"FESTUS HAGGEN"

256 Episodes
(December 8, 1962)
(January 18, 1964–March 31, 1975)

"I have to say the character of Festus is unique. In fact, I think it's the most unusual character ever created for any television series."

(Ken Curtis)

"Last but not least, we come to the question of Chester," critic Cleveland Amory wrote in an early 1964 review of *Gunsmoke*. "We have done our best to be philosophical about his departure, and we've tried to make friends with the new-uns. We love Burt Reynolds as Quint, and we're growing fond of Festus…"

After nine seasons of Dennis Weaver's immensely popular character, Ken Curtis, who had already done three half-hour episodes of *Gunsmoke*, was saddled with the unenviable task of wrangling his way into the position of Matt Dillon's right hand man. His initial appearance as Festus Haggen, in the 1962 episode "Us Haggens," was intended as a one-time shot, but audience response was so over-whelmingly positive that producer Norman Macdonnell had no qualms about bringing the character back when it was learned that Weaver had finalized a deal to star in the series *Kentucky Jones*. Coincidentally, the prototype for Festus had been created for a 1959 episode of *Have Gun-Will Travel* ("The Naked Gun"), written and directed by the same team (Les Crutchfield and Andrew McLaglen, respectively) who had done the same for "Us Haggens." McLaglen remembered Curtis as "a terrific guy, and it was me who got him to play the Festus character on *Gunsmoke*, in a recurring role that later became a regular. The roles were similar and I recommended he play the Festus part." On *Have Gun-Will Travel*, Curtis portrayed a scruffy drifter named Monk, of whom Festus was a slightly more refined extension. The next season, Monk returned in the 1960 episode "Love's Young Dream," which at one point was considered as a pilot for a spinoff series. Curtis instead went on to co-star with Larry Pennell as a skydiver in 76 episodes of the syndicated adventure *Ripcord*.

Curtis was born Curtis Gates in 1916. His father was a Colorado sheriff, and like the character with whom he would forever be identified, Curtis did chores around the jail. Originally interested in studying medicine, he ultimately gravitated to music as both a singer and composer. Migrating to Los Angeles, in 1939, he was judged a sufficiently skilled vocalist to replace Frank Sinatra in Tommy Dorsey's band. (On *Gunsmoke*, he would occasionally have the opportunity to sing, and recorded an album for Capitol Records, the cover a photograph of Festus and his mule Ruth.) World War II interrupted his career, and he served in the Army from 1942 to 1945. Back in Hollywood, Columbia Pictures offered him a movie contract after he was heard warbling "Tumbling Tumbleweeds" on a radio program.

Between 1945 and 1949, Curtis cranked out nearly a dozen low-budget "singing cowboy" films (*Song of the Prairie, Rhythm*

Roundup, Singing on the Trail, etc.) that were no challenge to the popularity Gene Autry and Roy Rogers. From 1949 to 1953, he was also a member of the Sons of the Pioneers, who can be heard in director John Ford's *Wagonmaster* (with a young James Arness) and seen performing in Ford's *Rio Grande*, both from 1950. Two years later, Curtis married Ford's daughter, Barbara, which led to parts in his father-in-law's films *The Quiet Man, Mister Roberts, The Searchers, The Wings of Eagles, The Last Hurrah* and *The Horse Soldiers* between 1952 and 1959. During this period he found additional work in *Spring Reunion, The Missouri Traveler, Escort West* and *The Young Land.* Trying his hand at producing, he was responsible for a pair of low budget 1959 drive-in classics, *The Giant Gila Monster* and *The Killer Shrews*, also acting in the latter.

More significant than his two science-fiction efforts and continued work in John Ford films (*The Alamo, Two Rode Together*) were Curtis' first roles in series television, beginning with the episode "Jayhawkers" toward the end of *Gunsmoke*'s fourth season. This was followed by his first appearance as Monk on *Have Gun-Will Travel*, and then two more *Gunsmoke*s ("The Ex-Urbanites," "Speak Me Fair"), broadcast just one month apart during season five. When John Ford agreed to direct an episode of *Wagon Train* ("The Colter Craven Story"), he insisted on giving bit parts to his stock company, including his son-in-law and even a heard-but-not-seen John Wayne. After producing a third film (1960's *My Dog, Buddy*), his second stint as Monk, and guest starring on *Perry Mason* and *Rawhide*, he had time for little more than *Ripcord.*

With the exception of the segment Ford directed for 1962's *How the West Was Won*, the "Us Haggens" episode was all Curtis did until returning to *Gunsmoke* not as Festus but as the title character in season nine's "Lover Boy." By then, the fall of 1963, the show was in its third year as an hourly program and had fallen out of the Top Ten for the first time since 1955. New blood was needed, and it arrived roughly three months later when Festus Haggen rode into Dodge on January 18, 1964. The episode, "Prairie Wolfer," was the first of only two to feature both Festus and Chester. "Once a Haggen," broadcast two weeks later, was the second, and in April Chester said adios.

Curtis and Arness

For a while, no one—not even Matt Dillon—knew quite what to make of Dodge City's newest citizen. Although it was hinted that Festus definitely had a shady past, it soon became obvious he was the most honest and reliable of the many Haggen relatives that occasionally passed through town. As Festus grew comfortable being around civilized folks, the possibility for more humor—particularly in scenes with Doc and Quint—increased. Compared to those moments, dramatic situations involving Festus had greater impact, and, as Dennis Weaver had done with Chester, Curtis was able to portray the character as much more than comic relief. Thanks to such episodes as "May Blossoms," "The Kite," "Comanches is Soft" and "Now That April's Here," Festus had been firmly integrated into the *Gunsmoke* family before his first season was over. Aside from John Ford's 1964 epic *Cheyenne Autumn*, Ken Curtis would play no one but Festus for the next eleven years.

Scenes centering around Festus and Doc, whether humorous or poignant, were always memorable, and Curtis' favorite episode, "Wishbone," finds him saving the life of Dodge City's snake-bitten "on'ry ol' scudder." Curtis and Milburn Stone became good friends off the set, making personal appearances together and socializing with one another's families on weekends. "Mil is one of the most entertaining fellows I've ever been around in my life," Curtis told a reporter after his first season as Festus. "He's one of the most honest guys I've ever met." When *Gunsmoke* was canceled, Curtis was quick to buy Doc Adams' roll top desk, at which Stone had sat for so many years. In 1979, the former co-stars, dressed as Festus and Doc, were the only cast members to participate in the ABC special *When the West Was Fun*, entering through batwing saloon doors as the *Gunsmoke* theme was played.

Curtis guest starred on *Petrocelli* and James Arness' *How the West Was Won* series, joined Buck Taylor in the feature *Pony Express Rider* (1976), made the television films *California Gold Rush* (1981) and *Lost* (1983), and played Hoyt Coryell on the one and only season of *The Yellow Rose* (1983-84). His final series work was an episode of *Airwolf*.

At a memorial service for actor Jim Davis, early in 1982, Curtis revealed that at one time James Arness thought about quitting *Gunsmoke*. "Only one other actor—Jim Davis—was considered to take over as Matt Dillon," he said.

When approached by producer John Mantley to reprise his iconic role as Festus Haggen in the first *Gunsmoke* movie, Curtis was reportedly insulted by the money he was offered and countered by asking for twice what Amanda Blake was getting. He and Mantley never spoke again.

His attempt at retiring was interrupted by the telefilm *Once Upon a Texas Train* (1988), starring Willie Nelson, and a reunion with his *Yellow Rose* co-star Sam Elliott for *Conagher*, another movie for television, whose cast included Buck Taylor. Curtis was not in the best of health during the production and would not live to see it broadcast. He suffered a heart attack on April 28, 1991, sitting next to Doc's old desk. *Conagher* aired in July.

Cast on the set of "Old Friend" (1967). Glenn Strange, Curtis, Roger Ewing, Arness, Blake, Stone

ROGER EWING
"CLAYTON THADDEUS GREENWOOD"

46 Episodes
(October 2, 1965–September 25, 1967)

"Any actor who was working on television at that time would say the best show to work on was **Gunsmoke.** *It was always a joy."*

(Roger Ewing, 1990)

The gradual transition from Chester to Festus went smoothly, but finding a replacement for Quint, someone who would attract younger viewers, was more problematic. Burt Reynolds was last seen in Dodge City on March 20, 1965, and a dozen episodes went by before Roger Ewing was introduced as Thad Greenwood the following season. James Arness balked at the notion of Matt having such a youthful deputy, but producers Mantley and Leacock felt there was a need to show a young person benefiting from the marshal's years of experience and instructed writer Calvin Clements to create the character.

In the October 2, 1965 episode "Clayton Thaddeus Greenwood," Thad, the son of an Oklahoma sheriff, travels to Dodge in search of his father's killers. Matt, while a lawman in Tulsa, knew the elder Greenwood and ends up making Thad his part-time deputy for $8 a month. The job lasted for two seasons (the series' final year in black-and-white and the first in color) and 46 episodes, the last installment ("The Prodigal") filmed for the twelfth season but not shown until the next. Aside from his debut, Thad's largest share of the spotlight occurred in the episodes "Harvest" and "Quaker Girl."

Roger Ewing, who played Thad as somewhat withdrawn but pleasant, had little acting experience prior to *Gunsmoke* and would not have looked out of place surfing the waves at Malibu Beach. His few credits were limited to the feature films *Ensign Pulver* (1964) and *None But the Brave* (1965) and guest roles on *Bewitched, The Farmer's Daughter,* and *The Eleventh Hour* before venturing out onto the television prairie. During *Gunsmoke*'s tenth season he landed a part in the episode "Song for Dying," followed six weeks later by an episode of *Rawhide,* "The Calf Women."

Although Ewing enjoyed his time on *Gunsmoke,* he found work hard to come by after leaving the show, and the allure of the entertainment industry quickly faded. He appeared in an episode of *Room 222* and the 1972 film *Play It As It Lays* before deciding to wander the globe and concentrate on this passion for photography.

Cast in 1972. Strange, Stone, Blake, Curtis, Arness, Buck Taylor

BUCK TAYLOR
"NEWLY O'BRIEN"

103 Episodes
(November 6, 1967–March 10, 1975)

"I think I've got one of the better jobs in Hollywood. If I never did anything but **Gunsmoke** *I'd be happy."*
(Buck Taylor, 1973)

Matt Dillon spent the first two months of *Gunsmoke*'s thirteenth year with only Festus to back him up. That changed with the ninth episode, "The Pillagers," when gunsmith and aspiring physician Newly O'Brien—after helping to rescue Miss Kitty from stagecoach bandits—settled in Dodge City for eight seasons. Chosen for the role was Buck Taylor, who only a month before had played an obnoxious gunslinger in the first half of the two-part episode "Vengeance," which was never seen again until the series went into syndication in the fall of 1975.

Taylor, the son of beloved character actor Dub Taylor, was born Walter Clarence Taylor, III, in 1938, and grew up on a ranch not far from Hollywood. Due to his size at birth—nine pounds—his father gave him his distinctive nickname before he could walk. As a young man he developed interests in both art and athletics, and in his early twenties tried out for the United States Olympic gymnastics team, nearly making the cut. He came by his physical skill naturally, his mother having once been a member of an acrobatic dance act known as the Dean Sisters. After a year of classes in art and cinema at the University of Southern California, Taylor spent two years in Japan as a Navy firefighter. Upon returning to civilian life, he decided to try his hand at acting and stunt work, quickly landing jobs on such shows as *Have Gun-Will Travel, Stoney Burke, Combat!, The Fugitive, Ben Casey, The Outer Limits, The Rebel, The Virginian, Branded, Bonanza, Wagon Train, The Legend of Jesse James, Daniel Boone, Death Valley Days, The Big Valley* and *Alfred Hitchcock Presents.* He also appeared with Roger Ewing in the feature film *Ensign Pulver* (1964), followed by *And Now Miguel* (1966), *The Wild Angels* (1966) and *The Devil's Angels* (1967). Although he made a second attempt at becoming an Olympic gymnast in 1964, he decided to stick to acting, eventually hired as a semi-regular on the short-lived series *The Monroes*, the last episode of which aired in March of 1967. By November viewers were being introduced to him as Newly O'Brien, which may not have occurred had Taylor accepted the offer of playing Dano opposite Jack Lord on *Hawaii Five-O.*

Of Newly, John Mantley observed, "The four characters—Matt, Kitty, Doc and Festus—are a cross section. The one category we neglected was the young man who learns from his elders." In reality, Taylor was already pushing thirty by the time he was added to the cast, but according to Glenn Strange, who made personal appearances with him on the county fair and rodeo circuit, "He captures the kids—they're his." (In honor of the Long Branch bartender, Taylor named one of his sons Glenn, and another Matthew.) Taylor did, however, admit to profiting from being around more experienced thespians. "I don't try to compete with 'em. Actually they help me. Milburn is sorta my acting coach—I go to him whenever I have problems."

Taylor's final episode was "The Busters," which aired three weeks before the series ended, and was the last rerun broadcast by the network in September 1975. Twelve years later, Newly was back, this time as Dodge City's marshal, in *Gunsmoke: Return to Dodge*. During the interim, Taylor guest starred on *The Fall Guy* and *Lottery*, in the television movies *The Sacketts, Wild Times, The Cherokee Trail, No Man's Land*, and the independent features *Beartooth, Doc Hooker's Gang* and *Pony Express Rider*, the latter with Ken Curtis. Prior to the first *Gunsmoke* movie, he was reunited with James Arness for the television film *Alamo: 13 Days to Glory*.

Between 1989 and 1999, while launching his successful career as an artist, Taylor guest starred on *Walker, Texas Ranger* and kept busy in the previous century with roles on *Paradise, The Young Riders* and one of the *Desperado* television movies. Another telefilm, *Conagher*, found him again co-starring with Ken Curtis. His feature work included *Gettysburg, Tombstone* and the big screen version of the *Wild, Wild West* series.

During most of his time on *Gunsmoke*, Taylor and his first wife lived on a ranch in Montana. "I'd like to have lived 100 years ago," he said in 1973. "That ranch is the next best thing." No surprise, then, that he and his second wife settled on a 100-acre western spread, this one north of Fort Worth, Texas, where he continues to pursue his love of painting and is the official poster artist for the Forth Worth Stock Show.

In 2000, Taylor told a reporter that people often come up to him and say he looks "kind of like Newly on *Gunsmoke*." When he reveals that they are correct, their response is usually, "Nah, you ain't him. But you do look like him."

GLENN STRANGE
"SAM NOONAN"

222 Episodes
(September 30, 1961–November 26, 1973)

"Well, I smoked all these dang cancer sticks. People warned me and everything, and I didn't listen. Now I'm payin' the price."

(Glenn Strange, 1972)

He was never included with the regular cast in the opening or closing credits, but Glenn Strange was very much a part of the *Gunsmoke* family. If Matt Dillon needed assistance, or Miss Kitty was being pestered by some variety of prairie scum, bartender Sam Noonan could be counted on to step up, often wielding the shotgun he kept out of sight but close at hand.

Strange was born in Weed, New Mexico, on August 16, 1899, and knew how to play the fiddle before entering his teens, a talent that would later grant him entrance into the world of show business. Before that, however, he spent years herding cattle, taking a stab at heavyweight boxing, and working as a deputy sheriff.

In 1928, he joined a musical outfit known as the Arizona Wranglers, performing throughout the southwest and eventually on radio in Hollywood. Like many other country and western bands, the Wranglers made a handful of B-Westerns, but after branching out on his own as a rodeo rider, Strange began his acting career around 1930. Usually cast as a villain, he appeared along with Hoot Gibson, Buck Jones, Tom Tyler, Ken Maynard, Dick Foran, Gene Autry, John Wayne and other classic cowboys in literally dozens of films for several studios, including Monogram, Republic, Paramount, Warner Bros., and Universal.

In 1944, Strange took over the role of the Frankenstein monster in Universal's *The House of Frankenstein*, coached in how to play the role by the character's originator, Boris Karloff, who was cast as a mad doctor. Strange briefly reprised the part the following year in a sequel, *The House of Dracula*. Three years later, he portrayed the monster for the last time—and even had some lines of dialogue—

in *Abbott and Costello Meet Frankenstein*. Generally acknowledged as the funniest horror spoof of all time, Strange managed to steal every scene he was in.

On September 15, 1949, *The Lone Ranger* debuted on ABC, with Strange as the hero's nemesis, Butch Cavendish, in the first three episodes and another later in the season. In addition to five more *Lone Ranger*s, he found steady employment on the video range in such series as *The Adventures of Champion, The Adventures of Rin Tin Tin, Annie Oakley, Buffalo Bill, Jr., The Cisco Kid, Colt .45, Death Valley Days, Frontier Doctor, The Gene Autry Show, Hopalong Cassidy, Judge Roy Bean, The Adventures of Kit Carson, The Life and Legend of Wyatt Earp, The Range Rider, Rawhide, The Restless Gun, Stories of the Century, Sugarfoot, Tales of Wells Fargo, Wagon Train* and *26 Men*. He also played North Fork's stagecoach driver on several early episodes of *The Rifleman*.

Sometime in 1959, James Arness, by then an associate producer of *Gunsmoke*, ran into Strange and invited him to appear on the show, saying he enjoyed working with other tall actors. Consequently, Strange guest starred as a Long Branch customer in the sixth season episode "Old Faces," and as a cowboy in the same year's "Melinda Miles."

When the show began its seventh season as an hour-long program in 1961, Strange was there as Sam—unbilled—behind the bar, sporting a large moustache. For a dozen full seasons, Sam was an amiable and reliable presence in Dodge City, pouring drinks, bouncing drunks, riding with posses, playing fiddle, and often simply lending a sympathetic ear.

In 1972, during production of the eighteenth season, Strange learned he had lung cancer but never stopped working. Thanks to Arness, he continued to play Sam until he was no longer able, completing five episodes the next year, all of which were broadcast after his death on September 20, 1973. Sam Noonan was seen smiling and drawing beers for the last time at the close of the November 26 episode "The Hanging of Newly O'Brien."

Glenn Strange was buried in Hollywood's Forest Lawn Memorial Park on September 24, with the entire cast and crew of *Gunsmoke* in attendance. James Arness was one of two honorary pall bearers. When the other, Strange's good friend Bob Burns, began to choke up, Arness offered comfort by saying, "Bob, we're all gonna miss him. But he's always alive in our minds and hearts. Always remember that. He's always with us, he's never really going to leave us. He's just left us in body only, because we've got so many wonderful memories of that man."

"Glenn was one of the nicest men the Lord ever made," executive producer John Mantley said in his eulogy. "*Gunsmoke* was his life. He was a marvelous professional."

"Our cast is the closest family of performers ever to do a television show," Amanda Blake remarked after the service. "Glenn was part of that family. He was very close to all of us."

CHAPTER 2
THE FAMILIAR FACES
OF DODGE CITY

Over the course of twenty seasons, no less than fifty-five regular or semi-regular characters joined the cast of *Gunsmoke*. As near as can be determined, all of the following appeared in at least two episodes.

HARRY BOTKIN/BODKIN, Bank President: Six different actors played Dodge City's leading banker, whose surname was spelled Botkin in the early episodes, then changed to Bodkin. At various times the role was given to Wilfred Knapp, Gage Clark, Richard Deacon, Fay Roope and Joe Kearns, but most often to Roy Roberts, who made sixteen episodes. Roberts, a veteran of more than 200 films, guest starred on nearly twenty different television Westerns.

EMMETT BOWERS, Rancher: Dodge's most prominent horse rancher was portrayed by Russ Thorson, Tyler McVey, Harry Shannon and Bartlett Robinson.

JUDGE BROOKING: Several judges passed through Dodge during the early years of the series, but Howard Wendell was the first to make return visits.

JUDGE BROOKER: Herb Vigran was the first judge to apparently make Dodge his base of operations, appearing in ten episodes.

JIM BUCK, Stagecoach Driver: Robert Brubaker, also cast in different parts during the run of the series, made fourteen episodes as Dodge's most frequently seen stage driver before replacing Glenn Strange as the Long Branch's bartender in Season 19.

NATHAN BURKE, Freight Office Manager: Ted Jordan, after playing several different guest roles on the series, finally settled in to make 108 episodes as one of Dodge's most opinionated and meddlesome residents. Jordan, who co-starred with James Arness in the 1950 Audie Murphy Western *Sierra*, once told reporters he had possession of a diary kept by Marilyn Monroe.

CALE, Drifter: Young cowboy played by Carl Reindel in two episodes.

DR. JOHN CHAPMAN: Pat Hingle signed on to temporarily replace Milburn Stone for six episodes as Dodge City's physician while Stone recuperated from heart surgery. In 1992, Hingle played the villainous Colonel Tucker in the third *Gunsmoke* movie, "To the Last Man."

CLEM, Bartender: One of the Long Branch's earlier barkeeps, portrayed by Clem Fuller in two dozen episodes.

APRIL CONLAN, Girlfriend of Festus: Four episodes featured Elizabeth MacRae as the daughter of a Texas farmer, whose last name is uttered only once, and not very distinctly, during an exterior scene in "Us Haggens."

PERCY CRUMP, Undertaker: The man responsible for preparing the dearly (and not so dearly) departed for Boot Hill was played by the same actor in nine episodes, but using three different names during his time on the series: Kelton Garwood, Jonathan Harper and John Harper.

BARNEY DANCHES, Telegrapher: Dodge City's most familiar communicator was Charles Seel, who appeared as Barney eleven times. Seel also played different characters in two additional episodes.

ROLAND DANIEL, Hillbilly: Victor French, who worked as both an actor and director in numerous episodes, appeared as Roland in two of the four episodes involving a troublesome clan of hill folk making a nuisance of themselves in Dodge City.

JIM DOBIE, Hotel Owner: Dodge's premier lodging was the property of four actors: Gage Clark, Joe Kearns, Dan Sheridan, and Hal Smith.

"DIRTY" SALLY FERGUS: Jeanette Nolan guest starred on eight episodes of *Gunsmoke*, most memorably as this amusing recluse in three. The character was so popular that CBS produced the short-lived *Dirty Sally* series in early 1974.

MERRY FLORENE: Lane Bradbury, who guest starred on two earlier episodes, left her mark on the series four times as the only reputable member of the hillbilly family who stirred up trouble every time they came to Dodge City.

FLOYD, Bartender: Robert Brubaker took over as the Long Branch's barkeep for eight episodes after the death of Glenn Strange.

HANK GREEN, Restaurant Owner: Delmonico's eatery had several owners over the years, but Western veteran Harry Swoger (nearly two dozen series, including four episodes of *Gunsmoke*) was given the most to do.

MOSS GRIMMICK, Stable Owner: Proprietor of Dodge City's livery stable, portrayed by George Selk in forty-three episodes.

EMERY HAGGEN: The colorful Shug Fisher, who co-starred with Ken Curtis on the *Ripcord* series, played Festus' cousin on two occasions. He made an additional fourteen episodes of *Gunsmoke* as different characters including several appearances as Oasis Saloon owner Obie.

LAMBERT HAGGEN: Yet another of Festus' many cousins, portrayed by the versatile Royal Dano, who appeared on more than thirty Western series, including thirteen episodes of *Gunsmoke*.

CHARLIE HALLIGAN, Townsman: Charles Wagenheim, an experienced character actor for many years before joining the series for twenty-nine episodes, once said he was not sure who Halligan was or what he did for a living.

MISS HANNAH: The second owner of the Long Branch Saloon, played by Fran Ryan in five episodes of the final season as well as the first *Gunsmoke* movie, "Return to Dodge." The late Ms. Ryan was often mistaken for actress Marjorie Main (film's Ma Kettle) and was misidentified as having portrayed Miss Kitty in some obituaries.

DUMP HART, Homesteader: Portrayed by Western stalwart Lane Bradford (nearly sixty different series), who guest starred as Dump and other characters in eleven episodes.

IKE HOCKETT, Farmer: Played by both John Reilly and David Soul in two episodes of the final season. David Soul later co-starred on the *Starsky and Hutch* series.

JED HOCKETT, Farmer: Portrayed by the late Harry Morgan, best known for his roles on *Dragnet* and *M*A*S*H*. Morgan appeared in two earlier *Gunsmoke* episodes as different characters.

LUKE HOCKETT: Herman Poppe as one of Jed Hockett's three sons.

SHEP HOCKETT, Farmer: Dennis Redfield as Jed Hockett's youngest son.

EMMET HOLLY, Army Sergeant: In addition to five other episodes, Forrest Tucker played this would-be suitor of Miss Kitty's two times.

JOE, Waiter: Mathew McCue played Delmonico's largely silent waiter, given only one close-up shot in twenty-eight episodes!

ABELIA JOHNSON, Homesteader: Jacqueline Scott, perhaps best known for her role as David Janssen's sister on *The Fugitive*, made three appearances as this single mother and possible object of Festus' affections. Ms. Scott was a guest on nine episodes in all.

JONATHAN JOHNSON: Played twice by Mike Durkin, once by Brian Morrison.

MARIEANNE JOHNSON: Played twice by Susan Olsen, once by Jodie Foster.

WILBUR JONAS, Storeowner: The late Dabbs Greer was possibly the busiest character actor in the history of television, on both Western and non-Western series. It would be easier to list the shows he did *not* guest on. Surprisingly, he was a regular on but three: *Hank, Little House on the Prairie* and *Gunsmoke*, in which he portrayed Wilbur Jonas in 36 episodes. He was also Chester's Uncle Wesley in another.

BULL LANDERS, Saloon Owner: The Bull's Head was Kitty Russell's main competition in Dodge, its owner played by Victor Izay in nine of ten episodes. Val Avery was cast as Bull in one. Izay also appeared as a minister in the third *Gunsmoke* movie, "The Long Ride."

WOODY LATHROP, Storekeeper: Operator of one of Dodge City's three general stores, and usually called Mr. Lathrop. The character was portrayed in thirty-one episodes by Woodrow Chambliss, who was occasionally cast as other characters as well.

SARAH LYNN, Prospective Bride: Played by Michele Marsh in two final season episodes.

MELANIE: Susan Morrow portrayed one of Chester's possible love interests in two episodes.

HANK MILLER, Stableman: Hank Patterson, known to sitcom fans as Fred Ziffel on *Green Acres*, appeared first as an assistant to livery owner Moss Grimmick, then as the sole proprietor of Dodge's stable in twenty-eight episodes. At one point, the sign over the stable door read "Hank Patterson" rather than Miller.

MILT, Telegrapher: Ollie O'Toole played Dodge City's telegrapher in the early seasons.

ELBERT MOSES, Hillbilly: Anthony James portrayed one of Merry Florene's half-brothers in all four episodes involving the mountain clan.

CALEB NASH, Mountain Man: Denver Pyle, once a leading contender for the part of Matt Dillon, was cast in this role twice even though he seemed to have been killed the first time. Pyle appeared in a total of fourteen *Gunsmoke* episodes.

ED O'CONNOR, Rancher: Played in thirteen episodes by Tom Brown, who also co-starred on the daytime drama *General Hospital* while making *Gunsmoke*.

BILL PENCE, Saloon Owner: Half-owner of the Long Branch, portrayed at various times by Joseph Mell, Judson Pratt, Steve Ellsworth and Barney Phillips. (An early episode features a rancher named Bill Pence.)

LOUIE PHEETERS, Town Drunk: Memorably brought to life by James Nusser in seventy-two episodes. Nusser also played bit parts before the series expanded to an hour.

MRS. RONIGER, Farmer's Wife: In addition to smaller roles, the remarkably fertile character—once said to have had a thirteenth child—was played by Peggy Rea.

CAL ROSS, Storeowner: Another of Dodge's three general store proprietors, played by Lou Vernon, Ben Wright and Stanley Adams.

ROY, Storeowner: Western veteran Roy Barcroft played the part, and was sometimes also referred to as Mr. Jonas, in a dozen episodes.

RUDY, Bartender: Rudy Sooter made six credited appearances as the Long Branch's other barkeep in six episodes, sometimes strumming guitar while Sam played fiddle.

MA SMALLEY, Boarding House Owner: Once played by Mabel Albertson, but most famously by Sarah Selby, an experienced radio and sitcom performer, in thirteen episodes.

BRECKINRIDGE "BRECK" TAYLOR, Attorney: Portrayed by Ben Cooper, a familiar face in dozens of Western films on screens large and small, as well as co-star of the Civil War series *The Americans*.

FRANK TEETERS, Barber: Dodge City's chatty hair clipper in the early years of the series, played by Jess Kirkpatrick.

TOBEEL, Indian Guide: Frank DeKova, arguably the most famous Hollywood Indian (after Iron Eyes Cody and Jay Silverheels), portrayed Matt Dillon's reliable assistant in three episodes.

HOWARD UZZEL, Hotel Clerk: Usually addressed as Howie, Howard Culver was the Dodge House's desk clerk for all twenty seasons, appearing in forty-eight episodes.

JEB WILLIS, Farmer's Son: Played by James Hampton in two episodes.

Arness, 1955

CHAPTER 3
THE GLORY YEARS
(1955–61)

Season One (1955–56)
39 Episodes / Rating: Unknown

"The stories the first year of **Gunsmoke** *were the greatest."*

(Jame Arness, 1981)

In August of 1955, CBS announced that its radio program *Gunsmoke* would debut on television the following month. Both John Meston and Norman Macdonnell had assumed that they would be in charge of production, but the network handed the reins to Charles Marquis Warren, a writer and director who had worked previously with Arness (*Hellgate*, 1952), Stone (*Arrowhead*, 1953) and most recently Weaver (*Seven Angry Men*, 1955). Although Meston and Macdonnell remained involved with the series (as writer and associate producer, respectively), Warren was at first reluctant to make the move from feature films to television, particularly when he learned that CBS had budgeted each episode at only $25,000, including the actors' salaries. However, he found the network's offer of seven thousand dollars a month hard to refuse and ended up producing all of the first thirty-nine episodes, as well as directing twenty-six and writing four scripts based on Meston's radio plays, and one of his own. The radio cast was allowed to audition, but Warren, for one reason or another, opted to go with Arness, Stone, Weaver and Blake instead, and CBS went along with his decisions. A proposal the network vetoed was his suggestion that the name of the show be changed to *The Outriders*. Warren felt that *Gunsmoke* sounded too much like a B-Western, and there indeed had been an Audie Murphy film with that title two years before. A few years later, Warren attempted to resurrect the title for his creation *Rawhide*, but it was again rejected by the network.

Prior to 1955, the television Western had been aimed almost exclusively at younger viewers whose heroes quickly became Gene Autry, Hopalong Cassidy, The Cisco Kid, The Lone Ranger, and Roy Rogers. At the end of the 1950-51 season, the first for which the A.C. Nielsen Media Research rating system tabulated the habits of the home audience, both *The Lone Ranger* and *Hopalong Cassidy* ranked in the Top 10. No Western would be so highly rated until 1956-57, when *Gunsmoke*, then concluding its second season, came in at #8.

Gunsmoke, one of only ten Westerns on network television at the time, debuted on Saturday, September 10, 1955, four days after ABC's *The Life and Legend of Wyatt Earp*, considered the first "adult Western" on network television despite the melodramatic and distracting background warbling of the Ken Darby Singers. While *Gunsmoke* easily beat *Tomorrow's Careers*, an instructional series on ABC, it ran second to NBC's very popular *The George Gobel Show*, then in its second year. The next season, when both *Gunsmoke* and *The Life and Legend of Wyatt Earp* made their first appearances in the Top 30 (*Earp* at #18), George Gobel was eating Matt Dillon's dust.

The *Gunsmoke* pilot was "Hack Prine," filmed roughly a year after the radio version was broadcast, but the network instead chose "Matt Gets It," the second episode to be shot, as the premiere. As a favor to his friend Warren, John Wayne, wearing Western garb, introduced the first airing of the series:

"Good evening. My name's Wayne. Some of you may have seen me before. I hope so. I've been kicking around Hollywood a long time. I've made a lot of pictures out here, all kinds. Some of them have been Westerns, and that's what I'm here to tell you about tonight—a Western, a new television show called *Gunsmoke*. No, I'm not in it. I wish I were though, 'cause I think it's the best thing of its kind to come along, and I hope you'll agree with me. It's honest, it's adult, it's realistic.

When I first heard about the show *Gunsmoke*, I knew there was only one man to play in it—James Arness. He's a young fella and may be new to some of you, but I've worked with him and I predict he'll be a big star. So you might as well get used to him, like you've had to get used to me. Now I'm proud to introduce my friend Jim Arness and *Gunsmoke*."

Wayne's admission that he wished he had been offered the role of Matt Dillon was pure whimsy. Nevertheless, to this day there are those who believe it to be true. Arness, who was not aware Wayne had done an introduction until it aired, lent credence to the myth in 1957 by telling TV Guide, "I have a hunch CBS first offered the part to Mr. Wayne, but that he turned it down and recommended me. He's the kind of guy who would do a generous thing like that and never let anyone know."

Another false belief among some *Gunsmoke* fans is that all of the half-hour episodes began with Matt Dillon surveying Dodge City from atop Boot Hill, with narration by Arness. Although several variations of this opening were used frequently during the earliest seasons, they gradually became occasional and had stopped altogether before the end of the fifth year. The famous title scene of Matt stepping out to confront his nemesis for a showdown on Front Street was not filmed until 1959, then later tacked onto the beginning of the older episodes.

The theme music, known variously as "Gunsmoke Trail" or "On the Trail," was composed by Rex Koury, who also scored the radio version of the show. In later years, the theme was somewhat rearranged by Morton Stevens and Fred Steiner, as well as used more often as background music than in the half-hour episodes. To date there have been over thirty recorded renditions of the theme, the first on RCA by the Prairie Chiefs, and sheet music was made available to high school and college marching bands. Much of the incidental music came from CBS's vast library, composed by either Lucien Moraweck or Rene Garriguenc, and was also heard on such series as *Have Gun-Will Travel, Rawhide,* and even the contemporary *Perry Mason.* Over the years other gifted composers who contributed scores included Elmer Bernstein, Jerry Goldsmith, Jerrold Immel, Leon Klatzkin, Jerome Moross, John Parker, and Franz Waxman.

A new half-hour episode—eventually 233 in all—was filmed approximately every four days, taking anywhere from forty to forty-eight hours to complete. Extensive location shooting took place mainly at Gene Autry's Melody Ranch and an area then usually referred to as Conejo Flats, with interiors filmed at a rather ramshackle facility across the street from Paramount Studios in Hollywood. Known at various times as California Studios and Producers Studios (and now named Raleigh Studios), it was built in 1914 and had been used for some of the later Marx Brothers and Sherlock Holmes films. By the 1950s it was being rented almost exclusively by independent producers and television series. Warren eventually convinced CBS to let him construct a phony exterior Dodge City set there, making trips out to Autry's ranch an unfortunate rarity. After the first five seasons, the *Gunsmoke* company moved to Paramount for the following three.

As a known commodity from radio, *Gunsmoke* had no trouble attracting sponsors, chiefly L&M Cigarettes, for which James Arness and Amanda Blake did occasional commercials, both on film and in print.

TV Guide listed *Gunsmoke* as "A new Western adventure series starring James Arness as Dodge City Marshal Matt Dillon." Amusingly, they misidentified Dennis Weaver's character as "Cheater." In the November 26 issue, the week the episode "The Hunter" aired, critic Robert Stahl said the show's "production and direction reflect skill and attention to detail." Of Kitty, he remarked, "...the writers don't let her interfere much with *Gunsmoke*'s taut, action-packed stories."

During the first season, only Matt and Chester appeared in all thirty-nine episodes, with interesting facts regarding their backgrounds scattered throughout. Viewers learned that Matt had been a soldier and spent time in Missouri and Arizona before coming to Dodge. Chester, whose last name was not revealed until the fourth episode ("Home Surgery"), mentions being raised by Ben Cherry, a friend of his father, and is visited by his brother Magnus. As for Doc, except for his old army outfit being the Third Illinois Cavalry, and having once been in love with a woman who married someone else and died giving birth, not much was disclosed. Kitty remained more or less a woman of mystery.

Aside from the four principal actors, the sole citizen of Dodge City introduced in the first episode was Howard Culver as Dodge House desk clerk Howard "Howie" Uzzel, who would go on to appear in forty-eight episodes spanning the entire duration of the series. Two other longtime residents making their initial bows before the season was over were Dabbs Greer as storeowner Wilbur Jonas, and George Selk as stableman Moss Grimmick.

The first season ran for nearly a year, from September 1955 to August 1956, and featured numerous episodes that would come to be considered among the best of the entire series, including "Matt Gets It," "Kite's Reward," "The Hunter," "No Handcuffs," "Reward for Matt," "Hack Prine," "The Killer, "Doc's Revenge," "The Guitar," "Cara," and "Unmarked Grave."

Gunsmoke had been on the air for only a few months when Dell Comics published the first of twenty-seven issues that would run through 1961, every cover featuring a full-color shot of Matt Dillon wielding—or about to draw—his trusty six-gun.

When the Emmy Awards were broadcast on March 17, 1956, *Gunsmoke*, barely through the first half of its first season, was among the nominees for Best Action or Adventure Series. It, along with *Alfred Hitchcock Presents, Dragnet,* and *The Lineup*, was beaten by ABC's *Disneyland*, whose standout segment had been "Davy Crockett and the River Pirates."

Before shooting for the second season began, Arness, Angie Dickinson, Robert Wilke, Emile Meyer and Harry Carey, Jr. made *Gun the Man Down*, a solid 78-minute B feature, for United Artists. The screenplay was written by the prolific writer/director Burt Kennedy, and was the first big screen assignment for director Andrew V. McLaglen, who allegedly got the job courtesy of his pal John Wayne, whose Batjac company produced the film. Known as *Arizona Mission* when shown on television, the original title was restored when finally released on home video in 2007. As a change of pace from the Matt Dillon character, Arness played a "good" outlaw. He also found time to shoot an episode of the dramatic anthology program *Front Row Center* and take a supporting role in *The First Traveling Saleslady*, a somewhat minor feature starring Ginger Rogers, notable as the last film produced by RKO, and the first appearance in a Western by a young Clint Eastwood.

The rest of the cast also took advantage of *Gunsmoke*'s first hiatus, guest starring on episodes of other series: Dennis Weaver on the newspaper drama *Big Town*, Amanda Blake on *Alfred Hitchcock Presents* and the afternoon drama *Matinee Theater*, Milburn Stone on *Front Row Center*.

James Arness

Season Two (1956–57)
39 Episodes / Rating: #8

"I just do what they tell me to do. I don't pretend to be a director or writer."

(James Arness, 1957)

Gunsmoke was still among ten network Westerns on the air in 1956, but it was one of only two to rank in the Top 30 shows at the end of the season, the other ABC's *The Life and Legend of Wyatt Earp*. Popularity was not all the two series had in common. Both shot exteriors at Melody Ranch, the largest Western location in Southern California (four streets, Mexican village, ranch house, barn) and for its second season, the *Earp* producers decided to change the setting to Dodge City. As if this were not confusing enough, *Gunsmoke* and *Earp* each featured regular supporting characters named Doc. (The first season of *Earp* co-starred Douglas Fowley first as Doc Fabrique, then switching to Doc Holliday in the third year.)

Producer Charles Marquis Warren, never thrilled to be working in television, was worn out after the first season of *Gunsmoke*. Not only had he supervised the casting, look and tone of the show, he directed most of the episodes and had a hand in writing several scripts. He was also weary of arguing with Arness and Stone about how their characters should behave in various situations. Consequently, he produced only thirteen of the second season's thirty-nine episodes before turning the reins over to Norman Macdonnell.

During the season, characterization became equally as important as plot. Matt, Doc, Chester and Kitty were more multi-dimensional, and the relationships between the four deepened. Some of Kitty's background was finally revealed, when she mentions having once worked on riverboats, and especially when her ne'er-do-well father shows up in Dodge. Viewers also learned that she was half-owner of the Long Branch Saloon. Also disclosed was the fact that Doc had once lived in both Tennessee and Missouri, where he once met Sam Clemens, the future Mark Twain. Chester, who is shot for the first time, continues to perfect his brewing of the jailhouse coffee, and there is a reference to his once being a cook in the army. Matt remarks that it has been a long time since he was in California and he has "lived around quite a few places." He is even more aggressive in his efforts to maintain law and order, particularly in such outstanding episodes as "The Round Up," "Spring Term," "Bloody Hands" and "No Indians," one of the best moments of the series. Other highlights of the season included "Cow Doctor," "Greater Love," "Kick Me," "Skid Row," "Cain," "Last Fling," and "Bureaucrat."

In January 1957, *Gunsmoke* was named the fourth Best Filmed Series by *Radio Daily*, and in March, Arness received an Emmy nomination for Best Continuing Performance by an Actor in a Dramatic Series. *Wyatt Earp*'s Hugh O'Brian was also nominated, but the award went to Robert Young for his role on, inexplicably, the sitcom *Father Knows Best*. In May, Arness made the first of his eleven appearances as Matt Dillon on the cover of TV Guide. The accompanying article described him as "Marshal from Minnesota."

Dennis Weaver and Amanda Blake kept their acting skills sharpened between seasons by working on other shows, Weaver on episodes of *The Silent Service* and *Climax*, Blake on *State Trooper* and *Red Skelton*.

In addition to the Dell comic books, the marketing of products to promote the series included two versions of Matt Dillon's gun from the Halco company, one with a leather holster and cap gun, the other just a gun with a plastic clip holding six bullets.

Season Three (1957–58)
39 Episodes / Rating: #1

"There are very few series that run longer than five years. I have to start thinking of other roles for the future, or else I'll be a sitting duck."
(James Arness, 1957)

Hollywood has always loved a sure thing, and the success of *Gunsmoke* had not gone unnoticed. At the beginning of the 1957-58 season, the number of network television Westerns had nearly doubled from the previous year, with eighteen being filmed at more than thirty different locations within fifty miles of Los Angeles. Some of the major series introduced that year were *Maverick, Tales*

James Arness

of Wells Fargo, Wagon Train and *Have Gun-Will Travel*. In the year-end ratings, nine Westerns placed in the Top 30, and *Gunsmoke* was in the lead, having attracted over forty-three percent of the viewing audience, a rare instance of true quality being rewarded with high numbers.

And the third season was indeed the strongest yet, with Dodge visited by Kitty's first love, now an outlaw. One of Matt's many jobs before becoming marshal was said to be a lawman in Dakota Territory. Doc says he was once a doctor on a riverboat called the Tennessee Belle, and that he mustered out of the army in 1865. Chester, who plays guitar for the first time, mentions being from Stone County, Missouri. Among the many outstanding episodes were "Blood Money," "Kitty's Outlaw," "Born to Hang," "Never Pester Chester," "How to Kill a Woman," "Doc's Reward," "Buffalo Man," "Claustrophobia," "The Cabin," "Texas Cowboys," "Amy's Good Deed," "The Big Con," "Chester's Hanging," and "Overland Express." Morgan Woodward, who would be cast in more major guest roles on the series than any other actor, made the first of his eighteen appearances with a very brief scene as Calhoun in "Potato Road." Kathleen Hite, who had written for the radio version, began turning out scripts for the show that were noticeably different from those being done by John Meston, Les Crutchfield and others. Toward the end of the following season, she was quoted as saying, "I approach a Western with less killing. I'm not a shoot-'em-up writer. I try to stress the character of the people and their problems." This is evident in this season's "Kitty's Outlaw," "Amy's Good Deed," "Cows and Cribs" and "Innocent Broad," and especially Hite's work in the early hour-long episodes.

TV Guide ran a brief profile of Dennis Weaver in January, and in March, Amanda Blake and James Arness were featured in a cover story for the magazine that addressed the matter of Kitty and Matt's relationship. Both actors, as well as producer Norman Macdonnell, came to the conclusion that if their characters were to launch an obvious romantic relationship, the show would suffer. "After he's declared his love, Matt could no longer be casual with her," Macdonnell said. "We'd have to start doing domestic problem stories."

Arness was more succinct when explaining why viewers would eventually object to Matt and Kitty becoming seriously involved:

"They don't want to see a U.S. marshal come home and help his wife wash the dishes." On a more personal note, he added: "If they ever get married—*Pow!*—that's all, man; we're finished! As far as I'm concerned, that would be my last show."

Another concern among fans of the show continued to be Chester's bad leg. As early as the first season episode "Chester's Mail Order Bride," the network received letters from viewers who mistakenly thought the character's limb had been fixed. In reality, a couple of scenes were edited so sharply that Dennis Weaver appeared to be walking normally. During the third year, CBS heard from a cancer researcher from the University of California's medical center who said he had "serious doubts" about Weaver's health. The doctor's concern stemmed from the position of Chester's footprints in a close-up shot from a recent episode. The network assured him that Weaver was just fine, thank you.

In January, Arness flew to New York for an appearance on *The Ed Sullivan Show*. Dressed as Matt Dillon, he answered Sullivan's questions regarding his height and birthplace, then participated in a dramatic *Gunsmoke* skit with two other actors.

At the 1957-58 Emmy Awards, held on April 15, *Gunsmoke* beat *Maverick*, *Wagon Train*, *Perry Mason* and *Lassie* in the category of Best Dramatic Series with Continuing Characters, the award accepted by producer Norman Macdonnell. Although Arness and Weaver were denied awards as Best Actor and Best Supporting Actor in a Drama or Comedy by, respectively, Robert Young (*Father Knows Best*) and Carl Reiner (*Caesar's Hour*), *Gunsmoke* editor Mike Pozen won for his work on the episode "How to Kill a Woman." John Meston's script for "Born to Hang" was nominated for Best Teleplay Writing for a show running a half hour or less, but lost to Paul Monash's "The Lonely Wizard," a segment of *Schlitz Playhouse of Stars*.

TV-Radio Mirror named *Gunsmoke* its favorite TV Western, and the series tied with *Wagon Train* as Radio Daily's Best Western Show of the Year for Television. But the greatest honor bestowed on *Gunsmoke* in 1958, perhaps even more prestigious than the Emmy, was the real Dodge City renaming Walnut Street "Gunsmoke" on August 1. James Arness, Milburn Stone and Amanda Blake, along with actors Chill Wills and David Janssen, flew to Kansas for the

James Arness

dedication ceremony. *Gunsmoke* had clearly become a masterwork of American popular culture after six years on radio and only three on television.

Before shooting commenced on the fourth season, Blake did an episode of *Studio One in Hollywood* and made the second of an eventual six appearances on *Red Skelton*. Stone guest starred on *Climax,* his last work outside *Gunsmoke* during the run of the series. Dennis Weaver was also on *Climax,* as well as *Playhouse 90*, but his most significant role was as a timid motel clerk in the film noir classic *Touch of Evil*, starring Charlton Heston and Orson Welles, who also directed.

Season Four (1958–59)
39 Episodes / Rating: #1

"Gunsmoke? *It proves that people will still go for folksy persiflage and that get-nowhere dialogue. But, you know, it's got something. Just don't ask me what."*
**(Former *Gunsmoke* producer
Charles Marquis Warren, 1958)**

Warren's statement was made in November, when his new series, *Rawhide*, had yet to find a sponsor or a slot on the CBS program schedule, the network understandably concerned that there were already too many six-gun sagas on the air. At the start of the 1958-59 season, there were twenty-six Westerns in prime time, a full dozen of which would end up in the Top 30 and be joined by *Rawhide*, an immediate hit when finally introduced in January. NBC became the first and only network to schedule a Western opposite *Gunsmoke*, the hour-long *Cimarron City*, starring George Montgomery, Audrey Totter, John Smith and Dan Blocker. Both Smith and Blocker would return the following season in, respectively, *Laramie* and *Bonanza*. *Cimarron City*, however, would not be back. Other short-lived and mostly forgotten series introduced that season included *The Californians, Rough Riders, Jefferson Drum* and *Buckskin*.

While several *Gunsmoke* stories focused on the problems of the guest stars, the relationships of the four principal characters continued to deepen during the fourth year, and fans were treated to more backstory revelations about each. Matt clarifies that he works for the War Department, not the state of Kansas, and says that five years before coming to Dodge he had been a lawman in Wichita. Most surprising is his admission that as a young man, he and a friend had been badly beaten when suspected of horse theft in Silver City. In another moment of candor, he confides to Kitty that he would like to quit being marshal, but that "something always comes up." Kitty says Matt is her best friend in the world, but that he still does not know much about women. Chester gives Kitty a couple of guitar lessons during the course of the season, and buys a nightcap because he is tired of sleeping with his head under the covers. The catfish Doc is periodically said to be after (all the way into the color years) is mentioned for the first time, and he is reunited with a nurse he worked with in the Civil War. The high caliber episodes included "Matt for Murder," "Monopoly," "Thoroughbreds," "How to Kill a Friend," "Love of a Good Woman," "Sky," "The F.U.," "Murder Warrant," "Print Asper," "The Constable," "Jayhawkers" and "Change of Heart," the latter two featuring the first guest spots by a pre-Festus Ken Curtis.

So prevalent were Westerns in the 1958-59 season that the Academy of Television Arts and Sciences created a one-time category of Best Western Series for that year's Emmy Awards, held in May. Scoring an upset was *Maverick*, then in its second (and best) season, beating out *Gunsmoke, Have Gun-Will Travel, The Rifleman* and *Wagon Train*. In January, *Maverick* had aired what was arguably its most famous episode, "Gun-Shy," a spoof of *Gunsmoke* with a marshal named Mort Dooley. Although he possessed a great sense of humor, James Arness was not amused, complaining, "It's poor taste and poor business for one show to rap another." In response, Marion Hargrove, who wrote the episode, said: "*Maverick* is perhaps the only Western that could poke fun at *Gunsmoke* and get away with it. *Gunsmoke* can do nothing in retaliation. It cannot parody *Maverick* without endangering its own impressive dignity, and *Maverick* has no dignity to attack." Time magazine reported that *Gunsmoke* did indeed plan to fight back by naming an outlaw in an upcoming episode after Roy Huggins, *Maverick*'s producer, but nothing came of the alleged threat.

Arness failed to earn an Emmy as the Best Actor in a Leading Role (Continuing Character) in a Dramatic Series for the third year in a row, the award going to *Perry Mason*'s Raymond Burr (James Garner of *Maverick* and *Have Gun-Will Travel*'s Richard Boone were also among the losers), and Barbara Hale of *Perry Mason* was chosen over Amanda Blake as Best Supporting Actress. But *Gunsmoke* did not walk away empty handed, Dennis Weaver winning as Best Supporting Actor.

Radio Daily once again dubbed *Gunsmoke* the Best Western Show of the Year, and TV-Radio Mirror said the series was its Favorite Half-Hour Dramatic Program. Look magazine honored it as the Best Action Series "that most effectively presented Western, mystery, or other adventure stories." The announcement was illustrated by a publicity shot taken during the production of the previous season's "Overland Express" episode. And Arness as Matt Dillon was featured on the cover of Time magazine's March 30 issue, along with Richard Boone, Ward Bond (*Wagon Train*), James Garner, Hugh O'Brian and Dale Robertson (*Tales of Wells Fargo*). The story, "The American Morality Play," attempted to explain the massive appeal of the television Western, and predicted that sales of merchandise promoting the shows would hit $125 million by the end of 1959.

Gunsmoke-related products then in the marketplace included a board game from Lowell, a Dodge City play set from Prestige, trading cards from Topps Gum, a children's book from Whitman, a target game, and even a Matt Dillon costume. How much income the stars saw from the sales of these items was, if anything, minimal, most of the money going to the network as license fees. But the cast was compensated for their work not only on the series itself (Arness was said to be making $78,000 per season), but also for appearing at rodeos and state fairs. "I can make $100,000 a year in personal appearances, just working weekends," claimed Arness.

While the Dodge City marshal eventually tired of this weekend work, these extracurricular activities provided his three co-stars with a secondary career. In February, Roy Rogers, in the midst of his performance at the Florida State Fair in Tampa, told the audience that Doc, Kitty and Chester happened to be in the audience. When

Stone, Blake and Weaver stood and waved, the crowd, according to Stone, nearly tore the place apart.

Season Five (1959–60)
39 Episodes / Rating: #1

"As far as I'm concerned, the show can go on forever."
(James Arness, 1960)

Arness had good reason to feel optimistic: CBS had not only made him associate producer, but *Gunsmoke* topped the annual ratings for the third year in a row, tying the record set by *I Love Lucy*. This accomplishment was even more impressive considering there were now nearly thirty Western series airing every week, the peak of the genre. However, fewer than half ended up among the top programs, an indication that viewers were, perhaps, tiring of a steady diet of "oaters." Not even the fact that the first season of the soon-to-be-classic *Bonanza* had the distinction of being broadcast in color could make it much more than a middling success, especially with it being scheduled opposite the very popular *Perry Mason*.

Before *Gunsmoke* began its fifth season, the famous opening showdown sequence was filmed. (This was grafted onto the episodes of the first four years when CBS later reran them as *Marshal Dillon* on Tuesday evening from fall 1961 through spring 1964.) The villain confronting Matt in the distance was Arvo Ojala, who taught several actors how to handle guns and perfect the fast draw.

Thanks to its combination of solid characterizations and exceptional writing, *Gunsmoke* could do no wrong, even as its focus continued to shift more toward the dilemmas of others rather than those of the main cast. Clem Fuller made the first of his two dozen appearances as Long Branch bartender Clem, and Ken Curtis was cast in two more episodes. Chester remarks that Boot Hill (now shown only rarely at the beginning of each show) is twenty minutes from Dodge, and Doc says the charge for removing a bullet is $5.50. Among the revelations are that Doc was in Dodge before Chester, and that Oklahoma was one of the many places Matt hung his hat before coming to town. There is a flashback to the first anniversary of the Long Branch, after which Kitty observes, "This place has an awful lot of history I'm glad I missed." Matt and Kitty are shown riding together on the prairie for the first time in "Kitty's Injury" (one of the best installments of the series) and "Horse Deal." Other above-average episodes were "Tail to the Wind," "Saludos," "Brother Whelp," "Odd Man Out," "Box O' Rocks," "False Witness," "Big Tom," "Doc Judge," "Unwanted Deputy," "The Ex-Urbanites" and "The Bobsy Twins." "Moo-Moo Raid," using footage shot for *Rawhide*, turned out to be the highest rated episode of *Gunsmoke*'s twenty-year run, although the audience could not have known in advance that the story revolved almost exclusively around the guest stars, not the four leads. At one point, Matt jokes that Dodge could stand to be rebuilt.

Now that Arness, as associate producer, had a degree of control over scripts and casting, he cut back on personal appearances but remained busy in the industry that provided him his livelihood. In October he was a guest on *The Red Skelton Chevy Special*, and he returned to the big screen in a brief cameo as Matt Dillon at the climax of the Bob Hope comedy *Alias Jesse James*.

Earlier in the year, Amanda Blake managed to squeeze in guest roles on *Steve Canyon, G.E. True Theater*, and another visit to *Red Skelton*.

Dennis Weaver went on *The Ed Sullivan Show* in character as Chester, responding to Sullivan's questions about Doc and Kitty, and giving the studio audience a taste of what he did when he, Stone and Blake performed on the fair and rodeo circuit. Accompanying himself on guitar, he sang "My Daddy Come West to Kansas," a tune familiar to *Gunsmoke* viwers, and then, stiff legged, jumped a pair of fences. He knocked the first one over, something, he told Sullivan, had never happened before.

So popular and lucrative (more than $3,000 apiece per engagement) was their act that Weaver, Stone and Blake took it on the road even when *Gunsmoke* was still in production. They appeared not only throughout the west but also as far east as North Carolina, where they were met at the airport in the dead of night by several hundred fans despite being thirteen hours late.

In January, all four members of the original *Gunsmoke* cast were featured on the cover of TV Guide for the first and only time. While

James Arness

the story inside the magazine concerned the activities of Arness' co-stars, the most interesting reading was an item in writer Dwight Whitney's column that Stone had asked CBS for a raise but had been turned down. Stone, a man of strong principles, said he would not be reporting to work until his demands were met. Evidently the network caved. In the same article, it was announced that CBS intended to continue with the series for another five seasons.

While *Gunsmoke* fell from first place to third in Radio Daily's fourth annual poll of Western Show of the Year for TV, Quigley Publications gave the series a Television Champion Award as Best Western, and Motion Picture Daily voted it Best Western Series. In May, Arness became the first television actor to win the Silver Spur award as Outstanding Western Actor of the Year from the Reno Chamber of Commerce.

There was no let up in the amount of *Gunsmoke* merchandise available to young fans of the show as the season drew to a close. In addition to eleven more comic books published by Dell during 1959 and 1960, Whitman came out with a jigsaw puzzle and coloring book, John-Henry Products manufactured a pair of toy steel handcuffs, and the Aladdin company issued the first of four lunchboxes.

Season Six (1960–61)
38 Episodes / Rating: #1

"Those half-hour episodes ultimately began to wear a little thin."

(James Arness, 1988)

A few years after *Bonanza* ended its fourteen-season run, Lorne Greene surprised fans of the series by saying that five years would have been enough. *Bonanza* was successful in reinventing itself and remaining both entertaining and interesting far beyond its fifth season, but in retrospect, that year was the peak of the six involving all four Cartwrights. Pernell Roberts' final season was not as compelling as the previous one, a certain degree of redundancy and predictability creeping in.

To a lesser extent, the same ennui affected *Gunsmoke* as it entered its last season as a half-hour program. Although it was once again the top rated show in the country, Westerns in general were beginning to lose favor with the public as the new decade unfolded. There were twenty-two "horse operas" in prime time, seven fewer than the year before, only eight of them in the Top 30, as opposed to eleven in 1959-60. Of the eight, four were an hour in length, including *Wagon Train* (#2), which would take over the top spot the following season, and *Rawhide* (#6). Farther down the list were *Bonanza* (#17) and *Cheyenne* (#28).

In the spring of 1960, production of *Gunsmoke* moved to Paramount Studios for the first of three seasons, and Matt Dillon's voice-over observations from Boot Hill at the beginning of the episodes were completely eliminated.

The relationships between the four main characters had become so firmly established that there was little room for surprise. Consequently, stories began to center even more on the guest stars, and some plots had an air of familiarity. But even at its most routine, *Gunsmoke* was still unsurpassed in relation to other dramas on the air, Western or otherwise. A good example of the show's potential as an hour-long adventure was the episode "Shooting Stopover," in which outlaws trap Matt, Chester, and a variety of fellow passengers inside a stage depot. Other highlights of the season were "The Badge," "Unloaded Gun," "Big Man," "Bless Me Til I Die," "The Peace Officer," "Chester's Dilemma," "Love Thy Neighbor," "Hard Virtue," and "Little Girl," the latter three the first of four episodes directed by Dennis Weaver. There were previews of things to come in the form of James Nusser as a pre-Louie Pheeters drunk, and two episodes with a pre-Sam Noonan Glenn Strange. Matt continues to run into old acquaintances and mention places he has been before Dodge City, Doc shoots someone for only the second time, Kitty is shown on Doc's operating table for the first time, and Chester has yet another ill-fated romance.

Arness appeared on *The Chevrolet Golden Anniversary Show*; Amanda Blake, who was given her first TV Guide profile in December, paid another visit to Red Skelton's show; Dennis Weaver landed guest roles on *Alfred Hitchcock Presents* and *The Twilight Zone*, and worked on what would be his last feature film for six years, *The Gallant Hours*, one of screen legend James Cagney's final efforts.

Motion Picure Daily voted *Gunsmoke* the Best Western Series for the second year in a row, and Hartland Plastics issued a four-inch Matt Dillon figure and horse as well as a full-size version. Whitman released another jigsaw puzzle, and kids could stash their weekly allowance in a *Gunsmoke* vinyl wallet.

Stone, Blake, Arness on set of "Marry Me," 1961

CHAPTER 4
SEASONS OF CHANGE
(1961–67)

Season Seven (1961–62)
34 Episodes / Rating: #3

*"If Gunsmoke goes ten more years, I'll be happy;
I'll swim with the tide, however it goes."*
(James Arness, 1961)

Wagon Train, which had been nipping at *Gunsmoke's* heels in the ratings for three seasons, finally claimed the top spot when the numbers were added up in April 1962. This development seems surprising today considering *Wagon Train* had lost the dynamic Ward Bond to a fatal heart attack half-way through the previous season, relied heavily on guest stars rather than the regular cast, and had begun to do less location filming.

Less of a surprise was *Bonanza's* ascendency from seventeenth to second place. NBC moved the show from Saturday to Sunday, where the television audience has always been traditionally largest, and it was one of the very few programs being broadcast in color.

The total number of Westerns dropped from twenty-two to fifteen at the beginning of the 1961-62 season, and one of them was *Marshal Dillon*, the Tuesday night reruns of the half-hour *Gunsmokes*. The genre claimed the top three positions, but only three other series (*Rawhide, The Rifleman, Have Gun-Will Travel*) made the Top 30. Sitcoms such as *Hazel, The Andy Griffith Show* and *My Three Sons* were proving more popular, as were the dramas *Perry Mason* and *Dr. Kildare*, and even *Candid Camera*.

Gunsmoke remained not only the most consistently well-written and authentic Western on the air, it offered superior storytelling of any type. If its half-hour episodes were akin to finely crafted short stories, the first season of hour-long shows were groundbreaking examples of what frontier drama could be when seasoned actors and genuinely creative writers came together. Although only thirty-four episodes were produced—the fewest to date until the eleventh season—nearly all of them were extraordinarily good. The writers and directors were credited up front instead of in the closing credits, with varying musical motifs indicating the general tone of the story that was about to unfold. Responsible for a majority of the best segments of the season were old hands John Meston, John Dunkel, and Kathleen Hite. Directorial chores were entrusted almost exclusively to Andrew McLaglen, Harry Harris and Ted Post. Thanks to these six individuals, producer Norman Macdonnell was able to avoid the erratic quality occasionally plaguing other series.

While stock footage from Gene Autry's Melody Ranch was utilized, *Gunsmoke* no longer filmed at the twenty-acre site, which had the misfortune of being almost entirely destroyed by a brush fire prior to the following season. Nor did the show make much use of the Western street at Paramount, known chiefly as Virginia City on *Bonanza*. Instead, Dodge City was most often depicted on either the soundstage or a partial exterior set constructed at the Conejo location.

The character of Matt Dillon remained central, of course, and Doc and Chester were given additional time in the spotlight. Kitty was, if possible, even prettier, and more forceful as, in Amanda Blake's words, "television's first liberated woman." Joining the cast were Glenn Strange as bartender Sam (with a larger mustache than in later episodes), James Nusser as town drunk Louie Pheeters, and Mathew McCue as Joe, Delmonico Restaurant's nearly mute headwaiter.

It would be easier to name the few lesser moments of the season, but more important to point out what will always be essential viewing for anyone who values truly memorable television: "Miss Kitty," "Long, Long Trail," "Chesterland," (Weaver's favorite) "Apprentice Doc," "Marry Me," (directed by Weaver) "A Man a Day," "Old Dan," "He Learned About Women," "The Gallows," (one of Arness' favorites), "Coventry," and "Chester's Indian."

Arness & Carl Reindel in "The Search," 1962

Due to it taking far longer to shoot thirty-four hour-long episodes than thirty-nine half-hours (frequently six days per installment), the four *Gunsmoke* stars understandably curtailed their personal appearances and guest turns on other series. This was particularly frustrating for Dennis Weaver, who, despite being allowed to direct several episodes, was anxious to branch out and avoid being typecast as Chester. Only ten weeks into the new season, CBS announced that Weaver had signed to host a new variety show (*TV Tonight*) and would not be returning to Dodge the following year. Fortunately, at least for *Gunsmoke* fans, Weaver agreed to continue as Chester on a limited basis during the 1962-63 season in exchange for his own series in 1963-64. That deal, however, was later pushed back another year, resulting in two more seasons of Chester Goode in Dodge City.

In November, TV Guide ran the first of a two-part profile of Arness (with him and Blake on the cover), and in June CBS informed the magazine that Burt Reynolds would be joining the cast as a blacksmith in the upcoming season.

In January, with the season still in progress, Motion Picture Daily and Radio Daily each voted *Gunsmoke* the second best Western on television, though history has proven the ranking one notch too low.

On the merchandise front, Whitman introduced another jigsaw puzzle, Hassenfeld Brothers, Inc., offered young fans a pencil box decorated with Marshal Dillon's face, and the final four comic books from Dell continued to be the most popular of those featuring television cowboys.

Season Eight (1962–63)
38 Episodes / Rating: #10

"I've exhausted the potential of Chester."
(Dennis Weaver, 1963)

Only ten series about the Old West were scheduled in prime time at the start of the 1962-63 season, and that included the Tuesday night reruns of the half-hour *Gunsmoke* episodes. For the first time since 1956, the top rated program in the country was not a Western, that honor going to *The Beverly Hillbillies*. Also for the first time since 1956, *Gunsmoke* was not one of the top three shows, and only four others (*Bonanza, Rawhide, Wagon Train, The Virginian, Have Gun-Will Travel*) made the Top 30, all but *Bonanza* (#4) lower than twentieth place. The most dramatic change was the drop of *Wagon Train* from number one to twenty-five after switching from NBC to ABC. An era was definitely coming to a close. Not that the networks were giving up entirely, as three "modern" Westerns (*Stoney Burke, Empire, Wide Country*) were trotted out.

Gunsmoke was still enormously popular and a ratings powerhouse on Saturday night, both it and *Have Gun-Will Travel* beating NBC's *Saturday Night Movie* and two sports programs on ABC. The addition of Burt Reynolds as half-breed blacksmith Quint Asper was also a hit with viewers—4,000 letters poured into the network's mailbag after his first episode, "Quint Asper Comes Home," three weeks into the season. "When Burt was on the show, more women were writing to him than to me," Arness recalled in 1988. "Wonder why." Reynolds, whom producer MacDonnell hoped could satisfactorily replace Dennis Weaver, would appear in forty-eight episodes through the tenth season.

Weaver had only twenty-seven episodes left as Chester (fifteen this year, a dozen the next), and he was contracted to be the lead character in all of them. Following the failure of *TV Tonight* to get off the ground, two dramatic roles he hoped for had fallen through: one as a high school vice-principal (*The Giant Step*), another as a pre-presidential Abraham Lincoln. Now there was a chance that a third series (*Kentucky Jones*) might have potential, and Weaver wanted to be through with *Gunsmoke* by October so he could shoot the pilot.

Although not planned at the time, Chester's eventual replacement—Ken Curtis as Festus Haggen—was introduced in the episode "Us Haggens," one of the season's highlights. Other solid entries included "Jenny" (with the only glimpse of the room Matt rented when away from the jail), "Phoebe Strunk," "The Hunger," "Abe Blocker," "The Way It Is," "Louie Pheeters," "The Renegades," "Cotter's Girl," "Shona," "Blind Man's Bluff," "Quint's Indian," "Anybody Can Kill a Marshal," "With a Smile," "Jeb," "The Quest for Asa Janin," and two episodes ("The Cousin," "Old York") dealing with Matt's past.

In June, Amanda Blake, Milburn Stone and Ken Curtis attended the wedding of Burt Reynolds to actress Judy Carne. The following month, Dennis Weaver and James Arness graced the cover of TV Guide for the second and final time, and Blake shot her sixth guest appearance on *Red Skelton*.

Dell was no longer issuing *Gunsmoke* comic books, but Aladdin put another lunchbox on the market.

Once again, Motion Picture Daily and Radio Daily both named *Gunsmoke* television's second best Western.

Stone & William Talman in "Legends Don't Sleep," 1963

Season Nine (1963–64)
36 Episodes / Rating: #20

"Gunsmoke is great for me emotionally. It's steady, secure—like a home away from home."

(Amanda Blake, 1964)

In the estimation of many fans and critics, 1963-64 was the final classic season of the Western on television, due largely to it being the last consistent year of *Rawhide*, the best season of *Bonanza* to date, and because Chester was still hanging around Dodge City. Of the nine series left, one (*Redigo*, a revamped *Empire* from the previous season) had a contemporary setting, and another was the *Marshal Dillon* reruns. Only three shows landed in the Top 30, the hugely popular *Bonanza* in second place, *The Virginian* seventeenth, and *Gunsmoke* falling to number twenty. *Wagon Train*, now filmed in color and expanded to ninety-minutes, failed to rank for the first time in its history, easily trounced Monday night by Lucille Ball, Danny Thomas and Andy Griffith on CBS.

Gunsmoke, pitted against *The Jerry Lewis Show* and NBC's *Saturday Night Movie*, was still winning its time slot, but it was obvious that fewer people were tuning in to Matt Dillon and his friends. While there was no lapse in quality, the pattern of less being seen of Marshal Dillon began, and stories revolving around guest stars took precedence over those featuring the regular cast. Both of these developments were very possibly responsible for all but the most loyal viewers turning away. Another factor was the anti-violence campaigns launched by Congress and various conservative groups in the wake of President Kennedy's assassination in November. This backlash would only continue to gain momentum, blunting the realism necessary in dramatic series.

Production moved from Paramount Studios to CBS Studio City, the former Republic Pictures lot the network had leased the previous season, and where *Rawhide* was already headquartered. Just as the coming year would be Dennis Weaver's swan song, it was also destined to be producer Norman Macdonnell's final season as *Gunsmoke's* main producer, a crucial blunder on the part of the network. And James Arness decided Season Nine would be the last year of the Arness Production Company.

After his last guest appearance ("Lover Boy"), Ken Curtis joined the cast on a permanent basis in "Prairie Wolfer," the first of only two episodes to feature both Festus and Chester, the other "Once a Haggen" two weeks later. Dennis Weaver departed in early April ("Bently") with no indication that Chester would never be seen again. The reasonably friendly but contentious relationship between Festus and Quint was presented in the entertaining "Comanches is Soft," and the first of the series' twelve two-part installments ("Extradition") was the template for several solo Matt Dillon epics to come. Writer Kathleen Hite won a prestigious National Headliner Award, and Paul Savage's story/script for "Owney Tupper Had a Daughter" was nominated for a Writers Guild Award. Despite a general lack of action overall, there were a number of first class episodes: "Quint's Trail," "Pa Hack's Brood," "Dry Well," "Friend," "No Hands," "The Bassops," "The Kite," "Caleb," "Now That April's Here," and "Kitty Cornered."

Viewership was dwindling, yet in March noted television critic Cleveland Amory observed: "The truly amazing thing about this show is that, these days, we are not only watching it less, but we are also enjoying it more...Over the long haul, no show has ever kept more interesting characters entirely in character...To say they are all fine performers is as much of an understatement as they magnificently understated way they themselves play their parts. They are, in short, superb...Furthermore, if they are, week after week, predictably the same, they somehow manage—and here director Andrew McLaglen and producer Norman Macdonnell should take a bow—never to be fatiguingly so. Finally, chief writer John Meston and his confreres deserve credit not only for the variations in their plots but also for a basic understanding of the Old West which, if basically fiction, is at least based on believable fact."

A few months later, in her second TV Guide cover story of 1964, Amanda Blake, then between husbands and living alone in Calabasas California, admitted that even on days she was not needed, she visited the *Gunsmoke* set. "I feel just as much at home in that saloon as I do here—more so, because I spend more time there! When the show ends, I'll have 'em pack up that set and move it out here. I don't know what I'd do without it—and besides the bar is practical!"

After the season wrapped up, critic Joyce Alban weighed in on the current state of Gunsmoke: "We don't see half enough of any of the series' 'regulars,' including half-Indian Quint (Burt Reynolds) and the new hillbilly type, Festus (Ken Curtis). The show's too busy filming the terrible things that happen to visiting performers who don't survive from one week to the next...Don't get me wrong—I don't mind the violence. It fits this wild and woolly period...But I do mind the unending grimness of it all, the grayness which makes the transient performers look alike."

Blake & Betty Conner in "Help Me, Kitty," 1964

Alban obviously disagreed with those who felt that the show's stark realism—"the unending grimness"—was what distinguished *Gunsmoke* from the rest of the video stampede. Ironically, she recommended viewers catch the half-hour reruns on Tuesday night, which were just as dark as the latest season.

Season Ten (1964–65)
36 Episodes / Rating: #27

"I wouldn't presume to know how to run a network, or be the producer of a show, but I do know the flavor of Gunsmoke. You can detect the changes."
(Milburn Stone, 1965)

If one considers *Daniel Boone* a Western—though its setting was east of the Mississippi—there were but six such series on the air in the fall of 1964, only half of them in the Top 30 when the season ended: Number One *Bonanza, The Virginian,* and *Gunsmoke,* continuing to beat the competition, but with fewer viewers than the year before. (Dennis Weaver's new show, the NBC comedy/drama *Kentucky Jones,* debuted on Saturday night, one week before the start of *Gunsmoke's* tenth year, but ran for only one season, coming in third behind ABC's *Lawrence Welk Show* and *Gilligan's Island* on CBS.)

Norman Macdonnell, who produced only fourteen of the season's thirty-six episodes, objected strongly to the network's proposal to add Jack Palance to the cast as a villain Marshal Dillon would have to contend with on at least a semi-regular basis. He also did not feel it was necessary to use aging stars from Hollywood's Golden Age (as *Wagon Train* routinely did) in an attempt to bolster ratings. Neither did Milburn Stone, who complained that including famous guest stars was a move "that I certainly don't agree with." The Palance idea was dropped. And so was Macdonnell, one of the show's creators. In a display of solidarity, chief writers John Meston and Kathleen Hite, not especially pleased with how the previous season had turned out, left the series, but not before contributing some top notch scripts.

To replace Macdonnell, CBS brought in British-born director Philip Leacock, who had impressed the network brass with his direction of such shows as *Rawhide, The Alfred Hitchcock Hour, Route 66* and *The Defenders.* Although he and Macdonnell were cordial to one another, Milburn Stone and Amanda Blake were, initially, staunchly against having someone new in charge. "I just felt awful about it," Blake said regarding Macdonnell's firing. "I felt like we were losing the head of the family. I was appalled." Arness, not satisfied with the way *Gunsmoke* had gradually changed during its ninth year, declined to continue as an associate producer. He was pleased, however, when the network agreed to alter his schedule so that he could see more of his family. Consequently, production started several weeks earlier than usual, with episodes involving Matt Dillon being filmed first, allowing Arness to be off most of the time while the remainder of the season was being shot.

The proverbial silver lining in the clouds gathering over the fictional Dodge City was writer John Mantley, hired as story consultant for the tenth season, and who would eventually restore *Gunsmoke* to its former glory.

A new opening sequence was directed by Vincent McEveety on the phony exterior Dodge City set at CBS Studio City, replacing the showdown between Arness and Arvo Ojala filmed at Melody Ranch in 1959. This time, Matt Dillon's opponent was played by Fred McDougall, a crew member.

Viewers who had stopped watching *Gunsmoke* on a regular basis missed out on several notable episodes: "Crooked Mile," "Old Man," "Chicken" and "Help Me, Kitty," all produced under Macdonnell's watch. And there were a number of strong moments turned out by Leacock as well: "Hung High," "Double Entry," "Twenty Miles from Dodge," and "Run, Sheep, Run." Ken Curtis and Burt Reynolds, who were seen more than during the previous season, concocted the storyline for the amusing "Eliab's Aim."

For the third year in a row, Motion Picture Daily and Radio Daily awarded the number two slot to *Gunsmoke* as the best Western on the air, and the Spiegel catalogue offered a new gun and holster set (plus badge, handcuffs, jail keys and a knife) for $4.88.

In a TV Guide article published a couple of weeks after the season ended, Milburn Stone remarked: "Everybody keeps saying we're a cinch for next year. I still don't believe it. I've made a bet every year for the past three years and lost them all—that *Gunsmoke* wouldn't be back." He added that he was contracted to the series for one more year, after which he intended to star in a show (to which he owned the rights) about a country doctor at the turn of the century. Fortunately, Dodge City continued to require the services of Doc Adams.

It was around this time that Stone, Arness and Blake sold their residual rights in the series to CBS, which the actors figured would put them on Easy Street for the rest of their lives. However, a few years later Blake confessed that, "We should have waited a few more years."

Arness & Robert Lansing on the set of "The Bounty Hunter," 1965

Season Eleven (1965–66)
32 Episodes / Rating: #30

"In eleven years of Gunsmoke *I don't think I got more than a handful of letters expressing anger over a show."*

(John Mantley, 1981)

John Mantley was promoted from story consultant to associate producer for his second year with the series, giving *Gunsmoke* the unique advantage of having a supervisor with a writing background.

The season began with what would become Mantley's all-time favorite episode, the powerful "Seven Hours to Dawn," written by Clyde Ware, a contributor to the radio version of the show. The episode earned composer Morton Stevens an Emmy nomination for Achievement in Music Composition, proof that some in the television industry were still paying attention to *Gunsmoke* even if the general public continued to stray.

There was a slight resurgence of the Western on television in 1965, with the addition of such series as *The Big Valley, Laredo, Branded, The Wild, Wild West, The Legend of Jesse James, A Man Called Shenandoah*, and *The Loner*, the latter three lasting less than a full season. Nor did *Rawhide* complete its final cattle drive, axed by CBS after thirteen episodes. Five Westerns, which included the adventure series *Daniel Boone*, wound up in the Top 30, with *Bonanza* at the very top, and *Gunsmoke* on the bottom, its lowest rating to date.

Producers Leacock and Mantley decided to fill the void left by Burt Reynolds' departure with a part-time deputy named Thad Greenwood, created by writer Calvin Clements and introduced in the season's third episode, "Clayton Thaddeus Greenwood." Played by Roger Ewing, the character was intended to appeal to *Gunsmoke's* more youthful audience. Arness initially felt that Ewing, who had guest starred the previous season in a different role, was a bit *too* young, but Thad gradually meshed comfortably with the rest of the Dodge City family, particularly Miss Kitty. And with John Mantley overseeing most of the creative aspects of the series, the main characters did indeed return to interacting more like a family, unlike much of the past couple of years. In addition to Thad, Ted Jordan, who had been cast in numerous guest roles, appeared in "Parson Comes to Town" as freight agent Nathan Burke for the first of an eventual 108 episodes. Woodrow Chambliss was also added to the show as Woody Lathrop, who would be seen around Dodge for thirty-one episodes.

To inject new blood into *Gunsmoke*, Mantley did away with the standard industry practice of requiring scripts to be submitted only by agents. Writers with ideas for the show were allowed to send their work directly to the producers, resulting in what was arguably the best season since the eighth year. Highlights included "Ten Little Indians," "The Bounty Hunter," "The Hostage," "Outlaw's

Woman," "The Avengers," "My Father, My Son," "Prime of Life," the two-part "The Raid," and "Wishbone," Ken Curtis' favorite episode of the entire series. Calvin Clements' script for "Death Watch" earned a Wrangler, the Western Heritage Award for Outstanding Fictional Television Western episode. ("Death Watch" was the first of twenty-nine episodes to include Charles Wagenheim as Dodge City citizen Charlie Halligan.)

The 1965-66 season was the last to be filmed in black-and-white. While some television historians have commented that the stark realism of such dramatic series as *Gunsmoke, The Fugitive,* and *Combat!* benefited from *not* being in color, and suffered to a degree when they switched, those shows had no choice. *The Big Valley*, which was now sharing the old Republic lot with *Gunsmoke*, was in color, and the next season was the first when all network programs would be.

With Radio Daily now defunct, it was left to Motion Picture Daily to alone vote *Gunsmoke* the second best Western on television, a position the show would continue to hold in the publication until the end of the 1971-72 season.

Before starting production on the twelfth year, Amanda Blake joined Red Skelton one last time (for the television film *Clown Alley*), unaware that she would be returning to *Gunsmoke* for what also could have been the last time.

Season Twelve (1966-67)
29 Episodes / Rating: #34

***"Gunsmoke** has been canceled. Go down and tell your people."*
(CBS to John Mantley, 1967)

Only two Westerns—*Bonanza* and *The Virginian*—garnered above average ratings during the 1966 season. The frontier drama *Daniel Boone* was still getting respectable numbers, but *Gunsmoke* and the other seven shows set before the twentieth century (*Iron Horse, The Big Valley, The Road West, The Monroes, Shane, Laredo, Wild, Wild West*) fell below the Top 30. A new contemporary Western, *The*

Arness & Blake in "The Jailer," 1966

Rounders, was regularly beaten by *The Red Skelton Hour,* and *Pistols 'n' Petticoats* an Old West CBS sitcom starring screen legend Ann Sheridan never stood a chance against NBC's *Get Smart* on Saturday night.

This was to be *Gunsmoke's* final season on Saturday night, scheduled after the new *Mission: Impossible* and coming in third opposite the more popular *Lawrence Welk Show* on ABC and NBC's *Saturday Night Movie.* (Burt Reynolds fared no better in his first post-*Gunsmoke* series, *Hawk,* a police drama which ran for only two months on ABC.)

Because of the switch to color, Matt's showdown on Front Street was filmed again, this time outdoors on the Western street of CBS Studio City, the former Republic Pictures lot that the network had been leasing and now owned. As a gag, Arness pretended to be outdrawn and fell to the ground. The footage was thought to have been destroyed (at Arness' request), but turned up nearly forty years later on DVD in the *50th Anniversary Collection* of *Gunsmoke*.

Also changed were the individual head shots of the main characters in the opening credits, a sequence which had been introduced the previous season. Roger Ewing as Thad was sometimes added.

The new season began with six strong episodes in a row: "Snap Decision" (Matt accidentally kills a friend and turns in his badge), "The Goldtakers" (in which Festus mentions Quint Asper), "The Jailer" (with guest star Bette Davis), "The Mission" (alone, Matt tangles with outlaws in Mexico) and "The Good People" (with Morgan Woodward).

The following episode, "Gunfighter R.I.P.," was not inferior, but featured only token appearances by Matt, Kitty, Doc and Sam. Fortunately, there were several more solid entries ahead: "The Wrong Man," "Stage Stop," "The Newcomers," "The Hanging," "Saturday Night," "The Lure," "Noose of Gold," "The Favor," and "Mistaken Identity" in particular. Instrumental in the high quality of the writing was new story consultant Paul Savage, as well as memorable scripts by Clyde Ware, Hal Sitowitz, Richard Carr, Calvin Clements, Les Crutchfield, and Preston Wood in particular.

In December, James Arness was on the cover of TV Guide for the eighth time, a rustic painting by Bernie Fuchs. The feature article described the actor as "the Greta Garbo of Dodge City" (a reference to the famously reclusive actress from Hollywood's Golden Age), now weary of the special treatment frequently accorded a star. "Fans, publicity men, writers, photographers," he said. "They usually wind up saying the same thing over and over. I'm sick of stories about being real tall."

Arness, however, remained devoted to the cast and crew of the show. On location in Thousand Oaks, he responded emotionally to the unexpected news that the show was being canceled by galloping wildly—some in the crew said recklessly—across the Hollywood prairie in the next scene filmed. Later, when the *Gunsmoke* company gathered for a farewell party, he was too emotional to attend. "I got into my car five times," he said. "Once I got as far as six blocks, but I couldn't face those people saying goodbye."

It was in late February, during production of the last episode of the season (a two-part story entitled "Nitro!"), that CBS informed Mantley it was also going to be the end of *Gunsmoke*. Michael Dann, the network's vice president in charge of programming, felt the show had succumbed to "program fatigue" and that the declining ratings and aging demographics would not be sufficiently attractive to advertisers. Jay Eliasberg, head of research, and Frank Smith, a vice-president in charge of sales, concurred.

Saying the announcement that *Gunsmoke* had reached the end of the trail did not go over well with the general public is indeed an understatement. The show still had an average audience of around eleven million, and the network was bombarded with letters from viewers and phone calls from local affiliates. Most significantly, the Kansas state legislature passed a resolution vowing that no CBS programs would be carried within its borders unless *Gunsmoke* was put back on the schedule.

In retrospect it is somewhat difficult to believe that Dann and his associates were unaware of how much the network's head honcho, CBS board chairman William S. Paley, enjoyed Westerns. And it was most likely no coincidence that they decided to kill *Gunsmoke* while their boss was vacationing in the Bahamas. Paley had vetoed two attempts to cancel *Rawhide*, so it should have not come as a surprise when he reacted negatively to the news that Matt Dillon himself was being ordered out of Dodge. *Gunsmoke* had always been one of Paley's personal favorites, making a point of visiting the set whenever he happened to be in Los Angeles. He called Tom Dawson, president of the network, and learned that the show was going to be replaced by *Mannix*, a new private eye series. Paley then asked how advertising revenue was stacking up for two half-hour sitcoms—a third season of *Gilligan's Island* and a new one called *Doc*—on Monday night. Dawson admitted that sales for both shows were far less than hoped. Never fond of confrontation or issuing direct orders, Paley made the following "suggestion": "I don't know why you fellows don't put *Gunsmoke* in that slot."

On March 8, CBS announced that Matt, Doc, Kitty and Festus were not dead. The network had "re-evaluated the situation" and determined that a mistake had been made. "All the indications were that the show had run its course," said Michael Dann. "How did we know that we had a mass phenomenon on our hands?" Allegedly, some CBS executives hoped that *Gunsmoke* would fare no better, and possibly even worse, on Monday night, proving Paley's instincts to be wrong. History proved otherwise.

A curious footnote to the twelfth year is that a thirtieth episode, "The Prodigal," was filmed but held over until the following season. Evidence of this is the brief glimpse of Roger Ewing, who was not asked to return as Thad Greenwood when the series continued.

With the future of *Gunsmoke* assured, John Mantley and Philip Leacock, who had collaborated in doing damage control on the creatively shaky CBS series *The Wild, Wild West* (described by several critics of the day as "James Bond Goes West"), teamed up to co-produce the theatrical feature *Firecreek*. Initially one of them would supervise the production for a week while the other attended to *Gunsmoke*, then trade duties for the next week. The process was an unwieldy one, so Leacock took over the film and Mantley worked exclusively on preparing the upcoming season of *Gunsmoke*. Both men received screen credit for *Firecreek*, an underrated Western with a superb cast: James Stewart, Henry Fonda, and a host of actors familiar to *Gunsmoke* fans, including Jack Elam, Jay C. Flippen, Jacqueline Scott, James Best, and Morgan Woodward.

After wrapping *Firecreek* (which would not be released until 1968), Leacock bid *Gunsmoke* adieu and became executive producer of *Cimarron Strip*, a new ninety-minute CBS Western from veteran *Gunsmoke* director Bernard McEveety. Mantley became executive producer of *Gunsmoke*, with Joseph Dackow taking over as associate producer.

CHAPTER 5
BACK ON TOP
(1967–74)

Season Thirteen (1967–68)
25 Episodes / Rating: #4

"Let's face it—this show has made us all."
(Amanda Blake, 1968)

In its new Monday night time slot, *Gunsmoke* stunned CBS by not only whipping the competition (Chuck Connors in *Cowboy in Africa* on ABC, *The Monkees* and *The Man from U.N.C.L.E* on NBC) but also surging to fourth place in the year-end ratings with more than fourteen million viewers, albeit tied with *Family Affair* and *Bonanza*. The last time Matt Dillon and Company had been that popular had been way back in 1961. Including *Daniel Boone*, there were thirteen Westerns on the air when the season began, but only *Boone* and *The Virginian* joined *Gunsmoke* and *Bonanza* in the Top 30. Three new series—*The Legend of Custer, Hondo, Dundee and the Culhane*—were gone before the year was over. (Dennis Weaver's new CBS series, *Gentle Ben*, debuted on Sunday night and would run for two seasons. A proposal for Weaver to make a one-time guest appearance as Chester was rejected by John Mantley, claiming the right script never came up.)

Cimarron Strip, which would at least finish out the season, now shared the CBS Studio City lot with *Gunsmoke* and more often than not monopolized the exterior Western sets. As a result, the filming of Dodge City was usually confined to the soundstage, though there were exceptions, such as "The Wreckers," "Stranger in Town" and "Death Train." As in the past, such desolate locations as Lancaster, California, were utilized to great effect.

Cast on the set of "Baker's Dozen," 1967

Paul Savage returned as story consultant, adding the uniquely talented Ron Bishop ("A Hat") to the show's stable of scribes, and continuing Mantley's unique policy of considering ideas or complete scripts from writers without agency representation. One example was "Baker's Dozen," although the author, Charles Joseph Stone, had the obvious advantage of being Milburn's brother.

"Baker's Dozen," in which Doc campaigns to keep orphaned triplets from being sent to different foster homes, was originally intended as a showcase for Chester a few years earlier. Although it first aired on Christmas Day and no doubt had a less than average audience, it finally earned Milburn Stone a long overdue Emmy as Outstanding Performance by an Actor in a Supporting Role in a Drama at the award ceremony on May 19, 1968. "Mention awards, and you have hit the sorest point in the world with me," Mantley said a few years later. "*Gunsmoke* got Emmys the first two years it was on the air. But it took more than a decade for Stone to get his award, and that was because of a fluke.

"You see," the producer continued, "the trade, the industry, votes on the Emmy awards, and the trade doesn't watch *Gunsmoke*. I ran that episode once and reran it. Then, because I had to lift the violent programs out of the series, I ran Milburn's show a third time, just before the voting took place. We saturated the country with that episode."

Composer Morton Stevens' score for "Major Glory" was nominated for an Emmy in 1968, but did not win.

A two-part episode, "Vengeance," was the second one filmed for the season, though it was shown as the fourth (and fifth). Among the guest cast was a young actor named Buck Taylor, son of veteran character actor Dub Taylor, portraying a hotheaded gunslinger killed by fellow guest star James Stacy in Part One. A month later, Taylor was back in "The Pillagers" as Newly O'Brien, a role he would own for a total of 103 episodes, though he was not included with the other cast members in the opening credits until the fifteenth season. While the episode introduced Newly as a gunsmith, it was disclosed that he had also studied medicine for a brief spell. "We designed him that way," said John Mantley. "We gave him wide range." The executive producer hoped Taylor would appeal to younger viewers, but regretted that adding him to the cast meant "Vengeance" could never be rerun. "We can never us it—he was the heavy. And it was a good show, too."

Not only did the character of Newly catch on with the youth crowd, so did *Gunsmoke* in its weeknight placement, with more televisions in use than on Saturday night. Viewers in the 18-34 age group, who had grown up with the series but had spent several years going out on dates or starting families, were now able to reconnect with the Dodge City family, bolstering the ratings considerably. The most faithful fans were still there, of course, as were, according to marketing research, pre-teens. "For no reason you can imagine, the show found a new audience waiting for it in the early time period," CBS West Coast programming chief Perry Lafferty reflected later.

The loyalty of the fans was rewarded with many exceptional moments during the season, including "I Call Him Wonder" (a humorous sequel to Kathleen Hite's 1963 episode "Wonder"), "Dead Man's Law," "The Gunrunners," "The Jackals," "The First People," and "A Noose for Dobie Price."

In June, following the assassinations of Martin Luther King and Robert Kennedy, all three networks canceled scheduled summer repeats of episodes considered too violent. NBC shelved segments of *The Virginian, Run for Your Life*, and postponed a first-run episode of *Bonanza* until 1971. On CBS, reruns of *Cimarron Strip, Gunsmoke* and *Wild, Wild West* were substituted by episodes containing less mayhem.

With the media spotlight back on the resurgent *Gunsmoke*, TV Guide devoted the cover of the August 17 issue to a drawing of Arness, Stone and Blake by artist James Hill. Instead of concentrating on the show's resurrection, the article inside brought viewers up to date on the lives of the stars, reporting that Milburn Stone and Ken Curtis in particular had become good friends both on and off the set. Curtis had replaced Amanda Blake, now married for the fourth time and living mainly in Phoenix, in the *Gunsmoke* act when he and Stone toured the county fair and rodeo circuit. Presumably in reference to the country doctor property he owned, Stone mentioned that he had an idea for a new show co-starring him and Curtis when *Gunsmoke* ran its course.

Season Fourteen (1968-69)
26 Episodes / Rating: #6

"This is a pretty good way to end a guy's career. Not that I have any intention of retiring."
(Milburn Stone, 1968)

Gunsmoke was one of nine "period" series in prime time at the beginning of the season, and one of only four that would rank among the top-rated programs the following spring. *Rowan & Martin's Laugh-In*, a politically-charged collection of comedy sketches on NBC, suddenly climbed from number twenty-one the previous year to the first position, running ahead of both *Gunsmoke* and ABC's *The Avengers* on Monday night. However, the size of the audience watching *Gunsmoke* barely changed, still averaging more than fourteen million.

Bowing to the pressure being exerted by politicians and various social groups demanding less violence on television, CBS replaced

Arness & Michael Burns in "The Hide Cutters," 1968

the opening scene of Matt Dillon preparing for a gun duel with the 1967 footage from "Nitro!" showing him riding swiftly across the plains.

The fourteenth season proved to be an exceptional one, beginning with Morgan Woodward's ninth appearance (now billed as a Special Guest, thanks to his nearly being Oscar-nominated for his role in *Cool Hand Luke*) in "Lyle's Kid." This was followed by four more classics in a row: "The Hidecutters," "Zavala," "Uncle Finney," and "Slocum." *Gunsmoke* was clearly on a creative roll, with several more "greatest hits" in store:

Abelia" introduced Jacqueline Scott as farming woman and single mother in a role written especially for Faye Dunaway. However, after the success of the theatrical feature *Bonnie and Clyde*, Dunaway considered guest starring on *Gunsmoke* to be a backward step in her career. Scott went on to play Abelia, a possible love interest for Festus, in two later episodes. "Railroad!" climaxed with Arness and guest star Jim Davis engaged in the biggest knockdown, drag out fistfight of the series, progressing through Dodge and ending on the banks of the CBS Studio City lagoon formerly used for *Gilligan's Island.* "Lobo" concerned the hunt for a marauding wolf, with Morgan Woodward in what he came to regard as his personal favorite of his numerous *Gunsmoke* appearances. And James Nusser gave perhaps his finest performance as town drunk Louie Pheeters in "The Long Night," refusing to drink a glass of whisky he has been promised for crawling across the floor of the Long Branch.

Other landmarks of the season included "9:12 to Dodge," "Waco," "Time of the Jackals," "Mannon," (inspiration for the first *Gunsmoke* movie nearly twenty years later), "The Mark of Cain," "Reprisal," "The Nightriders," "The Intruders," and "The Prisoner."

Toward the end of the season, Gold Key resumed where Dell had left off, issuing the first (of six) *Gunsmoke* comics since 1961.

More significantly, Amanda Blake became the first woman—and first living person—inducted into the Hall of Fame of Great Western Performers by the National Cowboy Hall of Fame in Oklahoma City, Oklahoma. Blake was described as "an active advocate of preserving our Western traditions."

Season Fifteen (1969-70)
26 Episodes / Rating: #2

"Oh, we've been forced to make certain alterations. No shootouts. Tighter censorship. Different twists. Sometimes we feel quite asinine, but we've adjusted."
(Amanda Blake, 1970)

Because *Gunsmoke* had slipped from fourth place in 1967-68 to sixth the following season, some critics claimed that the series was once again on its way out. Their predictions were ridiculously off the mark, to say the least. In its fifteenth year, *Gunsmoke*'s audience not only increased by over one million, it became the second most popular show in the country, ahead of *Bonanza* (#3) for the first time since the 1960-61 season. Westerns in general were waning, none of the four others still on the air (*Lancer, The Virginian, High Chaparral, Daniel Boone*) ranking among the Top 30, which was comprised primarily of sitcoms, variety programs and police dramas. The

James Arness

continuing popularity of *Gunsmoke* and *Bonanza* in the face of changing tastes can only be attributed to the excellence of their casts and quality storytelling.

John Mantley told the media that as a writer he hated clichés and wanted viewers to know that *Gunsmoke* would do its best to avoid them. He added that in an attempt to broaden the show's appeal, the writers were working on more stories aimed at women, a move instituted during the previous season.

Behind the scenes, CBS had cut the budget by approximately $50,000, necessitating less location shooting and more "bottle" shows (i.e. more interior scenes and fake exterior sets). Nevertheless, with Calvin Clements now executive story consultant, and with the addition of Jim Byrnes (writer of "Lobo" and "The Intruders," two of the best 1968-69 episodes) to the slate of regular contributors, there was no lapse in the number of consistently good scripts: "The Devil's Outpost," "Stryker," "Charlie Noon," "A Matter of Honor," "The Innocent," "Ring of Darkness," "Roots of Fear," "The Pack Rat," "The Judas Gun," "Kiowa," "Celia," "Morgan," "The Thieves," "Hackett," and "The Cage" in particular.

Significantly, "The Badge" found Kitty putting the Long Branch up for sale and leaving Dodge (temporarily, of course), fed up after watching Doc dig yet another bullet out of Matt. It is very likely that this episode was responsible for Amanda Blake being nominated for a Golden Globe as Best TV Actress in a Drama.

Buck Taylor, now pictured with the rest of the cast in the opening credits, was featured more often, and even Glenn Strange was finally allowed the spotlight for "The Thieves." Former *Gunsmoke* writer Kathleen Hite commented that the cast as a whole was "the nearly perfect arrangement for storytelling."

"Charlie Noon" earned an Emmy nomination for Outstanding Achievement in Sound Editing, Quigley Publications gave the series a Television Champion Award as Best Western, and Whitman Books published *Showdown on Front Street* by Paul S. Newman, a new hardcover book based on the series for young readers.

Season Sixteen (1970–71)
24 Episodes / Rating: #5

"Gunsmoke is popular because its characters represent a cross-section of humanity. We have a lawman with the power of life and death by the gun; a doctor with the power of life and death with his science; Kitty, who is the earth mother to all men, and a vagabond who lives with his wits and humor."

(John Mantley, 1971)

Gunsmoke continued as the most popular show on Monday night, trouncing NBC's *Laugh-In* for the second year in a row, as well as *The Young Lawyers* on ABC. Of the four Westerns remaining on the air, only *The High Chaparral*, then in its fourth and final year, failed to make the Top 30 network shows as the first season of the Seventies came to a close. *Bonanza* posted its lowest rating in a decade, dropping from number three to number nine. *The Men from Shiloh*, which NBC had renamed *The Virginian*'s ninth year, managed a respectable eighteenth place, impressive in light of the fact that for the first time ever, it had not numbered among the top shows the previous season. The network canceled it anyway. Elsewhere on NBC, Dennis Weaver starred as a detective from New Mexico transferred to New York in *McCloud*, a contemporary series rotating with three others on Wednesday night. It became Weaver's biggest post-*Gunsmoke* success, running until 1977.

The season began with "Chato," filmed in New Mexico, and one of James Arness' personal favorites. Paul F. Edwards' script earned a Golden Spur award from the Western Writers of America, which also recognized *Gunsmoke* itself for contributing "15 years of quality Western drama."

Nor did the accolades end there: Writer Jack Miller won a Black Image award for "The Scavengers," guest starring the dynamic duo of Yaphet Koto and Cicely Tyson, and in 1972 Miller was honored with a Golden Spur for "Pike," the two-part episode featuring Jeanette Nolan as Dirty Sally that concluded the 1970-71 season and was sufficiently popular to warrant a sequel the next season. "Pike" was also named Best Western Television Script by the Writers Guild of America.

The National Cowboy Hall of Fame gave a Wrangler award to composer John Parker for "Snow Train," a two-part episode filmed in Custer, South Dakota, that was almost scrapped until the production was blessed with a spring blizzard.

Quigley Publications once again gave *Gunsmoke* its Television Champion award as Best Western, Motion Picture Daily named the show the second best Western on television for the eleventh year in a row, and Amanda Blake received her second Golden Globe nomination.

Gold Key issued the final *Gunsmoke* comic at the beginning of the season, and Popular Library published a paperback novel by Chris Stratton simply entitled *Gunsmoke*, its cover illustrated by a color shot of a hatless Arness holding his gun on an unseen adversary.

In January, Arness graced the cover of TV Guide as Matt Dillon for the eleventh and last time for what was basically a photo feature illustrated by seven pictures taken on the sets of "Chato," "Snow Train," and "The Witness."

In addition to the superior episodes mentioned above, the season was filled with such vivid segments as "The Noose," "Stark," "The Noon Day Devil," "Mirage," "Cleavus" and "Sam McTavish, M.D." The latter two should have at least brought Emmy nominations for Ken Curtis and Milburn Stone, respectively, for the ceremony being held in March.

Instead, March found Stone, then 66, undergoing coronary bypass surgery. CBS announced that Pat Hingle would take over Doc's chores for perhaps a dozen episodes, with Stone expected to return to the set by September.

Season Seventeen (1971-72)
24 Episodes / Rating: #4

"I have to say that by far the character of Festus is the most enjoyable thing I've ever done. I would like to go on for twenty more years."

(Ken Curtis, 1971)

Gunsmoke and *Bonanza* were the sole Westerns in the Top 30 of the season as Old West programming became rapidly rare on the video range. CBS launched *Cade's County*, a contemporary series about a California sheriff, but it did not catch on despite having silver screen favorite Glenn Ford in the title role. ABC decided to try *Alias Smith and Jones*, a sort of *Butch Cassidy and the Sundance Kid* for television that was sufficiently successful to be granted a second season. While *Gunsmoke*'s audience increased somewhat, *Bonanza* sank from number nine to twenty. Toward the end of the season, NBC announced that the Cartwrights would be moving from

James Arness

Sunday to Tuesday, perhaps believing that scheduling the show on a weeknight would result in the same success that *Gunsmoke* was continuing to experience. Tragically, Dan Blocker, who played the much-loved character Hoss, died suddenly in May, a loss not even a new time slot could overcome.

Gunsmoke's seventeenth year opened with "The Lost," with Kitty stranded in the wilderness (actually Kanab, Utah) and attempting to befriend an uncivilized young woman. Had there been any justice in the universe, Amanda Blake would have won—or been nominated for—the Emmy she was denied in 1959.

Also filmed in Kanab was the two-part "Waste," guest starring Jeremy Slate, screen veteran Ruth Roman, and Ellen Burstyn, who had appeared in one of the first hour-long episodes ("Wagon Girls") and would soon star in the horror classic *The Exorcist* (1973).

"New Doctor in Town" introduced Pat Hingle as Dr. John Chapman, substituting for Doc Adams, who was said to be back East learning advancements in medicine. In reality, Milburn Stone was still recovering from heart surgery. Over the summer, the Associated Press had run a brief item ("Doc's On the Mend") accompanied by a photo of Stone practicing "with his favorite rod and reel." The dozen episodes CBS anticipated Hingle doing ultimately numbered only six, Stone returning for the epic three-part "The Bullet," (also known as "Gold Train") written by the ever-reliable Jim Byrnes. Ironically, Doc decides that his newly acquired skills are not enough to extract a bullet lodged near Matt's spine, necessitating a dangerous train trip to Denver. Along the way, Kitty, in a poignant scene, recounts her memory of the day she arrived in Dodge City and first saw Matt.

Ken Curtis, who in "No Tomorrow" logged his 200th episode as Festus, gave one of his best performances in "My Brother's Keeper," trying to help an aged Indian who wants only to be left alone to die in peace, and Jeanette Nolan returned as Dirty Sally in "One for the Road." ("No Tomorrow" was the last of James Nusser's 72 appearances as Louie Pheeters.)

Other notable episodes included "Trafton," "Lynott," "Lijah," "Hildalgo," "The Predators," (the third and final appearance of Jacqueline Scott as Abelia Johnson), "Blind Man's Bluff," "Alias Festus Haggin" (a new spelling of Festus' last name, previously

Haggen) and "The Wedding."

A couple of months after the season ended, TV Guide's Richard K. Doan reported: "Those recent TV violence hearings have triggered visible measures to rid police and Western dramas of some of their worst forms of mayhem. Under four new 'guidelines' laid down by CBS for such series as *Gunsmoke, Mannix, Hawaii Five-O, Mission: Impossible* and *Cannon*, teaser openings are banned; victims of shoot-outs and stabbings aren't to be pictured at the moment of impact; inordinate fascination with weaponry is frowned upon; and trailers promoting upcoming episodes aren't to excerpt the rough stuff unless it's part of a logical dramatic progression."

Arness made a rare extracurricular appearance to participate in a special saluting television's 25th anniversary, and in addition to the Sportsman's Award Amanda Blake was given at Arizona's Turf Paradise Race Track earlier in the season, she became the first woman to be honored with the Buffalo Bill Cody Award, presented that June in North Platte, Nebraska.

Gunsmoke itself received its third Television Champion Award as Best Western from Quigley Publications.

Season Eighteen (1972-73)
24 Episodes / Rating: #7

"The people involved in Gunsmoke *take great pride in the show. Our stars have always put the show ahead of themselves. The performers all like and respect one another, and there's absolutely no jealousy among them. I've never worked with a finer group of professionals."*

(John Mantley, 1973)

In November, after nearly fourteen full seasons, NBC abruptly canceled *Bonanza*, its last episode broadcast in January. "We're all by ourselves now, don't have a stablemate" Amanda Blake told reporter Joseph Finnigan. "That's too bad. I particularly felt bad about *Bonanza*. It was a household word and a living legend, kind of like *Gunsmoke*."

Gunsmoke, Alias Smith & Jones, Richard Boone's occasional *Hec Ramsey* on NBC, and ABC's new "Eastern/Western" *Kung Fu* were the sole representatives of the Old West on the air when the season ended. As its eighteenth year drew to a close, John Mantley told the press that he expected the citizens of Dodge City to be around for at least two more, "to an even twenty."

The producer had good reason to be optimistic as *Gunsmoke* was attracting more than fifteen million viewers and beating everything the competing networks scheduled against it on Monday night.

Altered somewhat were the opening credits, with announcer George Walsh now reading the actors' names, and a shot of Arness getting ready for a showdown, but, thanks to the antiviolence movement, not firing his gun.

"The River," a two-part episode shot largely on location around Grants Pass, Oregon, and on the Rogue River, featured the first ever aerial photography (helicopter) employed by the series. Befitting the story's epic scope, the writer (Jack Miller) and director (Herb Wallerstein) credits were shown at the beginning of the episode rather than at the end.

More location work was done in Arizona for "Sarah" and "Tatum," both above-average segments of yet another solid season that also included such highlights as "The Judgment," "The Fugitives" (another episode written by Milburn Stone's brother Charles), "Milligan," "The Brothers," "Whelan's Men," "Jesse," "Kimbro," "The Drummer," and the humorous "Quiet Day in Dodge."

Morgan Woodward made his fifteenth guest appearance in "The Sodbusters," his typically outstanding performance almost snaring an Emmy nomination.

Particular noteworthy were "Patricia," in which Newly becomes the lone member of the *Gunsmoke* family be (briefly) married, and the now-classic "Hostage!" with Matt taking off his badge and pursuing the "dog soldiers"who have nearly killed Kitty.

In March, James Arness was named Man of the Year at the 13th Annual International Broadcasting Dinner sponsored by the Hollywood Radio and Television Society, attended by his *Gunsmoke* co-stars. At the event, John Mantley told the press, "Reports that Jim has so much money he no longer wants to work are absolutely untrue. The problem is the antiviolence edict. I can't have him walking around tipping his hat to ladies. He's a lawman with a gun on his hip and when he's on he should function as a marshal. And if I can't have him function as a marshal I'm obliged to use less of him than before."

The National Conference of Christians and Jews gave *Gunsmoke* the Mass Media Award for the episode "This Golden Land," and the Western Writers of America named William Kelley's "Bohannan" the season's Best Western TV Script. For the twelfth and final time, the series was voted the second best Western in

Motion Picture Daily's Annual Television Poll, once again giving the top spot to sentimental favorite *Bonanza*.

The GAF Corporation, manufacturer of the View-Master portable "slide show" (twenty-one pictures on three reels), released "The Drummer" as "The Rat Trap," and Aladdin produced its final *Gunsmoke* lunchbox.

Season Nineteen (1973-74)
24 Episodes / Rating: #15

"When Gunsmoke *first started 18 years ago, Kitty was just another whore. We got a lot of complaints from people who didn't want her spreading her favors around to everyone."*

(John Mantley, 1973)

The new season of *Gunsmoke* included a pair of now-famous episodes dealing with Matt and Kitty's private lives ("Matt's Love Story," "Kitty's Love Affair"), a pair of excellent two-part episodes ("Women for Sale," "A Game of Death, An Act of Love"), and what would prove to be the final appearance of Kitty Russell ("Disciple"). And yet, the Dodge City saga, despite continuing to win its time slot, dropped from seventh place to fifteenth in its penultimate season. *Hec Ramsey*, airing once a month as part of *The NBC Sunday Mystery Movie*, came in one notch higher, while *Kung Fu* hung in at number twenty-seven, tied with *The Carol Burnett Show*. The era of the TV Western seemed to be finally coming to a close.

Ten days after the season began, Glenn Strange died, a victim of lung cancer. The disease had been discovered in late 1972, when he was hospitalized with pneumonia, but Strange continued working as long as he was able, finishing the eighteenth season and beginning the next. One of the few people who were aware of his condition was Arness, who told him, "Glenn, you can continue to work on the show just as long as you want to work. You just let me know. You just tell me." Often unable to speak any lines, and sometimes too weak to stand, Strange would sit on a stool behind the Long

Arness, Blake, Curtis, Stone

Branch bar that was high enough to make it look like he was erect. During the summer he managed to film the last of his 222 episodes as Sam Noonan: "The Widowmaker," the two-part "A Game of Death, An Act of Love," and "The Hanging of Newly O'Brien." By the time the latter aired on November 26, Strange, who sounds tired and is noticeably more slender, had been gone for over two months. Appropriately, the episode ends with a shot of a smiling Sam dispensing beers for the citizens of Dodge.

Robert Brubaker, who had portrayed stagecoach driver Jim Buck in more than a dozen half-hour episodes, was cast as Floyd, the new Long Branch bartender, a role he would play eight times. In January's "Like Old Times," when a customer asks where Sam is, Floyd replies, "We lost him a while back. Everybody around here misses him a lot." Kitty also mentions Sam in "The Foundling."

The season opened with two episodes filmed in Arizona, the two-part "Women for Sale" (with narration by none other than radio's Matt Dillon, William Conrad) and "Matt's Love Story," which would inspire the second *Gunsmoke* television movie in 1990. A third episode, "The Widow and the Rogue" was also shot partially in

Arizona. Other outstanding installments included "A Family of Killers," "The Iron Blood of Courage," and "The Deadly Innocent," in which Festus attempts to help a mentally challenged young man find a place in the world. Calvin Clements, Sr.'s script for the latter won a Golden Spur from the Western Writers of America as well as an award from the President's Council on Mental Retardation.

The concluding episode of the season, "The Disciple," though not the last to be filmed, was Amanda Blake's swansong as Kitty Russell. While there was no indication that she would not be back at the time, there is added poignancy today in Blake's final close-up and line of dialogue: "Oh, Matt..."

In January, CBS reunited Jeanette Nolan and Dack Rambo (from 1971's "Pike") in the short-lived spinoff series *Dirty Sally*, a mid-season entry taking the place of the canceled *Planet of the Apes* on Friday night. While the title character's escapades may have been popular on *Gunsmoke*, her own show was not, vanishing from the airwaves by July.

That summer, Award Books published two *Gunsmoke* paperback novels by Jackson Flynn. The first, *The Renegades*, was an adaptation of Paul F. Edwards' script for "A Game of Death, An Act of Love," and the second was entitled "Shootout."

As filming of the following season got underway, reporter Joseph Finnigan asked Amanda Blake, then working on a television movie (*The Companion*, changed to *Betrayal* before it aired) for ABC, if she missed the show. "No, I've been too busy," she said. "I went to Tucson, where they were shooting on location, and I thought I would get the pangs, but I didn't. I thought, there but for the grace of God go I."

CHAPTER 6
SUNDOWN IN
DODGE & BEYOND
(1974–75)

Season Twenty (1974-75)
24 Episodes / Rating: #28

"Hollywood hasn't watched Gunsmoke *in years, so it hasn't been considered for Emmys and the like. But the rest of the country always loved it."*
(John Mantley, 1975)

ABC's police drama *The Rookies*, in its third season, became the first series to finally beat *Gunsmoke* on Monday night. No doubt legions of viewers regretted the absence of Miss Kitty (replaced by Fran Ryan as new Long Branch owner Miss Hannah in just five episodes) after nineteen recording-breaking years, and there is no question the general flavor of the show changed without her. Even so, a little over twenty percent of the country's televisions were still tuned in to see what was happening in Dodge City. That number would qualify *Gunsmoke* as a huge hit in today's world of one hundred-plus channels, when a show attracting an audience half that size is considered a ratings giant. But nearly forty years ago, with approximately sixty series airing in prime time on the three major networks, anything near the bottom of the Top 30 was regarded as a middling success at best—especially if the main audience was older than the one preferred by sponsors. And the age of the average *Gunsmoke* viewer had been heading north of forty-nine for at least the past two seasons.

Arness & Curtis

Nearly half of the most popular shows during 1974-75 were comedies. The only other series in the top 30 set before the twentieth century besides *Gunsmoke* was Michael Landon's *Little House on the Prairie*, in thirteenth place. The novelty of *Kung Fu* had worn off in its third and final year, and a frontier drama called *The New Land* lasted barely a month. The following season would be the first with no "period" shows ranked in the Top 30 since A.C. Nielsen Media Research began tracking television viewership in 1950. It would also be the first in two decades without *Gunsmoke*.

Season Twenty began with new opening credits, segueing from bustling Front Street to shots of Doc at his desk, Festus and his mule Ruth outside the Long Branch, Newly in his gun shop, and Matt once again facing down an (unseen) opponent.

The episodes of the first five weeks all steered clear of Dodge. "Matt Dillon Must Die," the season premiere, was filmed at Cedar Breaks National Monument in Kanab, Utah, and featured Morgan Woodward in his eighteenth guest appearance, this time as the head of a mountain clan bent on getting even with Matt for killing one of their own. "Town in Chains" and the two-part "The Guns of Cibola Blanca" were filmed at Arizona's Old Tucson and Coronado National Forest, and "Thirty a Month and Found" at California's Big Sky Ranch and only briefly in Dodge.

Paul Savage's script for "The Guns of Cibola Blanca" was written before it was known that Amanda Blake would not be returning, which necessitated a quick rewrite to replace Kitty with a character named Lyla.

All in all, the end of the *Gunsmoke* trail was a strong one: "The Iron Men," "The Fourth Victim," "The Tarnished Badge," "In Performance of Duty," "The Squaw," "The Angry Land," "Larkin," The Hiders," "Hard Labor" (the last episode filmed), "The Busters" (the last to air, as a network rerun) and the two-part "Island in the Desert" all solid Western tales. Less noteworthy were a pair of light-hearted segments, "The Wiving" and its sequel, "Brides and Grooms." Nor was the final first-run episode, "The Sharecroppers," of any real consequence.

Offsetting those relative disappointments were the awards bestowed on "Thirty Month and Found" (Best Episodic Drama for Jim Byrnes from the Writers Guild of America as well as the Golden Spur from the Western Writers of America), "The Fires of Ignorance" (National Education Award) and "The Busters" (another Golden Spur for Jim Byrnes).

At the beginning of the season, Award Books published another paperback novel by Jackson Flynn, *Duel at Dodge City*, based on Ron Bishop's 1972 episode "The Sodbusters." A fourth novel, *Cheyenne Vengeance*, adapted from Richard Fielder's "The Drummer," also from 1972, followed in the spring.

On April 30, 1975, the Associated Press reported: "CBS has done something Indians, bad guys, bad whisky and not even CBS could do earlier: Kill off U.S. Marshal Matt Dillon. The move will put actor James Arness, for 20 years the hero of the long-running *Gunsmoke* TV western, on the unemployment rolls. A few years ago CBS tried to remove the show but was met by such audience protests that the network had to renew the series."

This time, William S. Paley did not ride to the rescue. Although *Gunsmoke* had avoided CBS's infamous purge of series it considered overly bucolic and not sufficiently urbane (*The Beverly Hillbillies, Mayberry R.F.D, Hee Haw*, etc.) a few years before, the network now regarded the show's audience as, in the words of one critic, "too old and too rural." Similar to NBC's lack of respect when suddenly ending the run of its former flagship, *Bonanza*, while scripts were still being written and locations scouted, CBS dropped *Gunsmoke* just as production was due to begin on the next season.

"All of us were ready, psychologically, for one more season of *Gunsmoke*," Arness said a couple of years later. "CBS had led us downstream and then, when we were down to the wire, they dropped the ax. Some horsefeathers about demographics. We knew it couldn't last forever. My God, we still had 20 years under our belt! Still, we were left hanging by the ropes."

Regarding those demographics, Alan Wagner, a CBS vice president in charge of program development, did indeed confess that *Gunsmoke*'s ratings were fine, but that the fan base—rural and older—was not the group being targeted by advertisers. Perhaps not coincidentally, CBS, which touted itself as the Tiffany Network, was to see its fortunes dwindle for the next few years after *Gunsmoke*, long their most prestigious series, left the air.

Amanda Blake was in New York shortly after the show was canceled. Riding past CBS headquarters, she remarked, "I think I'll go in there and hit Bill Paley over the head with a brickbat."

Dennis Weaver, whose *McCloud* series was still going strong, told the press, "I think primarily the reason for *Gunsmoke*'s longevity was the *Gunsmoke* family. These people were very likable, very human, very believable."

Critic Norman Mark, in the now-defunct Chicago Daily News, was not saddened by the show's demise despite having written admiring stories about it in recent years: "CBS has canceled *Gunsmoke* after 20 years on the air. I will not weep for it. Five years ago would have been time for a wake. Matt, Doc and Kitty were still interesting then. But I haven't watched a *Gunsmoke* adventure in months. And I don't know anyone else who has. Twenty years later, Kitty had become a den mother, Doc was lovable, Chester was gone, and Matt was hardly there. *Gunsmoke* was irrelevant. Good riddance."

Harsh words from one who obviously had little appreciation for consistently unsurpassed writing, convincing performances and a generally authentic depiction of the Old West. And who admittedly had stopped following the series, and was apparently unaware that Kitty was no longer in Dodge City.

But Mark's opinions were in the minority. Several other columnists lamented the passing of the series, and the week before the last network broadcast on September 1, 1975, TV Guide ran an appreciation of the show that featured comments from such *Gunsmoke* figures as Charles Marquis Warren, Kathleen Hite, John Mantley and Norman Macdonnell. Referring to writer/co-creator John Meston, Macdonnell said, "The biggest tragedy about *Gunsmoke* is that Meston and I never had a piece of it. The second biggest is that Meston, the best Western writer, has never been properly honored."

Five years after *Gunsmoke* left the air, the late Louis L'Amour, the most popular Western novelist of all time, told Writer's Digest, "The best video westerns to date have been in the *Gunsmoke* series. The writers really did try to picture the West as it was."

In the time between the end of *Gunsmoke* and Mr. L'Amour's assessment, the networks made few attempts to resurrect the genre. In 1975, ABC teamed Doug McClure and William Shatner in *The Barbary Coast*, which ran for only four months. The following year, NBC's *The Quest*, co-starring Kurt Russell and Tim Matheson (with a guest appearance in one episode by Amanda Blake), lasted just three months. Although not technically a Western, a much larger flop was CBS's *Young Dan'l Boone*, canceled after four episodes in 1977. That same season, NBC offered *The Oregon Trail*, starring Rod Taylor, gone in a month, with several episodes unaired.

The sole success story was, presumably to no one's surprise, the combination of producer John Mantley and James Arness as mountain man Zeb Macahan in a 1976 television movie for ABC entitled *The Macahans.* "I fell in love with the script," said Arness. "I said to the people at M-G-M: 'Forget about Matt Dillon. This Macahan guy's more colorful.'" After a lengthy but necessary pre-production period, Arness/Zeb returned in the epic mini-series *How the West Was Won,* debuting in February 1977 and becoming the eleventh top rated program in the annual ratings when the numbers were tallied after the second season. Reviewing the series, critic Robert MackKenzie observed, "James Arness, who had his engaging moments as Matt Dillon in *Gunsmoke,* is considerably grayer and sterner and even more close-mouthed as Zeb Macahan, a heavy-stepping mountain man." In early 1979 the show returned for a third season with eleven two-hour episodes.

That same year, Milburn Stone and Ken Curtis, dressed as Doc and Festus, joined numerous former stars of television Westerns for an ABC special entitled *When the West Was Fun: A Western Reunion,* hosted by Glenn Ford. It was to be Stone's last public appearance, and only his second since *Gunsmoke* had been canceled. The previous year he had participated in CBS's 50th anniversary celebration, later telling reporter Vernon Scott, "I really miss *Gunsmoke*! And I'd dearly love to go back to work. I'm really getting bored with retirement." Prior to having bypass surgery in 1971, Stone had suffered three heart attacks, and in December 1977 had a pacemaker installed. On June 12, 1980, he finally succumbed to heart failure. A week later, the Associated Press ran a photo showing Arness (in dark sunglasses), Blake and Curtis at a memorial service for Stone held in Los Angeles. Regrettably, Stone did not live long enough to see himself—along with Arness, Curtis and Dennis Weaver—inducted into the Hall of Great Western Performers by the National Cowboy Hall of Fame the following year.

In early 1981, NBC issued a press release proclaiming their sci-fi series *Buck Rogers in the 25th Century* "The *Gunsmoke* of the Future! If you're wondering what *Gunsmoke* has to do with *Buck Rogers,* you probably haven't seen the show this season. The new *Buck Rogers* is carrying on *Gunsmoke's* tradition of exciting stories featuring a cast of characters you'll care about. Here's what John Mantley, Executive Producer of *Buck Rogers* and the Emmy-winning Executive Producer of *Gunsmoke* says: 'I'm really excited about this show! It's the *Gunsmoke* of the 25th Century!'"

Mantley, who had a reputation of breathing new life into troubled series (most notably *Gunsmoke* and *The Wild, Wild West*) and had also written science-fiction, was recruited by the network to "fix" the third season of *Buck Rogers*, starring Gil Gerard. In the producer's estimation, the show's stories were "empty." "The holes in some scripts are embarrassing," said Mantley. "This is absolutely the most difficult project I've ever done." He also found the title character problematic, saying, "I want to stretch Gil Gerard as I did James Arness on *Gunsmoke*." While critics for Variety and the Associated Press agreed that the show had improved, *Buck Rogers* did not return in the fall.

Ken Curtis, who in 1976 had made the film *Pony Express Rider* (also starring Buck Taylor), landed a role in 1981's *California Gold Rush* before joining *The Yellow Rose*, a contemporary Western soap opera airing Saturday nights on NBC, in 1983. Despite an impressive cast that included Chuck Connors, Sam Elliott and Noah Berry, Jr., the show lasted only one season.

Also running for a single season (1981-82) was NBC's *McClain's Law*, starring James Arness as a modern day lawman who comes out of retirement to find the killer of his former partner. ("Old *Gunsmoke* fans won't necessarily be pleased," said one review. "That show had an unmistakable style. So far, *McClain's Law* looks a lot like a half-dozen other police shows.") The only projects he participated in between 1982 and the five *Gunsmoke* movies were *The Alamo: 13 Days to Glory*, a 1987 television film with, among others, Lorne Greene, Brian Keith and Gene Evans, and a remake of *Red River* the following year. When his brother, actor Peter Graves, proposed a contemporary series in which they would co-star, Arness turned him down, saying, "I only feel comfortable in the nineteenth century."

The three major networks, however, wanted little to do with the nineteenth century, attempting a very few short-lived programs (*The Quest, Sara, Father Murphy, Young Maverick, Bret Maverick*, and the Old West sitcom *Best of the West*) from 1976 to 1982, and then no Western series at all for the next decade. A chapter of television history certainly did seem to be permanently closed. In his 1994 memoir, *In the Company of Heroes: My Life as an Actor in the John Ford Company*, Harry Carey, Jr., who guest starred on *Gunsmoke* ten times, lamented: "There are acres and acres of houses now where we shot all those westerns. One beautiful area is called Thousand Oaks, and there were thousands of them before developers got to them. Out in the 'West Valley,' where we did all the chases and gunfights, there are golf courses, and malls, and condos. Smog lays out there like a dirty brown blanket. We drive by there often on our way to Santa Barbara to see our daughters and grandchildren, and I hate to see what has happened to the *Gunsmoke* country I loved."

Following the success of the first *Gunsmoke* movie in 1987, there was a modest resurgence of the television Western, beginning with CBS's *Paradise* (1988-91) and *Dr. Quinn, Medicine Woman* (1993-98), ABC's *The Young Riders* (1989-92), Fox's fanciful *The Adventures of Brisco County, Jr.* (1993-94), and numerous syndicated and cable series and movies. The most exceptional success was the 1989 CBS mini-series based on Larry McMurtry's Pulitzer Prize winning novel, *Lonesome Dove*, which eventually spawned four sequels of varying quality. After two brief seasons of *The Magnificent Seven* (CBS 1998-99), shot on the site of the former Melody Ranch, the networks appeared to once again be done with the genre, although as of this writing there are rumored to be several new pilots on the drawing board, one a CBS remake of *The Rifleman*.

The *Gunsmoke* legacy has continued to be celebrated in print and product, beginning with the 1989 publication of John Peel's *Gunsmoke Years*, highlighted by interviews with John Mantley and story editor Paul Savage. The next year saw the masterful *Gunsmoke: A Complete History* by SuzAnne Barabas and Gabor Barabas, as well as the first of 45 videotapes of memorable episodes from the CBS network's subsidiary Columbia House. A few years later, Pacific Trading Cards, Inc., released 110 cards illustrated with mainly black-and-white stills from the show. In 1994, to celebrate the upcoming 40th anniversary of the series, the Franklin Mint began issuing six collector plates on Royal Doulton Fine Bone China, all painted by artist Dick Bobnick. From 1998 to 2008, no less than nine paperback novels based on the series were written by authors Gary McCarthy, Joseph A. West, and T.T. Flynn, some better—and more accurate—than others.

In 2001, Dennis Weaver published his autobiography, *All the World's a Stage*. Later in the year came *James Arness: An Autobiography*, co-written by James E. Wise, Jr. and with a foreword by Burt

Reynolds. *Gunsmoke: An American Institution*, an excellent tribute by Ben Costello, commemorated the show's 50th anniversary. Five years later, Beckey Burgoyne's richly detailed valentine to Amanda Blake, *Perfectly Amanda: Gunsmoke's "Miss Kitty" To Dodge and Beyond*, was released.

Millions of *Gunsmoke* devotees are no doubt justified to be nervous as well as skeptical about a feature from CBS Films currently in development, said to be starring either Brad Pitt or Ryan Reynolds as Matt Dillon. Regardless of the outcome, nothing will ever beat the original.

Arness as Matt Dillon, 1987

CHAPTER 7
RESURRECTION: THE GUNSMOKE TELEFILMS (1987–94)

"Gunsmoke was something whose time had come. What made the difference was they didn't try to do an entertainment fictionalized Western. They really tried like hell to make it hot and dry and dusty, and people were ready for it."

(James Arness, 1987)

Word that another trace of *Gunsmoke* might be on the horizon came from an unexpected source: Miss Kitty herself. After her appearance on *The Quest* in 1976, nothing was seen of Amanda Blake until she showed up in a segment of *The Love Boat* in 1979, on the *Hart to Hart* series in 1983, and on the daytime drama *The Edge of Night* in 1984. The following March, she visited the Boot Hill Museum and historic Front Street in Dodge City, surprising fellow tourists with news that she and a Nebraska businessman named Robert Potter were busy rounding up investors for a proposed movie called *The Last Gunsmoke*. Thus far they had raised $60,000 of the $6 million the film was estimated to cost. "I think this movie will work because we still have good overcoming evil," she said. "People want to see that." Veteran *Gunsmoke* writer Paul Savage was hired to pen a script in which Matt is recruited to rescue Kitty's niece, who turns out to be Matt and Kitty's daughter. Blake and Potter were able to get the rights to Rex Koury's theme song for the series, and Savage later claimed that Arness liked the script.

However, in May entertainment columnist Marilyn Beck reported that representatives for James Arness had termed rumors that there was going to be a *Gunsmoke* film "pure fantasy." Beck added that

CBS still owned the rights to the series "and has not released those rights to anyone." Not mentioned was the fact that the network had been contemplating a *Gunsmoke* project initially scheduled to be ready by as early as November of 1985.

A year later, CBS announced that Matt Dillon would indeed be returning to the home screen in *Gunsmoke: Return to Dodge*. Among the guest stars under consideration were Bruce Dern, Nick Nolte, Jon Voight, Richard Dreyfuss and Victor French, all of whom had done episodes of the series. The television tabloid *Entertainment Tonight* mistakenly informed viewers that Dennis Weaver and Burt Reynolds would also be part of the reunion. Weaver said he had never been officially asked, but admitted his agent had been approached about the possibility. If fans were disappointed to learn there would be no sign of Chester Goode or Quint Asper, they were truly incensed by the news that Ken Curtis would not be included, nor was *Gunsmoke: Return to Dodge* going to be filmed in the United States. The original plan was to go on location in Montana and Utah, but because production costs were cheaper, the movie, budgeted at $3 million, was being shot in Canada, specifically Calgary, Alberta. Director Vincent McEveety admired the Canadian crew and the country's beauty, but admitted "it's sad we aren't doing it at home."

As for the exclusion of Ken Curtis, the issue was said to be money. John Mantley, back as executive producer, diplomatically told the press, "He wanted twice what Amanda is getting. I said, 'Ken, I can't do that.' He said, 'Then I'm not coming.' And that's how it ended." If subsequent accounts are accurate, Curtis also objected to alterations that were made to Jim Byrnes' original script, and told Mantley to never call him again. (Arness had his own problem with the script, complaining that the character of Jake Flagg—played by Earl Holliman—was more colorful than Matt Dillon. Needless to say, changes were made.)

Ultimately, *Gunsmoke: Return to Dodge* was a sequel to Ron Bishop's 1969 episode "Mannon," with Steve Forrest guest-starring as one of Matt Dillon's most loathsome foes, out of prison and once again menacing Miss Kitty.

Back on board was Buck Taylor as Newly O'Brien. Since the series ended, he had taken occasional jobs on such shows as *Lottery* and

The Fall Guy, the television movies *The Busters, Kate Bliss and the Ticker Tape Kid, The Sacketts, Wild Times, The Cherokee Trail* and *No Man's Land,* and the theatrical feature *Pony Express Rider* (with Ken Curtis). While primarily interested in sharpening his skills as an artist, Taylor did not have to be asked twice to come back, this time as Dodge City's marshal. Asked about the atmosphere on the set, he replied, "Jim came out grinning the first morning, and it hasn't stopped."

Mantley agreed. "I've been with Jim for fifteen years, and I've never seen him so excited."

"Jim is one of the nicest people I've ever known" Blake added. "Jim has absolutely a childlike quality, which is surprising for someone as big as he is. It's a little boy quality; he's shy, too. He's very funny and kept us cracked up over the years. Nobody ever pictured him that way."

Finding herself back as Kitty Russell proved to be a bittersweet experience for Amanda Blake, who told reporter Mike Hughes that when she saw that the Long Branch set had been replicated exactly as she remembered, "I just fell apart. I spent the first day crying." She had difficulty getting through her initial scene in the saloon, telling Fran Ryan (reprising her role as Miss Hannah) it was because she missed Doc. "Milburn Stone would just be in his glory here," she said afterward. "He was not only Doc but our technical adviser. He would straighten us out, even if we didn't need straightening out. I miss him so much."

Sitting for a rare interview between shots, Arness remarked, "It's more fun to go back a hundred years or so. Believe me, this is better than slamming car doors. I like it better every day, and every day I feel better about it. But we'll have to wait and see what the people think."

Gunsmoke: Return to Dodge—dedicated to Milburn Stone, Glenn Strange, James Nusser, Woodrow Chambliss, Charles Waggenheim, Charles Seel, Roy Barcroft—was broadcast on Saturday, September 26, 1987, and was a hit with viewers and most critics. Howard Rosenberg, writing in *The Los Angeles Times,* said "the characters are a bit rickety" but that it was good to have Matt and Kitty back even if "a single *Gunsmoke* movie won't recapture this lost genre." Regarding the future of the television Western, he added, "Contemporary audiences are probably too sophisticated to watch back-lot horse operas, and weekly location filming would be too expensive." Rosenberg was, in general, correct, although as already stated, the first *Gunsmoke* movie was followed by more Western programming than had been seen in many years.

Prominent film historian Leonard Maltin rated the movie above average, commenting, "it's nice to greet old friends" but that "Doc and Chester are sorely missed." Critic Steven H. Scheuer dubbed it "a pleasant reunion."

CBS deemed *Gunsmoke: Return to Dodge* sufficiently successful to warrant a sequel, giving John Mantley the green light soon after. The producer promised fans that the film would not be shot in Canada, and that Kitty would have a larger part. After several delays, *Gunsmoke: The Last Apache* went into production on several locations in Texas, but without Amanda Blake, the character of Miss Kitty having been totally eliminated from Earl W. Wallace's script by the time the cameras rolled. Blake died in August 1989, more than six months before the movie aired in March 1990. The closing credits stated: "This film is dedicated to the memory of our beloved friends and artists: Miss Amanda Blake, Stan Hough and writer emeritus, Mr. Ron Bishop."

Gunsmoke: The Last Apache, which took three weeks to shoot in unseasonably cool weather, was the last to have a connection to the original series, with Michael Learned returning in the role as Mike Yardner from the Season 19 episode "Matt's Love Story." Introduced as Matt and Mike's daughter Beth was Amy Stock-Poynton, fresh off her one season on the prime time drama *Dallas*, and the only character who would go on to co-star in the remaining three *Gunsmoke* movies. Others in the cast were Richard Kiley, who had appeared in four episodes of the series, including "Kitty's Love Affair" (also from Season 19), and Hugh O'Brian, whose *The Life and Legend of Wyatt Earp* had debuted four nights before *Gunsmoke* in 1955. The story was somewhat reminiscent of John Ford's 1956 classic *The Searchers*, as well as Paul Savage's rejected 1985 script for the first *Gunsmoke* film, with Matt's daughter being kidnapped.

Asked by reporter Art Chapman to compare himself to Matt Dillon, Arness, then 66, replied, "There's no comparison, no way. I couldn't hold down the job of a U.S. Marshal for a week. You might think playing the same character all these years must be a piece of cake, but if you look at it from the standpoint of reality, it is always a mountain to climb. In this case, we've been away from it for a long time. It is a matter of getting back into the feel of it, and it does take a certain amount of time."

Broadcast as the CBS Sunday Movie on March 18, 1990, *Gunsmoke: The Last Apache* was another hit, watched by 32 million viewers and ranking as the number seven show of the week. Arness hinted it might be the end of the trail for Matt Dillon, but in early 1991 said he was open to the idea of doing a couple of *Gunsmoke* movies a year. "But a weekly show would be too hard a workload for me these days."

A third film, *Gunsmoke: To the Last Man*, was supposed to begin production in February 1991, but was delayed due to revisions of Earl Wallace's script (loosely based on Arizona's Pleasant Valley range war) and problems with John Mantley's health. It eventually aired on January 10, 1992. Supervising the production, at Mantley's request, was former *Gunsmoke* writer Jim Byrnes. Joining Amy Stock-Poynton were Morgan Woodward and Pat Hingle, both very familiar to fans of the series.

Shot on location in Arizona and dedicated to *Gunsmoke* co-creator and writer John Meston, *Gunsmoke: To the Last Man* was the most violent installment to date. Critic Ed Weiner commented, "What makes Matt Dillon Matt Dillon, according to *Gunsmoke: To the Last Man*, is his uncanny ability to kill every living organism in sight— but nobly."

Once the film wrapped, Arness, said again that he would enjoy doing another. With that in mind, Jim Byrnes began contemplating not only story ideas but also inviting Ken Curtis back to play Festus. But Curtis, who had not worked since the 1988 television movie *Once Upon a Texas Train*, died on April 28, 1991, at virtually the same time production of the third *Gunsmoke* film was completed.

The fourth Matt Dillon adventure, *Gunsmoke: The Last Ride*, was broadcast on May 8, 1993, written by Bill Stratton, directed by Jerry Jameson, produced by Norman S. Powell, and Arness credited as Executive Producer. Pam Polifroni, who had taken over as casting director in the twelfth season of the original series, was able to secure the services of James Brolin (*Marcus Welby, M.D.*) and Seventies superstar Ali MacGraw (*Love Story*) for what turned out to be a most enjoyable saga of Matt tangling with bounty hunters after being falsely accused of murder.

Jeff Jarvis, a TV Guide critic, wrote: "Thirty-eight years after he first rode out as Matt Dillon, James Arness returns in another movie, and that's a feat worth watching. He has a voice like a dusty old trail and a face that shows 20,000 sunsets. The script creates more burial plots than plotlines—but who cares? Matt Dillon's back." On a scale of zero to ten, Jarvis gave *Gunsmoke: The Last Ride* an eight.

The title of the 1993 film may have led viewers to assume that they had seen the last of Dodge City's former lawman, but he was back in less than a year, in *Gunsmoke: One Man's Justice*, shown on February 10, 1994. For this last hurrah, Executive Producer Arness was reunited with Bruce Boxleitner, his *How the West Was Won* co-star, and with whom he had made 1988's *Red River*, a television remake of the 1948 John Wayne classic. Once again directed by Jerry Jameson and produced by Jameson and Norman S. Powell, the script by Harry and Renee Longstreet revealed that Matt's father had been a Texas Ranger killed in the line of duty, a fact never mentioned during the series. For old time's sake, Dillon's left arm is wounded for the umpteenth time.

Gunsmoke: One Man's Justice received only lukewarm reviews and played to a dwindling audience. It is doubtful that CBS would have ordered a sixth film (an unfounded rumor claimed there were plans for another), but network interference, as well as health concerns, convinced Arness that Matt had finally reached the end of the trail. Not that he will ever be forgotten. In the words of John Mantley, Arness was "the most exposed man in the history of any medium— there's more film on Jim Arness than any other human being."

EPISODE GUIDE
SEASON 1
September 10, 1955–August 25, 1956

#1: MATT GETS IT
(09-10-55)

STORY: John Meston
TELEPLAY: Charles Marquis Warren
DIRECTOR: Charles Marquis Warren
CAST: Paul Richards, Robert Anderson, Malcom
               Atterbury, Howard Culver

After crafty gunman Dan Grat wounds him in a showdown, Marshal Matt Dillon must think of a way to beat him the next time they face each other.

NOTES: The second episode filmed, but the first to air. Matt is shot twice, in the chest and creased along the forearm. First of 48 appearances by Howard Culver as Dodge House desk clerk Howie Uzzel.

#2: HOT SPELL
(09-17-55)

WRITER: E. Jack Neuman
DIRECTOR: Charles Marquis Warren
CAST: John Dehner, James Westerfield, Marvin Bryan

After Matt saves him from being lynched by a local rancher, lowlife Cope Borden kills the rancher's nephew in a fair gunfight.

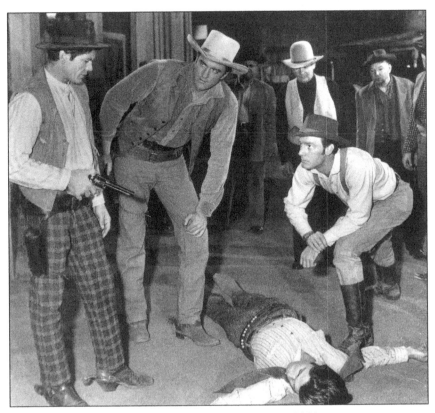

Charles Bronson, Arness, Weaver in "The Killer," 1956

NOTES: When Borden asks Matt if Kitty is his girl, Matt won't answer. First use of the now-famous command "Get out of Dodge!"

#3: WORD OF HONOR
(10-01-55)

STORY: John Meston
TELEPLAY: Charles Marquis Warren
DIRECTOR: Charles Marquis Warren
CAST: Robert Middleton, Claude Akins, Ray Boyle, Will J. Wright, Dick Paxton, Tom Carney

Outlaws kidnap Doc to tend to one of their wounded, agreeing to let him go if he promises not to send the law after them.

NOTES: Upset at the situation, Doc tells Matt and Chester he is "going to get good and drunk." At the episode's conclusion, however, he says, "This is no time for drinkin.'" Arness wears a coat, vest and black hat during the opening narration.

#4: HOME SURGERY
(10-08-55)

WRITER: John Meston
DIRECTOR: Charles Marquis Warren
CAST: Gloria Talbott, Joe De Santis, Wright King

Matt has to amputate the leg of a rancher suffering from gangrene, unaware that the old man's injury did not happen the way his daughter claims it did.

NOTES: First time revelations include Chester's last name and the fact that Matt fought in the Civil War, though for which side is not mentioned. No opening scene with narration on Boot Hill.

#5: OBIE TATER
(10-15-55)

STORY: John Meston
TELEPLAY: Charles Marquis Warren
DIRECTOR: Charles Marquis Warren
CAST: Royal Dano, Kathy Adams, Jon Sheppod,
               Pat Conway

A farmer rumored to be sitting on a pile of gold marries a saloon girl in cahoots with two men who are after the alleged fortune.

NOTES: Royal Dano guest starred on nearly 40 different television Westerns. Pat Conway later headlined his own series, *Tombstone Territory,* for three seasons (1957-60).

#6: NIGHT INCIDENT
(10-29-55)

WRITER: Charles Marquis Warren
DIRECTOR: Charles Marquis Warren
CAST: Peter Votrian, Robert Foulk, Amzie Strickland, Anne Warren, Lance Warren, Jeanne Bates, Lou Vernon

Matt is skeptical but feels he has to act when a young boy tells him an Indian girl's parents have been robbing and killing travelers.

NOTES: Matt brews tea rather than the usual jailhouse coffee, telling Chester it helps the body handle the heat better. When pretending to be drunk, Matt sings the "Daddy came west to Kansas" song later sung numerous times by Chester. The proprietor of Dodge's general store is revealed to be Cal Ross. Filmed at the legendary Iverson Ranch.

#7: SMOKING OUT THE NOLANS
(11-05-55)

STORY: John Meston
TELEPLAY: Charles Marquis Warren
DIRECTOR: Charles Marquis Warren
CAST: John Larch, Ainslie Pryor, Jeanne Bates, Ed Platt

Matt and Chester are forced to evict a farmer and his wife who insist they have been cheated out of rightful ownership to their land.

NOTES: Although best known as The Chief on the sitcom *Get Smart*, he appeared in more than a dozen television Westerns. John Larch guest starred on more than thirty.

#8: Kite's Reward
(11-12-55)

WRITER: John Meston
DIRECTOR: Charles Marquis Warren
CAST: Adam Kennedy, James Griffith

Matt attempts to protect a reformed outlaw from a gunman determined to a collect a reward still being offered for the young man.

NOTES: Matt, who wears a black hat in this episode, says that being a fast gun forced him into making a choice as to what side of the law he wanted to be on. First of 43 episodes with George Selk as stable owner Moss Grimmick.

#9: The Hunter
(11-26-55)

WRITER: John Dunkel
DIRECTOR: Charles Marquis Warren
CAST: Peter Whitney, Richard Gilden, Lou Vernon,
                Robert Keene

A deranged buffalo hunter who once gave Matt a vicious beating shows up in Dodge and threatens to start an Indian war.

NOTES: Matt's first encounter with an old foe. He tells Kitty that the fight with the hunter occurred when he first came to Dodge from Missouri and was "pretty green." Second appearance by Lou Vernon as storekeeper Cal Ross.

#10: The Queue
(12-03-55)

STORY: John Meston
TELEPLAY: Sam Peckinpah
DIRECTOR: Charles Marquis Warren

CAST: Keye Luke, Sebastian Cabot, Robert Gist, Devlin McCarthy

Matt is faced with a peculiar dilemma when a pair of Dodge City bigots cut off the pigtail of a presumably peaceful Chinese resident.

NOTES: Matt is once again shown on Boot Hill wearing a tie, vest and black hat. The bartender of the Long Branch saloon (which features slot machines in this episode) is called Sam for the first time. Familiar Western actors Charles Gray and Bing Russell appear unbilled. Writer Sam Peckinpah went on to create *The Rifleman* and direct several popular films, including *The Wild Bunch*. Keye Luke and Dennis Weaver later co-starred on the series *Kentucky Jones*.

#11: GENERAL PARCLEY SMITH
(12-10-55)

STORY: John Meston
TELEPLAY: John Dunkel
DIRECTOR: Charles Marquis Warren
CAST: Raymond Bailey, James O'Rear, John Alderson, Wilfred Knapp

An aged Civil War veteran with a habit of stretching the truth claims that Dodge's newest banker, Drew Holt, is not to be trusted.

NOTES: First reference to Dodge City banker Mr. Botkin, sometimes spelled Bodkin and played by several different actors over the years. Matt again mentions having once been in the army.

#12: MAGNUS
(12-24-55)

WRITER: John Meston
DIRECTOR: Charles Marquis Warren

CAST: Robert Easton, James Anderson, Than Wyenn, Tim
                     Graham, Dorothy Schuyler

Christmas in Dodge promises to be more than a little lively when
Chester's rough-hewn brother and a religious fanatic come to town
at the same time.

NOTES: First of only two holiday episodes in the series' history.
Chester says his brother Magnus has lived outdoors since he was
ten-years-old. According to stuntman Dick Stanford, the temperature
at Melody Ranch was well into the 90s while Dodge was shown to
be covered in snow. No opening scene on Boot Hill.

#13: REED SURVIVES
(12-31-55)

WRITER: Les Crutchfield
DIRECTOR: Charles Marquis Warren
CAST: Lola Albright, John Carradine, James Drury

Lucy Hunt, a former saloon girl, entices a love struck cowboy
into killing her elderly husband.

NOTES: It is implied that Matt and Lucy were close at one time.
This episode features Matt and Doc's first game of checkers. Arness'
first wife, Virginia, is listed as a gypsy woman in the credits, but her
scene is actually included in the later episode "The Killer." A major
error! Matt is again wearing a tie, striped vest and black hat in the
Boot Hill opening.

#14: PROFESSOR LUTE BONE
(01-07-55)

STORY: John Meston
TELEPLAY: David Victor & Herbert Little
DIRECTOR: Charles Marquis Warren

CAST: John Abbott, Jester Hairston, Gloria Castillo, Don Garner, Strother Martin, Sally Corner

When a bogus "doctor" shows up, Doc takes it upon himself to drive the charlatan out of Dodge.

NOTES: First of several encounters between Doc and various medicine men. Matt still dressed like a dandy in the opening Boot Hill scene.

#15: NO HANDCUFFS
(01-21-56)

STORY: John Meston
TELEPLAY: Les Crutchfield
DIRECTOR: Charles Marquis Warren
CAST: Vic Perrin, Charles Gray, Mort Mills, Marjorie Owens, Herbert Lytton, Cyril Delevanti

Matt travels to the town of Mingo to confront a crooked lawman.

NOTES: First time Matt leaves Dodge for business in another community. Charles Gray was a regular on the Warren-created series *Gunslinger* and *Rawhide*. No Boot Hill opening.

#16: REWARD FOR MATT
(01-28-56)

STORY: John Meston
TELEPLAY: David Victor & Herbert Little
DIRECTOR: Charles Marquis Warren
CAST: Helen Wallace, Paul Newlan, Val Dufour, Jean Inness, John G. Lee

Matt finds himself in more danger than usual when the vengeful widow of a man he was forced to shoot offers $1000 to anyone who kills Dillon.

NOTES: Matt refers to storekeeper Wilbur Jonas for the first time when he tells Chester to get a better blend of coffee. Chester, who wears a vest in one scene, mentions having breakfast at the Sunflower Restaurant instead of the usual Delmonico's.

#17: ROBIN HOOD
(02-04-56)

STORY: John Meston
TELEPLAY: Dan Ullman
DIRECTOR: Charles Marquis Warren
CAST: William Hopper, Nora Marlowe, Barry Atwater, James McCallion, Wilfred Knapp, S. John Launer

Matt must think of a way to trip up an outlaw who has been arrested several times but always manages to get out of doing any jail time.

NOTES: Chester again wears a vest in one scene. Matt's black hat in close-up shots does not match his regular hat worn in most of the episode. Another look at a slot machine in the Long Branch. William Hopper, first seen in the courtroom, would later spend a lot of time in court as Paul Drake on the long-running *Perry Mason* series.

#18: YORKY
(02-18-56)

STORY: John Meston
TELEPLAY: Sam Peckinpah
DIRECTOR: Charles Marquis Warren
CAST: Jeff Silver, Howard Petrie, Dennis Cross, Malcom Atterbury, Mary Gregory

Matt comes to the aid of a young Indian boy who has been wounded by horse thieves.

NOTES: Chester mentions his mother. First look at Dodge's general store with a sign reading Wilbur Jonas, Prop.

#19: 20-20
(02-25-56)

STORY:	John Meston
TELEPLAY:	David Victor & Herbert Little
DIRECTOR:	Charles Marquis Warren
CAST:	Wilton Graff, Martin Kingsley, Pitt Herbert, George Selk

Troy Carver, a former lawman as well as one of Matt's mentors, is looking forward to a comfortable retirement but has been marked for death.

NOTES: Carver, first in a long line of fellow lawmen Matt knew in the past, is from Arizona and had been working in a Wild West show in Chicago. No Boot Hill opening.

#20: REUNION '78
(03-03-56)

WRITER:	Harold Swanton
DIRECTOR:	Charles Marquis Warren
CAST:	Val Dufour, Marian Brash, Maurice Manson, Joe Perry, Mason Curry

Matt jails Jerry Shand before he can kill Andy Culley, but is understandably puzzled when Culley pays Shand's bail.

NOTES: Sam, the Long Branch bartender, mentions that Dodge City is seven-years-old. Doc presides over a coroner's inquest in the lobby of the Dodge House. Matt again wearing the black hat, striped vest and tie in the Boot Hill opening.

#21: HELPING HAND
(03-17-56)

STORY: John Meston
TELEPLAY: David Victor & Herbert Little
DIRECTOR: Charles Marquis Warren
CAST: Brett Halsey, Ken L. Smith, James Nusser, Russ
               Thorson, Michael Granger

Kitty is disappointed when a young man she saved from a lynching begins to idolize one of Dodge's no account troublemakers.

NOTES: Matt shot for the second of 33 times in the show's history. Doc tells Matt he bets someone gave him a push in the right direction once. Matt replies, "Maybe." The character Bill Pence, presented here as a ranch foreman, has the same name used later for the half-owner of the Long Branch. First mention of rancher Emmett Bowers, played by various actors early in the series. James Nusser would eventually become semi-regular character Louie Pheeters in 72 episodes. Different storekeeper than Mr. Ross.

#22: TAP DAY FOR KITTY
(03-24-56)

STORY: John Meston
TELEPLAY: John Dunkel
DIRECTOR: Charles Marquis Warren
CAST: John Dehner, Mary Adams, John Patrick, Evelyn
               Scott, Dorothy Schuyler, Charlene Brooks

Kitty is suspected of attempted murder when someone takes a shot at Nip Cullers, an aging rancher who has come to Dodge to lay claim to Kitty.

NOTES: First of Kitty's many unwanted suitors. A third Dodge storekeeper is depicted.

#23: INDIAN SCOUT
(03-31-56)

WRITER: John Dunkel
DIRECTOR: Charles Marquis Warren
CAST: Eduard Franz, DeForest Kelley, William Vaughn,
              Pat Hogan, Tommy Hart

Matt and Chester enter hostile Comanche country in search of an army scout who allegedly led troopers into a deadly ambush.

NOTES: The late DeForest Kelley will always be remembered as Dr. McCoy on the *Star Trek* series. No Boot Hill opening.

#24: THE PEST HOLE
(04-14-56)

WRITERS: David Victor & Herbert Little
DIRECTOR: Charles Marquis Warren
CAST: Patrick O'Moore, Howard McNear, Norbert
              Schiller, Evelyn Scott

When typhoid fever strikes the German citizens of Dodge, Doc and Chester put their lives at stake in order to discover the cause of the epidemic.

NOTES: Doc, who says his latest medical books are from St. Louis, is shown drunk for the first time. Howard McNear portrayed Doc in the radio version of *Gunsmoke*, but is best known as Floyd the barber on *The Andy Griffith Show*. Arness once again sports the black hat, vest and tie in the Boot Hill opening.

#25: THE BIG BROAD
(04-28-56)

STORY: John Meston
TELEPLAY: David Victor & Herbert Little
DIRECTOR: Charles Marquis Warren
CAST: Dee J. Thompson, Joel Ashley, Terry Becker,
                  Howard Culver, Heinie Brock

A different sort of gunslinger menaces Dodge: A six-foot tall Amazon named Lena Wave.

NOTES: Dodge House clerk Howie is referred to as Mr. Uzzel for the first time. Matt tells Lena she can have her gun back when she gets "out of Dodge." No Boot Hill intro.

#26: HACK PRINE
(05-12-56)

WRITER: John Meston
DIRECTOR: Charles Marquis Warren
CAST: Leo Gordon, George Wallace, Hal Baylor, Wally
                  Cassell, Tyler McVey

Matt is happy to be reunited with his old friend Hack Prine until he learns that Prine has been offered $800 to kill him.

NOTES: First episode filmed, with voice-over narration not only in the Boot Hill opening, but also during the first scene. Matt wears a tie in the fourth scene. Chester mentions his brother Magnus. The office sign for the jail is to the right of the jail door rather than the left. Inside, the rifle rack, the desk and the stove are in different places, and door swings to the right, not the left. The stairway in the Dodge House is on the opposite side of the lobby, and Howie is not the desk clerk.

#27: COOTER
(05-19-56)

STORY: John Meston
TELEPLAY: Sam Peckinpah
DIRECTOR: Charles Marquis Warren
CAST: Strother Martin, Vinton Hayworth, Brett King,
             Robert Vaughn

To get even with Matt, a cowardly gambler hires a slow-witted man to shoot the marshal.

NOTES: Matt orders Pate (Brett King) to "Get out of Dodge!" Brief appearance by Robert Vaughn, best remembered as *The Man from U.N.C.L.E.* Matt again in the "dude" clothing during the Boot Hill opening.

#28: THE KILLER
(05-26-56)

STORY: John Meston
TELEPLAY: John Dunkel
DIRECTOR: Charles Marquis Warren
CAST: Charles Bronson, David Chapman, James Nusser,
             Dabbs Greer

Dodge is plagued by a sadistic gunman who deliberately provokes fights and later claims he only acted in self-defense.

NOTES: Virginia Arness plays a gypsy woman in this episode but receives no credit. Her performance was erroneously listed as being in the earlier "Reed Survives." First of 36 appearances by Dabbs Greer as storekeeper Wilbur Jonas.

#29: DOC'S REVENGE
(06-09-56)

WRITER: John Dunkel
DIRECTOR: Ted Post
CAST: Ainslie Pryor, Harry Bartell, Chris Alcaide

Doc is the prime suspect when a man he intended to kill is shot.

NOTES: Matt says Doc, as the only doctor for miles, has a responsibility to the people of Dodge. Matt orders Clem (Chris Alcaide) to "get out of Dodge and stay out!" Delmonico's restaurant mentioned for the first time. Bert Rumsey's first appearance as the Long Branch barkeep. First of director Ted Post's 55 episodes.

#30: THE PREACHER
(06-16-56)

STORY: John Meston
TELEPLAY: John Dunkel
DIRECTOR: Robert Stevenson
CAST: Chuck Connors, Royal Dano, Paul DuBov, Jim
             Hyland

Bare knuckle fighter Sam Keeler is accustomed to bullying his way through life until he arrives in Dodge City and meets Matt Dillon.

NOTES: Chuck Connors will be forever known as Lucas McCain, *The Rifleman*. Kitty half-jokingly suggests Matt give up being a lawman. He asks her what he would do otherwise, adding, "I'm too lazy to work for a living."

#31: How to Die for Nothing
(06-23-56)

STORY: John Meston
TELEPLAY: Sam Peckinpah
DIRECTOR: Ted Post
CAST: Mort Mills, James Nolan, Maurice Manson, Larry
                Dobkin, Bill White, Jr., Herbert Lytton

When Matt is forced to kill a drunken cowboy, the man's brother vows revenge.

NOTES: Chester claims to be a light sleeper and reveals that he was raised by Ben Cherry, a friend of his father. Matt and Chester are shown eating in Delmonico's for the first time. Maurice Manson plays Mr. Reisling, owner of the Dodge House. No Boot Hill opening.

#32: Dutch George
(06-30-56)

STORY & TELEPLAY: John Dunkel
DIRECTOR: Robert Stevenson
CAST: Robert Middleton, Tom Pittman

Matt is dismayed to discover that Dutch George, whom he once admired, has become a horse thief.

NOTES: Moss Grimmick says Dutch George is "the biggest horse thief west of the Mississippi." First reference to Matt's childhood. No Boot Hill narration.

#33: Prairie Happy
(07-07-56)

STORY: John Meston
TELEPLAY: David Victor & Herbert Little

DIRECTOR: Ted Post
CAST: Robert Ellenstein, Anne Barton, Wilfred Knapp, Tyler McVey, Bruce Holland, Jack Holland, Roy Engel

Matt and Chester have their hands full when a crazy old timer convinces the citizens of Dodge that an Indian attack is imminent.

NOTES: Matt says that the Pawnee are peaceful, and that several have signed up to scout for Custer. Second appearance by Dabbs Greer as storekeeper Wilbur Jonas, who acts as more of a rabble rouser here than in later episodes. No Boot Hill scene.

#34: CHESTER'S MAIL ORDER BRIDE (07-14-56)

WRITERS: David Victor & Herbert Little
DIRECTOR: Robert Stevenson
CAST: Mary Carver, Joel Ashley, Russ Thorson

Chester unintentionally leads a young woman to believe he is interested in matrimony.

NOTES: First of Chester's many ill-fated romances. Chester tells Matt, "Nobody's fault but my own. I never should have learned how to write." When Matt remarks that Kitty is acting as though she at her engagement party rather than Chester's, she replies, "I'm just playing it safe—in case I don't get one of my own." First look at Dodge City's train depot. No Boot Hill opening.

#35: THE GUITAR (07-21-56)

STORY: John Meston
TELEPLAY: Sam Peckinpah
DIRECTOR: Harry Horner

CAST: Aaron Spelling, Jacques Aubuchon, Charles Gray, Duane Thorsen, Bill Hale, Joseph Mell

When two bullies torment a harmless drifter, some of the men in Dodge decide to even the score.

NOTES: Traditional *Gunsmoke* surprise ending. The late Aaron Spelling went on to become one of the most successful television producers in Hollywood history. First of five appearances by Joseph Mell as Long Branch owner Bill Pence.

#36: CARA
(07-28-56)

STORY: John Meston
TELEPLAY: David Victor & Herbert Little
DIRECTOR: Robert Stevenson
CAST: Jorja Curtwright, Charles Webster, Douglas Odney, Wilfrid Knapp, Howard Culver

Matt is unaware that one of his former girlfriends has come to Dodge to scout the town for a band of outlaws she has joined.

NOTES: Cara, the first of several women from Matt's past, knew him in Yuma, Arizona, twelve years before. Kitty is less than thrilled about helping his old flame, telling him he doesn't know much about women. Matt replies, "I'm learning." The bank is shown as Botkin Bank, Sam Botkin, President, although his name is later changed to Harry. Howard Culver is billed as Mr. Uzzel rather than Howie. Curiously, there are two Boot Hill openings, one with Matt wearing a tie, the other in a striped vest.

#37: MR. AND MRS. AMBER
(08-04-56)

STORY: John Meston

TELEPLAY: David Victor & Herbert Little
DIRECTOR: Ted Post
CAST: Gloria McGhee, Ainslie Pryor, Paul Richards, Bing Russell

An impoverished homesteader snaps after being harassed by his father-in-law, a religious fanatic.

NOTES: Second appearance by Paul Richards, who has the distinction of being the first actor to shoot Matt Dillon. The late Bing Russell, father of actor Kurt, portrayed deputy Clem Foster on *Bonanza*.

#38: UNMARKED GRAVE
(08-18-56)

WRITERS: David Victor & Herbert Little
DIRECTOR: Ted Post
CAST: Ron Hagerthy, Helen Kleeb, William Hopper, Than Wyenn, Joe Scudero, Boyd Stockman

Matt arrests a sly outlaw who plays on an elderly woman's sympathy in order to gain his freedom.

NOTES: Matt is shot for the third time. Plot somewhat reminiscent of the classic *3:10 to Yuma*, with Matt trying to get the outlaw on the train while under fire.

#39: ALARM AT PLEASANT VALLEY
(08-25-56)

WRITER: John Dunkel
DIRECTOR: Ted Post
CAST: Lew Brown, Helen Wallace, Dorothy Schuyler, Bill White, Jr., Dan Blocker

Matt, Chester and a farming family are pinned down by a band of Kiowa just as one of the women is about to give birth.

NOTES: Same ranch house as that used in the episode "Smoking Out the Nolans." No Doc, Kitty or Dodge City. Dan Blocker achieved immortality from 1959 to 1972 as Hoss Cartwright on *Bonanza*.

Weaver, Arness, Stone in "Young Man with a Gun," 1956

EPISODE GUIDE

SEASON 2
September 8, 1956–July 6, 1957

#40: COW DOCTOR
(09-08-56)

STORY: John Meston
TELEPLAY: John Dunkel
DIRECTOR: Andrew McLaglen
CAST: Robert H. Harris, Dorothy Adams, Tommy Kirk

Doc is stabbed by a homesteader who has no use for doctors.

NOTES: Chester mentions having been in the army. Same ranch set used as far back as "Obie Tater." First of a record 95 episodes directed by Andrew McLaglen, more than any other director.

#41: BRUSH AT ELKADER
(09-15-56)

STORY: John Meston
TELEPLAY: Les Crutchfield
DIRECTOR: Ted Post
CAST: Gage Clark, Paul Lambert, Alfred Linder, Dennis Cross, Malcom Atterbury

Matt and Chester ride to Elkader to arrest a murderer whom neither of them can identify, and no one in town feels inclined to help.

NOTES: Chester reveals that he makes only eight dollars a month. The Elkader Hotel set is the same one used for the Dodge House. Gage Clark (Hinkle) also portrayed both Dodge City banker Botkin and Dodge House owner Mr. Dobie in later episodes.

#42: CUSTER
(09-22-56)

STORY: John Meston
TELEPLAY: Gil Doud
DIRECTOR: Ted Post
CAST: Brian Hutton, Richard Keith, Herbert Lytton

Matt and an army major disagree on what to do with a deserter who has killed a rancher.

NOTES: Chester says he has never heard of Custer, although Matt mentioned him in the episode "Prairie Happy." Matt once again is "dressed up" in the Boot Hill opening.

#43: THE ROUND UP
(09-29-56)

STORY: John Meston
TELEPLAY: Sam Peckinpah
DIRECTOR: Ted Post
CAST: Barney Phillips, Jacques Aubuchon, John Dierkes, Michael Hinn, Mason Curry, John Patrick, Sam Schwartz

Matt's decision to shut down Front Street upsets both the trail weary cowboys who want to cut loose and the Dodge City business owners.

NOTES: The word marshal is misspelled ("marshall") on the sign Matt nails outside the Long Branch. Chester sprains both ankles.

Kitty is shown behind the bar for the first time. Barney Phillips also played Long Branch owner Bill Pence in later episodes.

No Boot Hill intro.

#44: YOUNG MAN WITH A GUN
(10-20-56)

STORY: John Meston
TELEPLAY: Winston Miller
DIRECTOR: Christian Nyby
CAST: Jack Diamond, Fredd Wayne, Clegg Hoyt, Sid
               Clute, Bert Rumsey

An outlaw's brother bent on revenge learns how to handle a gun in order to kill Matt.

NOTES: This episode reunited director Christian Nyby with Arness, who worked together in the 1951 sci-fi classic *The Thing*. No Boot Hill opening.

#45: INDIAN WHITE
(10-27-56)

STORY: Tom Hanley
TELEPLAY: David Victor & Herbert Little
DIRECTOR: Ted Post
CAST: Peter Votrian, Marian Seldes, Alexander Lockwood,
               Abel Fernandez, Stanley Adams, Clegg Hoyt,
               Kenneth Alton, George Archambeault

A young white boy raised as a Cheyenne has difficulty adjusting to life in Dodge City.

NOTES: Matt is shown at Fort Dodge for the first time. Kitty says, "Hats are the one virtuous weakness I have." Another *Gunsmoke* surprise ending.

#46: HOW TO CURE A FRIEND
(11-10-56)

STORY: John Meston
TELEPLAY: Winston Miller
DIRECTOR: Ted Post
CAST: Andrew Duggan, Simon Oakland, Joseph Mell,
              Jess Kirkpatrick

Matt's friend Nick Search is also a dishonest gambler who insists he has reformed.

NOTES: Chester says the richest man in Dodge is a man named Enoch Mills. First of Jess Patrick's four appearances as Dodge City barber Frank Teeters.

#47: LEGAL REVENGE
(11-17-56)

STORY: John Meston
TELEPLAY: Sam Peckinpah
DIRECTOR: Andrew McLaglen
CAST: Cloris Leachman, Philip Bourneuf, Robert Strong

Doc comes upon an injured man and a mysterious woman who may be on the verge of killing each other.

NOTES: Doc shown riding a horse for the first time, one of his coat sleeves torn.

#48: THE MISTAKE
(11-24-56)

STORY: John Meston
TELEPLAY: Gil Doud
DIRECTOR: Andrew McLaglen

CAST: Touch Connors, Gene O'Donnell, Cyril Delevanti, Robert Hinkle, Bert Rumsey

Matt chases after a murder suspect who claims to have been with Doc at the time the crime was committed.

NOTES: Chester mentions bartender Sam's last name (Noonan) for the first time. Kitty shown wearing a Stetson and riding skirt for the first time. Touch Connors is better known as Mike Connors, whose CBS series *Mannix* was canceled at the same time as *Gunsmoke* in early 1975. Matt again in tie, vest and black hat on Boot Hill.

#49: GREATER LOVE
(12-01-56)

STORY: John Meston
TELEPLAY: Winston Miller
DIRECTOR: Ted Post
CAST: Claude Akins, Ray Bennett, Amzie Strickland, Frank DeKova

An outlaw threatens to kill Doc if he fails to save a wounded man.

NOTES: Doc says he is fed up with Dodge and wants to move to San Francisco. First of three episodes featuring Frank DeKova as Matt's Indian friend Tobeel.

#50: NO INDIANS
(12-08-56)

STORY: John Meston
TELEPLAY: John Dunkel
DIRECTOR: Ted Post
CAST: Dick Rich, Herbert Rudley, Fintan Meyler, Joel Ashley, K.L. Smith, Mickey Simpson

Matt discovers that murders being blamed on Indians are actually the work of white horse thieves.

NOTES: Hard-hitting highlight of the series, with Matt itching for vengeance. "These aren't men," he tells Chester. "They're animals." No Boot Hill opening.

#51: SPRING TERM
(12-15-56)

STORY: John Meston
TELEPLAY: William F. Leicester
DIRECTOR: Ted Post
CAST: H.M. Wynant, Howard Culver, Harry Townes,
              Jack Kruschen, Paul Newlan, Ross Ford, Stanley
              Adams, Clayton Post

Matt learns that he was the real target when a Dodge City citizen is gunned down by an old enemy from Texas.

NOTES: Another episode with Matt driven to the edge. Doc calls Matt "Matthew." Chester calls Dodge House clerk Howie by his formal name, Mr. Uzzel. No Boot Hill opening.

#52: POOR PEARL
(12-22-56)

STORY: John Meston
TELEPLAY: Sam Peckinpah
DIRECTOR: Andrew McLaglen
CAST: Constance Ford, Denver Pyle, Michael Emmett,
              Jess Kirkpatrick, Bert Rumsey, John Hamilton,
              John McGough

Matt has to step in when two men in love with the same saloon girl attempt to shoot each other.

NOTES: First of several guest appearances by Denver Pyle, who was nearly cast as Matt Dillon.

#53: CHOLERA
(12-29-56)

STORY: John Meston
TELEPLAY: Les Crutchfield
DIRECTOR: Andrew McLaglen
CAST: Paul Fix, Bartlett Robinson, Peg Hillias, Stuart
              Whitman, Gordon Gebert, John Smith

Matt tries to avert certain trouble between a wealthy rancher and a stubborn homesteader who both lay claim to the same land.

NOTES: The guest cast includes future television Western stars of *The Rifleman* (Fix), *Cimarron Strip* (Whitman) and both *Cimarron City* and *Laramie* (Smith).

#54: PUCKETT'S NEW YEAR
(01-05-57)

WRITER: John Meston
DIRECTOR: Andrew McLaglen
CAST: Edgar Stehli, Grant Withers, Richard Deacon,
              Rocky Shahan, Bert Rumsey

Matt and Chester rescue an old buffalo hunter whose partner has left him to die on the prairie.

NOTES: Richard Deacon of *The Dick Van Dyke Show* plays banker Mr. Botkin in this episode. Rocky Shahan later portrayed trail drover Joe Scarlet on *Rawhide*.

#55: THE COVER UP
(01-12-57)

STORY: John Meston
TELEPLAY: William Robson
DIRECTOR: William D. Russell
CAST: Roy Engel, Vivi Janiss, Tyler McVey, Ted Marcuse,
             Malcom Atterbury

Matt finds he may have arrested the wrong man when a series of murders continues after the suspect has been locked up.

NOTES: Matt's arm is grazed by a bullet. Kitty, who again wears a riding skirt, says she has been out riding sidesaddle for the first time. She also reveals that she once worked at the Oasis Saloon in Abilene. Roy Engel played Virginia City's doctor in several early episodes of *Bonanza*.

#56: SINS OF THE FATHER
(01-19-57)

STORY: John Meston
TELEPLAY: John Dunkel
DIRECTOR: Andrew McLaglen
CAST: Peter Whitney, Angie Dickinson, Gage Clark, Paul
             Wexler

Dodge House owner Jim Dobie, upset when a buffalo hunter and his Arapahoe wife book a room, starts to spread rumors of impending Indian attacks.

NOTES: Kitty says Chester has owned the same one pair of pants ever since she has known him. First of four appearances by Gage Clark (who also occasionally played banker Botkin) as Mr. Dobie. Len Lesser, best known as Uncle Leo on the sitcom *Seinfeld,* is unbilled. No Boot Hill intro.

#57: KICK ME
(01-26-57)

STORY: John Meston
TELEPLAY: Endre Bohem & Louis Vittes
DIRECTOR: Andrew McLaglen
CAST: Robert H. Harris, Frank DeKova, Julie Van Zandt,
               Paul Lambert

Fred Myers takes Kitty hostage when Matt learns that Myers is really a bank robber.

NOTES: Second appearance as Frank DeKova as Matt's Indian friend Tobeel. Endre Bohem and Louis Vittes later worked extensively as, respectively, producer and writer on *Rawhide*.

#58: EXECUTIONER
(02-02-57)

STORY: John Meston
TELEPLAY: Gil Doud
DIRECTOR: Andrew V. McLaglen
CAST: Robert Keys, Michael Hinn, Liam Sullivan

Matt is unable to arrest a gunslinger who kills a farmer in a fair fight, but the farmer's brother has a plan to get even.

NOTES: Liam Sullivan later portrayed Major Mapoy on *The Monroes* (1966-67). Director McLaglen is billed with his middle initial for this episode.

#59: GONE STRAIGHT
(020-09-57)

STORY: John Meston
TELEPLAY: Les Crutchfield

DIRECTOR: Ted Post
CAST: Carl Betz, Tige Andrews, Joe De Santis, Marianne
              Stewart, Ward Wood, John Dierkes

Matt and Chester have a difficult time identifying and arresting a former outlaw who wants to leave his criminal past behind.

NOTES: John Dierkes portrayed North Fork's blacksmith in early episodes of *The Rifleman*. Tige Andrews and Joe De Santis would appear in the episode "The Jackals" during Season 13.

#60: BLOODY HANDS
(02-16-57)

WRITER: John Meston
DIRECTOR: Andrew McLaglen
CAST: Lawrence Dobkin, Russell Johnson, Gloria
              Marshall, Harvey Grant, David Saber

Matt, tired of having to kill in the line of duty, decides to resign as Dodge City marshal after being forced to shoot three men in the same gun battle.

NOTES: Not the first time Matt turns in his badge, declaring, "I've hated this job ever since I took it." He sends his resignation letter to the War Department in Washington, D.C. Matt and Kitty finally get some time alone. The cabin hideout is the same one used in "Greater Love." Particularly creative cinematography.

#61: SKID ROW
(02-23-57)

STORY: John Meston
TELEPLAY: Gil Doud
DIRECTOR: Ted Post
CAST: Susan Morrow, Joseph Sargent, Guinn Williams

A homesteader who has fallen on hard times refuses to meet with the woman who has come west to marry him.

NOTES: First mention of Ma Smalley and her boarding house. Joseph Sargent later turned to directing. Guinn Williams is better known as Big Boy Guinn to Western fans.

#62: SWEET AND SOUR
(03-02-57)

WRITER: John Meston
DIRECTOR: Andrew McLaglen
CAST: Karen Sharpe, John Alderson, Walter Reed, Ken Mayer

Matt gets a flirtatious young woman a job at the Long Branch, where she proceeds to deliberately provoke men into fighting over her.

NOTES: Kitty mentions being half-owner of the Long Branch for the first time. Karen Sharpe appeared on numerous television Westerns, including a regular role on the *Johnny Ringo* series.

#63: CAIN
(03-09-57)

WRITER: John Meston
DIRECTOR: Ted Post
CAST: Harry Bartell, Mark Roberts, Paul DuBov

A rancher who was once known as a fast draw is confronted by a drifter intent on goading him into one last gunfight.

NOTES: Chester says his mother was "a fine woman." Doc mentions knowing Mark Twain in St. Louis before the Civil War, referring to him by his given name, Sam Clemens. As in "The Executioner," an outmatched man finds a way to defeat an opponent even in death. No Boot Hill scene.

#64: BUREAUCRAT
(03-16-57)

STORY: John Meston
TELEPLAY: William F. Leicester
DIRECTOR: Ted Post
CAST: John Hoyt, Ned Glass, Ken Lynch

A government official arrives in Dodge determined to reform what he considers Matt's ineffective method of maintaining law and order.

NOTES: Chester's time in the army is mentioned again. Matt tells Procter (John Hoyt) that there was a deadline in Dodge when he became marshal, but that he did away with it.

#65: LAST FLING
(03-23-57)

WRITER: John Meston
DIRECTOR: Andrew McLaglen
CAST: Florenz Ames, Anne O'Neal, Frank DeKova, Susan Morrow

A pair of old farmers hit Dodge intent on raising a ruckus, leaving one of them shot and Kitty being shot at.

NOTES: A good indictment of domestic violence, as well as an example of Matt's more compassionate side. No Boot Hill opening.

#66: Chester's Murder
(03-30-57)

Story: John Meston
Director: Ted Post
Cast: Murray Hamilton, Peggie Castle, Tom Greenway,
               Gage Clark, Charles Conrad, Tim Graham

Matt reluctantly jails Chester when it seems as though his sidekick has killed a cowhand.

Notes: Matt is feeling a little under the weather. A predictable story made interesting by Chester's dilemma and how others react to it. Tim Graham rather than Dabbs Greer portrays Wilbur Jonas. Peggie Castle later co-starred on the *Lawman* series as a sort of Miss Kitty of Laramie, Wyoming. No Boot Hill opening.

#67: The Photographer
(04-06-57)

Writer: John Dunkel
Director: William D. Russell
Cast: Sebastian Cabot, Norman Fredric, Ned Glass,
               Charles Horvath, Howard Culver, Dorothy
               Schuyler

A photographer comes to Dodge and, after amusing the populace, rides out and stirs up trouble with the Indians.

Notes: Matt commands Jacoby (Cabot), "Get out! Get out of Dodge!" Howard Culver is billed as "Citizen" in the credits rather than Howie.

#68: WRONG MAN
(04-13-57)

WRITER: John Meston
DIRECTOR: Andrew V. McLaglen
CAST: Don Keefer, Catherine McLeod, Robert Griffin

Sam Rickers kills Jake Hanley, mistaking him for a wanted man, and is then targeted for death by Hanley's partner.

NOTES: Matt mentions a Judge Brookings. This episode title was reused during the color era.

#69: BIG GIRL LOST
(04-20-57)

STORY: John Meston
DIRECTOR: Ted Post
CAST: Gloria McGhee, Michael Pate, Judson Pratt, Gerald Milton

A judgmental Eastern dude comes to Dodge in search of his ex-fiancee, who now works at the Long Branch saloon.

NOTES: Kitty mentions once having worked on riverboats. Second mention of Ma Smalley. Different actor (Judson Pratt) as Bill Pence. Change of pace role for the late Michael Pate, usually cast as Indians or outlaws. No Boot Hill opening.

#70: WHAT THE WHISKEY DRUMMER HEARD
(04-27-57)

STORY: John Meston
TELEPLAY: Gil Doud
DIRECTOR: Andrew McLaglen
CAST: Vic Perrin, Robert Karnes, Robert Burton

Matt fakes his death to force a mysterious assailant into the open.

NOTES: Viewers learn that Chester was once an army cook. No Boot Hill opening.

#71: CHEAP LABOR
(05-04-57)

WRITER: John Meston
DIRECTOR: Andrew McLaglen
CAST: Andrew Duggan, Robert F. Simon, Peggy Webber, Alan Emerson, Tom Gleason, Susan Morrow, James Nusser

Homesteader Ben Stancil objects to his sister's relationship with reformed gunman Fos Capper.

NOTES: Susan Morrow's second appearance as Melanie, a girl Chester is sweet on. James Nusser is billed simply as Bum, the sort of role he would later develop to perfection as Dodge City's resident barfly Louie Pheeters.

#72: MOON
(05-11-57)

WRITER: John Meston
DIRECTOR: William D. Russell
CAST: Rebecca Welles, Phil Pine, Stafford Repp, Thomas Palmer, Jane Ray

It looks as though a cardsharp and a Long Branch saloon girl are going to literally get away with murder until a friend of the victim shows up.

NOTES: Matt to Vint (Pine): "There's a stage leaving at three o'clock. Be on it." Unusual episode in that no regular character shows up until it is nearly half over.

#73: WHO LIVES BY THE SWORD
(05-18-57)

WRITER: John Meston
DIRECTOR: Andrew McLaglen
CAST: Harold J. Stone, Steve Terrell, Robert C. Ross, Harry Wood

When Matt fails to stop a cunning gunman by using the law, he decides to use his fists.

NOTES: Matt to Delk (Stone): "You're leaving Dodge. I'll give you two hours to get out." No Boot Hill intro.

#74: UNCLE OLIVER
(05-25-57)

WRITER: John Meston
DIRECTOR: Andrew McLaglen
CAST: Earle Hodgins, Paul Wexler

After Chester is wounded by a unseen gunman, Matt has no choice but to use Chester and Doc as targets to lure the sniper out of hiding.

NOTES: Chester shot for the first time, the bullet creasing his head. Doc mentions having once lived in Memphis.

#75: DADDY-O
(06-01-57)

WRITER: John Meston
DIRECTOR: Andrew McLaglen
CAST: John Dehner, Judson Pratt

Kitty's father, once a gambler who deserted her when she was still a child, comes to Dodge and asks her to return with him to New Orleans—with all of her money.

NOTES: It is officially announced that Kitty is now half-owner of the Long Branch with Bill Pence although she already mentioned this in episode #62 ("Sweet and Sour").

#76: THE MAN WHO WOULD BE MARSHAL
(06-15-57)

STORY: John Meston
DIRECTOR: William D. Russell
CAST: Herbert Rudley, Alex Sharp, Rusty Westcoat,
               Clancy Cooper

A former army officer bored with civilian life believes he is just the man Matt needs to help maintain law and order in Dodge City.

NOTES: Matt says it has been a long time since he was in California. The late country singer June Carter Cash appears unbilled as saloon girl Clarice.

#77: LIAR FROM BLACKHAWK
(06-22-57)

STORY: John Meston
TELEPLAY: David Victor & Herbert Little
DIRECTOR: Andrew McLaglen
CAST: Denver Pyle, Strother Martin, John Doucette

The townsfolk of Dodge are unnerved by the presence of gunslinger Hank Shinn, unaware that Shinn is all bark and no bite.

NOTES: Al Janes (Doucette) knew Matt in New Mexico years before. By now it is evident that Chester has an eye for the ladies, considers himself an expert coffeemaker, likes to gamble but is always broke, and is no coward despite his peaceful demeanor. No Boot Hill opening.

#78: JEALOUSY
(06-29-57)

STORY: John Meston
TELEPLAY: Sam Peckinpah
DIRECTOR: Andrew McLaglen
CAST: Jack Kelly, Joan Tetzel, Than Wyenn, Jack Mann, Ken Drake, Barbara Dodd

An old friend of Matt's comes to Dodge to deal cards, later becoming convinced that Matt has eyes for his new bride.

NOTES: Matt says, "I've lived around quite a few places." Matt has two occasions to order men out of town: "Get out of here—all the way out." "When you're through at Doc's, why don't you just keep on goin'." Kitty rides sidesaddle. Jack Kelly portrayed Bart Maverick for the entire run of the *Maverick* series. As co-star James Garner once said, "Jack Kelly *was* Maverick."

EPISODE GUIDE
SEASON 3
September 14, 1957–July 7, 1958

#79: CRACK-UP
(09-14-57)

WRITER: John Meston
DIRECTOR: Ted Post
CAST: John Dehner, Jess Kirkpatrick, Jean Vaughn

When a known gun-for-hire arrives in Dodge, Matt tries to find out who has sent for him and why.

NOTES: Matt to Springer (Dehner): "You're leaving Dodge." Howard Culver appears unbilled as Dodge House clerk Howie. Different bartender than Sam. No Boot Hill opening.

#80: GUN FOR CHESTER
(09-14-57)

WRITER: John Meston
DIRECTOR: Louis King
CAST: Thomas Coley, George Selk, Howard Culver,
            Clayton Post

Although he will not explain why, Chester insists a new man in town intends to kill him.

NOTES: It is disclosed that Chester is from Stone County, Missouri. New Boot Hill opening with Matt wearing his traditional marshal's outfit.

Stone, Weaver, Blake, Arness in "Mavis McCloud," 1957

#81: BLOOD MONEY
(09-28-57)

WRITER: John Meston
DIRECTOR: Louis King
CAST: Vinton Hayworth, James Dobson, Lawrence Green

A man stranded on the prairie learns that his rescuer is wanted and kills him for the reward.

NOTES: This episode concerns poetic justice, one of the show's favorite themes. Long Branch barkeep is called Red. Speener

(Hayworth) is listed as "Spencer" in the credits. Episode title used again during the color seasons.

#82: KITTY'S OUTLAW
(10-05-57)

STORY: John Meston
TELEPLAY: Kathleen Hite
DIRECTOR: Andrew McLaglen
CAST: Ainslie Pryor, Dabbs Greer, Chris Alcaide, Howard Culver, Jack Mann

An old flame of Kitty's arrives in Dodge shortly before he and his partners rob the Dodge City bank.

NOTES: Kitty's first romantic episode. Chester sampling hair tonic in the general store is one of the funniest scenes in the show's history. Matt tells Kitty he grew up on Mexican food. First script by Kathleen Hite, who contributed several memorable stories when the series expanded to an hour.

#83: POTATO ROAD
(10-12-57)

WRITER: John Meston
DIRECTOR: Ted Post
CAST: Robert F. Simon, Jeanette Nolan, Tom Pittman

Matt and Chester are trapped in the potato cellar of a man who plans to rob the bank.

NOTES: The Grilk family is not the last bunch of deranged prairie rats Matt will encounter. Jeanette Nolan later starred in the short-lived *Dirty Sally*, a spinoff from *Gunsmoke*. In the first of his eventual 18 episodes, Morgan Woodward appears briefly and unbilled as Calhoun.

#84: JESSE
(10-19-57)

WRITER: John Meston
DIRECTOR: Andrew McLaglen
CAST: George Brenlin, Edward Binns, James Maloney

Matt befriends a young man who does not know the marshal killed his father.

NOTES: Matt mentions Doc having been in St. Louis the previous winter. Matt to Stapp (Binns): "There's a stage leavin' at eight o'clock in the morning—be on it." Rocky Shahan appears unbilled as stage driver Hank. The Long Branch bartender is again Red.

#85: MAVIS McCLOUD
(10-26-57)

WRITER: John Meston
DIRECTOR: Buzz Kulik
CAST: Fay Spain, Casey Adams, Robert Cornthwaite

Mavis McCloud comes west from St. Louis to land a husband, unaware that an angry former suitor is following her to Dodge.

NOTES: James Arness and Robert Cornthwaite co-starred in 1951's *The Thing*.

#86: BORN TO HANG
(11-02-57)

STORY: John Meston
DIRECTOR: Buzz Kulik
CAST: Wright King, Anthony Caruso, Mort Mills, Ken Lynch, Dorothy Adams

After Matt saves an alleged horse thief from men intending to lynch him, the young man has nothing on his mind but revenge.

NOTES: Chester is shot in the arm. Glick (Lynch) says bullets are seven cents apiece. No Boot Hill intro.

#87: ROMEO
(11-09-57)

STORY: John Meston
DIRECTOR: Ted Post
CAST: Barry Kelley, Robert Vaughn, Barbara Eden,
              Tyler McVey, Robert McQueeney, Bill McGraw,
              William Erwin

A range war seems to be inevitable when two young lovers from feuding ranchers defy their fathers' orders to stay away from each other.

NOTES: Matt refers to rancher Emmett Bowers (played this time by Tyler McVey) as Hank.

#88: NEVER PESTER CHESTER
(11-16-57)

WRITER: John Meston
DIRECTOR: Richard Whorf
CAST: Buddy Baer, Tom Greenway, Woodrow Chambliss,
              Paul Birch, Gary Vinson

Matt sees red after two cowboys drag Chester down Front Street, nearly killing him.

NOTES: Matt's rage gets the best of him, telling Stobo (Baer) that if he ever sees him in Dodge again, he will kill him. Matt's biggest fistfight to date. When Chester says that maybe he ought to quit,

Matt says he needs him, that Chester is the only person in Dodge besides Doc he can trust. No Boot Hill opening.

#89: FINGERED
(11-23-57)

WRITER: John Meston
DIRECTOR: James Sheldon
CAST: John Larch, Karl Swenson, Virginia Christine

Matt investigates charges that a homesteader is a wife killer after the man's second bride disappears.

NOTES: This episode features the first flashback sequence of the series.

#90: HOW TO KILL A WOMAN
(11-30-57)

WRITER: John Meston
DIRECTOR: John Rich
CAST: Robert Brubaker, Barry Atwater, Pernell Roberts

Matt and Chester stake out a remote stage depot in order to catch the bandit who has also been killing passengers.

NOTES: First of fourteen appearances by Robert Brubaker as stage driver Jim Buck. No scenes in Dodge City. Pernell Roberts rose to fame as Adam Cartwright on *Bonanza* for its first six seasons. This episode won an Emmy award for editing.

#91: COWS AND CRIBS
(12-07-57)

STORY: John Meston
TELEPLAY: Kathleen Hite

DIRECTOR: Richard Whorf
CAST: Judson Taylor, Val Avery, Kathie Browne

Matt suspects that a farmer with a bad drinking problem is responsible for cattle rustling and murder.

NOTES: Rancher Emmett Bowers is this time played by Bartlett Robinson. Ma Smalley portrayed by Mabel Albertson. Matt is shot in his left arm. Kathie Browne was later cast as Pernell Roberts' love interest on several episodes of *Bonanza* and later co-starred on the short-lived *Hondo* series.

#92: DOC'S REWARD
(12-14-57)

WRITER: John Meston
DIRECTOR: Richard Whorf
CAST: Jack Lord, Bruce Wendell, Netta Packer, Jean
              Fenwick, Brick Sullivan

Matt's decision to not throw Doc in jail for killing a man who tries to steal the physician's horse does not go over well with some of the Dodge citizens, nor the dead man's twin brother.

NOTES: Matt tells Doc, "The day I arrest you is the day I quit." Bartender Red is played by Brick Sullivan. Jack Lord later starred on the popular *Hawaii Five-0* series.

#93: KITTY LOST
(12-21-57)

WRITER: John Meston
DIRECTOR: Ted Post
CAST: Warren Stevens, Gage Clark, Brett King, Steve
              Ellsworth, George Selk

Matt and Chester search for Kitty, who has gone missing after accepting a gentleman's offer of a buggy ride in the country.

NOTES: Long Branch owner Bill Pence played by Steve Ellsworth this time. Veteran character actor Warren Stevens in nearly two dozen television Westerns.

#94: TWELFTH NIGHT
(12-28-57)

WRITER: John Meston
DIRECTOR: John Rich
CAST: William Schallert, Rose Marie, James Griffith,
            Dick Rich

Trouble comes to Dodge in the form of two mountain clans who have been feuding for four decades.

NOTES: Matt and Chester are shown wearing overcoats. Rose Marie co-starred as Sally Rogers on *The Dick Van Dyke Show.* Busy character actor William Schallert appeared on several different types of shows, including more than 30 television Westerns.

#95: JOE PHY
(01-04-58)

WRITER: John Meston
DIRECTOR: Ted Post
CAST: Morey Amsterdam, Paul Richards, William Kendis,
            Jack Reitzen, Ken Becker

Matt and Chester pursue a man who wounded Matt to Elkader, where they discover the town cowering under a lawman claiming to be the territorial marshal—Matt's job.

NOTES: The town of Elkader is the same set seen in numerous

episodes of *Have Gun-Will Travel, Wanted: Dead or Alive* and others. Comedian Morey Amsterdam is most familiar from his role on *The Dick Van Dyke Show*. No Boot Hill opening.

#96: BUFFALO MAN
(01-11-58)

STORY: John Meston
TELEPLAY: Les Crutchfield
DIRECTOR: Ted Post
CAST: Patricia Smith, John Anderson, Jack Klugman, Abel Fernandez

Matt and Chester are captured by a pair of uncivilized buffalo hunters who have been abusing a young woman.

NOTES: Chester says that when he was a kid he dreamed of running off and joining the circus. Jack Klugman starred in the television series *The Odd Couple* and *Quincy, M.E.* The fight scene between Arness and Anderson has been used in film schools as an example of good editing.

#97: KITTY CAUGHT
(01-18-58)

WRITER: John Meston
DIRECTOR: Richard Whorf
CAST: Bruce Gordon, Pat Conway, John Compton, William Keene, Charles Tannen

After two bank robbers take Kitty hostage, Matt and Chester trail them to their secluded hideout.

NOTES: Chester returns from Wichita wearing a coat and tie. Kitty shown riding side saddle. Banker Botkin portrayed this time by William Keene. No Boot Hill opening.

#98: CLAUSTROPHOBIA
(01-25-58)

WRITER: John Meston
DIRECTOR: Ted Post
CAST: Joe Maross, Vaughn Taylor, Willard Sage, James
            Winslow, Lynn Shubert, Jason Johnson

Matt has to jail a pig farmer whose mule and pigs have been killed by a pair of cattlemen so that the farmer will not take the law into his own hands.

NOTES: Filmed at the famed Iverson Ranch, mountainous and hardly flat Kansas prairie. No Boot Hill opening.

#99: MA TENNIS
(02-01-58)

WRITER: John Meston
DIRECTOR: Buzz Kulik
CAST: Nina Varela, Ron Hagerthy, Corey Allen

Matt attempts to arrest a young man for killing a gambler, but the murderer's hard edged mother is standing in the way.

NOTES: Ron Hagerthy appeared in numerous television Westerns and was a regular on the *Sky King* series.

#100: SUNDAY SUPPLEMENT
(02-08-58)

WRITER: John Meston
DIRECTOR: Richard Whorf
CAST: Werner Klemperer, Jack Weston, David Whorf,
            George Selk, Eddie Little Sky

A pair of newspapermen from New York cause trouble when they steal from the Pawnee in order to create a story.

NOTES: Doc mentions Kitty being half-owner of the Long Branch. Kitty thinks the New York newsmen can put Dodge on the map, but Matt says Texas cattle already have. Indian actor Eddie Little Sky is billed as Eddie Little. No Boot Hill opening.

#101: WILD WEST
(02-15-58)

WRITER: John Meston
DIRECTOR: Richard Whorf
CAST: Philip Bourneuf, Phyllis Coates, Paul Engle,
             Murray Hamilton, Robert Gist

A young man tells Matt that his father has been kidnapped, and that his stepmother is responsible.

NOTES: This episode takes place entirely out of Dodge. Phyllis Coates was one of two actresses to portray newspaperwoman Lois Lane on the *Superman* series.

#102: THE CABIN
(02-22-58)

WRITER: John Meston
DIRECTOR: John Rich
CAST: Patricia Barry, Claude Akins, Dean Stanton

Two homicidal outlaws hold Matt and a young woman hostage in a snowbound cabin.

NOTES: Matt, who is wearing chaps when he arrives at the cabin, tells Belle (Barry) he would not make a very good husband, that his job is a little too chancy. Dean Stanton later changed his name to

Harry Dean Stanton. No Boot Hill intro.

#103: Dirt
(03-01-58)

STORY: John Meston
TELEPLAY: Sam Peckinpah
CAST: June Lockhart, Wayne Morris, Ian MacDonald,
             Gail Kobe, Barry McGuire, Tyler McVey

When a newlywed rancher is shot, the suspects include the man's brother and former girlfriend.

NOTES: Matt and Chester attend the wedding in ties, where Chester catches the bouquet. Matt tells Beulah (Lockhart) she will have to go to prison for attempted murder even though he has let others off the hook for the same crime. Mainly a showcase for June Lockhart's sensitive performance. No Boot Hill opening.

#104: Dooley Surrenders
(03-08-58)

WRITER: John Meston
DIRECTOR: John Rich
CAST: Strother Martin, Ken Lynch, James Maloney, Ben
             Wright, George Selk, James Nusser

Matt determines that a simple-minded buffalo skinner has been framed for murder and sets the poor soul free in an attempt to attract the real killer.

NOTES: It is revealed that Doc has a storage shed. Ben Wright plays storekeeper Mr. Ross this time. James Nusser is listed in the credits but does not appear in the episode.

#105: JOKE'S ON US
(03-15-58)

WRITER: John Meston
DIRECTOR: Ted Post
CAST: Virginia Gregg, Bartlett Robinson, Michael Hinn,
               James Kevin, Kevin Hagen, Herbert C. Lytton,
               Craig Duncan

The wife and son of a man falsely hanged for horse theft vow to get even with the men responsible.

NOTES: Stories are beginning to concentrate more on guest stars and their problems than the regular cast. Kevin Hagen later played Doc Baker on *Little House on the Prairie.*

#106: BOTTLEMAN
(03-22-58)

WRITER: John Meston
DIRECTOR: John Rich
CAST: John Dehner, Ross Martin, Peggy McKay

The town drunk, usually easy going, suddenly turns violent and goes after a stranger who has come to Dodge.

NOTES: Dennis Weaver plays guitar and sings "Run, Rabbit, Run." No Matt for nearly the first half of the episode. First of Barney Phillips' four appearances as Bill Pence. Ross Martin later co-starred on *The Wild, Wild West.*

#107: LAUGHING GAS
(03-29-58)

WRITER: James Fonda
DIRECTOR: Ted Post

CAST: June Dayton, Dean Harens, Val Benedict, Cyril Delevanti, Jess Kirkpatrick

A former gunslinger running a medicine show featuring laughing gas, and who has promised his wife he will steer clear of violence, is badly beaten by two men.

NOTES: Matt takes credit for a shooting actually done by Stafford (Harens). James Nusser appears unbilled as a drunk named Ransom. No Boot Hill opening.

#108: TEXAS COWBOYS
(04-05-58)

WRITER: John Meston
DIRECTOR: John Rich
CAST: Allan Lane, Clark Gordon, Ned Glass, Stafford Repp, John Mitchum

Matt once again antagonizes trail drovers and Dodge's business community when he shuts Front Street down to flush out a murderer.

NOTES: Kitty to Matt: "I've worked in a lot of places, but Dodge is the worst." John Mitchum is the brother of actor Robert Mitchum.

#109: AMY'S GOOD DEED
(04-12-58)

STORY: John Meston
TELEPLAY: Kathleen Hite
DIRECTOR: John Rich
CAST: Jeanette Nolan, Lou Krugman

A woman comes to Dodge determined to murder Matt for killing her brother.

NOTES: Matt says he was once a lawman in Dakota Territory. A picture Chester hangs in the beginning of the episode is gone at the end. Another twist ending.

#110: HANGING MAN
(04-19-58)

WRITER: John Meston
DIRECTOR: John Rich
CAST: Luis Van Rooten, Robert Osterloh, Zina Provendie, Helen Kleeb, Dick Rich, K.L. Smith

Matt realizes he may have arrested the wrong man for the hanging of a Dodge City cattlebuyer.

NOTES: More crime and mystery in Dodge, illustrating that Matt is just as much a detective as he is a marshal. No Boot Hill intro.

#111: INNOCENT BROAD
(04-26-58)

STORY: John Meston
TELEPLAY: Kathleen Hite
DIRECTOR: John Rich
CAST: Ed Kemmer, Myrna Fahey, Aaron Saxon

Matt encounters an odd triangle when he takes an interest in a pretty young newcomer to Dodge City.

NOTES: Second appearance by Robert Brubaker as stage driver Jim Buck. No Boot Hill opening.

#112: THE BIG CON
(05-03-58)

WRITER: John Meston
DIRECTOR: John Rich
CAST: Joe Kearns, Alan Dexter, Gordon Mills, Raymond Bailey

Doc is taken hostage by a trio of crooked gamblers who swindle the bank out of $20,000 and ride out of town.

NOTES: Doc mentions once being a doctor on a riverboat called the Tennessee Belle. A clever story beginning to end. Joe Kearns played Mr. Wilson on the *Dennis the Menace* series. Raymond Bailey is better known as Mr. Drysdale on *The Beverly Hillbillies*.

#113: WIDOW'S MITE
(05-10-58)

WRITER: John Meston
DIRECTOR: Ted Post
CAST: Katharine Bard, Marshall Thompson, Ken Mayer

Gambler Leach Fields kills Zack Morton, a bank robber, then proceeds to make life difficult for Morton's poor widow.

NOTES: Marshall Thompson later starred on the *Daktari* series. Ken Mayer guest starred on more than 40 different television Westerns.

#114: CHESTER'S HANGING
(05-17-58)

WRITER: John Meston
DIRECTOR: Ted Post
CAST: Charles Cooper, Sam Edwards, Walter Barnes

Friends of a killer Matt has jailed threaten to hang Chester if their partner is not released.

NOTES: Matt deputizes two citizens of Dodge for the first time.

#115: CARMEN
(05-24-58)

WRITER: John Meston
DIRECTOR: Ted Post
CAST: Ruta Lee, Robert Patten, Tommy Farrell, Ray Teal, Alan Gifford

Unless Matt can find out who murdered three soldiers and stole the Fort Dodge payroll, the army will place Dodge City under martial law.

NOTES: Doc mentions being mustered out of the army in 1865. Matt is shown at Fort Dodge for the second time. Barney Phillips once again portrays Bill Pence. Ruta Lee was one of the busiest actresses on the Hollywood range, guest starring on nearly two dozen television Westerns. Ray Teal was Virginia City sheriff Roy Coffee on all but the first and last seasons of *Bonanza*. Len Lesser and Roy Engel appear unbilled.

#116: OVERLAND EXPRESS
(05-31-58)

WRITER: John Meston
DIRECTOR: Seymour Berns
CAST: Simon Oakland, Peter Mamakos, Clem Bevans, James Gavin, Forrest Stanley, Jan Arvan, Jimmy Cross, Alfred Hopson

Matt and Chester's horses are killed while apprehending a murder suspect, and the stagecoach they hitch a ride on is held up.

NOTES: This episode takes place entirely outdoors. The late Simon Oakland appeared on more than twenty television Westerns. Veteran character actor Clem Bevans is always a hoot to watch.

#117: THE GENTLEMAN
(06-07-58)

WRITER: John Meston
DIRECTOR: Ted Post
CAST: Jack Cassidy, Virginia Baker, Timothy Carey,
             Henry Corden

Matt steps in when a gambler with a secret falls for a woman whom another man claims is his.

NOTES: Second appearance of banker Botkin's daughter Tildy Mae. Another surprise ending. No Boot Hill opening.

EPISODE GUIDE
SEASON 4
September 13, 1958–June 13, 1959

#118: MATT FOR MURDER
(09-13-58)

WRITER: John Meston
DIRECTOR: Richard Whorf
CAST: Robert Wilke, Bruce Gordon, Elisha Cook

When Matt is framed for murder, none other than his old friend Wild Bill Hickok is sent from Abilene to arrest him.

NOTES: The opening *Gunsmoke* theme is now more ominous than sweeping. The famous "Pharaoh's Horses" painting, seen in several Western series, hangs in Doc's office. Sam back in the Long Branch instead of Red. In a foreshadowing of his eventual fate, Hickok (Wilke) says no one has tried to shoot him in the back—yet. Dennis Weaver sounds as if he has a cold. No Boot Hill opening.

#119: THE PATSY
(09-20-58)

STORY: John Meston
TELEPLAY: Les Crutchfield
DIRECTOR: Richard Whorf
CAST: Jan Harrison, Peter Breck, Martin Landau, John
            Alderman, Ken Lynch

Weaver & Arness in "The Patsy," 1958

Matt once again faces a lynch mob when a Long Branch saloon girl and the brother of a murdered man stir up trouble.

NOTES: Matt shown wearing a black vest. First look at the inside of Ma Smalley's boarding house. Arness sounds as if he has caught Weaver's cold from the previous week. (Both episodes were shot back-to-back.) Peter Breck later starred on the series *Black Saddle* and *The Big Valley*. No Boot Hill opening.

#120: GUNSMUGGLER
(09-27-58)

STORY: John Meston
TELEPLAY: Les Crutchfield
DIRECTOR: Richard Whorf
CAST: Frank DeKova, Paul Langton

Matt and an army officer disagree on who should pursue the men responsible for selling rifles to renegade Indians.

NOTES: Matt and Chester wear chaps. Chester says army coffee is good enough to make him consider re-enlisting. Third and final appearance of Frank DeKova as Tobeel.

#121: MONOPOLY
(10-04-58)

STORY: John Meston
TELEPLAY: Les Crutchfield
DIRECTOR: Seymour Berns
CAST: J. Pat O'Malley, Harry Townes, Robert Gist

An unethical St. Louis businessman attempts to take over all the freight lines in Dodge and hires a gunslinger to back him up. No Boot Hill opening.

NOTES: Matt reveals that he was a lawman in Wichita five years before. Doc says the only time Dodge looks good is after dark.

#122: LETTER OF THE LAW
(10-11-58)

STORY: John Meston
TELEPLAY: Les Crutchfield
DIRECTOR: Richard Whorf

CAST: Mary Carver, Harold J. Stone, Clifton James,
             Bartlett Robinson

Matt travels to Wichita to see a judge when homesteaders refuse to comply with an order to vacate their land.

NOTES: Matt wears a coat and tie on his visit to Wichita. Another infrequent look at Kitty on horseback. An airplane can be heard in the distance toward the end of the scene at the Teek ranch. No Boot Hill opening.

#123: THOROUGHBREDS
(10-18-58)

WRITER: John Meston
DIRECTOR: Richard Whorf
CAST: Ron Randell, Walter Barnes, Dan Blocker

The citizens of Dodge embrace a friendly stranger who likes to throw his money around, but Matt is certain the man is a horse thief.

NOTES: Kitty again mentions being half-owner of the Long Branch. Another surprise ending, leaving the resolution to the viewer's imagination. Second guest appearance by Dan Blocker, who by this time was co-starring on the series *Cimarron City*.

#124: STAGE HOLD-UP
(10-25-58)

STORY: John Meston
TELEPLAY: Les Crutchfield
DIRECTOR: Ted Post
CAST: John Anderson, Charles Aidman, Sandy Kenyon,
               Robert Brubaker, Bob Morgan

Three outlaws kill a passenger and rob the stagecoach carrying Matt and Chester to Dodge City.

NOTES: Chester mentions the cold winter Dodge experienced in 1868. The Boot Hill opening shows Matt dismounting from his horse.

#125: LOST RIFLE
(11-01-58)

WRITER:	John Meston
DIRECTOR:	Richard Whorf
CAST:	Charles Bronson, Paul Engle, Lew Gallow, Tom Greenway

Ben Tiple insists he did not kill a man with whom he had been seen arguing, and the sole witness is a young boy who says he only heard the shot.

NOTES: Second guest appearance by Charles Bronson, still a few years away from becoming an internationally famous film star.

#126: LAND DEAL
(11-08-58)

WRITER:	John Meston
TELEPLAY:	Les Crutchfield
DIRECTOR:	Ted Post
CAST:	Nita Talbot, Murray Hamilton, Ross Martin, Dennis Patrick

Matt believes a man trying to sell immigrants valuable railroad land at a discount is making an offer too good to be true.

NOTES: Second episode by the versatile Ross Martin. Dabbs Greer appears as storekeeper Wilbur Jonas. No Boot Hill opening.

#127: LYNCHING MAN
(11-15-58)

WRITER: John Meston
DIRECTOR: Richard Whorf
CAST: George Mcready, Bing Russell, Charles Gray,
             O.Z. Whitehead, Chuck Hayward

A man whose father was lynched years before goes on a crusade to rid the west of anyone who commits the crime.

NOTES: Actors Charles Gray and Bing Russell were also teamed in the first season episode "The Queue." *Gunsmoke* theme now begins with a tympani roll. No Boot Hill opening.

#128: HOW TO KILL A FRIEND
(11-22-58)

WRITER: John Meston
DIRECTOR: Richard Whorf
CAST: Philip Abbott, Pat Conway, James Westerfield

When Matt throws a pair of dishonest gamblers out of town, they return with a gunman who used to be a friend of Matt's.

NOTES: Matt and his friend Toque (Conway) were once suspected of being horse thieves and beaten by a mob in Silver City. Last line in this episode is Matt's famous "Get out of Dodge!" Veteran character actor Gregg Palmer appears unbilled. No Boot Hill opening.

#129: GRASS
(11-29-58)

WRITER: John Meston
DIRECTOR: Richard Whorf

CAST: Phil Coolidge, Chris Alcaide, Charles Fredericks

Matt is not only skeptical of homesteader Harry Pope's claim that he is being bothered by Indians, he also doubts another man's story about Pope killing an innocent cowhand.

NOTE: Chris Alcaide guest starred on more than 40 television Westerns. No Boot Hill opening.

#130: THE CAST
(12-06-58)

WRITER: John Meston
DIRECTOR: Jesse Hibbs
CAST: Robert F. Simon, Ben Carruthers

Doc again tangles with a farmer who hates doctors when the man's wife accidentally swallows a nail.

NOTES: Matt says, "There isn't a man on the frontier who doesn't respect Doc Adams. He's one of the most valuable men out here." Kitty continues to kid Matt about his not knowing much about women. He still insists that he is learning. No Boot Hill opening.

#131: ROBBER BRIDEGROOM
(12-13-58)

WRITER: John Meston
DIRECTOR: Richard Whorf
CAST: Burt Douglas, Jan Harrison, Donald Randolph,
            Frank Maxwell, Dan Sheridan, Clem Fuller, Tex
            Terry

A young woman says she is in love with the man who kidnapped her, provoking her fiancée into forming a mob to lynch her abductor.

NOTES: Jan Harrison also appeared in this season's "The Patsy." Richard Whorf directed 18 episodes in all. No Boot Hill opening.

#132: SNAKEBITE
(12-20-58)

WRITER: John Meston
DIRECTOR: Ted Post
CAST: Andy Clyde, Warren Oates, Charles Maxwell

Matt pursues an old Poney Thompson, suspected of killing the man who shot his dog, only to find Thompson dead before he can ask him any questions.

NOTES: The second dog to be shot down in the streets of Dodge, as well as the second prisoner who says he cannot stand to be cooped up in jail. No Boot Hill opening.

#133: GYPSUM HILLS FEUD
(12-27-58)

STORY: John Meston
TELEPLAY: Les Crutchfield
DIRECTOR: Richard Whorf
CAST: Anne Barton, William Schallert, Albert Linville,
             Hope Summers, Sam Edwards

Matt and Chester go to the high country to hunt antelope and find themselves caught between two feuding families.

NOTES: Hope Summers was a semi-regular character on both *The Rifleman* and *The Andy Griffith Show*. This was the first of her three appearances on *Gunsmoke*.

#134: Young Love
(01-03-59)

WRITER: John Meston
DIRECTOR: Seymour Berns
CAST: Joan Taylor, John Lormer, Wesley Lau, Charles
              Cooper, Stephen Chase

A wealthy rancher is murdered, and Matt discovers that the man's younger wife is in love with one of the hired hands.

NOTES: Matt tells Kitty he would like to quit, but something always seems to come up. Joan Taylor portrayed storeowner Millie Scott on *The Rifleman* for two seasons.

#135: Marshal Proudfoot
(01-10-59)

STORY: Tom Hanley
TELEPLAY: John Meston
DIRECTOR: Jesse Hibbs
CAST: Dabbs Greer, Charles Fredericks, Earl Parker,
              Robert Brubaker

Chester is embarrassed when Matt, Kitty and Doc learn that he has led his Uncle Wesley to believe he is the marshal of Dodge.
NOTES: Wesley describes Chester as "borderline ignorant." Dabbs Greer, familiar as storekeeper Wilbur Jonas, portrays Chester's uncle. No Boot Hill opening.

#136: Passive Resistance
(01-17-59)

WRITER: John Meston
DIRECTOR: Ted Post
CAST: Carl Benton Reid, Alfred Ryder, Read Morgan

Two cattlemen kill Gideon Seek's flock of sheep, but Seek refuses to tell Matt who did the deed.

NOTES: Same homestead used as far back as "Smoking Out the Nolans" in Season One. Dabbs Greer back as Wilbur Jonas.

#137: LOVE OF A GOOD WOMAN
(01-24-59)

WRITER: John Meston
DIRECTOR: Andrew McLaglen
CAST: Kevin Hagen, Jacqueline Scott

A paroled convict who comes to Dodge to kill Matt is stricken by a serious fever.

NOTES: Abby (Scott) is a nurse Doc knew in the hospital during the Civil War. Kitty complains about being stuck in Dodge running a saloon. Matt tells Coney (Hagen) he has not closed both eyes for as far back as he can remember. No Boot Hill opening.

#138: JAYHAWKERS
(01-31-59)

WRITER: John Meston
DIRECTOR: Andrew McLaglen
CAST: Ken Curtis, Jack Elam, Lane Bradford,
            Chuck Hayward, Earl Parker, Cliff Ketchum,
            Brad Payne

Matt and Chester join a cattle drive headed by an old friend of Matt's to help ward off attacks by marauding jayhawkers.

NOTES: Chester discloses that he once lived in Texas for several years. First of several guest appearances by Ken Curtis before joining the series as Festus. A jayhawker was a Kansas guerilla who fought on the Union side during the Civil War. Jayhawkers later harassed Texas cattlemen, claiming that the herds coming north carried Texas fever. Some of the stock footage used in this episode was shot for *Rawhide*, which debuted on CBS earlier in the month. No Boot Hill opening.

#139: KITTY'S REBELLION
(02-07-59)

STORY: Marian Clark
TELEPLAY: John Meston
DIRECTOR: Jesse Hibbs
CAST: Barry McGuire, Addison Powell, Robert Brubaker, Richard Rust

The brother of Kitty's best friend travels from New Orleans to Dodge and is not at all pleased to discover that she is half-owner of the Long Branch.

NOTES: "My life hasn't always been an easy one," says Kitty. No Boot Hill opening, which is quickly becoming a rarity.

#140: SKY
(02-14-59)

STORY: John Meston
TELEPLAY: Les Crutchfield
DIRECTOR: Ted Post
CAST: Allen Case, Charles Thompson, Linda Watkins, Olive Blakeney, Patricia Huston

Matt and Chester chase after a man accused of murdering his girlfriend for her life savings.

NOTES: Chester teaches guitar to Kitty, who sings. Allen Case co-starred with Henry Fonda on the series *The Deputy*. Western veteran Roy Barcroft appears unbilled.

#141: DOC QUITS
(02-21-59)

WRITER: John Meston
DIRECTOR: Edward Ludlum
CAST: Wendell Holmes, Fionna Hale, Bartlett
            Robinson, Jack Younger, Jack Grinnage,
            Bert Rumsey

A new doctor in town wants to merge his practice with Doc's, but Doc considers the man's alternative healing methods to be nothing but quackery.

NOTES: Doc tears down the shingle hanging at the bottom of the stairway to his office.
    First mention of the catfish Doc is always trying to land.

#142: THE BEAR
(02-28-59)

WRITER: John Meston
DIRECTOR: Jesse Hibbs
CAST: Denver Pyle, Norma Crane, Grant Williams,
            Russell Johnson, Guy Wilkerson

After fighting with one of his employees, Mike Blocker is suspected of murdering the man.

NOTES: Kitty gets a bouquet and figures all she can do is plant it.

#143: The Coward
(03-07-59)

WRITER: John Meston
DIRECTOR: Jesse Hibbs
CAST: Barry Atwater, Jim Beck, House Peters, Jr. William
             Phipps, John Close, Sheldon Allman

A man sore at Matt but not brave enough to confront him starts a rumor that someone is out to kill the marshal.

NOTES: "A man like me's got a lot of enemies," says Matt, who is shot in his right arm. Matt is so jumpy he shoots and kills an innocent man.

#144: The F.U.
(03-14-59)

WRITER: John Meston
DIRECTOR: Andrew McLaglen
CAST: Bert Freed, Joe Flynn, Fay Roope, Steve Raines, Ed
             Faulkner

While Matt and Chester hunt for a murder suspect, his cohorts rob the bank.

NOTES: Anyone who has served in the military—or with imagination—can guess what the episode title stands for. Fay Roope portrays Mr. Botkin. Steve Raines was, along with Clint Eastwood, the only member of the *Rawhide* cast to remain on the series for all of its eight seasons.

#145: Wind
(03-21-59)

WRITER: John Meston

DIRECTOR: Arthur Hiller
CAST: Mark Miller, Whitney Blake, Roy Engel, Dabbs
               Greer, Walter Burke, Allen Lurie, Stephen Roberts,
               George Douglas, Guy Teague, Robert Swan

A troublemaking saloon girl attempts to kill Matt after he orders her out of town.

NOTES: Matt to Dolly: "This stage'll leave in about five minutes, and you're gonna be on it." Another amusing scene between Chester and Mr. Jonas.

#146: FAWN
(04-04-59)

WRITER: John Meston
DIRECTOR: Andrew McLaglen
CAST: Peggy Stewart, Wendy Stuart, Robert Karnes,
               Robert Rockwell, Charles Fredericks, Phil Harvey,
               Raymond Guth, Mike Gibson, Joe Kearns

Matt comes to the rescue of a white woman and her half-Cherokee daughter when they are abducted by buffalo hunters.
NOTES: Chester buys a nightcap, saying his head has been cold ever since he was a young boy and is tired of sleeping with his head under the covers. Mr. Dobie of the Dodge House is played by Joe Kearns, who was a banker in "The Big Con."

#147: RENEGADE WHITE
(04-11-59)

STORY: John Meston
TELEPLAY: Les Crutchfield
DIRECTOR: Andrew McLaglen
CAST: Michael Pate, Barney Phillips, Robert Brubaker,
               Hank Patterson

Indians capture Matt, who has been trailing the man responsible for providing them with rifles.

NOTES: Chester gives Kitty another guitar lesson. Barney Phillips plays Ord Spencer rather than Bill Pence this time. Hank Patterson later replaced George Selk as proprietor of the Dodge City livery stable.

#148: MURDER WARRANT
(04-18-59)

WRITER: John Meston
DIRECTOR: Andrew McLaglen
CAST: Ed Nelson, Mort Mills, Onslow Stevens, Fay
             Roope, Joe Kearns, George Selk

Matt devises a way to avoid sending a popular Dodge City resident to a town where he will not get a fair trial for the crime he has been charged with.

NOTES: Ed Nelson and Mort Mills each appeared in literally dozens of television Westerns. No Boot Hill opening.

#149: CHANGE OF HEART
(04-25-59)

WRITER: John Meston
DIRECTOR: Andrew McLaglen
CAST: Lucy Marlowe, James Drury, Ken Curtis, Fay Roope

A rancher and a Long Branch saloon girl plot to cheat the rancher's brother out of his share of some land.

NOTES: Kitty says Matt is her best friend, and that about all there is to Dodge is heat and dust. Second pre-Festus appearance by Ken Curtis. James Drury was the star of NBC's *The Virginian* for nine years.

#150: BUFFALO HUNTER
(05-02-59)

WRITER: John Meston
DIRECTOR: Ted Post
CAST: Harold J. Stone, Garry Walberg, Lou Krugman,
            William Meigs, Sam Buffington, Tom Holland,
            Brett King, Scott Stevens

Matt and Chester tangle with the leader of some buffalo hunters who is needlessly rough on the men working for him.

NOTES: Second of Harold J. Stone's eventual seven appearances on *Gunsmoke*.

#151: THE CHOICE
(05-09-59)

WRITER: John Meston
DIRECTOR: Ted Post
CAST: Darryl Hickman, Robert Brubaker, Charles
            Maxwell, Dick Rich, Tyler McVey

After a young drifter comes to Kitty's aid, Matt arranges for him to ride shotgun on the Dodge City stage.

NOTES: Matt tells Chester someone once gave him help when he needed it. Darryl Hickman later co-starred on *The Many Loves of Dobie Gillis*. Charles Maxwell guest starred on more than a dozen television Westerns, including ten episodes of *Bonanza*.

#152: THERE WAS NEVER A HORSE
(05-16-59)

WRITER: John Meston
DIRECTOR: Andrew McLaglen
CAST: Jack Lambert, Joe Sargent, Bill Wellman, Jr.

Matt will not take the bait when a well-known gunslinger wants to add killing a marshal to his list of credits.

NOTES: Chester does the stitching when Matt is wounded in the right forearm. Jack Lambert appeared on nearly two dozen television Westerns.

#153: PRINT ASPER
(05-23-59)

WRITER:	John Meston
DIRECTOR:	Ted Post
CAST:	J. Pat O'Malley, Ted Knight, Lew Brown, Robert Ivers

An old rancher is the prime suspect when the crooked attorney who tried to swindle the rancher out of his property is shot.

NOTES: More *Gunsmoke* irony involving a crime that did not need to be committed. Ted Knight is better known as Ted Baxter on *The Mary Tyler Moore Show*.

#154: THE CONSTABLE
(05-30-59)

WRITER:	John Meston
DIRECTOR:	Arthur Hiller
CAST:	John Larch, Strother Martin, Pitt Herbert, William Bryant, Joel Ashley, Scott Peters, Joe Kearns, Joseph Breen, Dan Sheridan, John Mitchum, Lee Winters, Vic Lundin, Robert DeCost

The Dodge City business owners once again clash with Matt's tactics and hire a replacement to run the town their way.

NOTES: Steve Raines (*Rawhide*) appears unbilled as a drover. No Boot Hill opening.

#155: BLUE HORSE
(06-06-59)

STORY: Marian Clark
TELEPLAY: John Meston
DIRECTOR: Andrew McLaglen
CAST: Michael Pate, Gene Nelson, Monte Hale,
              Bob Murphy

An Indian being hunted by the army comes to Matt's aid after the lawman is stranded on the prairie with a broken leg.

NOTES: Matt again must choose between the letter of the law and what is morally right.

#156: CHEYENNES
(06-13-59)

WRITER: John Meston
DIRECTOR: Ted Post
CAST: Walter Brooke, Ralph Moody, Chuck Roberson,
              Tom Brown, Eddie Little Sky, Dennis Cross,
              Connie Buck, Edward Robinson, Jr.

Gunrunners are selling rifles to the Indians, and Matt wants to put a stop to it before the army can start a deadly uprising.

NOTES: Eddie Little Sky is billed under his full name this time. Tom Brown was later cast as semi-regular character Ed O'Connor during the color era of *Gunsmoke*.

EPISODE GUIDE

SEASON 5
September 5, 1959–June 11, 1960

#157: TARGET
(09-05-59)

STORY: Les Crutchfield
TELEPLAY: John Meston
DIRECTOR: Andrew McLaglen
CAST: Darryl Hickman, Suzanne Lloyd, John Carradine,
            Frank DeKova

Danny Kater falls in love with a young gypsy, but neither his father nor the girl's approves of the relationship.

NOTES: James Arness is now listed as associate producer. Writers Crutchfield and Meston switch duties, with the latter turning out a script based on the former's story. The Boot Hill openings become increasingly rare this season.

#158: KITTY'S INJURY
(09-19-59)

STORY: Marian Clark
TELEPLAY: John Meston
DIRECTOR: Buzz Kulik
CAST: Don Dubbins, Karl Swenson, Anne Seymour

When Kitty is seriously hurt in a riding accident, Matt is reluctant to leave her with an odd family of homesteaders.

Arness in "How to Kill a Friend," 1958

NOTES: First time Matt and Kitty are shown riding together. First of Clem Fuller's 24 appearances as Long Branch bartender Clem.

#159: HORSE DEAL
(09-26-59)

WRITER: John Meston
DIRECTOR: Andrew McLaglen
CAST: Bart Robinson, Harry Carey, Jr.,
             Trevor Bardette, Michael Hinn,
             Fred Grossinger, Bill Catching

When Matt is unwilling to go after a horse thief, several ranchers threaten to form a posse and lynch the suspect.

NOTES: Matt and Kitty go riding on the prairie again. Bartlett Robinson, once again portraying rancher Emmett Bowers, is billed as Bart. First of Harry Carey Jr.'s 13 *Gunsmoke* appearances. "Slim" rather than Moss Grimmick in charge of stable.

#160: JOHNNY RED
(10-03-59)

STORY: Les Crutchfield
TELEPLAY: John Meston
DIRECTOR: Buzz Kulik
CAST: James Drury, Josephine Hutchinson,
             Abel Fernandez, Dennis McMullen,
             Robert Brubaker

Matt suspects a man claiming to be a soldier previously believed dead is actually an outlaw scheming to cheat the woman he says is his mother.

NOTES: Josephine Hutchinson played Basil Rathbone's wife in the 1939 horror classic *The Son of Frankenstein*.

Arness & Blake on location for "Horse Deal," 1959

#161: KANGAROO
(10-10-59)

WRITER: John Meston
DIRECTOR: Andrew McLaglen
CAST: Peter Whitney, John Crawford, Richard Rust,
               Lew Brown, Clem Fuller

When Chester interferes with a religious zealot's method of meting out justice, the whip-wielding man vows to cut off Chester's right hand.

NOTES: Peter Whitney, who guest starred on dozens of television Westerns, appeared in half a dozen episodes of *Gunsmoke*.

#162: TAIL TO THE WIND
(10-17-59)

STORY: Les Crutchfield
TELEPLAY: John Meston
DIRECTOR: Christian Nyby
CAST: Harry Townes, Alice Backes, Harry Swoger,
               Alan Reed, Jr.

A homesteader being bullied by a rancher and his son declines Matt's offer to help.

NOTES: Typical unexpected *Gunsmoke* ending.

#163: ANNIE OAKLEY
(10-24-59)

WRITER: John Meston
DIRECTOR: Jesse Hibbs
CAST: Florence MacMichael, George Mitchell,
               John Anderson

Kate Dolliver insists that a neighbor has murdered her husband, but Matt has his doubts and asks the neighbor to assist him in finding the real killer.

Notes: Matt and Chester play checkers in Doc's office rather than the jailhouse.

#164: Saludos
(10-31-59)

Story: Les Crutchfield
Teleplay: John Meston
Director: Andrew McLaglen
Cast: Connie Buck, Gene Nelson, Jack Elam,
            Robert J. Wilke

Matt and Chester track down a trio suspected of wounding an Indian woman and murdering her husband.

Notes: Kitty turns an old cliché on its head by saying, "You know how all white men look alike to Indians." Chester mentions Boot Hill being 20 minutes from Dodge City, and boasts that he makes "the best coffee in Dodge, bar none."

#165: Brother Whelp
(11-07-59)

Story: Les Crutchfield
Teleplay: John Meston
Director: R.G. Springsteen
Cast: Lew Gallo, Ellen Clark, John Clarke, Clem Fuller,
            Dabbs Greer

An ex-con returns to Dodge only to discover his girlfriend married to his brother, and his brother sole owner of the family ranch.

NOTES: A rare upbeat if bittersweet ending.

#166: THE BOOTS
(11-14-59)

WRITER: John Meston
DIRECTOR: Jesse Hibbs
CAST: John Larch, Richard Eyer, Wynn Pearce

The town drunk's relationship with a young boy is threatened when a gunman comes to Dodge and presses the drunk into helping him rob the general store.

NOTES: The episode opens with a flashback to the first anniversary of the Long Branch. In the present day, Sam is back as bartender. Kitty says, "This place has a lot of history I'm awful glad I missed." Richard Eyer later co-starred on the series *Stagecoach West*.

#167: ODD MAN OUT
(11-21-59)

STORY: Les Crutchfield
TELEPLAY: John Meston
DIRECTOR: Andrew McLaglen
CAST: Elisha Cook, William Phipps, Elizabeth York,
              Dallas Mitchell, Dabbs Greer, George Selk,
              Clem Fuller

An old farmer claims his wife has deserted him, but Matt is doubtful after another man attempts to sell the woman's clothing.

NOTES: Kitty jokingly asks Matt if he has come into the Long Branch to propose marriage. Chester and Moss Grimmick "match dimes." Clem back as barkeep.

#168: Miguel's Daughter
(11-28-59)

STORY: Marian Clark
TELEPLAY: John Meston
DIRECTOR: Andrew McLaglen
CAST: Fintan Meyler, Simon Oakland, Wesley Lau, Ed Nelson

Matt hopes he can locate a couple of trail bums who harassed a young woman before her father does.

NOTES: Kitty makes a joke about being jealous of other women being around Matt. Rare instance of Doc riding a horse.

#169: Box O' Rocks
(12-05-59)

STORY: Les Crutchfield
DIRECTOR: R.G. Springsteen
CAST: Howard McNear, Vaughn Taylor, Larry Blake, William Fawcett, Gertrude Flynn

A suspicious Matt stops a burial service and finds no body in the coffin.

NOTES: No Boot Hill opening, but the first time a scene takes place there. Good story with a clever ending.

#170: False Witness
(12-12-59)

STORY: Marian Clark
TELEPLAY: John Meston
DIRECTOR: Ted Post
CAST: Wright King, Wayne Rogers, Robert Griffin,

Len Hendry, Richard Sinatra, Clem Fuller, Norman Sturgis, Brad Trumbull, Harold Goodwin

When he learns that an alleged eyewitness has lied, Matt believes an innocent man has been executed.

NOTES: First trial in Dodge in a long while, as well as the first photographer in town since "The Photographer" episode. Not the only time Matt disagrees with the court's verdict, believing Morey (Rogers) to be innocent. Matt loses his temper and throttles Crep (King). Wayne Rogers was one of the stars of the *Stagecoach West* series.

#171: TAG, YOU'RE IT
(12-19-59)

WRITER: Les Crutchfield
DIRECTOR: Jesse Hibbs
CAST: Paul Langton, Madlyn Rhue, Gregg Stewart, Clem Fuller, Harold Goodwin

Matt discovers that a gunman who earns $1000 per job has come to Dodge to kill one of Kitty's girls.

NOTES: Matt and Killion (Langton) knew each other "in the panhandle days." Killion is surprised to see that Matt is a lawman. A now rare Boot Hill opening.

#172: THICK 'N' THIN
(12-26-59)

STORY: Les Crutchfield
TELEPLAY: John Meston
DIRECTOR: Stuart Heisler
CAST: Robert Emhardt, Percy Helton, Tina Menard

Matt steps in when two quarreling farmers each lay sole claim to their jointly-owned property.

NOTES: Rare lighthearted episode for the 1959 holiday season. Kitty says Ma Smalley has gone back East. Matt asks Chester how much he has lost "matching dimes" with Moss Grimmick.

#173: GOAT'S GRUDGE
(01-02-60)

STORY: Marian Clark
TELEPLAY: John Meston
DIRECTOR: Andrew McLaglen
CAST: Ross Elliott, Thomas Coley, Ben Wright

Matt and Chester chase after a former Confederate soldier who intends to kill the man he believes murdered his wife during the war.

NOTES: Doc mentions taking a bullet out of Matt's leg the previous month and charging $5.50. Haskett (Coley) says Doc took a sliver out of his eye when he was in Libby Prison. Ross Elliott portrayed the sheriff of Medicine Bow on *The Virginian*.

#174: BIG TOM
(01-09-60)

STORY: Marian Clark
TELEPLAY: John Meston
DIRECTOR: Andrew McLaglen
CAST: Don Megowan, Robert J. Wilke, Harry Lauter,
              Howard Caine, Gregg Palmer, Rand Harper

Matt takes on a professional prizefighter when Doc determines that the original opponent is in no shape to fight.

NOTES: Matt's biggest fight scene since "Buffalo Man." Rare sympathetic role for Robert J. Wilke, who was usually cast as villains. Don Megowan also played fighters in episodes of *Bonanza* and *Laramie.*

#175: TILL DEATH DO US
(01-16-60)

WRITER: Les Crutchfield
DIRECTOR: Jean Yarbrough
CAST: Milton Selzer, Mary Field, Rayford Barnes

A religious fanatic with a habit of preaching to the Long Branch girls about their wicked ways becomes the target of a sniper.

NOTES: Matt shot in the left forearm.

#176: THE TRAGEDIAN
(01-23-60)

STORY: Les Crutchfield
TELEPLAY: John Meston
DIRECTOR: Arthur Hiller
CAST: John Abbott, Howard McNear, Harry Wood,
             Stanley Clements

Matt takes a liking to a Shakespearian actor who in reality is hardly an upstanding citizen.

NOTES: Howard McNear is cast this time as the owner of Delmonico's.

#177: HINKA DO
(01-30-60)

WRITER: Les Crutchfield
DIRECTOR: Andrew McLaglen

CAST: Nina Varela, Walter Burke, Mike Green, Richard Reeves, Ric Roman, Bob Hopkins

Matt suspects that the rough and tumble woman who assumes ownership of the Lady Gay Saloon has murdered the former proprietor.

NOTES: A humorous mystery. Doc uses a microscope for the first time. Matt refers to Kitty as the owner of the Long Branch, though her buying Bill Pence out has never been mentioned. Interior of the Lady Gay is the Long Branch set redressed. Final Boot Hill opening of the series.

#178: DOC JUDGE
(02-06-60)

WRITER: John Meston
DIRECTOR: Arthur Hiller
CAST: Barry Atwater, Dennis Cross, George Selk, Dabbs Greer

Chester comes to the rescue when a vengeful gunslinger insists Doc is the judge who sent him to prison.

NOTES: Good example of the unspoken affection Doc and Chester have for each other. Doc begins to list the medicals bills Chester has run up during his time in Dodge. First episode ever without much of Matt, who has three brief scenes.

#179: MOO MOO RAID
(02-13-60)

STORY: Les Crutchfield
TELEPLAY: John Meston
DIRECTOR: Andrew McLaglen
CAST: Raymond Hatton, Robert Karnes, Lane Bradford,

Richard Evans, Tyler McVey, Ron Hayes, John Close, Clem Fuller

The disappearance of an aging cow used for leading reluctant cattle herds across rivers may lead to an all-out range war.

NOTES: Matt says Dodge could stand to be rebuilt. This episode, the highest rated of the entire series, revolves mainly around guest cast rather than regulars.

#180: KITTY'S KILLING
(02-20-60)

STORY:	Marian Clark
TELEPLAY:	John Meston
DIRECTOR:	Arthur Hiller
CAST:	Abraham Sofaer, John Pickard, Clem Fuller

Mentally unstable Jacob Leech comes to Dodge to kill his former son-in-law, demanding that Kitty reveal the man's whereabouts.

NOTES: John Pickard, who was one of the actors who tried out for the part of Matt Dillon, appeared in more than 50 television Westerns, including regular roles on *Boots and Saddles* and *Gunslinger*.

#181: JAILBAIT JANET
(02-27-60)

WRITER:	Les Crutchfield
DIRECTOR:	Jesse Hibbs
CAST:	John Larch, Nan Peterson, Bartlett Robinson, Steve Terrell, Jon Lormer

Matt and Chester go after a train robber and find that his accomplices are his two teenage children.

NOTES: Matt complains about how slowly the War Department in Washington pays him. Infrequent use of the Dodge City railroad depot.

#182: UNWANTED DEPUTY
(03-05-60)

STORY: Marian Clark
TELEPLAY: John Meston
DIRECTOR: Andrew V. McLaglen
CAST: Charles Aidman, Mary Carver, Marlowe Jenson, Dick Rich, Ed Faulkner, Dick London, Craig Fox, Bob Wiensko, Joe Haworth

A man seeking revenge against Matt concocts a unique method of achieving his goal.

NOTES: Rare occasion of Chester getting drunk. Matt tells Chester he is not going to start making his own coffee after all these years.

#183: WHERE'D THEY GO
(03-12-60)

STORY: Les Crutchfield
TELEPLAY: John Meston
DIRECTOR: Jesse Hibbs
CAST: Jack Elam, Betty Harford, Dabbs Greer

A farmer accused of robbing the general store cons Matt and Chester into doing chores before they take him to jail.

NOTES: Second episode of "winter" in Dodge, though it certainly does not look like it.

#184: CROWBAIT BOB
(03-26-60)

WRITER: Les Crutchfield
DIRECTOR: Andrew McLaglen
CAST: Hank Patterson, Ned Glass, Shirley O'Hara,
               John Apone

An ailing prospector asks Matt to make out a will leaving all of his possessions to Kitty.

NOTES: Matt mentions a Judge Bent. After George Selk leaves the series, Hank Patterson (Bob) later takes over the stable in which he resides during this episode.

#185: COLLEEN SO GREEN
(04-02-60)

STORY: Les Crutchfield
TELEPLAY: John Meston
DIRECTOR: Jean Yarbrough
CAST: Joanna Moore, Harry Swoger, Dabbs Greer, Robert
               Brubaker, Harold Goodwin, Clem Fuller, Perry Ivins

A pretty Southern gal breezes into Dodge and casts a spell over Doc, Chester and a rich buffalo man.

NOTES: Another lighthearted episode. Joanna Moore (Colleen) played Sheriff Taylor's love interest on several episodes of *The Andy Griffith Show*.

#186: THE EX-URBANITES
(04-09-60)

WRITER: John Meston
DIRECTOR: Andrew McLaglen

CAST: Ken Curtis, Robert Wilke, Lew Brown

Chester is a wounded Doc's only hope when the two of them are stranded on the prairie.

NOTES: Another pre-Festus role for Ken Curtis, similar to both Festus and the Monk character he played in two episodes of *Have Gun-Will Travel.* Brief appearance by Matt at the end of the episode.

#187: I THEE WED
(04-16-60)

STORY: Les Crutchfield
TELEPLAY: John Meston
DIRECTOR: Jesse Hibbs
CAST: Allyn Joslyn, Alice Frost, Hank Patterson

Matt gets a bullet for his trouble when he takes on an unrepentant wife beater.

NOTES: Matt once again shot in the left arm, and is checked out by Doc after taking a bullet close to a lung six months earlier. Sam (Joslyn) goes to jail not for shooting Matt, but for disturbing the peace! Hank Patterson plays Judge Bent, with court held in the dining room of Delmonico's. Episode somewhat similar to "Last Fling."

#188: THE LADY KILLER
(04-23-60)

WRITER: John Meston
DIRECTOR: Andrew McLaglen
CAST: Jan Harrison, Ross Elliot, Harry Lauter,
              Charles Sterrett

Matt is skeptical when the saloon girl who kills an important witness in an upcoming trial claims the man was attempting to rob and murder her.

NOTES: Doc again mentions being a doctor on a riverboat, and Kitty says she knows how dealing cards on a Mississippi riverboat can make a woman hard.

#189: GENTLEMAN'S DISAGREEMENT
(04-30-60)

WRITER:	Les Crutchfield
DIRECTOR:	Jesse Hibbs
CAST:	Adam Kennedy, Fintan Meyler, Val Dufour, Tom Reese, Joseph Hamilton

Matt has no choice but to arrest a blacksmith for allegedly killing his wife's former lover.

NOTES: Beaudry (Dufour) says that Matt once knew Jeanne (Meyler) years ago in Louisville, Kentucky.

#190: SPEAK ME FAIR
(05-07-60)

WRITER:	Les Crutchfield
DIRECTOR:	Andrew McLaglen
CAST:	Douglas Kennedy, Ken Curtis, Chuck Roberson, Perry Cook

Matt believes a rancher upset about cattle rustlers has beaten a young Indian boy.

NOTES: Matt, Chester and Doc hunt game birds together. Another rare occasion of Doc on horseback rather than in his buggy. Fourth of Ken Curtis' six pre-Festus episodes.

#191: BELLE'S BACK
(05-14-60)

WRITER: Les Crutchfield
DIRECTOR: Jesse Hibbs
CAST: Nita Talbot, Nancy Rennick, Daniel White,
            Gage Clark

Matt has a hunch two sisters know where a wanted man is hiding.

NOTES: Chester gives Matt a haircut because Dodge barber Frank Teeters is out of town. Kitty says she wishes someone like Matt had given her advice when she was younger. Rare use of phony exterior set for night scenes.

#192: THE BOBSY TWINS
(05-21-60)

WRITER: John Meston
DIRECTOR: Jesse Hibbs
CAST: Morris Ankrum, Ralph Moody, Buck Young,
            Jean Howell, John O'Malley, Charles MacArthur,
            Richard Chamberlain, Paul Hahn, Hank Patterson,
            Clem Fuller

Two old hillbilly brothers who seem harmless at first are actually deranged killers with their own warped code of ethics.

NOTES: The brothers say they came west to kill Indians but cannot find any. When they ask for Matt's help locating some, he tells them, "Turn around and go on back home where you came from." A darkly humorous episode.

#193: Old Flame
(05-28-60)

STORY: Marian Clark
TELEPLAY: John Meston
DIRECTOR: Jesse Hibbs
CAST: Marilyn Maxwell, Lee Van Cleef, Peggy
              Stewart, Hal Smith

One of Matt's old girlfriends comes to Dodge claiming her husband is out to kill her.

NOTES: Matt describes being marshal as "just a job." Kitty refers to Chester as Matt's "assistant" rather than deputy. Dolly (Maxwell) last saw Matt in Texas when she was only eighteen-years-old. Hal Smith, best known as Otis on *The Andy Griffith Show*, plays Dodge House owner Mr. Dobie. First of Lee Van Cleef's three *Gunsmoke* episodes.

#194: The Deserter
(06-04-60)

STORY: Marian Clark
TELEPLAY: John Meston
DIRECTOR: Arthur Hiller
CAST: Rudy Solari, Joe Perry, Henry Brandon, Charles
              Fredericks, Harry Bartell, Jean Inness

Chester is wounded when he and Matt pursue two men who have robbed an army payroll.

NOTES: Matt goes to Fort Dodge for the third time. Chester tells Maddie (Inness) that he is an expert on coffee. Henry Brandon, usually cast as an Indian, plays an army major.

#195: CHERRY RED
(06-11-60)

WRITER: Les Crutchfield
DIRECTOR: Andrew McLaglen
CAST: Joanna Moore, Arthur Franz, Douglas Kennedy,
               Cliff Ketchum

A young widow has a feeling the man after her affections may have had something to do with the robbery of a stage coach that resulted in the death of her husband.

NOTES: Joanna Moore also appeared in this season's "Colleen So Green."

EPISODE GUIDE

SEASON 6
September 3, 1960–June 17, 1961

#196: FRIEND'S PAY-OFF
(09-03-60)

STORY: Marian Clark
TELEPLAY: John Meston
DIRECTOR: Jesse Hibbs
CAST: Mike Road, Tom Reese, George Selk, Jay Hector,
              Clem Fuller

A dying man shot by Matt tells the marshal that Ab Butler, Matt's friend, is really a thief and murderer.

NOTES: Series now filmed at Paramount Studios. James Arness again listed as associate producer. Doc uses a gun for the second time.

#197: THE BLACKSMITH
(09-17-60)

STORY: Norman Macdonnell
TELEPLAY: John Meston
DIRECTOR: Andrew McLaglen
CAST: George Kennedy, Bob Anderson, Anna-Lisa,
              Wesley Lau, Hank Patterson

Dodge City's German blacksmith marries a mail order bride, but their joy is cut short when a bigoted rancher burns down their house.

Susan Gordon & Arness in "Little Girl, 1961

NOTES: After hearing Doc and Chester's verbal sparring, Gretchen (Anna-Lisa) remarks, "I don't think they mean everything they say." Story contributed by the show's producer, Norman Macdonnell.

#198: Small Water
(09-24-60)

WRITER: John Meston
DIRECTOR: Andrew McLaglen
CAST: Trevor Bardette, Rex Holman,
            Warren Oates

Matt and Chester are on their way back to Dodge with an elderly man suspected of murder when they run into the man's two sons.

NOTES: Warren Oates appeared on more than two dozen television Westerns, including ten episodes of *Gunsmoke*. Rex Holman did fourteen in all. Trevor Bardette was a regular on *The Life and Legend of Wyatt Earp* for two seasons.

#199: Say Uncle
(10-01-60)

WRITER: John Meston
DIRECTOR: Andrew McLaglen
CAST: Richard Rust, Gene Nelson, Harry Lauter,
            Dorothy Green

A young man is certain his uncle killed his father, but without proof there is nothing Matt can do about it.

NOTES: Dorothy Green portrayed the sister-in-law of Gil Favor (Eric Fleming) on two episodes of *Rawhide*.

#200: Shooting Stopover
(10-08-60)

STORY: Marian Clark
TELEPLAY: John Meston
DIRECTOR: Andrew McLaglen

CAST: Patricia Barry, Anthony Caruso, Paul Guilfoyle, Robert Brubaker

Outlaws trap Matt, Chester, and their fellow stagecoach passengers in an isolated waystation.

NOTES: Jim Buck (Brubaker) is wounded. Would have made a good hour-long episode.

#201: THE PEACE OFFICER
(10-15-60)

STORY: Norman Macdonnell
TELEPLAY: John Meston
DIRECTOR: Jesse Hibbs
CAST: Susan Cummings, Lane Bradford, John Zaccaro, Arthur Peterson, Jr., John Close, Gilman Rankin, Stafford Repp, James Nusser

Matt goes to Tascosa to relieve a crooked sheriff of his duties, then encounters the sheriff's frightened former girlfriend on the ride back to Dodge City.

NOTES: "If I was worried about dying I would've quit this job a long time ago," Matt tells Rawlins (Bradford). Kitty obviously tells Stella (Cummings) how things are between her and Matt, although the conversation is never heard. *Bonanza* fans will recognize Tascosa as the Virginia City set at Paramount.

#202: DON MATTEO
(10-22-60)

STORY: Marian Clark
TELEPLAY: John Meston
DIRECTOR: Jesse Hibbs
CAST: Lawrence Dobkin, Bing Russell, Ben Wright,

Anne Whitfield, Barney Phillips, Roy Engel

Matt tries to talk an old friend out killing the man who ran off with his wife.

NOTES: Kitty tells Tabor (Russell), "I own this place" even though her partner Bill Pence (Phillips) is still there. Garcia (Dobkin) and Matt used to hire out to ranchers to chase rustlers back "in the border days."

#203: THE WORM
(10-29-60)

WRITER:	John Meston
DIRECTOR:	Arthur Hiller
CAST:	Kenneth Tobey, H.M. Wynant, Ned Glass, Stewart Bradley, Gage Clark, Howard Culver

A buffalo hunter's assistant decides he has taken all he is going to from his abusive employer and plots to do away with him in Dodge.

NOTES: Matt's arm gets cut. Gage Clarke portrays a judge rather than Dodge House owner Mr. Dobie. Kenneth Tobey and James Arness appeared together in *The Thing*.

#204: THE BADGE
(11-12-60)

STORY:	Marian Clark
TELEPLAY:	John Meston
DIRECTOR:	Andrew McLaglen
CAST:	John Dehner, Conlan Carter, Allan Lane, Harry Swoger, Michael Mikler

NOTES: This episode is significant for it being the very first in the series with no sign of Chester. Conlan Carter later played Doc on the *Combat!* series for four seasons, earning an Emmy nomination for the role. The episode title was used again in 1970.

#205: DISTANT DRUMMER
(11-19-60)

STORY: Marian Clark
TELEPLAY: John Meston
DIRECTOR: Arthur Hiller
CAST: Bruce Gordon, Jack Grinnage, George Mitchell, George Selk, William Newell, Phil Chambers

Raffie, an army drummer, is suspected of murdering a mule skinner who had been harassing him.

NOTES: Bruce Gordon, known mainly for playing gangster types, appeared in nearly two dozen television Westerns.

#206: BEN TOLLIVER'S STUD
(11-26-60)

STORY: Norman Macdonnell
TELEPLAY: John Meston
DIRECTOR: Andrew McLaglen
CAST: John Lupton, Jean Ingram, Roy Barcroft, Hank Patterson

A hired hand is accused of horse theft by the rancher for whom he works.

NOTES: John Lupton co-starred on the series *Broken Arrow*. Both Roy Barcroft and Hank Patterson would later join *Gunsmoke* as semi-regular characters. Patterson portrays stableman Carl Miller rather than Hank, later his character's name.

#207: NO CHIP
(12-03-60)

WRITER: John Meston
DIRECTOR: Jean Yarbrough
CAST: John Hoyt, Rex Holman, Leo Gordon,
             Guy Stockwell, Mark Allen

A hot-headed rancher has only his pacifist son to back him up when cattlemen drive their herd onto his land and refuse to leave.

NOTES: Once again the stories are beginning to revolve around guest actors rather than the main stars. When one (Kitty) shows up, the episode is nearly half over. Long Branch bartender is named Dan rather than Sam, Clem, Red or Freddy.

#208: THE WAKE
(12-10-60)

WRITER: John Meston
DIRECTOR: Gerald H. Mayer
CAST: Denver Pyle, Anne Seymour, George Selk,
             Michael Hinn

A wake is held for a man whom Matt discovers is still very much alive.

NOTES: The year in this episode is said to be 1873.

#209: THE COOK
(12-17-60)

WRITER: John Meston
DIRECTOR: Ted Post
CAST: Guy Stockwell, Gene Benton, Harry Swoger, Sue
             Randall, John Pickard, Ken Mayer, Tom Greenway,

John Milford, Brad Trumball, Craig Duncan, Sam Woody

The citizens of Dodge are up in arms when the finest cook to ever work at Delmonico's is arrested for accidentally killing a troublemaking buffalo hunter.

NOTES: Harry Swoger's first episode as Delmonico owner Hank Green. Sue Randall portrayed Theodore Cleaver's teacher Miss Landers on *Leave it to Beaver*. More stock footage shot for *Rawhide* is used.

#210: OLD FOOL
(12-24-60)

WRITER: John Meston
DIRECTOR: Ted Post
CAST: Buddy Ebsen, Hope Summers. Linda Watkins, Hampton Fancher

A scheming widow intrudes on the happiness of an elderly ranching couple.

NOTES: Token appearances by Doc and Kitty at beginning, Matt and Chester do not show up until more than half-way. First of Buddy Ebsen's three guest roles.

#211: BROTHER LOVE
(12-31-60)

WRITER: John Meston
DIRECTOR: Franklin Adreon
CAST: Lurene Tuttle, Kevin Hagen, Gene Lyons, Jack Grinnage, Jan Harrison, Dabbs Greer, Clem Fuller

A dying storeowner says one of two brothers attacked him, but which one?

NOTES: Another rare rainstorm in Dodge City.

#212: BAD SHERIFF
(01-07-61)

WRITER: John Meston
DIRECTOR: Andrew McLaglen
CAST: Russell Arms, Harry Carey, Jr. Kenneth Lynch,
             Don Keefer, Lane Chandler

Two men intending to steal from the stagecoach robber they have captured pretend to be lawmen when Matt and Chester arrive.

NOTES: Second of Harry Carey Jr.'s thirteen appearances. Ken Lynch was in eleven episodes and later co-starred with Dennis Weaver in the *McCloud* series.

#213: UNLOADED GUN
(01-14-61)

STORY: Marian Clark
TELEPLAY: John Meston
DIRECTOR: Jesse Hibbs
CAST: William Redfield, Lew Brown, Gregg Dunn,
             Hank Patterson, James Malcom, Clem Fuller,
             Bobby Goodwins, Rik Nervik

While Matt is bedridden with fever, Chester decides to clean the ailing marshal's gun, unaware that an outlaw seeking revenge is in Dodge.

NOTES: Another rare instance of Matt not feeling well. Hank Patterson appears once again as stableman Carl Miller.

#214: Tall Trapper
(01-21-61)

STORY: Marian Clark
TELEPLAY: John Meston
DIRECTOR: Harry Harris, Jr.
CAST: Tom Reese, Strother Martin, Jan Shepard

A trapper provides shelter for a traveling couple and is later suspected of murdering the wife.

NOTES: Tom Reese and Strother Martin are each cast against type for this episode. Jan Shepard, who appeared in nearly two dozen television Westerns, was a good friend of Amanda Blake. First of 65 episodes directed by Harry Harris, Jr.

#215: Love Thy Neighbor
(01-28-61)

WRITER: John Meston
DIRECTOR: Dennis Weaver
CAST: Jeanette Nolan, Jack Elam, Kenneth Lynch,
              Dean Stanton, Warren Oates, Nora Marlowe,
              David Kent, Cyril Delevanti, Wayne West

A deadly feud is caused by a stolen sack of potatoes.

NOTES: First of four episodes directed by Dennis Weaver, explaining why Chester appears briefly with very few lines. An especially strong guest cast.

#216: Bad Seed
(02-04-61)

STORY: Norman Macdonnell
TELEPLAY: John Meston

DIRECTOR: Harry Harris, Jr.
CAST: Anne Helm, Roy Barcroft, Burt Douglas

A young woman Matt rescues from an abusive father spreads ugly rumors about the marshal when he spurns her advances.

NOTES: Only the second episode without Chester. Anne Helm appeared in more than a dozen television Westerns.

#217: KITTY SHOT
(02-11-61)

WRITER: John Meston
DIRECTOR: Andrew McLaglen
CAST: George Kennedy, Joseph Mell, Rayford Barnes, Lew Brown

Matt chases after a rowdy Long Branch customer who accidentally shoots Kitty.

NOTES: Kitty's first time on Doc's operating table. Joseph Mell back as Bill Pence instead of Barney Phillips. Like other recent episodes, there are no windows and no door on the stairway wall of the Long Branch.

#218: ABOUT CHESTER
(02-25-61)

STORY: Frank Paris
TELEPLAY: John Meston
DIRECTOR: Alan Crosland, Jr.
CAST: Mary Munday, Charles Aidman, George Eldridge, House Peters, Jr., Harry Shannon

When Doc disappears for four days, Matt and Chester decide to split up in their search for him.

NOTES: Dodge rancher Emmett Bowers is played this time by Harry Shannon rather than Bartlett Robinson. Story contributor Frank Paris later became an associate producer on the series.

#219: HARRIET
(03-04-61)

WRITER: John Meston
DIRECTOR: Gene Fowler, Jr.
CAST: Suzanne Lloyd, Tom Reese, Ron Hayes,
            Howard Culver, Joseph Hamilton

A woman takes a job at the Long Branch in hopes that the men who killed her father will eventually come in.

NOTES: Harriet (Lloyd) tells Kitty that Chester has told her every man in the west eventually drops in at the Long Branch. Tom Reese appeared on the show 14 times.

#220: POTSHOT
(03-11-61)

WRITER: John Meston
DIRECTOR: Harry Harris, Jr.
CAST: Karl Swenson, Gage Clark, Joseph Mell,
            Dallas Mitchell, Barton Heyman,
            Wallace Rooney, Michael Harris,
            John Harmon

When Chester is shot by a sniper, Matt is puzzled to learn that neither of the men suspected were in Dodge at the time.

NOTES: Gage Clarke portrays banker Botkin rather than Dodge House owner Mr. Dobie. John Harmon played hotel owner Eddie on *The Rifleman*.

#221: OLD FACES
(03-18-61)

WRITER: John Meston
DIRECTOR: Harry Harris
CAST: James Drury, Jan Shepard, George Keymas,
              Ron Hayes, Robert Brubaker, Glenn Strange

Tilda Cook is a former riverboat entertainer whose husband challenges the man who insults her to a showdown.

NOTES: Kitty wields a shotgun for the first time. Contrary another source, Glenn Strange is cast as a Long Branch customer, not bartender Sam, which will become his role in the following season. The bartender in this episode is Freddy.

#222: BIG MAN
(03-25-61)

WRITER: John Meston
DIRECTOR: Gerald Mayer
CAST: George Kennedy, John McLiam,
              Chris Alcaide, Sandy Kenyon, Rayford Barnes,
              Barney Phillips, Steve Warren, James Nusser,
              Mathew McCue

Matt is suspected of murdering a man who had been bothering Kitty.

NOTES: Final appearance of Barney Phillips as Bill Pence. James Nusser plays another drunk, but not the Louie Pheeters character. Mathew McCue's role of Joe, the elderly Delmonico's waiter, will continue well into the hour-long episodes. Last half-hour episode to be filmed.

#223: LITTLE GIRL
(04-01-61)

STORY: Kathleen Hite
TELEPLAY: John Meston
DIRECTOR: Dennis Weaver
CAST: Susan Gordon, Wright King, Bill McLean,
              Doc Douglas

Matt and Chester come across an orphaned girl in a burned out house and take her back to Dodge.

NOTES: Not the last time Matt is faced with finding a home for an orphan. Moss Grimmick's having a wife is mentioned. The children of Hi Stevens (King) are played by the real life offspring of both Wright King and Dennis Weaver.

#224: STOLEN HORSES
(04-08-61)

STORY: Norman Macdonnell
TELEPLAY: John Meston
DIRECTOR: Andrew McLaglen
CAST: Buck Young, Shirley O'Hara, Jack Lambert, Guy
              Raymond, Henry Brandon, Charles Seel, Alex
              Sharp, Eddie Little Sky

A murderer being hunted by Matt and Chester takes a farmer hostage.

NOTES: Matt to Quick Knife (Brandon): "You know, Quick Knife, I can't agree with the way you do things, but I respect your law." Charles Seel (Cuff) would later portray Dodge City telegrapher Barney.

#225: MINNIE
(04-15-61)

WRITER: John Meston
DIRECTOR: Harry Harris, Jr.
CAST: Virginia Gregg, Alan Hale, Jr., George Selk, Joseph
    Mell, Barry Cahill, Robert Human, Mathew McCue

The wife of a jealous buffalo hunter comes to Dodge and decides Doc is truly the man for her.

NOTES: Minnie (Gregg) to Chester: "You're kinda country, even for Dodge, ain't ya?"
    Last of Joseph Mell's five appearances as Bill Pence.

#226: BLESS ME TILL I DIE
(04-22-61)

STORY: Ray Kemper
TELEPLAY: John Meston
DIRECTOR: Ted Post
CAST: Ronald Foster, Phyllis Love, Vic Perrin,
    Dabbs Greer

An aspiring doctor new to Dodge is accused of being an escaped convict.

NOTES: Kitty and Doc are both shown on horseback, Kitty trying out a new mount. Matt says Chester's coffee has been improving. Tragic episode with a surprise ending.

#227: LONG HOURS, SHORT PAY
(04-29-61)

WRITER: John Meston
DIRECTOR: Andrew McLaglen

CAST: John Larch, Lalo Rios, Frank Sentry, Allan Lane,
         Dawn Little Sky, Steve Warren, Fred McDougall

While tracking a gunrunner who has been selling to the Indians, Matt is captured by the man's customers.

NOTES: Matt tells Captain Graves (Lane) that no matter how successful he is in his job, Washington is not going to raise his pay.

#228: HARD VIRTUE
(05-06-61)

WRITER: John Meston
DIRECTOR: Dennis Weaver
CAST: Lew Brown, Lia Waggner, Robert Karnes,
            James Maloney, George Selk

When a jealous husband threatens to kill the man he believes has designs on his wife, Matt has to find out who it is before the husband can.

NOTES: A Western soap opera, directed by Dennis Weaver. The latest Long Branch bartender is named Lee.

#229: THE IMPOSTER
(05-13-61)

STORY: Kathleen Hite
TELEPLAY: John Meston
DIRECTOR: Byron Paul
CAST: Virginia Gregg, Harp McGuire,
            Paul Langton, Garry Walberg

A lawman from Texas claims that an upstanding citizen of Dodge is wanted for murder.

NOTES: Matt, who mentions once being in Miami, Texas, is shot in the right shoulder. Virginia Gregg looks a bit more glamorous than in the recent episode "Minnie." There is an amusing blooper from this episode in which Arness does not have the proper credentials the sheriff requests.

#230: CHESTER'S DILEMMA
(05-20-61)

WRITER: John Meston
DIRECTOR: Ted Post
CAST: Patricia Smith, John Van Dreelan, Vic Perrin

Chester falls for a pretty newcomer to Dodge, but all she seems interested in is the mail addressed to the jailhouse.

NOTES: Matt to Chester: "Look, I need you around here, Chester. You're the only person I can depend on." Yet another of Chester's doomed romances.

#231: THE LOVE OF MONEY
(06-03-61)

WRITER: John Meston
DIRECTOR: Ted Post
CAST: Cloris Leachman, Warren Kemmerling,
             Tod Andrews

A Long Branch saloon girl agrees to help Matt find the killer of an ex-lawman only if there is something in it for her.

NOTES: The ex-lawman is from Oklahoma Territory and another old friend of Matt's. Kitty mentions having once been in San Francisco. The boarding house Boni (Leachman) stays at is Ma Donovan's, not Ma Smalley's.

#232: MELINDA MILES
(06-03-61)

WRITER: John Meston
DIRECTOR: William Dario Faralla
CAST: Burt Douglas, Diana Millay, Walter Sande,
             Charles Gray, Rand Brooks, George Selk,
             Glenn Strange

When a ranch foreman is murdered, Matt figures the killer has to be the fiancée of a woman the foreman had his eye on.

NOTES: Although not seen, the character of Bill Pence is mentioned for the last time. Glenn Strange, soon to play Long Branch bartender Sam, plays a patron of the saloon.

Rand Brooks was a regular on the series *The Adventures of Rin Tin Tin*.

#233: COLORADO SHERIFF
(06-17-61)

WRITER: John Meston
DIRECTOR: Jesse Hibbs
CAST: Robert Karnes, Wright King,
             Kelton Garwood, Wayne West

NOTES: Final half-hour episode. Woodrow Chambliss, who later portrays Dodge City storekeeper Lathrop, appears as a telegrapher whom Matt addresses as Milt, although the closing credits identify him as Myles. Kelton Garwood later changed his name to Jonathan Harper, then John Harper, and went on to play Dodge City undertaker Percy Crump in a total of nine episodes.

EPISODE GUIDE

SEASON 7
September 30, 1961–May 26, 1962

#234: PERCE
(09-30-61)

WRITER: John Meston
DIRECTOR: Harry Harris, Jr.
CAST: Ed Nelson, Chuck Bail, Norma Crane,
             Kenneth Lynch, Robert Brubaker, James Nusser,
             John Mitchum, Chuck Hayward, Baynes Barron,
             Alex Sharp, Ted Jordan

Perce McCall helps Matt fight a band of outlaws, but will not take the marshal's advice to stay away from a particular Long Branch saloon girl.

NOTES: First hour-long episode, but the fourth to be filmed. Writer and Director credits now listed before each episode. Chester refers to Doc as their "star moocher" when Matt asks if there is any coffee left. First appearances of Glenn Strange as barkeep Sam (with a large moustache and unbilled) and James Nusser as Louie Pheeters, said to have been a friend of Perce's in Arizona. Robert Brubaker back as stage driver Jim Buck, Mathew McCue in his third (of 28) appearance as silent Delmonico waiter Joe. Ted Jordan, later freight agent Nathan Burke, plays Del.

Ed Nelson, Norma Crane, Arness in "Perce," 1961

#235: OLD YELLOW BOOTS
(10-07-61)

WRITER: John Meston
DIRECTOR: Ted Post
CAST: Warren Stevens, Joan Linville,
             Dean Stanton, Steve Brodie, Bing Russell

A boot print is all Matt has to go on when a rancher is murdered.

NOTES: Kitty is amused when Matt remarks that he did not think there were any single women left in Dodge City. First barn dance of the series. Dabbs Greer back as storekeeper Wilbur Jonas. Second of James Nusser's 72 episodes as Louie Pheeters.

#236: MISS KITTY
(10-14-61)

WRITER: Kathleen Hite
DIRECTOR: Harry Harris, Jr.
CAST: Roger Mobley, Harold Stone,
            Linda Watkins, John Lasell, Frank Sutton,
            Joseph Breen, Andy Albin

Kitty sneaks out of Dodge in the dead of night to meet a stage-coach carrying a young boy.

NOTES: This episode a showcase for Amanda Blake, who gets to wear pants for the first time, drive a wagon by herself, gather eggs, and blast an outlaw with a shotgun. Kitty tells Matt no one knows her as well as he does. Another amusing encounter between Chester and Wilbur Jonas. George Selk back as stableman Moss Grimmick.

#237: HARPER'S BLOOD
(10-21-61)

WRITER: John Meston
DIRECTOR: Andrew McLaglen
CAST: Peter Whitney, Dan Stafford,
            Conlan Carter, Moira Turner,
            Evan Evans, Warren Kemmerling

A stern rancher is convinced that both of his sons have inherited the negative traits of their notorious great-grandfather.

NOTES: Part of Dodge has been constructed at the filming location known as Conejo Flats. As in "Kangaroo," Peter Whitney again beats a son on Front Street.

#238: ALL THAT
(10-28-61)

WRITER: John Meston
DIRECTOR: Harry Harris, Jr.
CAST: John Larch, Buddy Ebsen, Frances Helm,
              Harry Lauter, Guy Raymond

A rancher loses everything and becomes a gold prospector, returning to Dodge with a partner and claiming to have made a big strike.

NOTES: First episode with Harold Innocent as bank clerk William. Harry Swoger returns as Delmonico owner Hank Green. Gage Clarke portrays Mr. Botkin this time.

#239: LONG, LONG TRAIL
(11-04-61)

WRITER: Kathleen Hite
DIRECTOR: Andrew McLaglen
CAST: Barbara Lord, Alan Baxter, Mabel Albertson,
              Peggy Stewart

Matt develops an attraction for the woman he reluctantly agrees to escort to Fort Wallace, 150 miles from Dodge.

NOTES: An Indian shoots Matt in his left arm. Matt says his first horse was a paint pony named Tortilla and liked to eat beans. One of the best episodes of the series.

Arness and Barbara Lord in "Long, Long Trail," 1961

#240: THE SQUAW
(11-11-61)

WRITER: John Dunkel
DIRECTOR: Gerald H. Mayer
CAST: John Dehner, Vitina Marcus, Paul Carr

The bigoted son of a wealthy rancher is appalled when his widowed father marries an Arapahoe woman.

NOTES: Another strong story of racial prejudice. The episode title was used again for a 1975 episode.

#241: CHESTERLAND
(11-18-61)

WRITER: Kathleen Hite
DIRECTOR: Ted Post
CAST: Sondra Kerr, Earle Hodgins, Harold Innocent, Arthur Peterson, Jr., Sarah Selby

Chester finally lands a prospective bride and attempts to transform a patch of scrubland into his vision of Paradise.

NOTES: Dennis Weaver regarded this Emmy-worthy episode, a major showcase for Chester, as one of his favorites. When Chester says he is going to be a farmer, Matt tells him his job will always be waiting for him. Doc brings Chester food on the pretense that he has too much. Kitty reminds Doc that he is "the local health officer." Sarah Selby makes the first of thirteen appearances as boarding house owner Ma Smalley.

#242: MILLY
(11-25-61)

STORY: Hal Moffett
TELEPLAY: John Meston
DIRECTOR: Richard Whorf
CAST: Jena Engstrom, Billy Hughes, Malcom Atterbury, Sue Randall, Don Dubbins

A young girl with a good-for-nothing father goes to Dodge in search of a husband to give her and her brother a better life.

NOTES: Amusing scene of Doc finding Chester practicing duck calls in the jailhouse. Harry Swoger appears as a farmer rather than Delmonico owner Hank Green.

Sondra Kerr & Weaver in "Chesterland," 1961

#243: INDIAN FORD
(12-02-61)

WRITER: John Dunkel
DIRECTOR: Andrew McLaglen
CAST: R.G. Armstrong, Pippa Scott, Robert Dix,
              Roy Roberts, Anthony Caruso, John Newton,
              Lane Chandler, Dawn Little Sky

Matt and Chester join an army troop attempting to secure the freedom of a white woman taken captive by a tribe of Arapahoe.

NOTES: Mountain man Gabe (Chandler) is yet another friend from Matt's past. Fancy bunting hangs from the balcony of the Long Branch. Henry Tabor is played by Roy Roberts, later cast as banker Botkin in sixteen episodes. Pippa Scott was a regular cast member for the first season of *The Virginian*. First hour-long episode filmed.

#244: APPRENTICE DOC
(12-09-61)

WRITER: Kathleen Hite
DIRECTOR: Harry Harris, Jr.
CAST: Ben Cooper, Crahan Denton, Robert Sorrells

An outlaw with a feel for medicine asks Doc to mentor him, but the young man's partners have other plans.

NOTES: Kitty chokes on her beer when Chester claims he is the last one to meddle in anyone's business. Doc says, "The cause of medicine always advances in time of war." Matt, watching Doc ride away, remarks, "We could use another one like you, old boy." Another outstanding episode written by Kathleen Hite.

#245: NINA'S REVENGE
(12-16-61)

WRITER: John Meston
DIRECTOR: Tay Garnett
CAST: Lois Nettleton, William Windom, Ron Foster,
              Glenn Strange, Johnny Seven

A rancher schemes to frame his wife and a hired hand in an extortion plot.

Blake, Warren Oates, Taylor McPeters in "Marry Me, 1961

NOTES: Chester claims he gets dizzy spells if he goes too long without eating. Doc mentions Dan Binny, owner of the Dodge City billiard parlor.

#246: MARRY ME
(12-23-61)

WRITER:	Kathleen Hite
DIRECTOR:	Dennis Weaver
CAST:	Don Dubbins, Warren Oates, Taylor McPeters, Glenn Strange

A trio of hill folk kidnap Kitty so she can marry the oldest son.

NOTES: Memorable shot of the four stars walking away at the episode's conclusion.

#247: A MAN A DAY
(12-30-61)

WRITER: John Meston
DIRECTOR: Harry Harris, Jr.
CAST: Val Dufour, Fay Spain, Leonard Nimoy

A gang of outlaws intent on robbing a shipment of gold vow to kill one man every day Matt remains in Dodge City.

NOTES: The portrait of "Pharaoh's Horses" which once hung in Doc's office is now in Kitty's backroom. Billiard parlor owner Dan Binny (Ben Wright) is shown for the first time. Leonard Nimoy played Mr. Spock on the original *Star Trek* series.

#248: THE DO-BADDER
(01-06-62)

WRITER: John Meston
DIRECTOR: Andrew McLaglen
CAST: Abraham Sofaer, Strother Martin, Warren Oates,
             Mercedes Shirley, Adam Williams, Roy Engel,
             Harry Bartell

Harvey Easter, a self-righteous prospector, comes to Dodge City and proceed to wreak havoc in his attempts to "clean up" the town.

NOTES: Doc says Louie Pheeters has been on a diet of whiskey for twenty years. Shug Fisher plays a saloon owner Harry Obie for the first time.

#249: LACEY
(01-13-62)

WRITER: Kathleen Hite
DIRECTOR: Harry Harris, Jr.
CAST: Sherry Jackson, Jeremy Slate, Dorothy Green,
              Oliver McGowan, Norah Hayden

When Lacey Parcher confesses to killing her father, Matt has no choice but to put the young woman behind bars.

NOTES: First of nine episodes guest starring the late Jeremy Slate. Sherry Jackson co-starred with Danny Thomas on the sitcom *Make Room for Daddy*.

#250: CODY'S CODE
(01-20-62)

WRITER: John Meston
DIRECTOR: Andrew McLaglen
CAST: Anthony Caruso, Robert Knapp, Gloria Talbott,
              Wayne Rogers

One of Dodge's upstanding residents gives refuge to a young outlaw who become's attracted to the man's intended bride.

NOTES: Anthony Caruso appeared in dozens of television Westerns, including five episodes of *Gunsmoke*. Wayne Rogers was a regular on *Stagecoach West* and *M*A*S*H*.

#251: OLD DAN
(01-27-62)

WRITER: Kathleen Hite
DIRECTOR: Andrew McLaglen
CAST: Edgar Buchanan, Philip Coolidge,

Gloria Talbott & Stone in "Cody's Code," 1962

William Campbell, Dabbs Greer, Hugh Sanders,
Dorothy Neumann, Joe Haworth

Doc attempts to help an old drunk kick the habit.

NOTES: The Lady Gay Saloon is the lobby of the Dodge House
redressed. One of Dabbs Greer's more prominent episodes as Wilbur
Jonas.

#252: CATAWOMPER
(02-10-62)

STORY: Gil Favor
TELEPLAY: John Meston
DIRECTOR: Harry Harris, Jr.
CAST: Sue Anne Langdon, Dick Sargent,
                Roy Wright, Frank Sutton, Robert Brubaker,
                Harold Innocent, Quentin Sondergaard,
                Warren Vanders, Joe Devlin, Jay Overholts,
                Robert Gravage

Chester becomes an unwitting pawn in a woman's scheme to get even with her former boyfriend.

NOTES: Amusing performance by Dennis Weaver, who once again gives a guitar lesson. Robert Brubaker appears not as Jim Buck but as a soldier. Harold Innocent plays a character named George rather than bank teller William. One of the weaker episodes of the season.

#253: HALF STRAIGHT
(02-17-62)

WRITER: John Meston
DIRECTOR: Ted Post
CAST: John Kerr, Elizabeth MacRae, William Bramley, J.
                Edward McKinley

A gunman hired to kill Matt falls in love and decides to pass the job along to someone else.

NOTES: Doc suggest Matt and Kitty get married and take up farming. Matt says Kitty would be happier if he ran the general store. Chester is shot in the left arm. Elizabeth MacRae later played April, Festus' love interest.

#254: HE LEARNED ABOUT WOMEN
(02-24-62)

STORY: John Rosser
TELEPLAY: John Meston
DIRECTOR: Tay Garnett
CAST: Barbara Luna, Claude Akins, Robert Wilke,
                Miriam Colon, Ted de Corsia, Jeff De Benning,
                Susan Petrone, Val Ruffino, Andy Romano,
                Joseph Ferrante, Miguel deAnda

Chester is captured by a band of Comancheros but escapes, accompanied by one of their women.

NOTES: Doc tells Chester he does not stop by the jail because the coffee is good, but because it is free. Good mixture of adventure and romance, partially filmed at Vasquez Rocks.

#255: THE GALLOWS
(03-03-62)

WRITER: John Meston
DIRECTOR: Andrew McLaglen
CAST: Jeremy Slate, Joseph Ruskin, Robert J. Stevenson,
                Richard Shannon, James Nusser, Orville Sherman,
                William Chamlee, Nancy Walters, Robert Gravage,
                Ollie O'Toole

Matt does not believe the outlaw who saved his life deserves to hang.

NOTES: According to Jeremy Slate, this outstanding episode was one of James Arness' all-time favorites. The Dodge City telegrapher is called Milt. Second use of Paramount's Virginia City set.

#256: REPRISAL
(03-10-62)

WRITER: John Meston
DIRECTOR: Harry Harris, Jr.
CAST: Dianne Foster, Jason Evers,
             George Lambert, Grace Lee Whitney,
             Tom Reese, Brad Trumbull

A widow woman falls in love with the gunman she hires to kill Matt.

NOTES: Cordelia (Foster) tells Kitty she knows Kitty is "the marshal's girl." Banker Botkin played this time by Harry Antrim. Harold Innocent now a bank clerk named Harold, not William or George. Stock footage from Melody Ranch still being used, although the series was no longer filmed there. Episode title used again in 1969.

#257: COVENTRY
(03-17-62)

WRITER: John Meston
DIRECTOR: Christian Nyby
CAST: Joe Maross, Paul Birch, Mary Field,
             Don Keefer

When a remorseless killer eludes justice, Matt suggests the people of Dodge act as though the man does not exist.

NOTES: Matt to Beard (Maross): "Take my advice and get out of this town." Trial is held in the Long Branch. Another episode featuring divine justice. Harold Innocent plays banker Botkin rather than a teller. Mathew McCue (Delmonico's Joe) gets his one close-up of the series.

#258: THE WIDOW
(03-24-62)

WRITER: John Dunkel
DIRECTOR: Ted Post
CAST: Joan Hackett, J. Edward McKinley,
             Alan Reed, Jr.

Matt warns a young widow against journeying to Indian territory to recover her husband's body.

NOTES: Matt mentions being in the Civil War. Chester has indigestion. A drunken frontier scout slugs Doc and dumps Kitty in a horse trough.

#259: DURHAM BULL
(03-31-62)

STORY: Jack Shettlesworth
TELEPLAY: John Meston
DIRECTOR: Harry Harris, Jr.
CAST: Andy Clyde, Ricky Kelman, John Kellogg, Gilbert
             Green, George Keymas, Ted Jordan, Richard
             Keene, Hank Patterson, George Selk, Howard
             Culver, Ted Jacques, Roger Torrey

An old man and his grandson who own a valuable bull become the target of cattle rustlers.

NOTES: Chester once again suffering from indigestion. Hank Patterson plays a cowboy rather than a stableman. Ted Jordan is one of the outlaws. Richard Keene portrays billiard parlor owner Dan Binny this time.

Arness & Joan Marshall in "Wagon Girls," 1962

#260: WAGON GIRLS
(04-07-62)

WRITER: John Meston
DIRECTOR: Andrew McLaglen
CAST: Arch Johnson, Kevin Hagen, Ellen McRae, Joan
            Marshall, Constance Ford

Matt joins a wagon train of husband-hunting women traveling through hostile Indian country.

NOTES: Kitty says, "I own this place" in reference to the Long Branch, partner Bill Pence apparently long gone. A good Matt Dillon adventure. Ellen McRae is known today as respected actress Ellen Burstyn.

#261: The Dealer
(04-14-62)

WRITER: John Dunkel
DIRECTOR: Harry Harris, Jr.
CAST: Judi Meredith, Gary Clarke, Roy Roberts, George Mathews

Against Matt's advice, Kitty hires a woman to deal faro, unaware that the man who killed the woman's father is on his way to Dodge City.

NOTES: Kitty says Dodge is no longer an all-night town, but was in the early days. Roy Roberts, the future Mr. Botkin of the Dodge bank, plays Billy Baskin. Ted Jordan appears as a Long Branch customer. Gary Clarke was a regular for the first two seasons of *The Virginian*.

#262: The Summons
(04-21-62)

STORY: Marian Clark
TELEPLAY: Kathleen Hite
DIRECTOR: Andrew McLaglen
CAST: Bethel Leslie, John Crawford, Cal Bolder, Robert J. Stevenson

When Matt refuses to give reward money to a gunslinger, the man prevails upon his girlfriend to help him get even with the marshal.

NOTES: Matt travels to Ashland, Kansas. Matt to Bishop (Crawford): "You'd better get on your horse and ride out of Dodge." Like "The Cabin," another episode where a woman gets the notion Matt wants to be her man.

#263: THE DREAMERS
(04-28-62)

WRITER: John Meston
DIRECTOR: Andrew McLaglen
CAST: Liam Redmond, J. Pat O'Malley,
             Valery Allen

Kitty spurns the advances of an old miner who decides to put the Long Branch out of business.

NOTES: First time Kitty puts the Long Branch up for sale. Touching scene where the co-stars offer to pool their money to keep her saloon open. Shug Fisher appears as Obie for the second time. Gage Clarke portrays Mr. Botkin this time.

#264: CALE
(05-05-62)

WRITER: Kathleen Hite
DIRECTOR: Harry Harris, Jr.
CAST: Carl Reindel, Ford Rainey, Robert Karnes, Joseph
             Hamilton, Peter Ashley

Matt comes across an injured young man who is more interested in revenge than the marshal's offer of help.

NOTES: First episode that will have a sequel. Hank Patterson portrays stableman Hank Miller rather than Carl Miller.

#265: CHESTER'S INDIAN
(05-12-62)

WRITER: Kathleen Hite
DIRECTOR: Joseph Sargent
CAST: Jena Engstrom, Karl Swenson, Eddie Little Sky,

Peggy Rea, Lew Brown, Garry Walberg, Michael Barrier, Shug Fisher, Gene Benton

Chester shoots an Indian who has been befriended by a young woman whose father dislikes her spending time with men.

NOTES: Chester leaves Dodge to visit his cousin Thurlow in Kalvesta, Kansas. Third appearance of Shug Fisher as barkeep Obie. Actress Peggy Rea also worked as casting director for *Have Gun-Will Travel* and later played Mrs. Roniger in two episodes of *Gunsmoke*.

#266: THE PRISONER
(05-19-62)

WRITER: Tommy Thompson
DIRECTOR: Andrew McLaglen
CAST: Andrew Prine, Nancy Gates, Conrad Nagel, Ed Nelson, William Phipps

An army officer and his son are determined to exact revenge on one of Matt's prisoners.

NOTES: The army fort at Vasquez Rocks can also be seen in episodes of *Bonanza* and *Star Trek*. This episode title was also used in 1969.

#267: THE BOYS
(05-26-62)

WRITER: John Meston
DIRECTOR: Harry Harris, Jr.
CAST: Malcom Atterbury, George Kennedy, Dean Stanton, Michael Parks, May Heatherly, Arthur Malet

Three men masquerading as Indians attack a stagecoach and kill a young woman, then tell Matt they will help him track down the murderers if he pays them.

NOTES: No Chester in this episode. Harry Swoger back as Delmonico's owner Hank Green. Stunt man Hal Needham plays the stagecoach driver.

Arness & Ruta Lee in "Jenny," 1962

Episode Guide
SEASON 8
September 15, 1962–June 1, 1963

#268: The Search
(09-15-62)

WRITER: Kathleen Hite
DIRECTOR: Harry Harris, Jr.
CAST: Carl Reindel, Ford Rainey, Virginia Gregg,
             Hank Patterson, Raymond Guth, Leonard Nimoy,
             Mike Ragan, Fred Coby, Mickey Morton

Matt encounters a variety of obstacles as he attempts to bring in an injured young man suspected of horse theft.

NOTES: Sequel to last season's "Cale." Chester and Kitty—in pants—go fishing.

#269: Call Me Dodie
(09-22-62)

WRITER: Kathleen Hite
DIRECTOR: Harry Harris, Jr.
CAST: Kathleen Nolan, Mary Patten, Jack Searl, Dianne
             Mountford, Carol Seflinger, Joby Baker

A young woman flees an orphanage run by a cruel brother and sister and becomes the proverbial babe in the woods when she hits Dodge City.

NOTES: No Chester in this episode. The stone house used as the orphanage can also be seen in episodes of *Have Gun-Will Travel, Rawhide, Bonanza, The Westerner* and several other series. Dan Binny of the billiard parlor played this time by Wallace Rooney. Kathleen Nolan co-starred on all but last season of *The Real McCoys*.

#270: QUINT ASPER COMES HOME
(09-29-62)

WRITER: John Meston
DIRECTOR: Andrew McLaglen
CAST: Burt Reynolds, Angela Clarke, William Zuckert, Harry Carey, Jr., Michael Keep, Lane Bradford, Myron Healey, Earle Hodgins, Robert Hinkle, Foster Brooks, Michael Barrier, Henry Beckman, John Vari, James Doohan, Ed Peck, Robert Gravage

Matt takes a liking to wounded half-breed Quint Asper, much to the displeasure of the Dodge City citizens.

NOTES: No Chester in this landmark episode, in which Burt Reynolds joins the series. Main story takes place three years after the character of Quint is introduced. The late James Doohan later achieved popular culture immortality as Scotty on *Star Trek*.

#271: ROOT DOWN
(10-06-62)

WRITER: Kathleen Hite
DIRECTOR: Charles Martin
CAST: Sherry Jackson, John Dehner, Robert Doyle

Chester faces a shotgun wedding when a young woman lies about her relationship with him.

NOTES: Matt to Grudie (Doyle) "Now, you get out of Dodge and stay out. Next time I see you around here, I'll throw you in jail until you dry up." Howard McNear appears as Howard Rudd in Jonas' store. Bartender at the Long Branch is Fred, not Sam.

#272: JENNY
(10-13-62)

WRITER: John Meston
DIRECTOR: Andrew McLaglen
CAST: Ruta Lee, Ron Hayes, John Duke, James Nusser,
            Barry Cahill, Ken Hudgins, Monte Montana, Jr.

Matt must contend with the girlfriend of an outlaw he has thrown in jail.

NOTES: First look at the room Matt keeps away from the office. First appearance of Burt Reynold's as the Dodge City blacksmith. Again, no Chester in sight.

#273: COLLIE'S FREE
(10-20-62)

WRITER: Kathleen Hite
DIRECTOR: Harry Harris, Jr.
CAST: Jason Evers, Jacqueline Scott, James Halferty,
            William Bramley

A resentful ex-con blames Matt in particular for the trouble he has adjusting to life out of prison.

NOTES: Matt shown delivering a prisoner to Kansas State Prison for the first time. No Chester. Jason Evers later co-starred on *The Guns of Will Sonnett*.

#274: THE DITCH
(10-27-62)

WRITER: Les Crutchfield
DIRECTOR: Harry Harris, Jr.
CAST: Joan Linville, Christopher Dark,
            Jay Lanin, Dehl Berti, Hardie Albright,
            Ted Jordan, Gail Bonney, Miguel deAnda

A woman rancher hires a gunman to protect her interests when neighboring ranchers object to her changing the route of the creek running through her land.

NOTES: Matt and Chester mention a Judge Blake. Long Branch bartender is again Fred, not Sam.

#275: THE TRAPPERS
(11-03-62)

WRITER: John Dunkel
DIRECTOR: Andrew McLaglen
CAST: Strother Martin, Richard Shannon, Doris
            Singleton, Robert Lowery, Lane Chandler, Chal
            Johnson, Robert Brubaker

A fur trapper leaves his wounded partner behind and heads for Dodge, where he becomes the target of two con artists.

NOTES: No Chester. Glenn Strange back in the Long Branch as Sam.

#276: PHOEBE STRUNK
(11-10-62)

WRITER: John Meston
DIRECTOR: Andrew McLaglen
CAST: Virginia Gregg, Joan Freeman,

Don Megowan, Dick Peabody,
Gregg Palmer, Harry Raybould

Matt and Quint track a mean-spirited woman and her four sons after they kidnap a young woman.

NOTES: Matt mentions Judge Brooking. No Chester or Kitty. Dick Peabody (Simsie) was also portraying G.I. Little John on the *Combat!* series at this time.

#277: THE HUNGER
(11-17-62)

WRITER: Jack Curtis
DIRECTOR: Harry Harris, Jr.
CAST: Elen Willard, Robert Middleton,
            Hampton Fancher, Linda Watkins, Joe Flynn,
            Sarah Selby, Byron Foulger, Kelton Garwood,
            Henrietta Moore, Robert McQuain, Sue Casey

A grateful young woman falls in love with Doc after he and Matt rescue her from her abusive family.

NOTES: Essentially a Doc story featuring another fine job by Milburn Stone. No Chester. Matt mentions a Judge Blood. (Apparently all the judges around Dodge had names beginning with the letter B: Bent, Brooking, Brooker, Blood, etc.).

#278: ABE BLOCKER
(11-24-62)

WRITER: John Meston
DIRECTOR: Andrew McLaglen
CAST: Chill Wills, Wright King, Miranda Jones, Harry
            Carey, Jr., Robert Adler, Marshall Reed, Lane
            Bradford, Wallace Rooney, Chuck Roberson

Arness & Chill Wills in "Abe Blocker," 1962

Matt is forced to go after an old friend, a mountain man determined to rid the prairie of encroaching settlers.

NOTES: No Chester or Doc. Standout performance by veteran character actor Chill Wills as the title character.

Blake & Claude Akins in "The Way It Is," 1962

#279: THE WAY IT IS
(12-01-62)

WRITER: Kathleen Hite
DIRECTOR: Harry Harris, Jr.
CAST: Claude Akins, Garry Walberg, Virginia Lewis,
             Duane Grey, George Selk, Bob Murphy

Upset with Matt for breaking yet another engagement, Kitty rides off to see some friends and comes across an injured man to whom she is attracted.

NOTES: Kitty to Matt, Doc and Chester: "I'm through being one of the boys." Sam to Kitty regarding Matt: "He's an awful good man to have around." Kitty: "He's the best." First time Kitty truly angered by her erratic relationship with Matt.

#280: Us Haggens
(12-08-62)

WRITER: Les Crutchfield
DIRECTOR: Andrew McLaglen
CAST: Ken Curtis, Denver Pyle, Elizabeth MacRae, Billy Hughes, Howard Wright

Matt and Festus Haggen track down Festus' outlaw uncle and the young woman with whom he is on the run.

NOTES: Another landmark episode this season, introducing both Ken Curtis as Festus Haggen and Elizabeth MacRae as his eventual girlfriend April, though neither will join the series until the next season. Matt shot in the left arm once again. Festus mentions having a dead brother named Jeff and a twin brother named Fergus, killed by his uncle. April from a farm in west Texas. No Chester or Kitty.

#281: Uncle Sunday
(12-15-62)

WRITER: John Meston
DIRECTOR: Joseph Sargent
CAST: Henry Beckman, Joyce Bulifant, Ed Nelson

Chester learns that his uncle has come to Dodge intending to rob the bank.

NOTES: Chester and Doc sing! Uncle Sunday originally from Texas.

#282: FALSE FRONT
(12-22-62)

STORY: Hal Moffett
TELEPLAY: John Meston
CAST: William Windom, Andrew Prine, Art Lund,
              Charles Fredericks, Shary Marshall, Wallace
              Rooney, Robert Fortier, Brett King, K.L. Smith,
              William Bryant, Roy Thinnes, Michael Mikler

Matt's livelihood is threatened by a politician who feels Dodge can do without a marshal, not to mention a would-be gunman who is a pawn in a scheme devised by two city slickers.

NOTES: Episode begins in Kansas City, Kansas. The senator tells Matt he is trying to save money for the Department of the Interior (although Matt works for the War Department) and says Matt can have "a good, safe job" back East. No Chester. Last of Robert Brubaker's fourteen appearances as stage driver Jim Buck.

#283: OLD COMRADE
(12-29-62)

WRITER: John Dunkel
DIRECTOR: Harry Harris, Jr.
CAST: J. Pat O'Malley, Frank Sutton, Ralph Moody

The friend of General Marston is saddened to discover that the general's son is the town clown of Dodge City.

NOTES: Wayne Treadway plays Delmonico owner Hank Green. Roy Roberts, later banker Botkin, plays Dodge House owner Mr. Dobie. Frank Sutton is best remembered as Sgt. Carter on the sitcom *Gomer Pyle, U.S.M.C.* Ted Jordan has a bit role.

#284: LOUIE PHEETERS
(01-05-63)

WRITER: John Meston
DIRECTOR: Harry Harris, Jr.
CAST: John Larkin, Larry Ward,
             Gloria McGhee, James Nusser,
             Woodrow Parfrey

Town drunk Louie Pheeters makes the mistake of telling some murderers he saw what they did but thinks it was just a dream.

NOTES: James Nusser's eighth appearance as Louie Pheeters, as well as his largest to date. Matt calls Louie one of Doc's "drinking buddies" and offers to let Louie help clean up around the jail if he gives up drinking. Matt shot in the left arm yet again. No Chester or Sam. Ted Jordan plays a character called Gus Thompson.

#285: THE RENEGADES
(01-12-63)

WRITER: John Meston
DIRECTOR: Andrew McLaglen
CAST: Audrey Dalton, Ben Wright,
             Jack Lambert, Donald Barry,
             John Pickard

Quint finds himself stranded in Indian territory with a woman prejudiced against Indians, including half-breeds such as Quint.

NOTES: Chester receives a letter from his brother Magnus. Kitty claims she cannot cook. Bob Steele, veteran of B-Westerns, plays Sam Gordon.

Arness & Reynolds on the set of "The Renegades," 1963

#286: COTTER'S GIRL
(01-19-63)

WRITER: Kathleen Hite
DIRECTOR: Harry Harris, Jr.
CAST: Mariette Hartley, Roy Barcroft, John Clarke,
            Jesslyn Fax, Sarah Selby

A young woman with several rough edges mistakes Matt's concern for love.

NOTES: This episode was reportedly one of James Arness' favorites. When Clarey (Hartley) says it is hard to leave Matt be, Kitty replies, "Takes years of practice." Impressive, natural performance by Mariette Hartley, who remembers that it took hours to film the scene with her, Arness and Weaver in Delmonico's because they all kept cracking up.

#287: THE BAD ONE
(01-26-63)

WRITER:	Gwen Bagni Gielgud
DIRECTOR:	Charles Martin
CAST:	Chris Robinson, Dolores Sutton, Booth Colman, Dabbs Greer, Michael Mikler, Ken Kenopka, Gil Lamb, Sue Casey, Robert Gravage

When a young woman begins seeing a stagecoach bandit, her strict father is less than pleased.

NOTES: Matt to Jett (Robinson): "You're through in Dodge. You've got until tomorrow morning to get out of town." No Chester or Doc.

#288: THE COUSIN
(02-02-63)

STORY:	Marian Clark
TELEPLAY:	Kathleen Hite
DIRECTOR:	Harry Harris, Jr.
CAST:	Michael Forest, Gloria Talbott, John Anderson, Joseph Perry

An ex-con who knew Matt when they were both very young takes advantage of their friendship in order to carry out a robbery.

NOTES: Rare reference to Matt's childhood. Matt and Chance (Forest), whom Matt used to call Runt, were orphans raised by the same folks on a ranch in Texas. The last time they saw each other Matt was seventeen, Chance ten.

#289: Shona
(02-09-63)

WRITER: John Meston
DIRECTOR: Ted Post
CAST: Miriam Colon, Robert Bray, John Crawford,
            Robert Palmer, Bart Burns

Quint and Kitty shield an ailing Indian woman from the bigoted citizens of Dodge City.

NOTES: Kitty tells Quint the Long Branch "was made to stay open 24 hours as long as there's one customer." Quint and Shona (Colon) knew each other as children in the same Comanche tribe. Sign for a Chinese laundry at the bottom of Doc's stairway. Roy Roberts as the Dodge House's Mr. Dobie in this episode. No Chester.

#290: Ash
(02-16-63)

WRITER: John Meston
DIRECTOR: Harry Harris, Jr.
CAST: John Dehner, Anthony Caruso, Dee Hartford,
            Adam West, Sheldon Allman, William Fawcett,
            Robert Bice, Richard Bartell, Michael Mikler

Dodge businessman Ash Farior (Caruso) must step in after his partner sustains a severe blow to the head and begins bothering another man's woman.

NOTES: John Dehner (Galt) appeared in a dozen episodes. Adam West is best remembered as television's *Batman*.

Anthony Caruso, Dee Hartford & Arness in "Ash," 1963

#291: Blind Man's Bluff
(02-23-63)

WRITER: John Meston
DIRECTOR: Ted Post
CAST: Will Hutchins, Crahan Denton, Herbert Lytton,
            John Alderson, Gregg Palmer, Judson Pratt

With his eyesight affected following a fight, Matt's only hope in a hostile town is a young man accused of murder.

NOTES: Matt mentions Judge Brooking, whom Kitty calls "the hanging judge." Another use of Paramount's Virginia City set for the town of Elkader. Ted Jordan appears as a drunken cowboy. Will Hutchins starred as the title character in the underrated *Sugarfoot* series for four seasons. No Chester. Episode title used again in 1972.

#292: QUINT'S INDIAN
(03-02-63)

STORY: Marian Clark
TELEPLAY: John Meston
DIRECTOR: Fred H. Jackman
CAST: Will Corry, James Brown,
              Patrick McVey, James Griffith

After being roughed up for something he did not do, Quint decides he has had enough of Dodge City.

NOTES: Shug Fisher appears again as Obie, the bartender of the Oasis Saloon. James Brown played Lt. Masters on *The Adventures of Rin Tin Tin.* No Chester.

#293: ANYBODY CAN KILL A MARSHAL
(03-09-63)

WRITER: Kathleen Hite
DIRECTOR: Harry Harris, Jr.
CAST: Milton Selzer, Warren Stevens,
              James Westerfield, Brenda Scott,
              Joyce Van Patten

When Matt is forced to shoot the otherwise harmless old man who tried to kill him, he is determined to learn who was behind the attempt.

NOTES: After Matt makes light of Kitty's concern for his safety, she says, "You make me sick!" not once, but twice. Howard McNear appears as store clerk Howard. No Chester.

#294: TWO OF A KIND
(03-16-63)

WRITER: Merwin Gerard
DIRECTOR: Andrew McLaglen
CAST: Richard Jaeckel, Michael Higgins,
            Kent Smith, Gary Walberg, Ben Wright,
            John Mitchum, Earle Hodgins,
            Bee Tompkins

Matt obtains a court order declaring that two feuding partners are responsible for one another's life.

NOTES: Earle Hodgins plays Judge Brooking. No Chester. Both Sam and Freddy tend bar at the Long Branch. No Chester.

#295: I CALL HIM WONDER
(03-23-63)

WRITER: Kathleen Hite
DIRECTOR: Harry Harris
CAST: Ron Hayes, Edmund Vargus, Sandy Kenyon,
            Leonard Nimoy, Duane Grey, Harry Bartell,
            William Zuckert, Eddie Little Sky, Alex Sharp,
            George Selk, Gilman Rankin

An Indian boy refuses to get along with anyone except a shiftless cowboy who takes the orphan under his wing.

NOTES: Episode begins in Caldwell, Kansas. Chester says Dodge is getting too overcrowded, and that he likes to get away from town. Episode had a sequel many years later in Season Thirteen.

#296: WITH A SMILE
(03-30-63)

STORY: Bud Furillo
TELEPLAY: John Meston
DIRECTOR: Andrew McLaglen
CAST: R.G. Armstrong, James Best, Dick Foran,
             Linden Chiles, Sharon Farrell, Dan Stafford

An army major must accept the fact that his outwardly cocky son is really a sad excuse for a human being after the young man murders a woman and expects to avoid hanging.

NOTES: There is a map on the wall behind Matt's desk for the first time. Solid episode with another surprise ending.

#297: THE FAR PLACES
(04-06-63)

WRITER: John Dunkel
DIRECTOR: Harry Harris, Jr.
CAST: Angela Clarke, Rees Vaughn,
             Bennye Gatteys

Matt becomes involved when a prospective buyer for a woman's ranch is chased away by her son.

NOTES: Freddy tends bar at the Long Branch instead of Sam.

#298: PANACEA SYKES
(04-13-63)

WRITER: Kathleen Hite
DIRECTOR: William Conrad
CAST: Nellie Burt, Dan Tobin, Charles Watts,
             Lindsay Workman, Charlie Briggs, John Clarke,

Nellie Burt & Blake in "Panacea Sykes, 1963

Jan Brooks, Carl Prickett, Charles Seel,
Robert Nash, John Lawrence, Ollie O'Toole

A petty thief who helped raise Kitty in New Orleans tells her fellow stage passengers she is Kitty's mother.

NOTES: Episode beings in Park City, Kansas. Directed by William Conrad, radio's Matt Dillon and best remembered as television's Cannon. The map behind Matt's desk is gone. Charles Seel later played Dodge City telegrapher Barney. No billing for Glenn Strange. No Chester.

#299: TELL CHESTER
(04-20-63)

WRITER: Frank Paris
DIRECTOR: Joseph Sargent
CAST: Mitzi Hoag, Lonny Chapman, Jo Helton

Chester is disgusted when he discovers that a former girlfriend has married a man who already has a wife.

NOTES: Part of episode takes place in Garden City, Kansas. Doc and Kitty dance with each other. Chester shot in left shoulder. Interesting story with good ending.

#300: QUINT-CIDENT
(04-27-63)

WRITER: Kathleen Hite
DIRECTOR: Andrew McLaglen
CAST: Mary La Roche, Ben Johnson, Don Keefer, Catherine McLeod

A vengeful widow tells Matt that Quint attacked her.

NOTES: Matt has a rowdy fistfight with Crown (Johnson) lasting nearly a full minute. Map back on the jailhouse wall. No Chester.

#301: OLD YORK
(05-04-63)

WRITER: John Meston
DIRECTOR: Harry Harris, Jr.
CAST: Edgar Buchanan, H.M. Wynant, Robert Knapp, Michael Constantine, Roy Roberts, Edward Madden, Howard Culver, Dorothy Neumann, Lou Krugman, Don Spruance, Robert S. White

An aging outlaw from Matt's past thinks their friendship will make it easy for him and a partner to rob the Dodge City Bank.

NOTES: Episode begins with a flashback to Redwater, Texas, 1858, when Matt was only eighteen-years-old. Years later, when Matt decides to hand in his resignation, the date is May 8, 1875. First of Roy Roberts' sixteen appearances as banker Botkin, later spelled Bodkin.

#302: DADDY WENT AWAY
(05-11-63)

STORY: John Rosser
TELEPLAY: Kathleen Hite
DIRECTOR: Joseph Sargent
CAST: Mary Carver, Suzanne Cupito,
             William Schallert

It looks as if Chester has finally found romance when he befriends a seamstress and her young daughter, but he learns he has taken on more entanglement than he bargained for.

NOTES: Kitty says she does not know if she can handle another of Chester's romances. Kitty to Lucy (Carver): "He's Chester. His friends learn to take him the way he is. And to love him. 'Cause there's no way in the world to understand him." Chester mentions both Uncle Sunday and brother Magnus. Dress shop is former freight office set.

#303: THE ODYSSEY OF JUBAL TANNER
(05-18-63)

WRITER: Paul Savage
DIRECTOR: Andrew McLaglen
CAST: Beverly Garland, Peter Breck, Denver Pyle,
             Gregg Palmer, Kevin Hagen

Cowboy Jubal Tanner is attracted to saloon girl Leah Brunson, unaware that the same man who stole his horse murdered Leah's fiancée.

NOTES: Coincidentally, guest star Peter Breck appeared in another episode with this exact title in October, 1965, when co-starring on *The Big Valley*. No Chester.

#304: JEB
(05-25-63)

WRITER: Paul Savage
DIRECTOR: Harry Harris, Jr.
CAST: James Hampton, Roy Thinnes, Emile Genest

A good natured young rancher is accused of stealing a horse he found loose on the prairie.

NOTES: Matt mentions barber Frank Teeters for the first time in years. Third episode to have a sequel. No Chester.

#305: THE QUEST FOR ASA JANIN
(06-01-63)

WRITER: Paul Savage
DIRECTOR: Andrew McLaglen
CAST: Anthony Caruso, Richard Devon,
            Gene Darfler, George Keymas, Jack Lambert,
            Harry Carey, Jr., Ed Faulkner

Matt has only a week to track down a murderer a save a friend from the hangman's noose.

NOTES: One of the best episodes of the series. Matt is shot in the left arm and right leg. Shug Fisher appears again as Obie. Rare voice-over narration (by Darfler): "Wearin' that badge ain't the easiest, but it's the right man wearin' it." No Chester.

Gilbert Roland and Arness in "Extradition," 1963

EPISODE GUIDE
SEASON 9
September 28, 1963–June 6, 1964

#306: KATE HELLER
(09-28-63)

WRITER: Kathleen Hite
DIRECTOR: Harry Harris, Jr.
CAST: Mabel Albertson, Tom Lowell,
               Betsy Jones-Moreland

Matt is ambushed and is taken to recover in the home of the young man who shot him.

NOTES: *Gunsmoke* now being filmed CBS Studio Center, the former Republic Studios.

Matt shot in the back and shoulder. The "Pharaoh's Horses" painting once on the wall of Doc's office and later Kitty's, can be seen in Kate's house. Ted Jordan appears as a character named Bo. Tom Lowell was also co-starring on the *Combat!* series at this time. No Chester. Dennis Weaver's last season.

#307: LOVER BOY
(10-05-63)

WRITER: John Meston
DIRECTOR: Andrew McLaglen
CAST: Sheree North, Alan Baxter, Ken Curtis,
               Dorothy Konrad, Richard Coogan

Kyle Kelly, who has a habit of loving and leaving the women he becomes involved with, goes too far when he comes to Dodge and begins an affair with married Avis Fisher.

NOTES: Episode starts in Wichita, Kansas, then picks up in Dodge six months later. Matt is again shot in his left arm. Ken Curtis' last guest appearance before joining the series as Festus. A bald bartender in the Long Branch instead of Sam.

#308: LEGENDS DON'T SLEEP
(10-12-63)

WRITER: Kathleen Hite
DIRECTOR: Harry Harris, Jr.
CAST: William Talman, Scott Marlowe,
             Hope Summers, Robert Bice, Don Haggerty,
             James Nusser, Alan Dexter, Ken Kenopka

A former gunfighter who returns to Dodge after five years in prison is determined to go straight, but a young tough has different ideas.

NOTES: Matt tells two outlaws to "turn right around and ride back out." Brief scene in Olathe, Kansas. William Talman played attorney Hamilton Burger on *Perry Mason*. No Chester.

#309: TOBE
(10-19-63)

WRITER: Paul Savage
DIRECTOR: John W. English
CAST: Harry Townes, Mary La Roche,
             Philip Abbott, L.Q. Jones, Sarah Selby

A down and out farmer feels he has found happiness with a Long Branch saloon girl until her jealous former boyfriend shows up.

NOTES: Chester fills in for Matt, who goes to Abilene. Sam mentions barber Teeters. L.Q. Jones, a semi-regular on *The Virginian*, *Cheyenne* and the final season of *Rawhide*, made seven guest appearances on *Gunsmoke*.

#310: EASY COME
(10-26-63)

WRITER: John Meston
DIRECTOR: Andrew McLaglen
CAST: Andrew Prine, Carl Reindel,
            George Wallace, Charles Briggs

A seemingly benign young man is in reality a cold-blooded killer.

NOTES: Matt and Chester go to Elkader. Shug Fisher portrays Harry at the Bull's Head Saloon rather than Obie of the Oasis. Storekeeper Wib Smith is played by Orville Sherman. Brief appearance by Peggy Rea.

#311: MY SISTER'S KEEPER
(11-02-63)

WRITER: Kathleen Hite
DIRECTOR: Harry Harris, Jr.
CAST: Nancy Wickwire, James Broderick,
            Jennifer Billingsley

A lonely widower unwittingly sets the stage for trouble when he goes to work for an old maid and her pretty young sister.

NOTES: Date on a grave marker in April 7, 1878; episode takes place four months later. Gage Clarke rather than Roy Roberts back as Mr. Botkin. Jennifer Billingsley looks like a refugee from a Malibu beach party rather than a frontier girl.

#312: QUINT'S TRAIL
(11-09-63)

WRITER: Kathleen Hite
DIRECTOR: Harry Harris, Jr.
CAST: Everett Sloane, Sharon Farrell,
               Shirley O'Hara, Don Haggerty,
               Charles Seel

Quint agrees to act and guide for a family headed for Oregon, unaware that their young daughter is mentally disturbed.

NOTES: Chester tries on Matt's extra badge. Map and poster board are switched on the jailhouse wall. North Platte, Nebraska, is the famous Corriganville set.

#313: CARTER CAPER
(11-16-63)

WRITER: John Meston
DIRECTOR: Jerry Hopper
CAST: Jeremy Slate, William Phipps,
               Anjanette Comer, Rayford Barnes,
               Barney Phillips, I. Stanford Jolley,
               George Selk, Michael Fox,
               William Fawcett, Jacque Shelton,
               Dennis Cross

After Billy Hargis beats Joe Stark for attempting to steal his horse, Stark gets even by telling everyone Hargis is a well-known gunslinger.

NOTES: Matt to Carter (Shelton): "I'm gonna have to ask you to leave Dodge. You've caused enough trouble around here already."

#314: EX-CON
(11-30-63)

WRITER: John Meston
DIRECTOR: Thomas Carr
CAST: Jeanne Cooper, John Kellogg,
               Richard Devon, Raymond Guth,
               Howard Wendell, Roy Roberts,
               Harry Lauter, Tommy Alexander

A feverish Matt is suspected of killing an unarmed man who had planned on starting fresh in Dodge after several years in prison.

NOTES: Chester walking a bit less stiff-legged than in early episodes. Roy Roberts back as Mr. Botkin. First appearance by Howard Wendell as Judge Brooking. Stairway of the Dodge House now different than before.

#315: EXTRADITION, PART ONE
(12-07-63)
#316: EXTRADITION, PART TWO
(12-14-63)

WRITER: Antony Ellis
DIRECTOR: John W. English
CAST: Gilbert Roland, Gene Evans,
               Anna Navarro, Rico Alaniz, Alex Montoya,
               Walter Burke, Miguel Landa, Pepe Hern,
               Lisa Seagram, Ricky Vera

Matt tracks a friend's killer to Chupadero, Mexico, where they are both taken prisoner by a crooked army captain.

NOTES: First of the series' thirteen multi-part episodes. Matt's first trip across the U.S./Mexican border.

#317: THE MAGICIAN
(12-21-63)

WRITER: John Kneubuhl
DIRECTOR: Harry Harris, Jr.
CAST: Lloyd Corrigan, Brooke Bundy,
               Barry Kelley, Tom Simcox,
               Sheldon Allman, William Zuckert,
               Ken Tyles

A wealthy rancher accuses a kindly old man of using his skill as a magician to cheat at cards.

NOTES: Freddy back as the Long Branch bartender. Burt Reynolds' twentieth episode as Quint. No Chester.

#318: PA HACK'S BROOD
(12-28-63)

WRITER: Paul Savage
DIRECTOR: Jerry Hopper
CAST: Milton Selzer, Lynn Loring,
               Jim Hampton, Charles Kuenstle,
               George Lindsey, Russell Thorson,
               Marianna Hill

A conniving old drifter decides to take over the Willis ranch and force the owner's son to marry his daughter.

NOTES: A sequel to the previous season's "Jeb." Matt shown going to barber Teeters for the first time in years. George Lindsey is best known for his role as Goober Pyle on *The Andy Griffith Show.* No Chester.

#319: THE GLORY AND THE MUD
(01-04-64)

WRITER: Gwen Bagni Gielgud
DIRECTOR: Jerry Hopper
CAST: Kent Smith, Marsha Hunt,
               James Best, Robert Sorrells,
               Joseph Hamilton, Rick Murray,
               Jenny Lee Arness

A former lawman recently employed by a Wild West show returns to Dodge hoping to resume his relationship with an old flame.

NOTES: Matt tells Doc that Jack Dakota (Smith) was once "the best peace officer on the prairie." Dan Binney of the billiard parlor now played by Joseph Hamilton. The late Jenny Lee Arness was James Arness' daughter.

#320: DRY WELL
(01-11-64)

WRITER: John Meston
DIRECTOR: Harry Harris, Jr.
CAST: Karen Sharpe, Tom Simcox,
               Ned Glass, John Hanek,
               Bill Henry

After Quint witnesses a murder, the killer's father throws him down an empty well.

NOTES: Matt tells Quint he has not had a vacation since becoming marshal of Dodge. No Chester.

Curtis and Arness in "Prairie Wolfer," 1964

#321: PRAIRIE WOLFER
(01-18-64)

WRITER: John Dunkel
DIRECTOR: Andrew V. McLaglen
CAST: Noah Beery, Jr., Don Dubbins,
                     Holly McIntire, Fred Coby, James Drake

Festus Haggen is hired by the Dodge City ranchers to track wolves that have been killing cattle, but he has a good idea who the real culprits are.

NOTES: Ken Curtis joins the series on a regular basis. One of only two episodes to feature both Chester and Festus, who claims he does not know his exact age. Orville Sherman appears again as storekeeper Wib Smith. Episode title used again in 1967.

#322: FRIEND
(01-25-64)

WRITER: Kathleen Hite
DIRECTOR: Harry Harris, Jr.
CAST: Tom Reese, George Keymas, Jan Shepard, Ben
            Wright, Butch Patrick, Frank Kreig, Ralph Moody

After being reunited with an old friend who once saved his life, Matt learns that he has been killed in the town of Friend, Kansas.

NOTES: Matt mentions being marshal "about eight years" and that ten years earlier he had intended to become a rancher. Door to the right of the Long Branch bar is revealed to be a washroom. Interesting episode with unpredictable ending.

#323: ONCE A HAGGEN
(02-01-64)

WRITER: Les Crutchfield
DIRECTOR: Andrew McLaglen
CAST: Slim Pickens, Elizabeth MacRae,
            Kenneth Tobey, Roy Barcroft, John Hudson

Festus' friend Bucko is framed for the murder of a man who beat them in a poker game.

NOTES: Ken Curtis, who once replaced Frank Sinatra in Tommy Dorsey's band, sings. Second of only two episodes with both Festus and Chester. Elizabeth MacRae reprises her role as April. Howard Wendell returns as Judge Brooking.

#324: No Hands
(02-08-64)

WRITER: John Meston
DIRECTOR: Andrew McLaglen
CAST: Strother Martin, Denver Pyle, Kevin Hagen,
            Rayford Barnes, Conlan Carter, Wright King,
            Orville Sherman, Shug Fisher, Mark Murray

A family of worthless drifters breaks the hand of a carpenter then leaves him to die on the prairie.

NOTES: Matt to Pa Ginnis (Pyle): "I want you to get out of Dodge, and I don't want to see you, or him, or any of your sons around here ever again." Shug Fisher at the Oasis Saloon, but as Pete instead of Obie. No Chester.

#325: May Blossom
(02-15-64)

WRITER: Kathleen Hite
DIRECTOR: Andrew McLaglen
CAST: Lauri Peters, Charles Gray, Richard X. Slattery,
            Roger Torrey, Sarah Selby

Festus hunts down the man responsible for having his way with Festus' cousin May Blossom, who has come to Dodge from Texas.

NOTES: First of many Haggen relatives to visit Dodge City. Charles Gray replaced Sheb Wooley on *Rawhide*.

#326: The Bassops
(02-22-64)

WRITER: Tom Hanley
DIRECTOR: Andrew McLaglen

CAST: Robert Wilke, Warren Oates, Enuice Pollis
Christopher, Mickey Sholdar, James Griffith,
Ollie O'Toole, Robert Bice, Patricia Joyce

A family crossing the prairie comes across Matt handcuffed to a prisoner who claims to be the marshal.

NOTES: Quint is shot in the left arm by Kelby (Wilke), whom Matt captures in Tascosa. A particularly solid episode. No Chester.

#327: THE KITE
(02-29-64)

WRITER: John Meston
DIRECTOR: Andrew McLaglen
CAST: Lyle Bettger, Michael Higgins,
Betsy Hale, Allyson Ames

A farmer goes to Dodge in search of the man who murdered his wife, taking along the only witness to the crime—his young daughter.

NOTES: Kitty says Letty (Hale) is the first child that has ever been in the Long Branch. No Chester.

#328: COMANCHES IS SOFT
(03-07-64)

WRITER: Kathleen Hite
DIRECTOR: Harry Harris, Jr.
CAST: Kathy Nolan, Don Megowan, Ted Jordan,
Dean Stanton, Rex Holman

Quint and Festus go Wichita and become involved with a saloon girl who happens to have a jealous brute of a boyfriend.

Kathy Nolan & Curtis on the set of "Comanches is Soft," 1964

NOTES: Festus good naturedly refers to Quint simply as Comanche. A rare episode with no Doc, Kitty or Chester. Ted Jordan appears as a townsman.

#329: FATHER'S LOVE
(03-14-64)

WRITER: John Meston
DIRECTOR: Harry Harris, Jr.
CAST: Ed Nelson, Shary Marshall, Robert F. Simon,
           Anthony Caruso

Saloon girl Cora Prell wants nothing to do with Jesse Price, only to discover later that she has married Jesse's uncle.

NOTES: Episode begins with Matt in a Wichita saloon. Glenn Strange is given more to do than usual as Long Branch bartender Sam. Return of storekeeper Mr. Ross. No Chester or Festus.

#330: NOW THAT APRIL'S HERE
(03-21-64)

WRITER: Les Crutchfield
DIRECTOR: Andrew McLaglen
CAST: Elizabeth MacRae, Royal Dano,
                   Hal Baylor

When April tells Festus and Quint that she has seen a murder, the killers overhear the conversation.

NOTES: Third episode with Festus' girlfriend April. No Chester.

#331: CALEB
(03-28-64)

WRITER: Paul Savage
DIRECTOR: Harry Harris, Jr.
CAST: John Dehner, Ann Loos, Lane Bradford,
                   Dorothy Green, Vickie Cos, Christopher Barrey,
                   Dennis Robertson, Ted Jordan

Destitute farmer Caleb Marr leaves his shrew of a wife and befriends a saloon girl who happens to have a jealous gunslinger for a boyfriend.

NOTES: Sad episode with an outstanding performance by John Dehner. Last of 43 appearances by George Selk as stableman Moss Grimmick. No Chester or Festus.

#332: OWNEY TUPPER HAD A DAUGHTER
(04-04-64)

WRITER: Paul Savage
DIRECTOR: Jerry Hopper
CAST: Jay C. Flippen, Adrea Darvi,
               Noreen Corcoran, James Seay,
               Howard Wendell, Orville Sherman,
               Hank Patterson, Dolores Quinton,
               Vernon Rich, Berkeley Harris,
               Steve Gaynor

After the court judges him to be an unfit father, an widowed farmer offers to act as hangman in order to earn money and get his young daughter back.

NOTES: An especially poignant episode. Hank Patterson takes over from George Selk as operator of the Dodge City livery stable. Howard Wendell appears again as Judge Brooking. No Chester or Kitty.

#333: BENTLY
(04-11-64)

WRITER: John Kneubuhl
DIRECTOR: Harry Harris, Jr.
CAST: Jan Clayton, Charles McGraw,
               June Dayton, Bill Erwin, Gene Lyons

A dying homesteader confesses to a murder Chester is certain he did not commit.

NOTES: A significant episode in that it is Dennis Weaver's last. Chester is targeted for murder, and is last seen walking down the boardwalk of Front Street toward the railroad depot. No mention that he will never be seen again.

#334: Kitty Cornered
(04-18-64)

WRITER: Kathleen Hite
DIRECTOR: John Brahm
CAST: Jacqueline Scott, Shug Fisher,
             Joseph Sirola

Stella Damon, whose saloon in Pueblo burned to the ground, arrives in Dodge intent on opening an even grander place—and driving the Long Branch out of business.

NOTES: Festus to Stella: "I do as little as I can, and mostly what I please." Kitty calls Doc "Curly" for the first time. Festus calls Matt "Matthew" for the first time. Festus makes use of the level he acquired in the episode "May Blossom." Shug Fisher is again Obie in the Oasis Saloon.

#335: The Promoter
(04-25-64)

WRITER: John Meston
DIRECTOR: Andrew McLaglen
CAST: Vic Perrin, Allen Case, Robert Fortier,
             Wilheim Von Homburg, Peggy Stewart,
             John Newman, Larry Blake

Penniless Henry Huckaby thinks staging a prizefight between a German immigrant and a black soldier is the key to finally making his fortune.

NOTES: Matt to Shell (Blake): "I want you on the next stage. You know, I threw you out of town last year, I threw you out of town the year before. Don't you ever get tired of coming back here?"

#336: Trip West
(05-02-64)

WRITER: John Dunkel
DIRECTOR: Harry Harris, Jr.
CAST: Herbert Anderson, Vinton Hayworth,
            Sharon Farrell, H.M. Wynant,
            Percy Helton, Elizabeth Shaw,
            Henry Rowland, Angela Clarke

Convinced he has only three months to live, a timid bank clerk quits his job and moves to Dodge City to enjoy the time he believes he has left.

NOTES: Except for a brief opening scene with Doc and Festus, no regular cast members appear for more than twenty minutes into the story. Herbert Anderson played the father on the sitcom *Dennis the Menace*.

#337: Scot Free
(05-09-64

WRITER: Kathleen Hite
DIRECTOR: Harry Harris, Jr.
CAST: Patricia Owens, Jay Lanin, Anne Barton

Matt and Chester discover the dead body of Nora Brand's husband, but she claims she does not recognize the man.

NOTES: Barkeep Freddy, not Sam, tends the Long Branch bar.

#338: The Warden
(05-16-64)

WRITER: Les Crutchfield
DIRECTOR: Andrew McLaglen

CAST: Julie Parrish, Anthony Caruso,
                 George Kennedy, Christopher Connelly

Festus rescues an Indian girl who has been sold into servitude, only to have her steal his horse and ride away the first chance she gets.

NOTES: Another rare flashback sequence. Ollie O'Toole plays telegrapher Milt.

#339: HOMECOMING
(05-23-64)

STORY: Shimon Wincelberg
TELEPLAY: John Meston
DIRECTOR: Harry Harris, Jr.
CAST: Harold J. Stone, Jack Elam,
                 Phyllis Coates, Tom Lowell

An ex-con returns to his ranch and discovers that his wife has remarried and his son wants nothing to do with him.

NOTES: Story contributor Shimon Wincelberg wrote extensively for *Have Gun-Will Travel*. Second guest appearance by Tom Lowell of *Combat!* this season. Unexpected conclusion. The title was used again for a 1973 episode.

#340: THE OTHER HALF
(05-30-64)

WRITER: John Dunkel
DIRECTOR: Andrew McLaglen
CAST: Lee Kinsolving, Donna J. Anderson,
                 Paul Fix, Patric Knowles

The twin sons of Dodge City's feed storeowner have designs on the same young girl, although she clearly prefers one over the other.

NOTES: Festus sings "Shall We Gather At the River" at a funeral service on Boot Hill. The late Lee Kinsolving also appeared on *Black Saddle, Have Gun-Will Travel, The Rifleman* and *Zane Grey Theatre* during his brief career. Patric Knowles co-starred in the 1941 horror classic *The Wolf Man.*

#341: JOURNEY FOR THREE
(06-06-64)

WRITER: Frank Paris
DIRECTOR: Harry Harris, Jr.
CAST: William Arvin, Michael J. Pollard,
               Mark Goddard, Margaret Bly, Ollie O'Toole

Quint runs into three odd partners on the prairie, one of whom has accidentally killed a young woman.

NOTES: Louie Pheeters to Matt: "I'm not a man of habit, Marshal." Michael J. Pollard was nominated for a Best Supporting Actor Oscar for 1967's *Bonnie and Clyde.* Mark Goddard is known to sci-fi enthusiasts for his role on *Lost in Space.*

EPISODE GUIDE
SEASON 10
September 26, 1964–May 29, 1965

#342: BLUE HEAVEN
(09-26-64)

WRITER: Les Crutchfield
DIRECTOR: Michael O'Herlihy
CAST: Tim O'Connor, Kurt Russell, Diane Ladd,
             Karl Swenson, Jan Merlin, Eddie Hice

Despite being an outlaw on the run, Kip Gilman stops in Dodge to return a young boy to his alcoholic mother.

NOTES: New opening scene with Matt facing his opponent on the obviously phony exterior set of Dodge City's Front Street. Closing theme faster paced. Arness no longer listed as an associate producer. Norman Macdonnell shares production duties with Philip Leacock. Kitty says Rat Hole Alley, south of the railroad tracks, is the bad side of Dodge. Gilman says he knows Catfish Haggen, one of Festus' many cousins.

#343: CROOKED MILE
(10-03-64)

WRITER: Les Crutchfield
DIRECTOR: Andrew V. McLaglen
CAST: Katharine Ross, George Kennedy,
             Royal Dano

Arness & Glenn Corbett in "Chicken," 1964

A prejudiced homesteader calls his family's enforcer when Quint refuses to stop seeing his daughter.

NOTES: Katharine Ross, who appeared in such popular films as *The Graduate* and *Butch Cassidy and the Sundance Kid*, is married to well-known Western actor Sam Elliott, who also guest starred on *Gunsmoke*.

#344: OLD MAN
(10-10-64)

WRITER: John Meston
DIRECTOR: Harry Harris, Jr.
CAST: Ned Glass, Robert Hogan,
            Ed Peck, Rayford Barnes

Matt has a feeling an old man accused of murder is being framed for the crime.

NOTES: Brief flashback scene. Howard Wendell appears again as Judge Lucias C. Brooking.

#345: THE VIOLATORS
(10-17-64)

WRITER: John Dunkel
DIRECTOR: Harry Harris, Jr.
CAST: Denver Pyle, James Anderson, Art Batanides,
            Garry Walberg, Michael Pate

Two men whose partner has been scalped threaten to spark a war between the citizens of Dodge and the Cheyenne.

NOTES: First of two appearances by Denver Pyle as Caleb Nash.

#346: DOCTOR'S WIFE
(10-24-64)

WRITER: George Eckstein
DIRECTOR: Harry Harris, Jr.
CAST: James Broderick, Phyllis Love, Harold Gould,
            Anne Barton, Helen Kleeb, James Nusser,
            Robert Biheller, Dorothy Neumann,
            Howard Culver, Jewel Jaffe, Buck Young

The wife of a new doctor in town attempts to drum up business for her husband by starting a rumor that Doc drinks too much and cannot be trusted to provide quality care.

NOTES: Second guest role for the late James Broderick, father of actor Matthew Broderick.

#347: TAKE HER, SHE'S CHEAP
(10-31-64)

WRITER: Kathleen Hite
DIRECTOR: Harry Harris, Jr.
CAST: Malcom Atterbury, Lauri Peters,
              Willard Sage, Mort Mills, Linda Watkins

A young woman with feelings for Matt leaves her lazy family and heads to Dodge, but is attacked by a man Matt has thrown out of town.

NOTES: Humorous moment when Matt lectures the Carps: "What kind of people are you anyway? You couldn't be born this way—you work at it!" Lauri Peters played Festus' cousin May Blossom in the episode of the same name (#325).

#348: HELP ME, KITTY
(11-07-64)

WRITER: Kathleen Hite
DIRECTOR: Harry Harris, Jr.
CAST: Betty Conner, Jack Elam, James Frawley, Peggy
              Stewart

When the unmarried daughter of one of Kitty's friends discovers she is pregnant, she turns to Kitty for guidance.

NOTES: One of Kitty's ill-fated stagecoach trips. At the end of the episode, Matt says, "I'm proud of you, Kitty." Stage driver Carl played by Joe Conley, better known as shop owner Ike on *The Waltons.*

#349: HUNG HIGH
(11-14-64)

WRITER: John Meston
DIRECTOR: Mark Rydell
CAST: Robert Culp, Harold J. Stone,
             Scott Marlowe, Ed Asner, George Lindsey,
             Elisha Cook, Michael Conrad

Outlaw Joe Costa frames Matt for the hanging of a prisoner yet to be given a trial.

NOTES: First episode with future producer John Mantley as story consultant. Harold J. Stone plays another lawman mentor Matt knew several years ago in Abilene. First time Matt rides bareback. Matt to George (Cook), whom he barely knows: "What do you say we belly up to this bar here and talk about old times or something, huh?" One of the better episodes produced by Philip Leacock rather than Norman Macdonnell.

#350: JONAH HUTCHINSON
(11-21-64)

WRITER: Calvin Clements
DIRECTOR: Harry Harris, Jr.
CAST: Robert F. Simon, Richard Anderson,
             June Dayton

An aging ex-con returns to Dodge and asks his grandson to help him restore his once thriving ranch.

NOTES: Kitty acquired the painting in the Long Branch of the fight at Hutchinson House from a painter paying off a bar tab five years before. Rocky Shahan of *Rawhide* plays the stage driver. First of numerous scripts by Calvin Clements.

#351: BIG MAN, BIG TARGET
(11-28-64)

WRITER: John Mantley
DIRECTOR: Michael O'Herlihy
CAST: Mike Road, Mariette Hartley,
            J.D. Cannon

A wanted man frames a young farmer for horse theft so he can romance the man's wife.

NOTES: Matt is shot in the right arm. Ellie (Hartley) mentions Enoch Miller, a character from an earlier episode. First script by story consultant Mantley.

#352: CHICKEN
(12-05-64)

WRITER: John Meston
DIRECTOR: Andrew V. McLaglen
CAST: Glenn Corbett, Gig Perreau,
            L.Q. Jones, Bob Anderson,
            John Lupton

A cowboy lets the citizens of Dodge mistakenly assume that he killed four outlaws single-handed, a decision he comes to regret.

NOTES: Particularly well-written episode. Future freight office manager Ted Jordan appears unbilled.

#353: INNOCENCE
(12-12-64)

WRITER: John Meston
DIRECTOR: Harry Harris, Jr.
CAST: Bethel Leslie, Claude Akins,
             Michael Forest, Jason Evers

Long Branch saloon girl Elsa Poe stirs up trouble when two cowhands who have eyes for her object to her seeing a Dodge businessman.

NOTES: Quint mentions Moss Grimmick, although Hank Miller has taken over the stable. Matt faces a mob outside the jail for the first time in a long while. Glenn Strange plays fiddle for the first of many times.

#354: AUNT THEDE
(12-19-64)

WRITER: Kathleen Hite
DIRECTOR: Sutton Roley
CAST: Jeanette Nolan, James Stacy,
             Dyan Cannon, Frank Cady,
             Howard McNear, Hap Glaudi,
             Jenny Lee Aurness

Festus' Aunt Thede comes to Dodge in search of a husband, but ends up uniting two young lovers despite the disapproval of the girl's father.

NOTES: The late Jenny Lee Aurness, James Arness' daughter, appears as Laurie, credited with the original spelling of the Arness name.

#355: HAMMERHEAD
(12-26-64)

WRITER: Antony Ellis
DIRECTOR: Chris Nyby
CAST: Arch Johnson, Linda Foster, Chubby Johnson,
               John Fiedler, William Henry, Peter Dunn,
               Don Briggs, Tommy Richards, Ray Hemphill,
               Gene Redfern, Bill Catching, Daniel M. White,
               Chuck Hayward

Festus gets mixed up in a 350-mile horse race from Dodge City to Cheyenne, Wyoming, and Matt figures the high gambling stakes involved will lead to big trouble.

NOTES: Chubby Johnson was a familiar fixture in Westerns ranging from Hollywood's Golden Age all the way through the heyday of the genre on television, guest starring on more than two dozen series.

#356: DOUBLE ENTRY
(01-02-65)

WRITER: Les Crutchfield
DIRECTOR: Joe Sargent
CAST: Forrest Tucker, Cyril Delevanti, Mel Gallagher,
               Lew Brown, Nora Marlowe

Matt is not sure whether an old friend who has come to Dodge is a legitimate businessman or up to no good.

NOTES: Another dance in the Long Branch, with Doc doing the calling and Festus clog dancing. Brad (Tucker) says that when he and Matt rode together on the border of Texas fourteen years before, Matt was the wildest of their old bunch. Good episode with an effective performance by Forrest Tucker.

#357: RUN, SHEEP, RUN
(01-09-65)

WRITER: John Meston
DIRECTOR: Harry Harris, Jr.
CAST: Burt Brinkerhoff, Peter Whitney,
             Davey Davison, Arthur Malet

A rancher who believes he has killed the man who tried to swindle him persuades his wife they have to make a run for it.

NOTES: Louie Pheeters claims he gave up the habit of drinking years ago. Episode strong on irony, much like the half-hour installments.

#358: DEPUTY FESTUS
(01-16-65)

WRITER: Calvin Clements
DIRECTOR: Harry Harris, Jr.
CAST: Royal Dano, Shug Fisher,
             Denver Pyle, Carl Reindel,
             Don Beddoe, Bill Zuckert,
             Michael Petit, Ken Mayer,
             Harold Ensley

After Matt locks up three of Festus' cousins and leaves town, the men beg Festus to let them out.

NOTES: First time Festus puts on a badge. Moss Grimmick is mentioned, though long gone. Don Beddoe plays townsman Halligan, a role later taken over on a regular basis by Charles Wagenheim. Denver Pyle has now portrayed an uncle to Festus as well as a cousin.

John Drew Barrymore, Anne Helm, Arness in "One
Killer on Ice," 1965

#359: ONE KILLER ON ICE
(01-23-65)

WRITER: Richard Carr
DIRECTOR: Joseph Lewis
CAST: John Drew Barrymore, Philip Coolidge,
               Anne Helm, Dennis Hopper

A bounty hunter asks Matt to help him bring in a wanted man he
says his partner is guarding in a remote cabin.

NOTES: First appearance by the late John Drew Barrymore who, like
fellow guest star the late Dennis Hopper, specialized in playing rather
eccentric characters.

#360: Chief Joseph
(01-30-65)

STORY: Thomas Warner
TELEPLAY: Clyde Ware
DIRECTOR: Mark Rydell
CAST: Victor Jory, Robert Loggia,
              Joe Maross, Leonard Stone

An Indian chief being escorted to peace talks with President Grant becomes ill and must stop in Dodge City, much to the great displeasure of its citizens.

NOTES: Matt's right arm is cut by a bottle. Matt to Charlie (Maross): "You get out of here. I don't want to see you around Dodge for a month." Leonard Stone plays Wiley, now owner of the Dodge House rather than Mr. Dobie.

#361: Circus Trick
(02-06-65)

WRITER: Les Crutchfield
DIRECTOR: William F. Claxton
CAST: Elizabeth MacRae, Ken Scott,
              Warren Oates, Walter Burke,
              Isabelle Jewell

Matt is wary when a traveling carnival that might be linked to a series of bank robberies rolls into Dodge.

NOTES: Fourth and final appearance of Elizabeth MacRae as Festus' girlfriend April. Roy Roberts back as banker Botkin. Roy Barcroft as storekeeper Roy, a role he would play in a dozen episodes.

#362: Song for Dying
(02-13-65)

WRITER: Harry Kronman
DIRECTOR: Allen Reisner
CAST: Theodore Bikel, Robert F. Simon, Lee Majors,
             Roger Ewing, Russell Thorson, Sheldon Allman,
             Ford Rainey, Glenn Strange

Doc recognizes the weary musician who wanders into the Long Branch as a former physician.

NOTES: Matt deputizes Festus again. Doc's first name—Galen—finally revealed. Brief appearance by Lee Majors, later one of the stars of *The Big Valley*. Ben played by Roger Ewing, future *Gunsmoke* regular Thad Greenwood. Name on the undertaker sign reads Elias Foley rather than Percy Crump.

#363: Winner Take All
(02-20-65)

WRITER: Les Crutchfield
DIRECTOR: Vincent McEveety
CAST: Tom Simcox, John Milford, Margaret Bly

Matt attempts to settle matters between a pair of brothers who fight over everything from selling cattle to women.

NOTES: Matt is again shot in the left arm. First of 47 episodes directed by Vincent McEveety.

#364: Eliab's Aim
(02-27-65)

WRITER: Will Corry
DIRECTOR: Richard Sarafian

Stone & Jean Arthur in "Thursday's Child," 1965

CAST: James Hampton, Dee J. Thompson, Donald O'Kelly, Gregg Palmer

Doc and Quint become involved when Festus' nephew comes to Dodge determined to shoot off part of his uncle's ear.

NOTES: Matt does not appear for the first 40 minutes. Hank Patterson back as stableman Hank Miller. Based on a story idea by Burt Reynolds and Ken Curtis.

#365: THURSDAY'S CHILD
(03-06-65)

WRITER: Robert Lewin
DIRECTOR: Joseph H. Lewis

CAST: Jean Arthur, Scott Marlowe, Joe Raciti, Suzanne
               Benoit, Roy Barcroft, Hank Patterson, Fred Coby

Kitty's old friend Julie Blane claims she is on her way to Wichita to visit her son, who is really an outlaw hiding out with his pregnant wife.

NOTES: Julie, played by veteran film star Jean Arthur, is from New Orleans and taught Kitty everything she knows about the saloon business. Doc calls Roy Barcroft's character Jonas although he is listed in the credits as Roy.

#366: BRECKINRIDGE
(03-13-65)

WRITER: Les Crutchfield
DIRECTOR: Vincent McEveety
CAST: Ben Cooper, Robert Sorrells,
               Elisha Cook, John Warburton

A brash young Eastern attorney believes he can make the letter of the law work in a frontier town like Dodge City.

NOTES: Glenn Strange is on hand as Sam, although Elisha Cook plays a Long Branch barkeep named Jocko. Kitty is kidnapped again. Ben Cooper, who portrays the title character, would reprise the role in a follow-up episode.

#367: BANK BABY
(03-20-65)

WRITER: John Meston
DIRECTOR: Andrew V. McLaglen
CAST: Jacques Aubuchon, Gail Kobe,
               Virginia Christine, Hampton Fancher,
               Roy Roberts, Harry Carey, Jr.

A man planning to rob the Dodge City bank kidnaps a baby to make his ragged family seem more respectable when they drive their wagon into town.

NOTES: Matt and Doc play billiards in the Dodge House rather than at Boss Billiards. Burt Reynolds' 48th and final episode as Quint Asper.

#368: THE LADY
(03-27-65)

WRITER: John Mantley
DIRECTOR: Mark Rydell
CAST: Eileen Heckart, Katharine Ross,
               R.G. Armstrong, Walter Sande,
               Hank Patterson, Clifton James,
               Michael Forest

A self-centered young woman dreaming of going to San Francisco hires a gunman to kill her aunt's beau when it becomes apparent that the trip might be off.

NOTES: Good episode featuring poetic justice. Imprressive performance by future Oscar winning actress Eileen Heckart, who would later return to Dodge in another role.

#369: DRY ROAD TO NOWHERE
(04-03-65)

WRITER: Harry Kronman
DIRECTOR: Vincent McEveety
CAST: James Whitmore, Julie Sommars, John Saxon,
               Read Morgan, Howard Culver, L.Q. Jones

A preacher who considers drinking a sin comes to Dodge and angers both Kitty and a young man he has warned to stay away from his daughter.

NOTES: First of four guest appearances by James Whitmore, who co-starred with James Arness in the 1954 sci-fi classic *Them*!

#370: TWENTY MILES FROM DODGE
(04-10-65)

WRITER: Clyde Ware
DIRECTOR: Mark Rydell
CAST: Darren McGavin, Edward Sloane,
              Aneta Corseaut

Outlaws detain Kitty and her fellow stagecoach passengers in the middle of nowhere and demand money for their release.

NOTES: Kitty is returning to Dodge from a wedding in Wichita. Aneta Corseaut had a regular role as Helen Crump on *The Andy Griffith Show* at this time.

#371: THE PARIAH
(04-17-65)

WRITER: Calvin Clements, Sr.
DIRECTOR: Harry Harris, Jr.
CAST: John Dehner, Ilka Windish,
              Donald Losby, Steve Ihnat, Tom Reese,
              Lee Van Cleef, Don Keefer

Everyone in Dodge is proud of farmer Paolo Scanzano for killing a wanted man until it is revealed that the outlaw was shot in the back.

NOTES: Unfortunately brief appearance by veteran badman Lee Van Cleef. Ted Jordan plays an unbilled townsman.

Betty Hutton, Curtis & Arness in "Bad Lady from Brookline," 1965

#372: GILT GUILT
(04-25-65)

WRITER: Kathleen Hite
DIRECTOR: Harry Harris, Jr.
CAST: Jan Clayton, Peter Brooks, Andrew Duggen

Doc comes to the aid of a poor farm widow and her son who are suffering from scurvy.

NOTES: Roy Barcroft appears as storekeeper Roy. Jan Clayton preceded June Lockhart as the mother on the *Lassie* series.

#373: BAD LADY FROM BROOKLINE
(05-01-65)

WRITER: Gustave Field
DIRECTOR: Michael O'Herlihy

CAST:　Betty Hutton, Claude Akins, Billy Bowles, John Hubbard, Jonathan Kidd, Ollie O'Toole, Eddie Hice, Tom McCauley

A naïve woman comes to Dodge expecting to be reunited with her husband, unaware that he had turned outlaw and been killed by Matt.

NOTES: Not one of the better episodes, due largely to an over-the-top performance by musical comedienne Hutton, for whom this was apparently a showcase.

#374: Two Tall Men
(05-08-65)

WRITER:　Frank Q. Dobbs & Robert C. Stewart
DIRECTOR:　Vincent McEveety
CAST:　George Lindsey, Jay Ripley, Harry Townes, Ben Cooper

Matt is away in Hays, so it falls to Festus and attorney Breck Taylor to handle things when Doc is badly beaten and robbed.

NOTES: Second episode with Ben Cooper as Breckinridge. Some scenes shot at Iverson Ranch. Matt does not show up until the last quarter of the episode. George Lindsey was also appearing as Goober Pyle on *The Andy Griffith Show* at this time.

#375: Honey Pot
(05-15-65)

WRITER:　Clyde Ware
DIRECTOR:　Vincent McEveety
CAST:　Rory Calhoun, Joanna Moore, John Crawford, Dick Wessel, Harry Bartell, Harry Lauter, Hank Patterson, Roy Barcroft, Charles Maxwell

Matt is upset to discover that an old friend and a saloon girl have killed the woman's husband and pinned the crime on someone else.

NOTES: Matt to Evers (Maxwell): "I'm going to ride out in the country for a couple hours, and when I get back you'd better be out of Dodge." Matt and Ben (Calhoun) rode together in Arizona for five years. Sign over the livery stable still reads Moss Grimmick although Hank is now proprietor. Rory Calhoun starred and co-produced the series *The Texan* for two seasons (1958-60).

#376: THE NEW SOCIETY
(05-22-65)

WRITER:	Calvin Clements, Sr.
DIRECTOR:	Joseph Sargent
CAST:	James Gregory, Jeremy Slate,
	Elizabeth Perry, Jack Weston

Matt is far from welcome when he travels to Ridgetown to investigate a 12-year-old murder.

NOTES: Ridgetown saloon is the redressed set of the Dodge House lobby. Unusual episode with no Festus, Doc or Kitty.

#377: HE WHO STEALS
(05-29-65)

WRITER:	John Meston
DIRECTOR:	Harry Harris, Jr.
CAST:	Russ Tamblyn, Harold J. Stone,
	Len Wayland, Stanley Adams

When he defends an old buffalo hunter accused of cattle rustling, a young cowboy loses his job and the men he thought were his friends.

NOTES: Russ Tamblyn, who appeared in such films as *Peyton Place* and *West Side Story*, is the father of actress Amber Tamblyn. Harold J. Stone's seventh and final guest role on *Gunsmoke*.

EPISODE GUIDE

SEASON 11
September 18, 1965–May 7, 1966

Curtis and Arness in "The Raid," 1966

#378: SEVEN HOURS TO DAWN
(09-18-65)

WRITER: Clyde Ware
DIRECTOR: Vincent McEveety
CAST: John Drew Barrymore, Michael Vandever,
            Al Lettier, Allen Jaffe, Charles Seel, Morgan
            Woodward, Jerry Douglas, Johnny Seven

An army of outlaws swoops in to plunder Dodge, disarming everyone—including Matt.

NOTES: One of the best episodes of the series, with John Mantley, now associate producer, putting the emphasis back on the main cast. Writer Paul Savage new story consultant. Writer and Director credits now back in the closing credits rather than preceding episodes, with main title and star credits shown after a "teaser" scene. Matt shot by four rifles. Doc calls undertaker Percy Crump "Hank." First look at the cellar of the Long Branch. Second of an eventual 18 guest appearances by Morgan Woodward.

#379: THE STORM
(09-25-65)

WRITER:	Paul Savage
DIRECTOR:	Joseph Sargent
CAST:	Forrest Tucker, Ruth Warrick, Tim McIntire, Richard Evans, Kelly Thordsen, Willard Sage, Mary Lou Taylor, Lincoln Demyan, Charles Seel, Steven Darrell, Stuart Margolin, Victor Izay, Shug Fisher, Rudy Sooter

Two sons of one of Matt's best friends kill a hunter and remain silent when another man is arrested for the crime.

NOTES: Increasing banter between Festus and Doc. Festus sings with guitarist/barkeep Rudy. Court held in the Dodge House lobby. First of nine appearances by Victor Izay as Bull Anders, owner of the Bull's Head Saloon.

#380: CLAYTON THADDEUS GREENWOOD
(10-02-65)

WRITER:	Calvin Clements
DIRECTOR:	Joseph Sargent

CAST: Roger Ewing, Jack Elam, William Henry, Paul Fix, Sherwood Price, Robert Sorrells, Allen Jaffe

The son of an Oklahoma marshal tracks the men responsible for his father's death to Dodge City.

NOTES: First of 46 episodes with Roger Ewing as cast regular Thad Greenwood. Matt says he knew Thad's father as Sheriff John Greenwood of Tulsa. Thad tells Kitty he has a brother named Clayton Lowell Greenwood. Matt offers Thad $8 a month to help out. Festus mentions the long gone Moss Grimmick.

#381: TEN LITTLE INDIANS
(10-09-65)

WRITER: George Eckstein
DIRECTOR: Mark Rydell
CAST: Nehemiah Persoff, Warren Oates, Bruce Dern, Zalman King, Rafael Campos, John Marley, Stanja Lowe, Don Ross, Nina Roman

Outlaws begin to gather in Dodge after hearing there is a $25,000 bounty being paid for the murder of Matt Dillon.

NOTES: Jack Pinto (Persoff) yet another former lawman acquaintance of Matt's. Pringle (Marley) tells Matt his son was named Thad Ewing, an unintentional combination of Thad Greenwood and Roger Ewing? Some scenes filmed at Iverson Ranch. First of four guest roles by Bruce Dern, best known to Western enthusiasts as the man who shot John Wayne in the back in *The Cowboys*.

#382: TAPS FOR OLD JEB
(10-16-65)

WRITER: Les Crutchfield
DIRECTOR: James Sheldon

CAST: Ed Begley, Wayne Rogers,
                 Morgan Woodward, Arthur Batanides,
                 Don Keefer, Rudy Sooter

An old prospector strikes it rich and starts throwing his money around Dodge even though it may well get him killed.

NOTES: Doc does the calling at a square dance held in the Long Branch, with Sam on fiddle and Rudy on guitar.

#383: KIOGA
(10-23-65)

WRITER: Robert Lewin
DIRECTOR: Harry Harris, Jr.
CAST: Neville Brand, Teno Pollick, Howard Culver,
                 John War Eagle, Hank Patterson, Roy Roberts,
                 Ken Renard, John Hubbard, Nina Roman,
                 Catharine Wyles

A young Indian tracks the man who killed his father to Dodge, but is not interested in Matt's offer to help.

NOTES: Banker Botkin (Roberts) now spelled Bodkin. Guest star Neville Brand was co-starring on the NBC series *Laredo* at the time this episode aired.

#384: THE BOUNTY HUNTER
(10-30-65)

WRITER: Paul Savage
DIRECTOR: Harry Harris, Jr.
CAST: Robert Lansing, Bert Freed, Gregg Palmer,
                 Hal Lynch, Jon Kowal, Wright King,
                 Lisabeth Hush, Amber Flower, Charles Seel,
                 James Anderson, Victor Izay, Jason Johnson

A rancher offers to give a former bounty hunter 1,000 acres of land if he will kill the man the rancher says murdered his son.

NOTES: Ken Curtis' 50th episode as Festus. The last name of telegrapher Barney (Seel) is revealed to be Danches. Robert Lansing, star of *12 O'Clock High* for its first season, was considered one of the best actors working in television by *TV Guide* columnist Cleveland Amory.

#385: THE REWARD
(11-06-65)

STORY: Gilbert Ralston
TELEPLAY: Beth Keele & Scott Hunt
DIRECTOR: Marc Daniels
CAST: James Whitmore, David Ladd,
Peter Whitney, Julio Medina, Fred J. Scollay,
Gil Rankin, Roy Roberts, Berkeley Harris,
Normann Burton

An ex-con returns to Dodge after finishing his sentence and attempts to rebuild his life, only to find the citizens of Dodge are not in a forgiving mood.

NOTES: Banker Bodkin back to being Botkin. Rudy tending bar in the Long Branch. David Ladd is the son of actor Alan Ladd.

#386: MALACHI
(11-13-65)

WRITER: Paul Savage
DIRECTOR: Gene Nelson
CAST: Harry Townes, Edward Andrews, Jack Elam,
Robert Sorrells, Woodrow Chambliss, Joey Wilcox,
Rex Holman, Hank Patterson

With Matt out of town, Doc, Festus and Kitty help a drunken buffalo hunter pretend to be Dodge marshal to impress his successful brother.

NOTES: Although Hank Miller (Patterson) runs the livery stable, the sign still indicates that it belongs to Moss Grimmick.

#387: THE PRETENDER
(11-20-65)

WRITER: Calvin Clements
DIRECTOR: Vincent McEveety
CAST: Tom Simcox, Tom Skerritt, Gregg Palmer,
            Julie Sommars, Rusty Lane, Rudy Sooter,
            Nehemiah Persoff, Athena Lorde, Sam Edwards,
            Harry Davis, Ed McCready, Allen Jaffe

Two brothers return to their father's ranch after being imprisoned for rustling cattle, but only one of them has seen the error of his ways.

NOTES: Doc again does the calling at a square dance. Second guest appearance this season by Nehemiah Persoff.

#388: SOUTH WIND
(11-27-65)

WRITER: Jack Bartlett
DIRECTOR: Allen Reisner
CAST: Pat Cardi, Bruce Dern, Bob Random,
            Michael Davis, Ryan Hayes, Michael Whitney,
            Gregg Palmer, Michelle Breeze

On the prairie, Doc comes to the aid of an injured boy bent on vengeance.

NOTES: Second episode of the season guest starring Bruce Dern. Western veteran Gregg Palmer appears as the Dodge City black-smith.

#389: THE HOSTAGE
(12-04-65)

STORY: Joe Ann Johnson
TELEPLAY: Clyde Ware
DIRECTOR: Vincent McEveety
CAST: Darren McGavin, Simon Oakland, Tom Reese,
              I. Stanford Jolley, Vito Scotti, Willis Bouchey,
              Jimmy Cross, Charles Seel

Matt is taken hostage by four escaped convicts fleeing to Mexico.

NOTES: One of the best episodes of the series, with a top notch guest cast. Episode title was used again in 1972.

#390: OUTLAW'S WOMAN
(12-11-65)

WRITER: Clyde Ware
DIRECTOR: Mark Rydell
CAST: Lane Bradbury, Lou Antonio, Vincent Beck,
              Lonny Chapman, Gene Tyburn, Ted Jordan,
              Peggy Rea, Roy Barcroft

A young woman who has been riding with a band of outlaws decides to change her ways until she hears that Matt killed her brother.

NOTES: Storekeeper Roy Barcroft is again referred to as Wilbur Jonas rather than Roy. Some scenes filmed at Iverson Ranch.

#391: THE AVENGERS
(12-18-65)

WRITER: Don Mullally
DIRECTOR: Vincent McEveety
CAST: James Gregory, John Saxon,
             Les Brown, Jr., Olan Soule,
             Howard Culver, Ed McCready

A deranged judge is convinced that Kitty and Festus deliberately planned the murder of his dead son.

NOTES: Matt to Judge Strom (Gregory): "I suggest that you and your boys get out of Dodge—before midnight would be just about right." Matt shot in left leg. Kitty once again kidnapped from her room. Date on grave marker reads August 21, 1873.

#392: GOLD MINE
(12-25-65)

WRITERS: Scott Hunt & Beth Keele
DIRECTOR: Abner Biberman
CAST: John Anderson, Paul Carr, Michael Vandever,
             Tom Nardini, Argentina Brunetti, Russ Bender

Matt sends Thad to the town of Pick Axe to watch over Kitty, who has inherited a gold mine there.

NOTES: First Kitty episode in a while. Lighthearted in tone for Christmas 1965.

#393: DEATH WATCH
(01-08-66)

WRITER: Calvin Clements
DIRECTOR: Mark Rydell

CAST: Albert Salmi, Willard Sage, Frank Silvera,
                     Richard Evans

Matt protects a wounded outlaw from a pair of bounty hunters eager to collect the reward the Mexican government has put on the man's head.

NOTES: First of Charles Wagenheim's 28 appearances as Dodge townsman Halligan. Albert Salmi was a regular on the *Daniel Boone* series. Frank Silvera's last regular role was on *The High Chaparral*. Mark Rydell later directed *On Golden Pond*, Henry Fonda's final film. This episode earned a Western Heritage award from the National Cowboy Hall of Fame.

#394: SWEET BILLY, SINGER OF SONGS (01-15-66)

WRITER: Gustave Field
DIRECTOR: Alvin Ganzer
CAST: Bob Random, Brooke Bundy,
                     Royal Dano, Slim Pickens

More of the Haggen clan arrives in Dodge when Festus' nephew Billy comes courting a young woman whose father insists on collecting a dowery.

NOTES: A character named Sweet Billy appeared in the Season 7 episode "Marry Me" (#246). A sequel of sorts to "Eliab's Aim" (#364).

#395: THE RAID, PART 1 (01-22-66)
#396: THE RAID, PART 2 (01-29-66)

WRITER: Clyde Ware
DIRECTOR: Vincent McEveety

CAST: Gary Lockwood, John Kellogg, Richard Jaeckel,
             Jeremy Slate, Preston Pierce, John Anderson,
             Jim Davis, Ted Jordan, Michael Conrad,
             Percy Helton

A large band of outlaws rob the Dodge City bank, kidnap Doc
and torch the town.

NOTES: Second two-part episode of the series, as well as one of the
very best, and the first time the episode title has been shown.
Excellent guest cast. Olan Soule's second appearance as Dodge barber Tim. Brief glimpse of James Nusser as Louie Pheeters.

#397: KILLER AT LARGE
(02-05-66)

WRITER: Calvin Clements
DIRECTOR: Marc Daniels
CAST: Geraldine Brooks, Robert Ballew, Craig Hundley,
             Tim O'Kelley, Hardie Albright, Cyril Delevanti,
             John Pickard, Stuart Erwin, James Beggs, Gilman
             Rankin, Jonathan Lippe, Morgan Jones

Festus goes on the run after he is forced to kill the drunken sharp-
shooter who has come to town with another "medicine" show.

NOTES: Roger Ewing's tenth episode as Thad. First of guest star
Jonathan Lippe's dozen episodes.

#398: MY FATHER'S GUITAR
(02-12-66)

WRITER: Hal Sitowitz
DIRECTOR: Robert Totten
CAST: Beau Bridges, Charles Dierkop, Steve Ihnat,
             William Bramley, Dub Taylor, Robin Blake

Kitty hires a young man to play guitar in the Long Branch, unaware that he has just killed a man who tried to smash the instrument.

NOTES: At a party in the Long Branch it is disclosed that Doc is allegedly 64-years-old. Beau Bridges is son of the late Lloyd Bridges and brother of Jeff. First of two dozen episodes directed by Robert Totten.

#399: WISHBONE
(02-19-66)

WRITER: Paul Savage
DIRECTOR: Marc Daniels
CAST: Lew Gallo, Victor French, Lyle Waggoner, Billy
              Beck, Michael Fox, Don Happy, Adar Jameson,
              Natalie Masters, William Meader, Joan Granville

While Matt trails a trio of stagecoach robbers, Festus comes across Doc, who has been bitten by a rattlesnake.

NOTES: One of the best episodes of the series, as well as Ken Curtis' personal favorite. Matt shot in the left arm. The late Victor French (Travers), a frequent *Gunsmoke* guest star, also directed five episodes. He is best remembered as Mr. Edwards on *Little House on the Prairie* and Mark Gordon on *Highway to Heaven*, both starring Michael Landon.

#400: SANCTUARY
(02-26-66)

WRITER: Calvin Clements
DIRECTOR: Harry Harris, Jr.
CAST: Sean Garrison, Richard Bradford, Joan Blackman,
              Virginia Gregg, Larry Wood, Bill Hart,
              Martin Place, Jack Grinnage, Charles Wagenheim,
              Marsha Blakesley, Woodrow Chambliss

A wounded bank robber demands that Dodge City's preacher grant him sanctuary in the church.

NOTES: Woodrow Chambliss, later to portray regular character Lathrop, plays a porter at the Dodge House.

#401: HONOR BEFORE JUSTICE
(03-05-66)

WRITERS: Frank Q. Dobbs & Robert C. Stewart
DIRECTOR: Harry Harris, Jr.
CAST: France Nuyen, Noah Berry,
              Michael Ansara, Barton MacLane, Harry Bartell,
              George Keymas, Richard Gilden, Ken Renard,
              James Almanzar, Ted Jordan

Against Doc's advice, Thad decides to become involved in a matter of Indian justice.

NOTES: Ted Jordan appears as an Indian policeman. Michael Ansara starred in two television Westerns, *Broken Arrow* and *Law of the Plainsman*, a spinoff from *The Rifleman*. Some scenes filmed at Iverson Ranch.

#402: THE BROTHERS
(03-12-66)

WRITER: Tom Hanley
DIRECTOR: Tay Garnett
CAST: Scott Marlowe, Bobby Crawford,
              Joseph Hoover, Mark Sturges, Eddie Firestone,
              Tom Reese, Warren Vanders, Edmund Hashim

An outlaw vows to go after Matt's friends if the marshal does not release his brother from jail.

NOTES: Matt shot in the left arm yet again. Will (Sturges) is Thad's friend from Oklahoma. Bobby Crawford co-starred on *Laramie* and is brother of *The Rifleman*'s Johnny Crawford. Episode title used again in 1972.

#403: WHICH DR.
(03-19-66)

WRITER: Les Crutchfield
DIRECTOR: Peter Graves
CAST: George Lindsey, R.G. Armstrong,
            Shelley Morrison, Gregg Palmer, Claire Wilcox,
            Elizabeth Frazer

Buffalo hunters take Doc and Festus captive, figuring Doc will make good husband material for their boss's daughter.

NOTES: Directed by the late Peter Graves, brother of James Arness, whose participation in this episode is minimal.

#404: HARVEST
(03-26-66)

WRITER: Les Crutchfield
DIRECTOR: Harry Harris, Jr.
CAST: James MacArthur, Leslie Ann Warren,
            George Kennedy, Alma Platt, Ted Jordan,
            Fred Coby, Karl Swenson

Two men feud over the same rangeland while one man's son and the other man's daughter strike up a romance.

NOTES: The late James MacArthur co-starred on the original *Hawaii Five-0* series. Leslie Ann Warren co-starred on the cable series *In Plain Sight*.

#405: BY LINE
(04-09-66)

WRITER: Les Crutchfield
DIRECTOR: Allen Reisner
CAST: Chips Rafferty, Denver Pyle,
              Stefan Arngrim

Illiterate Festus goes to work for the Clarion, Dodge's newest newspaper, creating chaos by spreading rumors and setting off price wars among the town's merchants.

NOTES: Dabbs Greer back as storeowner Wilbur Jonas after a long absence. Stefan Arngrim is the brother of Alison Arngrim, best known as Nellie on *Little House on the Prairie*.

#406: TREASURE OF JOHN WALKING FOX
(04-16-66)

STORY: Gwen Bagni
TELEPLAY: Clyde Ware
DIRECTOR: Marc Daniels
CAST: Leonard Nimoy, Richard Webb,
              Jim Davis, Lloyd Gough, Ted Gehring,
              Tom McCauley

Matt and most of Dodge are curious as to where Indian John Walking Fox got a gold piece from a treasure trove believed to be lost.

NOTES: Kelton Garwood's second appearance as Dodge City's undertaker, but the first time he is identified as Percy Crump. Garwood would later change his name to Jonathan Harper.

#407: MY FATHER, MY SON
(04-23-66)

WRITER: Hal Sitowitz
DIRECTOR: Robert Totten
CAST: Jack Elam, Teno Pollick, Lee Van Cleef

After a gunslinger kills a young man, his own son vows vengeance.

NOTES: Rare opportunity to see two classic badmen—Elam and Van Cleef—in the same episode.

#408: PARSON COMES TO TOWN
(04-30-66)

WRITER: Verne Jay
DIRECTOR: Marc Daniels
CAST: Sam Wanamaker, Lonny Chapman, John McLiam, Joan Granville, Kevin Burchett, Kelton Garwood

A mysterious stranger arrives in Dodge and informs Matt, Doc and Percy Crump that he has come to town to witness a death.

NOTES: Matt shot in the left side. Doc and Festus split another wishbone, as they did in "Wishbone." First episode with Ted Jordan as freight agent Nathan Burke and Woodrow Chambliss as Mr. Lathrop.

#409: PRIME OF LIFE
(05-07-66)

WRITER: Dan Ullman
DIRECTOR: Robert Totten
CAST: Douglas Kennedy, Jonathan Lippe, Victor French, Joe Don Baker, Martin West, Lyn Edington, Cal Naylor, Ted French

Matt and Festus become involved when a former lawman will not accept that his two sons are responsible for robbery and murder.

NOTES: Final black-and-white episode, and one of the best of the series. Festus badly beaten. Humorous closing scene, when Doc compares Festus to a cactus and skunk cabbage.

EPISODE GUIDE

SEASON 12
September 17, 1966–April 15, 1967

James Daly & Blake in "The Favor," 1967

#410: SNAP DECISION
(09-17-66)

WRITER: Richard Carr
DIRECTOR: Mark Rydell
CAST: Claude Akins, Michael Strong, Michael Cole,
            Sam Gilman, Orville Sherman

Matt turns in his badge when he discovers there was no reason for him to kill an old friend who had turned outlaw.

NOTES: Series now filmed in color. Last season on Saturday night. New opening with Matt facing his opponent on one of the Western streets of the former Republic Studios. Roger Ewing not always shown in opening credits. Matt's friend Ray (Gilman) saved his life during the Civil War. Impressive performance by Arness, who wears a blue shirt rather than the usual red. Sign above stable still indicates Moss Grimmick as owner.

#411: THE GOLDTAKERS
(09-24-66)

WRITER: Clyde Ware
DIRECTOR: Vincent McEveety
CAST: Martin Landau, Denver Pyle, Roy Jenson, Brad Weston, Charles Francisco, Michael Greene, William Bramley, John Boyer, Woodrow Chambliss, Charles Wagenheim

Outlaws masquerading as soldiers take over the Dodge City blacksmith shop to melt down the gold they have stolen from the army.

NOTES: Matt attempts to take a vacation, visiting Caleb Nash (Pyle), who was evidently not killed in "The Violators" (#345). Festus remarks that Dodge's latest blacksmith is its best since "the Comanche" (Quint Asper) left town. Although already introduced previously as Lathrop, Woodrow Chambliss plays a character named Tim Garvey. The whole town backs Matt up, unlike earlier days when he usually stood alone with Chester. Episode partially filmed in Bronson Canyon.

#412: The Jailer
(10-01-66)

WRITER: Hal Sitowitz
DIRECTOR: Vincent McEveety
CAST: Bette Davis, Bruce Dern, Robert Sorrells,
                Zalman King, Tom Skerritt, Julie Sommars

A bitter widow has her sons kidnap Kitty as part of her plan to get revenge on Matt.

NOTES: Kitty to Matt: "Thanks for all the wonderful years, Matt." Colorful performance by screen legend Davis, billed as Special Guest, who told a reporter, "There is something about doing a show quickly, but I think doing an hour show in six days is cutting it a little close."

#413: The Mission
(10-08-66)

WRITER: Richard Carr
DIRECTOR: Mark Rydell
CAST: Robert F. Simon, Bob Random, Warren Oates,
                Steve Ihnat, Arch Johnson, Jim Davis, Rafael
                Campos, Robert Tafur, Ruben Moreno, Mike
                Avelar, Bert Madrid

Matt's trip to Mexico to retrieve a prisoner proves disastrous when he is shot and the only one he can count on is the father of the man he has come to arrest.

NOTES: Second of several times Matt journeys down to Mexico. Lafe (Oates) mentions that the Civil War has been over for ten years.

#414: THE GOOD PEOPLE
(10-15-66)

WRITER: James Landis
DIRECTOR: Robert Totten
CAST: Morgan Woodward, Allen Case,
    Tom Simcox, Shug Fisher, Frederic Downs,
    James O'Hara, Clyde Howdy,
    Charles Wagenheim, Steve Gravers

Matt devises a scheme to get the real perpetrator to confess when an old bounty hunter is accused of lynching an innocent man.

NOTES: Trial held in the lobby of the Dodge House. Morgan Woodward's fourth appearance, the first in color. Woodrow Chambliss back as Lathrop.

#415: GUNFIGHTER, R.I.P.
(10-22-66)

WRITER: Hal Sitowitz
DIRECTOR: Mark Rydell
CAST: Darren McGavin, France Nuyen,
    Allen Emerson, Stefan Gierasch,
    Michael Conrad, H.T. Tsiang,
    Don Hanmer, Michael Fisher

A gunslinger hired to kill Matt comes to the aid of an old Chinese man and is seriously wounded before he can confront the marshal.

NOTES: Largely a character study with token appearances by Matt, Kitty and Doc. Third guest appearance by the late Michael Conrad, best known for his role as the police sergeant on *Hill Street Blues*.

#416: THE WRONG MAN
(10-29-66)

WRITER: Clyde Ware
DIRECTOR: Robert Totten
CAST: Carroll O'Connor, Clifton James,
                Kevin O'Neal, Charles Kuenstle,
                James Anderson, James Almanzar, Mel Gaines,
                Gilman Rankin, Victor Izay, Terry Frost

Matt and Festus loan money to a down and out farmer, who proceeds to lose it all to a gambler who is later found murdered and robbed.

NOTES: Doc mentions Wilbur Jonas to Thad. Victor Izay appears again as the bartender in the Bull's Head, but his name is given as Dutch rather than Bull. The late Carroll O'Connor rose to fame as the iconic bigot Archie Bunker on *All in the Family*. Episode title was used previously in 1957.

#417: THE WHISPERING TREE
(11-12-66)

WRITER: Calvin Clements, Sr.
DIRECTOR: Vincent McEveety
CAST: John Saxon, Jacqueline Scott, Edward Asner,
                Kathleen O'Malley, Stephen McEveety, Morgan
                Woodward, Donald Losby, Christopher Pate, Rex
                Holman, Allen Jaffe, Fred Coby, Lane Chandler

An ex-con whose loot was never recovered returns to Dodge and is plagued by not only his former partner, but also a relentless lawman.

NOTES: Jacqueline Scott's role was originally intended for Faye Dunaway. Second guest appearance by Ed Asner, who played Lou Grant on *The Mary Tyler Moore Show*.

#418: THE WELL
(11-19-66)

WRITER: Francis Cockrell
DIRECTOR: Marc Daniels
CAST: Guy Raymond, Joan Payne,
              Lawrence Casey, Elizabeth Rogers,
              Woodrow Chambliss, Charles Wagenheim,
              Ted Gehring, Karl Lucas, Pete Kellett,
              Robert Ballew

Drought strikes Dodge, and Matt allows a supposed rainmaker to keep everyone's minds off the dilemma while he thinks of a practical way to solve the problem.

NOTES: Extensive use of the outdoor Dodge City street at CBS Studio City, now being shared with *The Big Valley*, rather than phony "bottle" exterior set.

#419: STAGE STOP
(11-26-66)

WRITER: Hal Sitowitz
DIRECTOR: Irving Moore
CAST: John Ireland, Anne Whitfield, Jack Ging,
              Steve Raines, Michael Vandever,
              Joseph Ruskin, Sig Haig, Andy Albin

Gold robbers trap Doc and his fellow passengers at a stage station, where all was not well before they arrived there.

NOTES: Doc participates in shooting it out with the robbers. John Ireland and Steve Raines reunited after their abbreviated season together on *Rawhide*.

#420: THE NEWCOMERS
(12-03-66)

WRITER: Calvin Clements, Sr.
DIRECTOR: Robert Totten
CAST: Karl Swenson, Jon Voight, Ben Wright,
               James Murdock, Laurence Aten,
               Robert Sorrells, Charles Dierkop,
               John Pickard, Daniel Ades

Father and son immigrants from Sweden look forward to life in Dodge City until they encounter death and blackmail.

NOTES: First of three guest appearances by Jon Voight, who later earned the Best Actor Academy Award for *Coming Home*. According to fellow thespian Bruce Dern, Voight "always chose his *Gunsmoke* scripts carefully." One of the few jobs James Murdock had after seven seasons of portraying Mushy on *Rawhide*.

#421: QUAKER GIRL
(12-10-66)

WRITER: Preston Wood
DIRECTOR: Bernard Kowalski
CAST: William Shatner, Ariane Quinn, Liam Sullivan,
               Ben Johnson, Warren Vanders, Timothy Carey,
               Anna Karen, Nancy Marshall, Ed McCready,
               William Bryant, Joseph Breen, Tom Reese

Thad tries to convince a family of Quakers that the man they found him with in the desert is a criminal, not him.

NOTES: William Shatner was starring on the *Star Trek* series at this time.

#422: The Moonstone
(12-17-66)

WRITER: Paul Savage
DIRECTOR: Dick Colla
CAST: Michael Kellin, Tom Skerritt, Gail Kobe,
            Warren Kemmerling, Jeff Palmer,
            Larry Barton, Fred Coby, Fred Dale,
            Chick Sheridan

A mentally challenged young man comes across a poster that reveals his brother, now a simple farmer, is actually a wanted man.

NOTES: Second appearance by Tom Skerritt this season.

#423: Champion of the World
(12-24-66)

WRITER: Les Crutchfield
DIRECTOR: Marc Daniels
CAST: Alan Hale, Dan Tobin, Ralph Rose,
            Jane Dulo, Gale Robbins, Arthur Peterson,
            John McLiam, Jr. Don Keefer,
            Pete Kellett, Troy Melton, Ted Jordan,
            Charles Wagenheim

Kitty refuses to sell the Long Branch to a former prizefighter, so he partners with a con man in a scheme to drive her out of business.

NOTES: Lighthearted episode for Christmas Eve 1966. Alan Hale, Jr., was the son of veteran character actor Alan Hale, who appeared in many Hollywood classics. He is best remembered as the Skipper on *Gilligan's Island*, also then being filmed at CBS Studio City.

#424: The Hanging
(12-31-66)

WRITER: Calvin Clements, Jr.
DIRECTOR: Bernard Kowalski
CAST: Tom Stern, Kit Smythe, Robert Knapp,
                    Henry Darrow, Anna Navarro,
                    Richard Bakalyan, Edmund Hashim,
                    Larry Ward, Morgan Woodward,
                    Byron Foulger

Gallows are being constructed for a rare hanging in Dodge City, and the condemned man is confident the execution will never take place.

NOTES: First hanging in Dodge in two years. Henry Darrow starred as Manolito for four seasons on *The High Chaparral*. Third appearance of Morgan Woodward this season.

#425: Saturday Night
(01-07-67)

WRITER: Clyde Ware
DIRECTOR: Robert Totten
CAST: Leif Erickson, William C. Watson,
                    Victor French, Dub Taylor, Link Harget,
                    Rudy Sooter, Frederick Downs

Matt finds himself in the awkward position of having to discipline the rowdy drovers working for the trail boss who saved his life.

NOTES: Matt, on his second trail drive of the series, is stabbed in the left arm. No Kitty, which is unusual in an episode involving wild cowboys carousing in Dodge's saloons.

George Lindsey & Curtis in "Mad Dog, 1967

#426: MAD DOG
(01-14-67)

WRITER: Jay Simms
DIRECTOR: Charles Rondeau
CAST: Denver Pyle, George Murdock, Iggie Wolfington,
             Hoke Howell, George Lindsey, Sammy Reese,
             Butch Patrick, Dub Taylor

Festus, bitten by a possibly rabid dog, figures the outcome does not matter if he has a showdown with three men who believe he is a hired killer.

NOTES: Second guest appearance by Butch Patrick, best known as little vampire Eddie on the sitcom *The Munsters*. Denver Pyle, Hoke Howell and George Lindsey all worked on *The Andy Griffith Show*.

#427: MULEY
(01-21-67)

WRITER: Les Crutchfield
DIRECTOR: Allen Reisner
CAST: Zalman King, Lane Bradbury,
             Anthony Call, Marc Cavell,
             Ross Hagen, Howard Culver

After wounding Matt, a young outlaw goes to Dodge to finish the job, but ends up falling for one of the Long Branch hostesses.

NOTES: Matt is shot in the back. Second of six guest appearances by Lane Bradbury.

#428: MAIL DROP
(01-28-67)

WRITER: Calvin Clements
DIRECTOR: Robert Totten
CAST: Eddie Hodges, John Anderson,
             Bing Russell, Woodrow Chambliss,
             Steve Raines, Ted French, Pete Kellett,
             Fred McDougall, Chick Sheridan,
             Robert Miles, Jr.

Young Billy Roberts thinks Matt and Festus are pretending to be his friends so he will lead them to his father, a wanted man.

NOTES: Steve Raines, who for eight seasons portrayed drover Jim Quince on *Rawhide*, finally gets the opportunity to play a trail boss in this episode.

#429: OLD FRIEND
(02-04-67)

WRITER: Clyde Ware
DIRECTOR: Allen Reisner
CAST: Fritz Weaver, Delphi Lawrence,
               William Benedict, Valentin de Vargas,
               Carlos Rivas, David Renard, Lew Brown,
               Pat Cardi, Robert B. Williams

A lawman from Arizona arrives in Dodge searching for the men who burned a town and ran off with his girlfriend.

NOTES: Yet another peace officer who happens to be an old friend of Matt's.

#430: FANDANGO
(02-11-67)

WRITER: Don Ingalls
DIRECTOR: James Landis
CAST: Mario Alcalde, Torin Thatcher,
               Diana Muldaur, Paul Fix,
               Shug Fisher, Joe Higgins,
               Walter Baldwin, Fletcher Brian

Matt captures a killer and is taking him back to Dodge, but the brother of one of the man's victims is determined to cut the trip short.

NOTES: Paul Fix and Joe Higgins appeared regularly on *The Rifleman*. Diana Muldaur played Dennis Weaver's love interest on *McCloud*.

Arness & Mario Alcalde in "Fandango," 1967

#431: THE RETURNING
(02-18-67)

WRITER: James Landis
DIRECTOR: Marc Daniels
CAST: Michael Ansara, Lois Nettleton,
               Steve Sanders, Johnnie Whitaker,
               Jonathan Lippe, Richard Webb,
               Kenneth Mars, Roy Barcroft,
               Roy Roberts, Billy Halop, Troy Melton

A former outlaw is tired of being a destitute farmer and throws in with his old partners when they decide to rob the freight office in Dodge City.

NOTES: Roy Barcroft appears as storekeeper Wilbur Jonas rather than Roy. Script by James Landis, who directed the previous week's episode.

#432: THE LURE
(02-25-67)

WRITER: Clyde Ware
DIRECTOR: Marc Daniels
CAST: Stephen McNally, Kim Darby,
            Warren Vanders, John Pickard,
            Paul Picerni, Fred Coby, Len Wayland,
            Martin Brooks, Val Avery,
            Woodrow Chambliss

Outlaw Del Neely avoids being captured by the lawmen who have set a trap, taking his daughter and Kitty with him.

NOTES: Kim Darby later co-starred with John Wayne in *True Grit*. Woodrow Chambliss appears as Swiger instead of in his regular role as Dodge City's Lathrop.

#433: NOOSE OF GOLD
(03-04-67)

WRITER: Clyde Ware
DIRECTOR: Irving Moore
CAST: Vincent Gardenia, Steve Ihnat,
            Sam Gilman, Jan Shepard, Barton MacLane,
            Michael Preece, Jack Bailey, Harry Basch,
            Robert B. Williams, Charles Wagenheim

Matt must prevent a devious government agent from murdering a wanted man who was once the marshal's friend.

NOTES: The late Steve Ihnat made six guest appearances on *Gunsmoke*.

#434: THE FAVOR
(03-11-67)

WRITER: Don Ingalls
DIRECTOR: Marc Daniels
CAST: James Daly, William Bramley,
              Diane Ladd, Troy Melton, Shirley Wilson,
              Fred J. Scollay, Lew Gallo

Kitty helps a wanted man who saved her life hide from Matt.

NOTES: The livery stable still identified as belonging to Moss Grimmick. The late John Daly, best known from the *Medical Center* series, was the father of actors Tim and Tyne Daly.

#435: MISTAKEN IDENTITY
(03-18-67)

WRITERS: Les Crutchfield & Paul Savage
DIRECTOR: Robert Totten
CAST: Albert Salmi, Hal Lynch, Ken Mayer,
              Sam Melville

An outlaw switches identities with a dying man, only to discover the man has been brought to Dodge by Matt and Thad, and still alive.

NOTES: One of the best episodes of the season, written by two long-time *Gunsmoke* scribes. Ted Jordan's largest role as Nathan Burke to date. Second look at the cellar of the Long Branch.

#436: LADIES FROM ST. LOUIS
(03-25-67)

WRITER: Clyde Ware
DIRECTOR: Irving Moore
CAST: Claude Akins, Josephine Hutchinson,

Aneta Corseaut, Kelly Jean Peters, Venita Wolf, Lois Roberts, Henry Darrow, John Carter, Ralph Roberts, Lew Brown, Vic Tayback

Nuns bring a wounded outlaw to Dodge, but do not want to hand him over to Matt because the man saved their lives.

NOTES: Ninth of ten guest appearances by veteran character actor Claude Akins. The late Vic Tayback achieved fame as Mel on the sitcom *Alice*.

#437: NITRO, PART 1
(04-08-67)
#438: NITRO, PART 2
(04-15-67)

WRITER: Preston Wood
DIRECTOR: Robert Totten
CAST: David Canary, Bonnie Beecher,
             Tom Reese, Eddie Firestone,
             Robert Rothwell, Dub Taylor, Sue Collier,
             Michelle Breeze, Rudy Sooter, Anthony Redondo,
             John Breen, Scott Hale, Howard Culver

An impoverished drifter takes a job making nitroglycerine for bank robbers to earn enough money to marry a Long Branch saloon girl with expensive tastes.

NOTES: Closing credits of Part 1 give special billing to James Nusser as Louie Pheeters. Part 2 was Ken Curtis' 100th episode as Festus Haggen. Guest star David Canary went on to portray ranch foreman Candy on *Bonanza*. Matt's desperate ride in Part 2 was employed as the show's opening title for Season 14. *Gunsmoke* was briefly canceled as this episode was being shot. Although the final episode of the season to air, there was another ("The Prodigal") that was held over to the following season. Had the series been canceled, it may have never been seen.

EPISODE GUIDE

SEASON 13
September 11, 1967–March 4, 1968

Chill Wills & Arness in "A Noose for Dobie Price," 1968

#439: THE WRECKERS
(09-11-67)

WRITER: Hal Sitowitz
DIRECTOR: Robert Totten
CAST: Edmund Hashim, Warren Oates, Warren Vanders,
           Rex Holman, Gene Rutherford, Charles Kuenstle,

Charles Seel, Trevor Bardette, James Almanzar, Lew Brown, Charles Wagenheim, Joe Haworth, Bobby E. Clark, Jerry Brown, Joe Yrigoyen, Sr.

After a stagecoach carrying Kitty, Matt and a wanted man crashes, Kitty pins Matt's badge on his unconscious prisoner so the outlaws responsible for the wreck will not discover the marshal's true identity.

NOTES: Now on Monday evening, followed by a major uptick in the ratings. With John Mantley now head producer, a return to more stories focused on the principal characters. Last season with Matt shown facing a gunman on Front Street. (*Gunsmoke* now sharing the Western backlot with *The Big Valley* and *Cimarron Strip*.) Episode titles now shown on a regular basis. Kitty and Matt on yet another failed vacation, and not the last time Matt will impersonate an outlaw. Charles Seel as Eli rather than his usual character, Dodge City telegrapher Barney Danches. Stage crash becomes stock footage used in later episodes and on other series.

#440: CATTLE BARONS
(09-18-67)

WRITER: Clyde Ware
DIRECTOR: Gunnar Hellstrom
CAST: Forrest Tucker, Robert Wilke, Brad Johnson, John Milford, Lew Brown, Robert Sampson, Fred Coby, Woodrow Chambliss, Charles Wagenheim, Roy Barcroft, Steve Liss, Mike Howden, Clyde Howdy, Henry Wise

Two feuding trail bosses, one a friend of Matt's, drive their herds to Dodge, and Matt's friend seems to be on the losing end.

NOTES: Matt to Smith (Milford): "All right, Smith, I want you out of town. You've got ten minutes to saddle up."

#441: THE PRODIGAL
(09-25-67)

WRITER: Calvin Clements
DIRECTOR: Bernard McEveety
CAST: Lew Ayers, Charles Robinson, Richard Evans,
Lamont Johnson, Lee Krieger, Ted Gehring,
Kelly Thordsen

Two brothers come to Dodge in search of the unknown killer of their father, but Matt feels the question should remain unanswered.

NOTES: Episode filmed for the previous season, with an unbilled Roger Ewing shown briefly in his 46th and final appearance as Thad Greenwood. Kitty tells the brothers that she has been owner of the Long Branch for 13 years. The circuit judge now referred to as Brooker. Director Bernard McEveety is brother of director Vincent, who between them helmed 108 episodes.

#442: VENGEANCE, PART 1
(10-02-67)
#443: VENGEANCE, PART 2
(10-09-67)

WRITER: Calvin Clements
DIRECTOR: Richard Sarafian
CAST: John Ireland, James Stacy, Morgan Woodward,
James Anderson, Buck Taylor, Kim Darby,
Paul Fix, Royal Dano, Victor French,
Sandy Kevin, Rudy Sooter

When a wealthy rancher falsely accuses a man and his two sons of cattle rustling he sets off a disastrous chain of events which reach Dodge City and beyond.

NOTES: Festus rather than Doc does the calling at a barn dance. Fourth two-part episode of the series. Excellent guest cast, including Buck

Taylor, future Dodge gunsmith and part-time deputy Newly O'Brien. Part one Morgan Woodward's seventh guest appearance.

#444: A HAT
(10-16-67)

WRITER: Ron Bishop
DIRECTOR: Robert Totten
CAST: Chill Wills, Gene Evans, Tom Simcox,
H.M. Wynant, Robert Sorrells, Hank Patterson,
Scott Hale, Gene O'Donnell, Bill Erwin,
Ed McCready, Lee De Broux, Don Happy,
Shirley Wilson

An argument over the importance of a hat leads to a senseless killing.

NOTES: The stable in Dodge still advertised as belonging to Moss, although Hank continues to run it. First of numerous scripts by Ron Bishop.

#445: HARD LUCK HENRY
(10-23-67)

WRITER: Warren Douglas
DIRECTOR: John Rich
CAST: John Astin, Royal Dano, Ken Drake,
Michael Fox, Mary Lou Taylor,
Bobby Riha, Anthony James, John Shank,
Charles Kuenstle, Bo Hopkins, Mayf Nutter

Festus and Henry, one of his many cousins, tangle with a clan of hill folk who want to get their hands on the Confederate gold Henry has found.

NOTES: The name Moss Grimmick on the stable sign is shown being painted over. The lake setting was formerly used as the lagoon on *Gilligan's Island*, canceled to make room on the CBS schedule when *Gunsmoke* was renewed and moved to Monday.

#446: Major Glory
(10-30-67)

STORY: Dick Carr & Clyde Ware
TELEPLAY: Dick Carr
DIRECTOR: Robert Totten
CAST: Carroll O'Connor, Victor French, Robert F. Lyons, Link Wyler, Lawrence Mann, Don G. Ross, Cal Naylor, Chris Stephens, Russ Siler, William L. Sumper

Festus is accused of murdering an army sergeant killed by two soldiers caught deserting.

NOTES: Another of what will be several episodes using the lake on the CBS backlot. Composer Morton Stevens received an Emmy nomination for this episode.

#447: The Pillagers
(11-06-67)

WRITER: Calvin Clements
DIRECTOR: Vincent McEveety
CAST: Buck Taylor, John Saxon, Joseph Schneider, Vito Scotti, Paul Picerni, William Bramley, Allen Jaffe, Harry Harvey, Sr.

Kitty and a gunsmith are taken hostage by outlaws who believe the gunsmith is a doctor who can tend to one of their seriously wounded partners.

NOTES: First of 103 episodes with Buck Taylor as Newton "Newly" O'Brian of Pennsylvania, whose surname was later changed to O'Brien. Partially filmed in Los Angeles' Bronson Canyon.

#448: PRAIRIE WOLFER
(11-13-67)

WRITER: Calvin Clements
DIRECTOR: Robert Butler
CAST: Jon Voight, Lou Antonio,
     Kelly Jean Peters, I. Stanford Jolley,
     Charles McGraw, Matt Emery

Two trappers resort to robbery when Festus mistakenly tells them no bounty is being paid for wolf pelts.

NOTES: Second of Jon Voight's guest appearances before his break-out role in the film *Midnight Cowboy* (1969). "Prairie Wolfer" was also the title of the 1964 episode in which Ken Curtis joined the series full-time.

#449: STRANGER IN TOWN
(11-20-67)

STORY: John Dunkel & Emily Mosher
TELEPLAY: John Dunkel
DIRECTOR: Daryl Hallenbeck
CAST: Pernell Roberts, Jacqueline Scott,
     R.G. Armstrong, Henry Jones,
     Eric Shea, Jon Kowal

A gunslinger finds out the man he has been hired to kill is romantically involved with his estranged wife and little son.

NOTES: Opening scene filmed on the *Cimarron Strip* saloon set. Second appearance by Pernell Roberts, fifth of Jacqueline Scott's nine episodes.

#450: DEATH TRAIN
(11-27-67)

WRITER: Ken Trevey
DIRECTOR: Gunnar Hellstrom
CAST: Dana Wynter, Morgan Woodward,
               Ed Bakey, Mort Mills, Trevor Bardette,
               Zalman King, Sam Melville

Doc quarantines a railroad car carrying a man suffering from spotted fever, and the citizens demand that Matt get the car out of Dodge.

NOTES: According to the sign at the railroad station, the population of Dodge is 996. Doc is called "a real porcupine" and "a cowtown pill roller." In a change of pace from his usual casting, Morgan Woodward portrays a refined manufacturer of buggies. Second appearance of Buck Taylor as Newly, but listed among the guest cast.

#451: ROPE FEVER
(12-04-67)

WRITER: Chris Rellas
DIRECTOR: David Alexander
CAST: Ralph Bellamy, Anna Lee, George Murdock,
               Sam Gilman, Ken Mayer, Ted Gehring,
               Dennis Cross, Hal Baylor, Hank Patterson,
               Gertrude Flynn

Festus stops to help a wounded bank robber and is thrown in jail after an old sheriff accuses him of being in on the holdup.

NOTES: Ralph Bellamy, a veteran of Hollywood's Golden Age (*The Awful Truth, His Girl Friday, The Wolf Man, Sunrise at Campobello*), guest starred on several television Westerns, including *Bonanza* and *Rawhide*.

#452: WONDER
(12-18-67)

STORY: William Blinn & Mary Worell
TELEPLAY: William Blinn
DIRECTOR: Irving J. Moore
CAST: Richard Mulligan, Tony Davis,
              Norman Alden, Warren Berlinger,
              Jackie Russell, Fay Spain, Ken Swofford

A young Indian boy asks for Matt's help when his guardian is being harassed by three surly no-goods.

NOTES: Sequel to "I Call Him Wonder" from Season 8. Two funny scenes, the first Matt's reaction to Wonder's (Davis) glee when Matt says he will allow himself to be beaten up by Jud (Mulligan), the other when Festus spills a bag of crawdads on Doc's office floor.

#453: BAKER'S DOZEN
(12-25-67)

WRITER: Charles Joseph Stone
DIRECTOR: Irving J. Moore
CAST: Denver Pyle, Peggy Rea, Harry Carey, Jr.,
              Harry Lauter, Mitzi Hoag, Ed McCready,
              Sam Greene, Phyllis Coghlan, Charles Wagenheim,
              Tyler MacDuff, William Murphy, Dana Dillaway,
              Keith Schultz, Gary Grimes

Doc is desperate to keep newborn and orphaned triplets from being placed in an orphanage in Topeka.

NOTES: Milburn Stone won the Best Supporting Actor Emmy for this episode. When Kitty observes Matt holding one of the babies, she sadly sees a future she will never have. Festus urges Doc to "stay in the buggy" in the courtroom, as he did when Doc was suffering from the snakebite in "Wishbone." Doc tells Festus the coldest winter in Dodge was 1863. Stable sign now reads Hank Patterson, the real name of the actor who portrays stableman Hank Miller. First appearance by Peggy Rea as Mrs. Roniger. This episode, originally conceived as a story for Chester, was written by Milburn Stone's brother. One of Amanda Blake's favorites.

#454: THE VICTIM
(01-01-68)

STORY: Hal Sitowitz
TELEPLAY: Arthur Rowe
DIRECTOR: Vincent McEveety
CAST: Beverly Garland, James Gregory,
             Cliff Osmond, John Kellogg, Kevin Hagen,
             Warren Vanders, Edmund Hashim,
             Roy Jenson, Gregg Palmer, Tim O'Kelley,
             Willis Bouchey

Matt goes to the town of Martin's Bend to stop a slow-witted giant of a man from being hanged illegally.

NOTES: Solo Matt story. First of Beverly Garland's four guest roles on the series. John Kellogg, Roy Jenson and Gregg Palmer in particular are all very familiar faces to Western fans.

#455: DEADMAN'S LAW
(01-08-68)

WRITER: Calvin Clements, Jr.
DIRECTOR: John Rich
CAST: John Dehner, Gunnar Hellstrom,
             Eddie Little Sky, Craig Curtis, Ralph Manza,
             Gregg Palmer, Robert Brubaker, Steve Raines,
             Baynes Barron, Woodrow Chambliss,
             Alex Sharp, Hank Patterson, Jonathan Harper

Shady businessmen attempt to take over Dodge City when it is believed Matt has been killed.

NOTES: Matt shot again in the left shoulder. Doc to Festus: "Don't think—that's when you get dangerous." Doc reminds citizens that Matt has been marshal for 12 years. Sam intervenes when Doc is being beaten. Director Hellstrom cast as Eriksson. Robert Brubaker was formerly stage driver Jim Buck. Steve Raines of *Rawhide* once more plays a trail boss. Filmed partly at Vasquez Rocks. One of the best episodes of the season.

#456: NOWHERE TO RUN
(01-15-68)

STORY: Robert Totten
TELEPLAY: Ron Honthaner
DIRECTOR: Vincent McEveety
CAST: J. Robert Porter, Bob Random, Dan Ferrone, Mark Lenard, Ikla Windish, Michael Burns, Tom Brown, Harry Harvey, Sr., William Tannen

The men of Dodge attempt to rescue a young man trapped down a well, but two of his friends would rather he stay there.

NOTES: First of 13 appearances by Tom Brown as rancher Ed O'Connor. Michael Burns was a regular cast member on the last two seasons of *Wagon Train*.

#457: BLOOD MONEY
(01-27-68)

WRITER: Hal Sitowitz
DIRECTOR: Robert Totten
CAST: Nehemiah Persoff, Anthony Zerbe, Donna Baccala, James Anderson, Hank Brandt, Mills Watson, Lee De Broux, Troy Melton

The father of a notorious gunfighter shoots his son's gun hand, setting the stage for more violence rather than ending it.

NOTES: First scene in Newly's gun shop. Anthony Zerbe later co-starred on *The Young Riders*.

#458: HILL GIRL
(01-29-68)

WRITER: Calvin Clements
DIRECTOR: Robert Totten
CAST: Lane Bradbury, Victor French, Anthony James

Newly meets an unrefined young woman wanting a fresh start in life and brings her to Dodge, followed by her disreputable hillbilly half-brothers.

NOTES: Matt gives Festus a badge for the first time. Kitty tells Merry Florene (Bradbury) of her experiences when she decided to leave home. Dabbs Greer back as Wilbur Jonas after a long absence. First of four appearances by Lane Bradbury as Merry Florene.

#459: THE GUNRUNNERS
(02-05-68)

WRITER: Hal Sitowitz
DIRECTOR: Irving J. Moore
CAST: Michael Constantine, Dan Ferrone, Jim Davis,
            Dick Peabody, James Griffith, John McLiam,
            Lane Bradford, X Brands

A fur trapper brings his badly beaten Indian son to Doc, then leaves to hunt down the men responsible.

NOTES: Festus shot in the left arm. Patch (Peabody) refers to Doc as "one of the best docs in the state."

#460: THE JACKALS
(02-12-68)

WRITER: Calvin Clements, Jr.
DIRECTOR: Alvin Ganzer
CAST: Paul Richards, Tige Andrews, Joe De Santis,
            Felice Orlandi, Ward Wood, Michael Vandever,
            Alex Montoya, David Renard, Martin Garralaga,
            Rico Alaniz, Jorge Moreno, Ruben Moreno,
            Ellen Davalos, Carmen Austin, Olga Velez

Matt faces a gang of Mexican bandits when he crosses the border in search of the four men who murdered his friend.

NOTES: It is disclosed that Matt was a deputy for Sheriff Mark Handlin (De Santis) in Texas fifteen or sixteen years ago. One of the best episodes of the season.

#461: THE FIRST PEOPLE
(02-19-68)

WRITER: Calvin Clements
DIRECTOR: Robert Totten
CAST: Todd Armstrong, Gene Evans, Jack Elam,
            James Almanzar, James Lydon, Richard Hale,
            Felix Locher, Bill Erwin, Eddie Little Sky

Matt investigates trouble on an Indian reservation, only to lose his badge and be accused of murder.

NOTES: Matt's left arm broken by Indian agents. Rare "good guy" role for Elam.

#462: MR. SAM'L
(02-26-67)

WRITER: Harry Kronman
DIRECTOR: Gunnar Hellstrom
CAST: Ed Begley, Mark Richman, Sandra Smith,
               Larry Pennell, Duke Hobbie, Tom Brown

Drought once again plagues Dodge, and no one believes the old man who says he can locate water, including his own daughter.

NOTES: Matt mentions the dry spell of 1868. James Nusser (Louie Pheeters) witnesses one of the many beatings and killings he has a knack for seeing.

#463: A NOOSE FOR DOBIE PRICE
(03-04-68)

WRITER: Antony Ellis
DIRECTOR: Richard C. Sarafian
CAST: Chill Wills, Shug Fisher, Sheldon Allman,
               Robert Donner, E.J. Andre, Rose Hobart,
               Owen Bush, Michael Greene, Raymond Mayo,
               John "Bear" Hudkins, Bob Herron

Matt joins forces with a former outlaw when two prisoners break jail, but it is never entirely clear if the man can be trusted.

NOTES: A rare hanging in Dodge. Chill Wills' second appearance of the season.

Arness & Miriam Colon in "Zavala," 1968

EPISODE GUIDE

SEASON 14
September 23, 1968–March 24, 1969

#464: LYLE'S KID
(09-23-68)

WRITER: Calvin Clements
DIRECTOR: Bernard McEveety
CAST: Morgan Woodward, Charlotte Considine,
Robert Pine, Sam Melville, Ken Mayer,
Mills Watson, Lew Palter, Joe De Santis,
I. Stanford Jolley, Jonathan Harper

Another former lawman from Matt's past comes to Dodge to kill a man about to be released from prison.

NOTES: New opening title sequence showing James Arness' frantic ride shot for the 1967 episode "Nitro!" Buck Taylor's tenth appearance as Newly, still listed among the supporting cast rather than with regular characters. Morgan Woodward's ninth guest appearance. Dodge City holds an anniversary celebration.

#465: THE HIDE CUTTERS
(09-30-68)

WRITER: Jack Turley
DIRECTOR: Bernard McEveety
CAST: Joseph Campanella, Michael Burns, Cliff Osmond,
Eddie Firestone, Ken Swofford, Conlan Carter,
Gregg Palmer, Steve Raines, Mike Howden

Matt and Festus are caught in the middle of trouble between a trail drive and a band of hide hunters.

NOTES: Steve Raines of *Rawhide* fame plays drover Lawson. Joseph Campanella was a regular on the first season of *Mannix.* Partially filmed at Vasquez Rocks.

#466: ZAVALA
(10-07-68)

WRITER: Paul Savage
DIRECTOR: Vincent McEveety
CAST: Miriam Colon, Manuel Padilla, Jr., Jim Davis, Jonathan Lippe, Larry D. Mann, Rex Holman, Rico Alaniz, Robert Sorrells, Warren Vanders, Nacho Galindo, Jose Chavez, Elizabeth Germaine, Bobby E. Clark

Matt pursues some outlaws to the Mexican town of Zavala, where a young boy gets the notion that the marshal is just the man to clean up the town.

NOTES: Matt shot in the left side. The border guard remembers Matt from other times he has crossed into Mexico. The late Manuel Padilla, Jr., appeared on *Rawhide,* played Jai on the *Tarzan* series and a hoodlum in the classic *American Graffiti.* One of executive producer John Mantley's favorite episodes.

#467: UNCLE FINNEY
(10-14-68)

WRITER: Calvin Clements
DIRECTOR: Bernard McEveety
CAST: Victor French, Anthony James, Lane Bradbury, Burt Mustin, Roy Roberts, Steve Raines, John Dolan, Monte Hale, Pete Kellett, Margaret Bacon

Merry Florene returns to Dodge with her two half-brothers, who want Festus to pay them a $50 reward for turning in their 103-year-old uncle, wanted for horse theft.

NOTES: The freight office where Nathan Burke (Ted Jordan) works is named the Kiskadden Freight Company, later changed to Adams Express. Matt shows up at literally the last minute of the episode. A comparison between the script and the episode illustrates how many liberties Ken Curtis could take with his lines yet retain the essence of a scene.

#468: SLOCUM
(10-21-68)

WRITER: Ron Bishop
DIRECTOR: Leo Penn
CAST: Will Geer, Dub Taylor, James Wainwright, Ross Hagen, Lee Lambert, Mills Watson, Steve Sandor, Bill Erwin, Lew Brown, Charles Kuenstle

An aging mountain man figures he owes Matt a favor, so he makes sure no harm comes to the marshal at the hands of a disgruntled family.

NOTES: Matt shot in the left arm again. Dub Taylor is the father of Buck Taylor. Will Geer portrayed the grandfather on *The Waltons*.

#469: O'QULLIAN
(10-28-68)

WRITER: Ron Bishop
DIRECTOR: John Rich
CAST: John McLiam, Victor French, Lou Antonio, Vaughn Taylor, Ken Drake, Anthony James, Steve Raines, Iron Eyes Cody, Peggy Rea, Woodrow Chambliss, Jerry Summers, Roy Barcroft

Leary O'Quillian, a troublemaking Irishman, drifts into Dodge and proceeds to cause chaos for nearly everyone, including Kitty.

NOTES: Peggy Rea appears briefly as a saloon girl on the saloon set used for *Cimarron Strip*. Victor French and Anthony James had just played brothers in "Uncle Finney."

#470: 9:12 to Dodge
(11-11-68)

WRITER: Preston Wood
DIRECTOR: Marvin Chomsky
CAST: Todd Armstrong, Joanne Linville, Frank Marth,
                Tom Water, Robert Emhardt, Harry Lauter,
                Troy Melton, Link Wyler, Fred Coby,
                Lee De Broux, William Murphy,
                Harry Harvey, Sr., Ed Long, Dan Terranova,
                Rush Williams, Johnny Haymer, Bobby E. Clark,
                Pete Kellett

Matt, Doc and a wounded prisoner are returning to Dodge in a train also carrying men intent on freeing the marshal's captive.

NOTES: Harry Lauter, who appeared on more than fifty television Western series, had guest roles on eight episodes of *Gunsmoke*.

#471: Abelia
(11-18-68)

WRITER: Calvin Clements
DIRECTOR: Vincent McEveety
CAST: Jacqueline Scott, Jeremy Slate, Tom Stern,
                Jack Lambert, Gregg Palmer, Mike Durkin,
                Susan Olsen, Jack Chaplain

Festus pretends to be a farmer in order to protect a widow and her children from the gang of outlaws who are hiding at the woman's house.

NOTES: First of three episodes with Jacqueline Scott as Festus' potential love interest Abelia Johnson. Badman Jack Lambert appeared in more than two dozen Western series, including six episodes of *Gunsmoke*.

#472: RAILROAD!
(11-25-68)

WRITER: Arthur Rowe
DIRECTOR: Marvin Chomsky
CAST: Shug Fisher, Jim Davis, Buck Holland,
                     Ramon Bieri, Roy Jenson, Don Hanmer,
                     James McCallion

Matt steps in when the Kansas and North Platte Railroad Company attempts to force a stubborn homesteader off his legally owned land.

NOTES: When Matt shoots holes in illegal barrels of whiskey, town drunk Louie Pheeters protests that it is "a crime against nature." Arness and Jim Davis engage in a knock down, drag out fist fight that ends in the *Gilligan's Island* lagoon.

#473: THE MIRACLE MAN
(12-02-68)

WRITER: Calvin Clements
DIRECTOR: Bernard McEveety
CAST: Don Chastain, Sandra Smith, William Bramley,
                     Joey Walsh, Bruce Watson, Margie De Meyer,
                     Lisa Gerritsen, Kevin Cooper, John Crawford,
                     Christopher Knight

In spite of Festus' warning, a sympathetic widow hires a conman before the citizens of Dodge run him out of town.

NOTES: Lisa Gerritsen was later a semi-regular cast member on *The Mary Tyler Moore Show* before dropping out of show business at an early age.

#474: WACO
(12-09-68)

WRITER: Ron Bishop
DIRECTOR: Robert Totten
CAST: Victor French, Harry Carey, Jr.,
             Louise Latham, Tom Reese, Lee De Broux,
             Mills Watson, Lawrence Mann, Pat Thompson,
             Joy Fielding, Liz Marshall, Fred McDougall

Matt, being pursued by four outlaws who want to free his prisoner, comes across a pregnant Indian woman badly in need of help.

NOTES: Matt tracks his prey to Spivey, Kansas. Third guest role for Victor French this season.

#475: LOBO
(12-16-68)

WRITER: Jim Byrnes
DIRECTOR: Vincent McEveety
CAST: Morgan Woodward, David Brian,
             Sheldon Allman, Sandy Kenyon,
             Ken Swofford, Eddie Firestone, Fred Coby,
             William Murphy

Luke Brazo, an old mountain man, asks for Matt's assistance in tracking down a marauding wolf before it can be killed by bounty hunters with no respect for wildlife.

NOTES: Morgan Woodward's tenth guest appearance, as well as his personal favorite.

#476: JOHNNY CROSS
(12-23-68)

WRITER: Calvin Clements
DIRECTOR: Herschel Daugherty
CAST: Jeff Pomerantz, Dean Stanton,
             John Crawford, Shug Fisher,
             Charles Thompson, Kelly Jean Peters

Two bounty hunters threaten to kill a witness unless he swears an innocent man committed a stage robbery.

NOTES: Partially filmed at Iverson Ranch.

#477: THE MONEY STORE
(12-30-68)

WRITER: William Blinn
DIRECTOR: Vincent McEveety
CAST: Eric Shea, Pamelyn Ferdin,
             William Schallert, Charles Aidman,
             Virginia Vincent

When his two young children take some money from the bank, a destitute farmer claims he committed the crime.

NOTES: Ezra Thorpe (Schallert) is said to be in charge of loans at Bodkin's bank, unlike previous episodes where Bodkin decided who deserved a loan.

#478: The Twisted Heritage
(01-06-69)

STORY:	Robert Haverly & Jack Turley
TELEPLAY:	Paul Savage & Arthur Rowe
DIRECTOR:	Bernard McEveety
CAST:	Virginia Gregg, Lisa Gerritsen, John Ericson, Nora Marlowe, Conlan Carter, Charles Kuenstle, Richard O'Brien, David McLean, Robert Luster, Steve Raines, Robert Karnes, Joshua Bryant

After the driver is killed, Kitty is forced to drive a stagecoach carrying a wounded passenger.

NOTES: Kitty in yet another stage mishap. Interior and exterior of the large ranch house is the set of the Barkley Ranch on *The Big Valley*. David McLean portrayed the title character on the underrated and seldom seen Western series *Tate*.

#479: Time of the Jackals
(01-13-69)

STORY:	Richard Fielder
TELEPLAY:	Paul Savage & Richard Fielder
DIRECTOR:	Vincent McEveety
CAST:	Leslie Nielsen, Beverly Garland, Jonathan Lippe, Edmund Hashim, Robert Knapp, Charles Maxwell, Sig Haig, Art Stewart, Kip Whitman

Matt discovers the woman he has wounded in a gun battle with outlaws is one of his ex-girlfriends.

NOTES: Matt first met Leona (Garland) in Colorado, where her father ran a trading post. Kitty mentions being owner of the Long Branch for 14 years.

#480: Mannon
(01-20-69)

WRITER: Ron Bishop
DIRECTOR: Robert Butler
CAST: Steve Forrest, Charles Seel, Howard Culver,
               Charles Wagenheim, Michelle Breeze,
               Woodrow Chambliss, Tom Brown

A psychotic gunslinger seriously wounds Festus, intimidates the citizens of Dodge City, and beats up Kitty while waiting for Matt to return to town.

NOTES: This episode was used as the basis for the first *Gunsmoke* television movie, "Return to Dodge," in 1987. Dillon shot in the left arm again. All of the regular Dodge City characters are present except banker Bodkin and undertaker Percy Crump. John Mantley considered this one of the most powerful episodes of the series.

#481: Goldtown
(01-27-69)

WRITER: Calvin Clements
DIRECTOR: Gunnar Hellstrom
CAST: Anthony James, Lane Bradbury, Lou Antonio,
               Kathryn Minner, Harry Davis, Chubby Johnson,
               Paul Wexler, Jack Searl, Pete Kellett,
               Jimmy Bracken, Eve Plumb

Merry Florene's dishonest half-brother Elbert Moses establishes his own "town" outside Dodge City as part of a scheme to swindle fortune hunters with a phony gold mine.

NOTES: Anthony James' and Lane Bradbury's third appearances as Elbert Moses and Merry Florene.

#482: The Mark of Cain
(02-03-69)

WRITER: Ron Bishop
DIRECTOR: Vincent McEveety
CAST: Nehemiah Persoff, Louise Latham, Robert Totten,
             Kevin Coughlin, Stanley Clements, Olan Soule,
             Robert DoQui, Roy Barcroft

A pair of buffalo hunters discovers that a prominent Dodge City rancher was in charge of the prison where they were incarcerated during the Civil War.

NOTES: No name on the Dodge City stable. Robert Totten, who plays Corley, also directed two dozen episodes of *Gunsmoke*. Robert DoQui the first black actor to appear on the series since "The Promoter" in Season 9.

#483: Reprisal
(02-10-69)

WRITER: Jack Hawn
DIRECTOR: Bernard McEveety
CAST: Joe Don Baker, Eunice Christopher,
             I. Stanford Jolley, John Pickard, Dennis Cross,
             Jack Lambert

A griefstricken farmer vows that Doc will pay for tending to a wounded outlaw instead of coming to the aid of his pregnant wife, who loses the baby.

NOTES: Even though Roy Barcroft now portrays storeowner Roy, Wilbur Jonas is mentioned but not seen. When Joe Don Baker knocks Doc down in front of the general store, it is obviously a stuntman, not Milburn Stone, taking the blow.

#484: THE LONG NIGHT
(02-17-69)

STORY: Dick Carr
TELEPLAY: Paul Savage
DIRECTOR: John Rich
CAST: Bruce Dern, Lou Antonio, Russell Johnson,
               Susan Silo, Robert Totten, Robert Brubaker,
               Rex Holman, Matt Emery, Victor Tayback

Doc, Kitty, Sam and Louie Pheeters are taken captive by bounty hunters who want to trade them to Matt for a prisoner worth a large reward.

NOTES: James Nusser (Louie), an alcoholic in real life, was applauded by the cast and crew after finishing a scene where he is forced to crawl across the Long Branch in order to get a drink, which he turns down.

#485: THE NIGHT RIDERS
(02-24-69)

WRITER: Calvin Clements
DIRECTOR: Irving J. Moore
CAST: Jeff Corey, Robert Pine, Bob Random,
               Norman Alden, Warren Vanders,
               Robert Karnes, Scott Hale, Ed Bakey

A deranged "judge" and men still fighting the Civil War take over Dodge in Matt's absence.

NOTES: In addition to acting and directing, Jeff Corey also ran an acting school in Los Angeles for several years. Bob Random appeared in seven episodes of *Gunsmoke*.

#486: THE INTRUDERS
(03-03-69)

WRITER: Jim Byrnes
DIRECTOR: Vincent McEveety
CAST: Charles Aidman, John Kellogg, Gail Kobe,
             Eric Shea, Ralph James, Robert Gravage

Festus and his prisoner stop at a ranch owned by the prisoner's wife, who assumed her husband was dead and has remarried.

#487: THE GOOD SAMARITANS
(03-10-69)

WRITER: Paul Savage
DIRECTOR: Bernard McEveety
CAST: Brock Peters, Rex Ingram, L.Q. Jones,
             Sam Melville, Hazel Medina, Paulene Myers,
             Robert DoQui, Davis Roberts, Lynn Hamilton,
             Dan Ferrone, John Brandon, Pepe Brown,
             Alycia Gardner

A wounded Matt is sheltered from bounty hunters by a family of former slaves.

NOTES: Matt shot in the left side. First predominantly black cast on the series, led by the dynamic Brock Peters. Lynn Hamilton is best known as Redd Foxx's long suffering fiancé Donna on *Sanford and Son.*

#488: THE PRISONER
(03-17-69)

WRITER: Calvin Clements
DIRECTOR: Leo Penn
CAST: Jon Voight, Ramon Bieri, Kenneth Tobey,

Ned Glass, Paul Bryar, Tom Brown, Jan Peters, David Fresco, Don Happy

Kitty's life is saved by a young man being mistreated by a band of bounty hunters.

NOTES: Festus is looking after the stable for an ailing Hank. Buck Taylor's 25th appearance as Newly O'Brien. Jon Voight's third and final *Gunsmoke* episode. Director Leo Penn was the father of actor Sean Penn.

#489: EXODUS 21.22
(03-24-69)

WRITER: Arthur Rowe
DIRECTOR: Herschel Daugherty
CAST: Steve Ihnat, Kaz Garas, Brandon Carroll, William Bramley, Lane Bradford, Sarah Hardy, Hank Brandt

A friend of Matt, Kitty and Doc returns to Dodge in search of three men who he holds responsible for the death of his Indian wife.

NOTES: The date on a grave marker reads 1874. Matt gets to deliver the famous "Get out of Dodge!" line for the first time in a long while.

Blake & Stone

EPISODE GUIDE

SEASON 15
September 22, 1969–March 23, 1970

#490: THE DEVIL'S OUTPOST
(09-22-69)

STORY: Robert Barbash
TELEPLAY: Jim Byrnes & Robert Barbash
DIRECTOR: Philip Leacock
CAST: Robert Lansing, Jonathan Lippe, Karl Swenson,
                Sheila Larkin, Ken Swofford, Warren Vanders,
                Val de Vargas, Charles Kuenstle, Sabrina Scharf,
                Troy Melton, Joe Higgins, I. Stanford Jolley,
                Sam Edwards, William Tannen, Joe Haworth,
                Ed Long

Outlaws make the mistake of attempting to rob a stagecoach carrying Matt.

NOTES: Newly shot in left arm. Buck Taylor now included with the regular cast in the opening credits. Writer Calvin Clements promoted to executive story consultant. Episode directed by former *Gunsmoke* producer Philip Leacock. Location shooting includes Vasquez Rocks.

#491: STRYKER
(09-29-69)

WRITER: Herman Groves
DIRECTOR: Robert Totten

CAST: Morgan Woodward, Joan Van Ark, Royal Dano,
             Andy Devine, Mills Watson, Walter Sande,
             Ted French, Don Happy

Josh Stryker, once marshal of Dodge City, returns after spending 15 years in prison because of Matt's testimony.

NOTES: Matt tells Doc that testifying against Stryker was the hardest thing he ever had to do. Stryker hits Doc. Stableman is named Dish.

#492: COREYVILLE
(10-06-69)

WRITER: Herman Groves
DIRECTOR: Bernard McEveety
CAST: Nina Foch, Ruth Roman, Jo Ann Harris,
             Bruce Glover, Kevin Coughlin, Thomas Hunter,
             John Schuck, James Almanzar, Charles Fredericks,
             Bill Erwin, Pete Kellett, Bill Catching,
             Gary Combs

Matt interrupts a farce of a murder trial in the town of Coreyville and tries to determine who is really guilty.

NOTES: Largely a showcase for Hollywood veterans Nina Foch and Ruth Roman. Saloon in Coreyville is the set of the Dodge House lobby.

#493: DANNY
(10-13-69)

WRITER: Preston Wood
DIRECTOR: Bernard McEveety
CAST: Jack Albertson, Scott Brady, Vito Scotti,
             Frank Marth, Rayford Barnes, Jonathan Harper,
             Tom Brown, Steve Raines

After learning he does not have long to live, con artist Danny Wilson devises a final ruse that will pay for an extravagant funeral.

NOTES: Kitty knew Danny (Albertson) in San Francisco 15 years ago.

#494: HAWK
(10-20-69)

WRITER: Kay Lenard & Jess Carneol
DIRECTOR: Gunnar Hellstrom
CAST: Brendon Boone, Louise Latham,
    Michael-James Wixted, Hilarie Thompson,
    Robert Brubaker, X Brands, Bill Hart,
    Hal Needham, Glen Randal, Jr.

A half-breed policeman chasing after four renegades is reunited with his mother, who abandoned him 20 years before.

NOTES: Legendary stunt artist Hal Needham portrays one of the renegade Indians. Robert Brubaker was Dodge City stagecoach driver Jim Buck in 14 episodes.

#495: A MAN CALLED "SMITH"
(10-27-69)

WRITER: Calvin Clements
DIRECTOR: Vincent McEveety
CAST: Earl Holliman, Jacqueline Scott,
    Susan Olsen, Michael Durkin, Val Avery,
    Roy Roberts, Sid Haig, William Fawcett,
    Margarita Cordova

An outlaw who deserted his family returns and promises to move on if his wife will sell the gold he has stolen.

NOTES: Ken Curtis' 150th episode as Festus Haggen. Jacqueline Scott's second appearance as Abelia. Val Avery rather than Victor Izay portrays the owner of the Bull's Head Saloon.

#496: CHARLIE NOON
(11-03-69)

WRITER: Jim Byrnes
DIRECTOR: Vincent McEveety
CAST: James Best, Miriam Colon, Ronny Howard,
             Edmund Hashim, Kip Whitman

Matt and his prisoner stumble upon an Indian woman and her white stepson in Comanche territory.

NOTES: This episode earned an Emmy for Outstanding Achievement in Film Sound Editing. Ronny Howard had just completed eight years on *The Andy Griffith Show* the previous season. James Best appeared on nearly 50 different television Westerns.

#497: THE STILL
(11-10-69)

WRITER: Calvin Clements
DIRECTOR: Gunnar Hellstrom
CAST: Lane Bradbury, Anthony James,
             Shug Fisher, James Westerfield, J. Edward
             McKinley, Trent Lehman

Merry Florene's half-brother Elbert Moses and her uncle hide a still and a stolen bull in the cellar of the school where she is teaching the children of Dodge City.

NOTES: Lane Bradbury and Anthony James reprise their roles as Merry and Elbert for the fourth time. Mr. Franks (Westerfield), not Victor Izay as Bull Landers, runs the Bull's Head Saloon this time.

#498: A MATTER OF HONOR
(11-17-69)

WRITER: Joy Dexter
DIRECTOR: Robert Totten
CAST: John Anderson, Katherine Justice,
               Tom Simcox, Dan Ferrone, Dan Bakalayan,
               Walter Sande, Jack Bailey, Lawrence Mann,
               Bob Burrows

Town drunk Louie Pheeters witnesses another killing, but this time he is the one charged with the crime.

NOTES: Louie occasionally pawns his father's watch at the Long Branch, then works off his debt. Festus does the calling at the Admission Day barn dance. Judge Brooker played by Jack Bailey.

#499: THE INNOCENT
(11-24-69)

WRITER: Walter Black
DIRECTOR: Marvin Chomsky
CAST: Eileen Heckert, Barry Atwater, Lee de Broux,
               Anthony James, Robert B. Williams, Eddie Little
               Sky, Manuel Padilla, Jr., Tom Nolan,
               Rush Williams

Festus is escorting a teacher and her wagonload of supplies to an Indian school when they are taken captive by backwoods thieves.

NOTES: Episode begins in Phelps, Kansas. Festus said to be hauling freight for Mr. Jonas. Partially filmed at Indian Dunes, site of the *Twilight Zone* accident which took the life of actor Vic Morrow.

#500: RING OF DARKNESS
(12-01-69)

WRITER: Arthur Dales
DIRECTOR: Bernard McEveety
CAST: Pamela Dunlap, Tom Drake, John Crawford, Anthony Caruso, Rex Holman

A farmer who has been forced to steal horses tells his blind daughter that Newly is the real culprit.

NOTES: Tom Drake played Judy Garland's love interest in the 1944 classic *Meet Me in St. Louis*.

#501: MACGRAW
(12-08-69)

WRITER: Kay Lenard & Jess Carneol
DIRECTOR: Philip Leacock
CAST: J.D. Cannon, Michael Larrain, Diana Ewing, Sam Melville, Charles Kuenstle, Ned Wertimer, Tom Brown, Sig Haig, Allen Jaffe, Bobby Hall, Sam Edwards

A former gunslinger is released from prison and takes a job playing piano at the Long Branch, but Matt suspects the man has other plans.

NOTES: Matt mentions once being a deputy in Hays. The livery stable once again advertised as belonging to Hank Patterson.

#502: ROOTS OF FEAR
(12-15-69)

STORY: Arthur Browne, Jr.
TELEPLAY: Jim Byrnes & Arthur Browne, Jr.
DIRECTOR: Philip Leacock

CAST: John Anderson, Louise Latham,
        Warren Vanders, Cliff Osmond, Jody Foster,
        Walter Burke, Arthur Peterson, Robert Karnes,
        Paul Micale, Hank Wise, Roy Roberts

A desperate homesteader worried about losing his farm breaks into the Dodge City bank, which has recently locked its doors over financial worries of its own.

NOTES: Banker Bodkin's first name revealed to be Harry. Judge Brooker now played by Arthur Peterson. Child actress Jody Foster later changed her name to Jodie as an acclaimed actress and director.

#503: THE SISTERS
(12-29-69)

WRITER: William Kelley
DIRECTOR: Philip Leacock
CAST: Jack Elam, Lynn Hamilton, Susan Batson,
           Gloria Calomee, Erica Petal, Chris Hundley,
           Cece Whitney

Unreliable Pack Landers pretends to change his drunken ways when a trio of nuns reunites him with his two young children.

NOTES: Typical good performance by Western veteran Jack Elam, who appeared in 15 episodes of *Gunsmoke*.

#504: THE WAR PRIEST
(01-05-70)

WRITER: William Kelley
DIRECTOR: Bernard McEveety
CAST: Forrest Tucker, Richard Anderson, John Crawford,
           Richard Hale, Sam Melville, Link Wyler,
           Tom Sutton, Pete Kellett, Vincent Deadrick

Kitty is taken captive by an escaped Apache war priest being hunted by a disreputable army sergeant.

NOTES: First appearance by Forrest Tucker as Sergeant Emmett Holly. The "Pharaoh's Horses" portrait which once hung in Doc's office, then Kitty's, can be seen in the bedroom of the stage depot.

#505: THE PACK RAT
(01-12-70)

STORY: Arthur Browne, Jr.
TELEPLAY: Jim Byrnes & Arthur Browne, Jr.
DIRECTOR: Philip Leacock
CAST: William C. Watson, Loretta Swit,
               Manuel Padilla, Jr., Heidi Vaughn,
               Robert Rothwell, Robert Brubaker,
               Bill Catching, Tom Sutton

Matt's job is complicated by a wounded prisoner, a pregnant woman and a young Mexican pickpocket.

NOTES: Partially filmed at Vasquez Rocks. Loretta Swit is best known for her role as Margaret "Hot Lips" Houlihan on the *M*A*S*H* series.

#506: THE JUDAS GUN
(01-19-70)

WRITER: Harry Kronman
DIRECTOR: Vincent McEveety
CAST: Ron Hayes, Peter Jason, Richard X. Slattery,
               Laurie Mock, Sean McClory, Tom Brown,
               Margarita Cordova, William Fawcett,
               Brad David, Ralph Neff

Two ranchers with no use for one another go at it again when their children fall in love.

NOTES: Ron Hayes appeared on more than two dozen television Westerns, including eight episodes of *Gunsmoke*.

#507: DOCTOR HERMAN SCHULTZ, M.D. (01-26-70)

STORY: Benny Rubin
TELEPLAY: Calvin Clements
DIRECTOR: Bernard McEveety
CAST: Benny Rubin, Pete Kellett, Howard Culver

An old friend and colleague of Doc's with a special interest in hypnosis comes to Dodge.

NOTES: Both Matt and Kitty are surprised to hear Doc's first name (Galen) used. Story contributed by comic actor Benny Rubin, who portrays Dr. Schultz.

#508: THE BADGE (02-02-70)

WRITER: Jim Byrnes
DIRECTOR: Vincent McEveety
CAST: Beverly Garland, Henry Jones, John Milford,
              Roy Jenson, Jack Lambert, William O'Connell,
              Mary Angela, John Flinn, Fred Coby

Upset by seeing Matt shot for at least the 30th time, Kitty puts the Long Branch up for sale and travels to visit a friend in a corrupt town.

NOTES: Matt is shot in the left side of his chest, above the heart. Doc is a bit off the mark when he tells Kitty he has dug bullets out of Matt 11 times in 15 years. When Doc says he is 51, Matt says he is lying. Matt to Kitty: "We've never needed explanations." Scenes from this episode were used in *Return to Dodge* in 1987.

#509: ALBERT
(02-09-70)

WRITER: Jim Byrnes
DIRECTOR: Vincent McEveety
CAST: Milton Selzer, Patricia Barry, L.Q. Jones,
              Bob Random, William Schallert,
              Dorothy Neumann, Natalie Masters,
              Roy Roberts

Bank teller Albert Schiller prevents an attempted robbery, but decides to steal $5000 and blame the would-be thieves.

NOTES: First and only appearance of Harry Bodkin's wife (Masters). At one point Albert's time at the bank is given as eight years, but Jake (Schallert) later says he has been there 15 years.

#510: KIOWA
(02-16-70)

WRITER: Ron Bishop
DIRECTOR: Bernard McEveety
CAST: Dub Taylor, Victor French, John Beck, Lucas
              White, Joyce Ames, Jean Allison, Richard Lapp,
              Richard Angarola, Angela Carroll

A rancher's daughter is abducted by a band of Kiowa, and Matt suspects her father knows why the Indians are leaving a trail easy to follow.

NOTES: Matt once again disappoints Kitty when he has to leave her birthday celebration.

#511: CELIA
(02-23-70)

WRITER: Harry Kronman
DIRECTOR: Philip Leacock
CAST: Cliff Osmond, Melissa Murphy, Frank Marth,
               Roy Roberts, Charles Seel, George Petrie,
               Walker Edmiston

Newly is certain a mail order bride is only interested in his friend's money.

NOTES: Blacksmith Ben Sommars (Osmond) co-signed a $1200 loan so Newly could open a gun shop. Steve Raines appears as a stagecoach driver.

#512: MORGAN
(03-02-70)

WRITER: Kay Lenard & Jess Carneol
DIRECTOR: Bernard McEveety
CAST: Steve Forrest, Hank Brandt, Charlotte Stewart,
               Ed Long, Mills Watson, Jonathan Lippe,
               Charles Seel, Jack Garner, I. Stanford Jolley,
               Fletcher Bryant, Read Morgan

A gang of outlaws packing a Gatling gun invade Dodge and wait for a shipment of gold Matt and a company of army troopers are bringing to town.

NOTES: Steve Forrest made such an impact as Mannon in the episode of the same name that viewers could be excused for thinking this is a sequel. Charlotte Stewart later played Miss Beadle on *Little House on the Prairie*. The late Jack Garner was the brother of James Garner.

#513: The Thieves
(03-09-70)

WRITER: Thomas Thompson
DIRECTOR: Philip Leacock
CAST: Michael Burns, Bill Callaway, Timothy Burns,
Royal Dano, Daphne Field, John Schuck

Bartender Sam takes pity on a young man headed for county jail and is able to arrange for him to work at the Long Branch.

NOTES: Glenn Strange's largest role ever as Sam, who says he once faced jail time but a marshal gave him a break. Louie Pheeters claims he has given up drinking, going on five days, then later nine after one relapse.

#514: Hackett
(03-16-70)

WRITER: William Kelley
DIRECTOR: Vincent McEveety
CAST: Earl Holliman, Morgan Woodward,
Jennifer West, Ken Swofford, Robert Totten,
Bill Erwin, Allen Jung

An ex-con hounds his cowardly ex-partner into planning a train robbery.

NOTES: Holliman (ex-con Hackett) and Woodward (ex-partner Sargent) switched roles at the suggestion of executive producer John Mantley, giving the latter an opportunity to display his versatility as an actor.

#515: The Cage
(03-23-70)

Writer: Calvin Clements
Director: Bernard McEveety
Cast: Steve Carlson, Laura Figueroa, Hank Brandt, Jorge
              Moreno, Paul Stewart, Gregg Palmer, Ken Mayer,
              Robert Swan, Allen Jaffe, Joaquin Martinez, Renata
              Vanni, Pedro Vegas, Araceli Rey

A convict trapped in a prison wagon agrees to help Matt and Festus track down gold robbers.

NOTES: Some scenes shot in Bronson Canyon, a well known filming location in Los Angeles' Griffith Park.

Arness in "Chato," 1970

EPISODE GUIDE
SEASON 16
September 14, 1970–March 8, 1971

#516: CHATO
(09-14-70)

WRITER: Paul F. Edwards
DIRECTOR: Vincent McEveety
CAST: Ricardo Montalban, Miriam Colon,
              William Bryant, Peggy McCay,
              Pedro Regas, Rodolfo Hoyos, Robert Knapp,
              Jim Sheppard

   Matt goes to New Mexico in search of the Indian warrior who killed a friend, ending up in need of his quarry's help.

NOTES: A favorite of both Arness and executive producer John Mantley. Filmed around Taos, New Mexico. *Gunsmoke* began more shooting outside California this season, one of the series' strongest. Edwards' script won a Golden Spur Award from the Western Writers of America. Arness and Montalban later worked together on the *How the West Was Won* series, for which Montalban won an Emmy.

#517: THE NOOSE
(09-21-70)

WRITER: Arthur Browne, Jr.
DIRECTOR: Vincent McEveety
CAST: Tom Skerritt, Hank Patterson,
              William Fawcett

Fifteen years after his father's hanging, a young man returns to Dodge determined to get even with Matt in a very unique way.

NOTES: Matt shot in right leg. Although there has never been mention of Dodge City being relocated, the former locale—now a ghost town—is referred to variously as "Dodgetown," "Old Dodge" and "Old Town." Freight office now called Adams Express. Hank Patterson back to portraying Hank Miller rather than Patterson.

#518: STARK
(09-28-70)

WRITER: Donald S. Sanford
DIRECTOR: Robert Totten
CAST: Richard Kiley, Suzanne Pleshette,
             Henry Wilcoxon, Shelly Novak,
             Bob Burrows, Rusty Lane

A bounty hunter turns blackmailer when he discovers that his prisoner is the son of a wealthy rancher.

NOTES: Bartender other than Sam at the Long Branch.

#519: SAM McTAVISH, M.D.
(10-05-70)

WRITER: Gerry Day & Bethel Leslie
DIRECTOR: Bernard McEveety
CAST: Vera Miles, Arch Johnson, Dee Carroll,
             Lisa Gerritsen, Amzie Strickland, Tom Fadden,
             Kathleen O'Malley, Harry Harvey, Sr., Read
             Morgan, Robert Rothwell, Lance Thomas,
             Glenn Redding

Doc sends for a temporary replacement so he can attend building dedication in honor of his mentor, and is not at all pleased when he learns that Doctor Sam McTavish is a woman.

NOTES: Milburn Stone deserved another Emmy for this episode. Doctor Eldred Hudkins paid Doc's way through medical school. Only third time Doc's first name is mentioned. A rare but tragic romance for Doc. Vera Miles was involved in a similarly ill-fated relationship with Lorne Greene in an episode of *Bonanza* later this season. Co-written by actress Bethel Leslie.

#520: GENTRY'S LAW
(10-12-70)

WRITER: Jack Miller
DIRECTOR: Vincent McEveety
CAST: John Payne, Peter Jason, Robert Pine,
Don Keefer, Louise Latham, Shug Fisher,
Darlene Conley, John Flinn, Robert Totten

When the sons of Matt's friend Amos Gentry accidentally hang a man, Gentry refuses to turn them over for trial.

NOTES: Matt's days as a deputy in Hays mentioned. Hollywood veteran John Payne (Gentry) played Vint Bonner for two seasons on *The Restless Gun*.

#521: SNOW TRAIN, PART 1
(10-19-70)
#522: SNOW TRAIN, PART 2
(10-26-70)

WRITER: Preston Wood
DIRECTOR: Gunnar Hellstrom
CAST: Clifton James, Gene Evans, Ken Lynch,
Roy Engel, Pamela Dunlap, Richard Lapp,
Loretta Swit, Tim Considine, Richard D. Kelton,
John Milford, Dana Elcar, Ron Hayes, X Brands

Arness on location for "Snow Train," 1970

The train carrying Matt, Doc and Festus back to Dodge after testifying at a trial in Denver is stranded in the mountains by Sioux Indians who want two passengers responsible for selling poisoned whiskey to their tribe.

NOTES: First two-part episode in more than three years, filmed near Custer, South Dakota. Matt being pursued on foot by Indians reminiscent of Henry Fonda's race for his life in the 1939 classic *Drums Along the Mohawk*. Guest star credits are run over the closing scenes of Part 2. Composer John Parker won a Western Heritage Wrangler Award for his score.

#523: LUKE
(11-02-70)

WRITER: Jack Miller
DIRECTOR: Bernard McEveety
CAST: Morgan Woodward, Anthony Costello,
              Howard Culver, Katherine Justice, Rex Holman,
              Victor Izay

A seriously wounded outlaw wants his young partner to find his school teacher daughter, unaware that she was a saloon girl and is dead.

NOTES: Morgan Woodward's 13th guest appearance. Victor Izay back as Bull Landers.

#524: THE GUN
(11-09-70)

WRITER: Donald S. Sanford
DIRECTOR: Bernard McEveety
CAST: Kevin Coughlin, L.Q. Jones, Patricia Morrow,
              Robert Phillips, Sam Melville, Ken Mayer,
              Stanley Clements, Jack Garner, Jon Jason Mantley,
              Marie Mantley, Foster Brooks, Frank Biro,
              Henry Wise, Bert Madrid, Eric Chase

After a young man outdraws a notorious gunslinger purely by chance, a sleazy newspaper reporter schemes to turn him into a famous—and profitable—hero.

NOTES: Matt to Pasco (Melville): "Get out of Dodge—tonight." Another town celebration on Front Street, this time the Dodge Day Turkey Shoot. Jon Jason Mantley and Marie Mantley are the offspring of executive producer John Mantley.

#525: THE SCAVENGERS
(11-16-70)

WRITER: Jack Miller
DIRECTOR: Bernard McEveety
CAST: Yaphet Kotto, Cicely Tyson,
               Slim Pickens, Roy Jenson, Link Wyler,
               Victor Holchak, Steve Raines, James Almanzar,
               Eddie Little Sky, Victor Izay, Jerelyn Fields,
               Henry Wise

Innocent Indians are going to be executed for attacking a wagon train unless a man who knows the truth but has lied comes forward.

NOTES: Dynamic performances by Kotto and Tyson. Script won a Black Image Award. Victor Izay credited as Barkeep rather than Bull.

#526: THE WITNESS
(11-23-70)

WRITER: Shimon Wincelberg
DIRECTOR: Philip Leacock
CAST: Harry Morgan, Tim O'Connor,
               I. Stanford Jolley, Dack Rambo,
               Barry Brown, Robert Swan, June Dayton,
               Annette O'Toole, Ray Young, Herb Vigran

Matt has no choice but to release an accused murderer when the eyewitnesses are intimidated into changing their stories.

NOTES: First of Herb Vigran's eleven appearances as Judge Brooker. The late Harry Morgan co-starred with Dennis Weaver on the *Kentucky Jones* series.

#527: McCabe
(11-30-70)

WRITER: Jim Byrnes
DIRECTOR: Bernard McEveety
CAST: Dan Kemp, Tani Phelps, Mitch Vogel,
              Jim Davis, David Brian, Jon Lormer,
              Robert Sorrells, Mills Watson, Lew Brown,
              Marie Cheatham, Trevor Bardette,
              Tom Sutton, Pete Kellett

Before bringing an outlaw in, Matt allows the man to visit the family he deserted, leading to unexpected circumstances.

NOTES: Shot on a Western set near Vasquez Rocks. Mitch Vogel was portraying Jamie Hunter on *Bonanza* by the time this episode aired.

#528: The Noonday Devil
(12-07-70)

WRITER: William Kelley
DIRECTOR: Philip Leacock
CAST: Anthony Zerbe, John Dullaghan,
              Warren Vanders, Ernest Sarracino,
              Annette Cardona, Natividad Vacio,
              Bert Madrid, Pepe Callahan, Anthony Cordova,
              Fred Coby, Tony Davis, Julio Medina

Matt learns that a robbery blamed on a priest was actually committed by the priest's twin brother, now seeking refuge in the church.

NOTES: A solo adventure for Matt, with a brief appearance by Doc at the end.

#529: SERGEANT HOLLY
(12-14-70)

WRITER: William Kelley
DIRECTOR: Bernard McEveety
CAST: Forrest Tucker, Albert Salmi, Med Flory,
             Read Morgan, David Renard, Victor Eberg,
             Gregg Palmer, Vito Scotti, Bob Morgan,
             Frank Hotchkiss

Sergeant Holly, falsely accused of stealing an army payroll, asks for Kitty's help in clearing his name.

NOTES: Sequel to last season's "The War Priest." More filming at Vasquez Rocks.

#530: JENNY
(12-28-70)

WRITER: Jack Miller
DIRECTOR: Robert Totten
CAST: Lisa Gerritsen, Steve Ihnat, Rance Howard,
             Steve Raines, Bob Burrows

A prisoner agrees to return to jail if Newly will allow him to visit with his little girl, a deal Newly later regrets.

NOTES: Newly tracked Pritchard (Ihnat) to Oklahoma the previous spring. Rance Howard is actor/director Ron Howard's father.

#531: CAPTAIN SLIGO
(01-04-71)

WRITER: William Kelley
DIRECTOR: William Conrad
CAST: Richard Basehart, Salome Jens, Royal Dano,

Stacy Harris, Robert Totten, Bob Eilbacher,
Geri Reischl, Larry Finley, Matt Emery,
Brian Foley, Boyd "Red" Morgan,
Fred Stromsoe, Troy Melton, Bob Herron

A retired sea captain and his pet buffalo arrives in Dodge City and decides that a widow who already has two children is just the woman to give him ten sons.

NOTES: Minimal participation of any series regulars. Second of two episodes directed by radio's Matt Dillon, William Conrad. Television fans know Richard Basehart best as the star of *Voyage to the Bottom of the Sea*.

#532: MIRAGE
(01-11-71)

WRITER: Jack Miller
DIRECTOR: Vincent McEveety
CAST: John Anderson, Gary Wood, Mary Rings,
             Bill Zuckert, Harry Raybould, Robert Knapp,
             Dan White, Kevin Burchett

A delirious Festus staggers into a ghost town and shoots a man whose father later says was innocent of any wrongdoing.

NOTES: John Anderson, who appeared in a dozen *Gunsmoke* episodes, portrayed Virgil Earp for three seasons of *The Life and Legend of Wyatt Earp*.

#533: THE TYCOON
(01-25-71)

WRITER: Robert Vincent Wright
DIRECTOR: Bernard McEveety
CAST: Shug Fisher, John Beck, Nora Marlowe,

James Minotto, Gwynne Gilford,
Herman Poppe, Walker Edmiston,
Charles Wagenheim

Festus goes from being Matt's part-time deputy to a wealthy man when he inherits $500.

NOTES: Shug Fisher had guest roles of varying sizes on nearly 20 episodes of *Gunsmoke*. Haggen is misspelled "Haggin" on a freight wagon. Charles Wagenheim plays Parson Mueller instead of his regular part as Dodge City's Halligan.

#534: JAEKEL
(02-01-71)

STORY: True Boardman
TELEPLAY: Calvin Clements
DIRECTOR: Bernard McEveety
CAST: Eric Braeden, Julie Gregg, Mia Bendixen,
              John Crawford, Victor Tayback, James Chandler,
              Scott Edmonds, Bob Golden

An ex-con returns to Dodge City and discovers that the woman who promised to wait for him is married and has a young daughter.

NOTES: Eric Braeden got his start playing German soldiers on *Combat!* using his real name, Hans Gudegast. He was also a regular co-star of *The Rat Patrol* series and later the daytime drama *The Young and the Restless*.

#535: MURDOCH
(02-08-71)

WRITER: Jack Miller
DIRECTOR: Robert Totten

CAST: Jack Elam, Bob Random, Jim Davis, Anthony
Caruso, Clint Howard, Tom Water, Tim Burns,
Liz Marshall, Bobby Clark, Gary Combs

Lawman Lucas Murdoch asks Matt to help him catch some outlaws, unaware that his son is one of the gang.

NOTES: Banner on Front Street advertises a Fourth of July Celebration
on River Street, complete with fireworks and a barn dance. Clint
Howard, son of actor Rance Howard and brother of Ron, co-starred
with Dennis Weaver on the *Gentle Ben* series. Episode title frequently
misspelled as "Murdock" in other references.

#536: CLEAVUS
(02-15-71)

WRITERS: Donald Z. Koplowitz & Richard D. Scott
DIRECTOR: Vincent McEveety
CAST: Robert Totten, Arthur Hunnicutt,
William Challee, Robert Cornthwaite,
Robert B. Williams, Henry Wise

One of Festus' childhood buddies accidentally kills a prospector,
takes his gold, and proceeds to court a reluctant Miss Kitty.

NOTES: Festus beds down in Hank's stable rather than his own
rarely-seen shack or the Dodge jail. Buck Taylor's 50th episode as
Newly. Outstanding performance by Robert Totten. Only *Gunsmoke*
appearance by Western veteran Arthur Hunnicutt.

#537: LAVERY
(02-22-71)

WRITER: Donald S. Sanford
DIRECTOR: Vincent McEveety
CAST: Anthony Costello, Judi West, David Carradine,

Karl Swenson, David Huddleston, Chanin Hale, Jack Perkins, Hank Patterson

Matt's life is saved by a young man on probation and fearful of a horse theft charge.

NOTES: The late David Carradine, son of famed character actor John Carradine, starred on the Western series *Shane* and *Kung Fu*.

#538: PIKE, PART 1
(03-01-71)
#539: PIKE, PART 2
(03-08-71)

WRITER: Jack Miller
DIRECTOR: Bernard McEveety
CAST: Jeanette Nolan, Dack Rambo, Cliff Osmond,
              William Murphy, Ross Hagen, William Mims,
              Jim Boles, Jon Jason Mantley, Maria Mantley,
              John Puglia, Susan Newmark, Billy McMickle

Eccentric homesteader Sally Fergus cares for an ailing young outlaw who is on the run from the partners he double-crossed.

NOTES: "Pike" was retitled "Dirty Sally" in syndication and, due to its popularity, spawned not only a sequel but also the 1974 series *Dirty Sally*, which ran for 14 weeks. The Cowboy Hall of Fame voted "Pike" the Outstanding Western Episode, and the story earned the Best Western Television Script from the Western Writers of America.

EPISODE GUIDE

SEASON 17

September 13, 1971–March 13, 1972

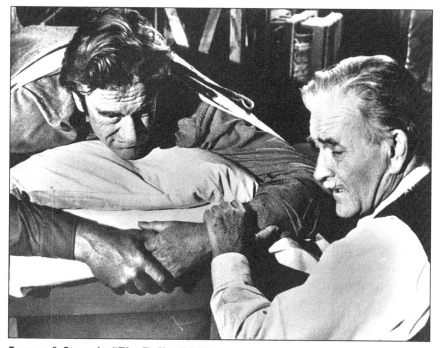

Arness & Stone in "The Bullet," 1971

#540: THE LOST
(09-13-71)

STORY: Warren Vanders
TELEPLAY: Jack Miller
DIRECTOR: Robert Totten
CAST: Mercedes McCambridge, Laurie Prange,
             Royal Dano, Link Wyler, Charles Kuenstle,
             Dee Carroll, Peggy Rea, Jerry Brown, Jon Jason
             Mantley, Maria Mantley, Heather Cotton

Kitty is stranded in the wildnerness after yet another stagecoach mishap and befriends an uncivilized young girl.

NOTES: Stock footage of the stagecoach crash from "The Wreckers." Second appearance of Peggy Rea as Mrs. Roniger. Story contributed by actor Warren Vanders, who guest starred on eleven episodes of *Gunsmoke*.

#541: PHOENIX
(09-20-71)

WRITER: Anthony Lawrence
DIRECTOR: Paul Stanley
CAST: Glenn Corbett, Mariette Hartley,
             Gene Evans, Ramon Bieri,
             Frank Corsentino

An ex-con takes a job at the ranch of a retired peace officer he has been hired to kill.

NOTES: Seventh of ten *Gunsmoke* episodes guest starring Western veteran Gene Evans, who appeared on more than two dozen series, including a regular role on *My Friend Flicka*.

#542: WASTE, PART 1
(09-27-71)
#543: WASTE, PART 2
(10-04-71)

WRITER: Jim Byrnes
DIRECTOR: Vincent McEveety
CAST: Ruth Roman, Jeremy Slate, Ellen Burstyn,
             Johnnie Whitaker, David Sheiner, Lieux Dressler,
             Shug Fisher, Rex Holman, Merry Anders

While chasing an outlaw across the desert, Matt is saddled with a young boy and a group of saloon girls whose wagon contains a stash of gold dust.

NOTES: Filmed in Utah. Ellen Burstyn, in her 2006 autobiography, says that in a diary she kept while shooting this episode, she wrote: "I'm doing good work in this show. I really understand how to act now." In 1962 she was billed as Ellen McRae in the episode "Wagon Girls" (#260). Final appearance on *Gunsmoke* by the late Jeremy Slate.

#544: NEW DOCTOR IN TOWN
(10-11-71)

WRITER:	Jack Miller
DIRECTOR:	Philip Leacock
CAST:	Pat Hingle, Lane Bradford, Jon Lormer,
	Glenn Strange, Ted Jordan, Woodrow Chambliss,
	Sarah Selby, Charles Wagenheim

The citizens of Dodge City are slow to accept Dr. John Chapman of New Orleans in place of Doc Adams, who has gone back to medical school in Baltimore after losing a patient to a blood disease with which he was unfamiliar.

NOTE: First of six appearances by Pat Hingle as Dr. Chapman, substituting for Milburn Stone, who was recuperating after heart surgery. Veteran character actor Lane Bradford appears in the occasional role of Dump Hart.

#545: THE LEGEND
(10-18-71)

WRITER:	Calvin Clements, Jr.
DIRECTOR:	Philip Leacock
CAST:	Kim Hunter, Jan-Michael Vincent,
	Richard D. Kelton, Greg Mullavey,
	Lloyd Nelson, Pat Dennis-Leigh, Victor Izay,

Pat Hingle, Michael Greene,
Read Morgan, Bryan O'Byrne,
Ken Mayer, Red Currie, Dick Cangey

A woman whose two oldest sons and late husband took the outlaw trail struggles to keep her youngest son on a straighter path.

NOTES: Kim Hunter won an Academy Award for her performance in *A Streetcar Named Desire*. Jan-Michael Vincent co-starred on the *Airwolf* series.

#546: TRAFTON
(10-25-71)

WRITER: Ron Bishop
DIRECTOR: Vincent McEveety
CAST: Victor French, Clay Tanner, Bill Catching,
             Fred Stromoe, Sharon Acker, John Dullaghan,
             Mike Mazurki, Marie Windsor, Philip Carey,
             Jon Lormer, Paul Stevens, Patti Cohoon,
             Manuel Padilla, Jr.

A gunman starts to lose his nerve after he is forgiven by the priest he has fatally shot.

NOTES: Only episode with Marie Windsor, who guest starred on more than a dozen television Westerns. Philip Carey starred as Captain Parmalee on the *Laredo* series.

#547: LYNOTT
(11-01-71)

WRITER: Ron Bishop
DIRECTOR: Gunnar Hellstrom
CAST: Richard Kiley, Peggy McCay,
             Anthony Caruso, Jonathan Lippe

Matt's life is saved by a former lawman who agrees to fill in while the marshal recovers from his wounds.

NOTES: Matt shot in left arm and side.

#548: LIJAH
(11-08-71)

WRITER: William Blinn
DIRECTOR: Irving J. Moore
CAST: Denny Miller, Howard Culver,
              Tom Brown, Lane Bradford,
              Erin Moran, Pat Hingle, Harry Townes,
              William Wintersole, Herb Vigran,
              Pete Kellett, Dan Flynn, Jr., Henry Wise

Doctor Chapman recognizes the deaf and dumb mountain man accused of murder to be a former patient.

NOTES: Denny Miller co-starred as Duke Shannon on *Wagon Train*.

#549: MY BROTHER'S KEEPER
(11-15-71)

WRITER: Arthur Dales
DIRECTOR: Paul Stanley
CAST: John Dierkes, Malcom Atterbury,
              Pippa Scott, Charles McGraw,
              Pat Hingle

Festus refuses to accept that an aging Indian abandoned by the tribe is waiting to die.

NOTES: Touching story featuring a standout performance by Ken Curtis.

#550: DRAGO
(11-22-71)

WRITER: Jim Byrnes
DIRECTOR: Paul Stanley
CAST: Buddy Ebsen, Ben Johnson, Mitchell Silberman, Del Monroe, Edward Faulkner, Rick Gates, Pat Hingle, Tani Phelps Guthrie, Jim Skaggs, Larry Randles

A hired hand and his dog, accompanied by Newly, track down the killers of the woman he worked for.

NOTES: Sixth and final appearance of Pat Hingle as Doctor Chapman.

#551: THE BULLET, PART 1
(11-29-71)
#552: THE BULLET, PART 2
(12-06-71)
#553: THE BULLET, PART 3
(12-13-71)

WRITER: Jim Byrnes
DIRECTOR: Bernard McEveety
CAST: Eric Braeden, Alejandro Rey, Katherine Justice, Robert Hogan, Pepe Callahan, Sian Barbara Allen, Warren Kemmerling, Walter Sande, Harry Carey, Jr., Sam Melville, Eddie Firestone, Robert Sorrells, John Crawford, Jonathan Lippe, Mills Watson, Harry Harvey, Sr., Dan Ferrone

Doc does not feel qualified to operate on a seriously wounded Matt, so he and the marshal, accompanied by Kitty, Festus and Newly, board a train for Denver that carries a gold shipment targeted by bandits.

NOTES: Matt shot in the back. Milburn Stone's return to the series after heart surgery. Memorable scene where Kitty reminisces about her first impressions of Dodge City and Matt for over three minutes. Alternate title for the episode is "Gold Train." The guest cast reads like a Who's Who of *Gunsmoke*, as virtually every actor had appeared on at least one previous episode.

#554: P.S. MURRY CHRISTMAS
(12-27-71)

WRITER: William Kelley
DIRECTOR: Herb Wallerstein
CAST: Jeanette Nolan, Jack Elam, Patti Cohoon, Jodie Foster, Erin Moran, Josh Albee, Brian Morrison, Willie Aames, Todd Lookinland

When the caretaker of a Kansas orphanage is fired, seven of the children decide to join him and travel to Dodge City.

NOTES: Second Christmas episode of the series. Kitty kisses Matt on the cheek. Seems to co-star nearly every child actor working in Hollywood at the time.

#555: NO TOMORROW
(01-03-72)

WRITER: Richard Fielder
DIRECTOR: Irving J. Moore
CAST: Sam Groom, Pamela McMyler, H.M. Wynant, Steve Brodie, Henry Jones, Richard Hale, Herb Vigran, Liam Dunn, Robert Nichols, Joe Haworth, Leo Gordon, Dan Flynn, Allan Fudge

Matt and Festus track an escaped prisoner they believe to be innocent of the crimes that have made him a wanted man.

NOTES: Kitty tacks up a sign behind the bar reading "No fighting, no loud mouth drunks, and that means you." Ken Curtis' 200th episode as Festus. Last of James Nusser's 72 appearances as Louie Pheeters.

#556: HIDALGO
(01-10-72)

WRITER: Colley Cibber
DIRECTOR: Paul Stanley
CAST: Alfonso Arau, Thomas Gomez,
            Fabian Gregory, Linda Marsh,
            Stella Garcia, David Renard, Julio Medina,
            Edward Colmans

After being seriously wounded by Mexican bandits, Matt is rescued by a young boy and his grandfather.

NOTES: Matt shot in the right side of his chest.

#557: TARA
(01-17-72)

WRITER: William Kelley
DIRECTOR: Bernard McEveety
CAST: Michele Carey, L.Q. Jones,
            Laurence Delaney

Newly falls for an attractive but dishonest young woman being harassed by her husband's murderer.

NOTES: Michele Carey (Tara) spends most of the episode looking more glamorous than any woman ever pictured in an Old West history book. Sarah Selby's thirteenth and final episode as Ma Smalley.

#558: ONE FOR THE ROAD
(01-24-72)

WRITER: Jack Miller
DIRECTOR: Bernard McEveety
CAST: Jack Albertson, Jeanette Nolan,
             Victor Holchak, Melissa Murphy,
             Herb Vigran, Dorothy Neumann,
             Jack Perkins

Wealthy Lucius Prince runs into fellow eccentric Sally Fergus while attempting to keep his distance from his granddaughter and her fortune hungry boyfriend.

NOTES: Second appearance by Jeanette Nolan as Dirty Sally.

#559: THE PREDATORS
(01-31-72)

WRITER: Calvin Clements
DIRECTOR: Bernard McEveety
CAST: Claude Akins, Jacqueline Scott,
             Tom Brown, Jodie Foster, Brian Morrison,
             George Murdock, Mills Watson,
             Lew Brown, Read Morgan

A gunman out for revenge comes to Abelia's ranch at the same time her children's long lost dog is being hunted by men from Dodge for killing sheep.

NOTES: Jacqueline Scott's third and final appearance as Abelia. Sam (Glenn Strange) joins Festus and Burke in the hunt for the dog.

#560: Yankton
(02-07-72)

WRITER: Jim Byrnes
DIRECTOR: Vincent McEveety
CAST: James Stacy, Forrest Tucker, Nancy Olson,
            Pamela Payton-Wright, Hank Patterson,
            Margaret Bacon, Tom Sutton, Bill Hart,
            Bennie Dobbins

A saddle bum pretends to be serious about the daughter of a wealthy rancher who cleaned him out in a poker game.

NOTES: James Stacy co-starred for two seasons on the CBS Western series *Lancer*.

#561: Blind Man's Bluff
(02-21-72)

WRITER: Ron Honthaner
DIRECTOR: Herb Wallerstein
CAST: Anne Jackson, Victor French,
            George Lindsey, Charles Kuenstle

A lonesome old maid tells a wounded man with no memory that he is her husband.

NOTES: Festus does the calling at another barn dance. Realistic story by associate producer Honthaner with no sugar-coated ending.

#562: Alias Festus Haggin
(03-06-72)

WRITER: Calvin Clements
DIRECTOR: Vincent McEveety
CAST: Ramon Bieri, Lieux Dressler, Robert Totten,

Booth Colman, Gregg Palmer, William Bryant,
Rayford Barnes, Herb Vigran, Jon Lormer,
Bill Erwin, Tom McFadden, Rusty Lane,
Ed McCready, Louie Elias, Lloyd Nelson

Festus has the misfortune of being mistaken for a notorious outlaw, and the outlaw's wife claims that he is indeed her husband.

NOTES: Haggen once again misspelled as "Haggin." Kitty testifies that Festus is not an educated man, but one of the smartest she has ever known. Festus jailed the day before his birthday, and he admits he is not sure of his age. More details of Festus' past than previously disclosed.

#563: THE WEDDING
(03-13-72)

WRITER: Harry Kronman
DIRECTOR: Bernard McEveety
CAST: Morgan Woodward, Sam Elliott, Melissa Murphy,
              James Chandler, Lane Bradford, Fran Ryan, Larry
              Barton, George Wallace, Byron Mabe, Troy
              Melton, Jason Wingreen

To prevent a young man from marrying his daughter, a rancher accuses him of horse stealing.

NOTES: Festus tells Doc he has opened a charge account at the Long Branch. Another Matt and Kitty date foiled by duty. Fran Ryan took over the Long Branch in *Gunsmoke*'s final season.

Arness

EPISODE GUIDE

SEASON 18
September 11, 1972–March 5, 1973

#564: THE RIVER, PART 1
(09-11-72)
#565: THE RIVER, PART 2
(09-18-72)

WRITER: Jack Miller
DIRECTOR: Herb Wallerstein
CAST: Slim Pickens, Miriam Colon,
             Clay O'Brien, Patti Cohoon, Roger Torrey,
             Read Morgan, Jerry Gatlin, Jack Elam

To elude the outlaw gang chasing him, Matt dives into a raging river and ends up on a raft being piloted by a pair of children making an escape of their own.

NOTES: Announcer now reads the stars' names in the show's opening sequence, including a shot of Matt facing his opponent on Front Street from earlier color seasons. Writer and director credits are shown at the beginning of this particular episode.

#566: BOHANNAN
(09-25-72)

WRITER: William Kelley
DIRECTOR: Alf Kjellin
CAST: Richard Kiley, Linda Marsh, Vincent Van Patten,
             Ed Bakey, Helen Kleeb, Rege Cordic

Doc comes to realize that a faith healer who comes to Dodge City is not a total charlatan.

NOTES: Distinguished actor Richard Kiley appeared on TV Westerns so rarely that the only one he did besides five episodes of *Gunsmoke* was a 1970 *Bonanza*. Ted Jordan (Nathan Burke) wearing his hair longer.

#567: THE JUDGMENT
(10-02-72)

WRITER: Shimon Wincelberg
DIRECTOR: Philip Leacock
CAST: Ramon Bieri, William Windom, Katherine
             Helmond, Tim O'Connor, Mariette Hartley,
             Richard Kelton, Jon Locke, Melissa Gilbert

An ex-con seeking revenge on the coward who turned him in comes to Dodge and shoots both Festus and Newly.

NOTES: Melissa Gilbert later played Laura Ingalls on *Little House on the Prairie.*

#568: THE DRUMMER
(10-09-72)

WRITER: Richard Fielder
DIRECTOR: Bernard McEveety
CAST: Victor French, Fionnula Flanagan, Brandon Cruz,
             Bruce Glover, Kiel Martin, Herb Armstrong,
             Hank Patterson, Paul Sorensen

A guilt-ridden former army officer who led troopers that wiped out an Indian village runs into two survivers of the attack when he arrives in Dodge City.

NOTES: Kitty enjoys Matt's discomfort when Shay (French) asks him why he is not married. Hank Patterson is billed as Liveryman rather than Hank Miller. Fionnula Flanagan later co-starred with Arness on *How the West Was Won*. The Viewmaster company released this episode in a set of picture reels. Jackson Flynn based the 1975 *Gunsmoke* paperback novel on Richard Fielder's script.

#569: SARAH
(10-16-72)

WRITER: Calvin Clements
DIRECTOR: Gunnar Hellstrom
CAST: Anne Francis, Anthony Caruso, Jonathan Lippe,
             Michael Lane, John Orchard, Kay E. Kuter,
             Rex Holman, George Keymas, Larry Duran,
             Ronald Manning, Alberto Pina

Matt is reunited with a woman from his past and pretends to be her husband when a gang of outlaws show up at the stage station she operates.

NOTES: Sarah (Francis) knew Matt when he was a deputy in San Antonio. Particularly good episode, featuring a standout performance by frequent guest star Caruso. Partially filmed at Old Tucson, Arizona.

#570: THE FUGITIVES
(10-23-72)

WRITER: Charles Joseph Stone
DIRECTOR: Irving J. Moore
CAST: James Olson, Darrell Larson, Victor Tayback,
             Russell Johnson, Troy Melton

Needing medical attention for his injured brother, outlaw Bede Stalcup kidnaps both Doc and Festus.

NOTES: Festus shot in the back. Another especially good episode, the second written by Milburn Stone's brother.

#571: ELEVEN DOLLARS
(10-30-72)

WRITER: Paul Savage
DIRECTOR: Irving J. Moore
CAST: Susan Oliver, Josh Albee,
           Ike Eisenmann, Diane Shalet

On a long ride across the Kansas prairie to deliver an inheritance, Festus is beset by not only threatening hide cutters but also a couple of scheming children.

NOTES: Charlie Halligan (Charles Wagenheim) shown working for storekeeper Lathrop (Woodrow Chambliss). Only episode with the late Susan Oliver, who guest starred on more than a dozen television Westerns.

#572: MILLIGAN
(11-06-72)

WRITER: Ron Bishop
DIRECTOR: Bernard McEveety
CAST: Harry Morgan, Joseph Campanella,
           Lynn Carlin, Sorrell Booke, Patti Cohoon,
           Scott Walker, John Pickard, Lew Brown,
           Read Morgan, Gene Tyburn, Robert Swan,
           Charles Magaulay, Todd Bass,
           Sammee Lee Jones

After a mild-mannered farmer shoots a well-liked outlaw in the back, he and his family are shunned by the citizens of Dodge City.

NOTES: Story similar to 1965 episode "The Pariah" (#371). The late Harry Morgan's performance is quite a contrast to his role in "The Witness" (#526).

#573: TATUM
(11-13-72)

WRITER: Jim Byrnes
DIRECTOR: Gunnar Hellstrom
CAST: Gene Evans, Ana Korita, Sandra Smith,
                   Jay MacIntosh, Sheila Larkin, Jeff Pomerantz,
                   Ken Tobey, Lloyd Nelson, Neil Summers,
                   Robert Tindall, Duncan Inches

Matt runs into trouble when he discovers that a dying man is not welcome in the town where he wants to be buried.

NOTES: The town of Spearville is actually the Old Tucson film set. Joe Beel is played by veteran stuntman Neil Summers.

#574: THE SODBUSTERS
(11-20-72)

WRITER: Ron Bishop
DIRECTOR: Robert Butler
CAST: Morgan Woodward, Alex Cord,
                   Katherine Justice, Leif Garrett, Dawn Lyn,
                   Harrison Ford, Robert Viharo, Richard Bull,
                   Joe di Reda, Jim Boles, Colin Male, Paul Prokop,
                   Norman Bartold, Evans Thornton

On the trail of an outlaw, Matt encounters a range war involving water rights.

NOTES: Morgan Woodward's dynamic performance—his 15th *Gunsmoke*—resulted in executive producer John Mantley's unsuccessful attempt to secure an Emmy nomination for him. Richard Bull later co-starred as storeowner Nels Oleson on *Little House on the Prairie*. Harrison Ford, of course, went on to more expansive productions. Ron Bishop's script was adapted by Jackson Flynn for the 1974 *Gunsmoke* paperback novel "Duel at Dodge City."

#575: THE BROTHERS
(11-27-72)

WRITER: Calvin Clements
DIRECTOR: Gunnar Hellstrom
CAST: Steve Forrest, Joe Silver, Angus Ducan,
Richard O'Brien, Regis J. Cordic, Eddie Ryder,
Edward Faulkner, Reid Cruickshanks,
Terry Wilson, Daniel Thorpe, John Harper,
Howard Culver, Nancy Fisher, Jon Kowal,
Al Berry, Daniel M. White, Phil Chambers

Both Kitty and a fellow stagecoach passenger shoot a wanted outlaw and become targets of the man's brother.

NOTES: Kitty in peril at the hands of Steve Forrest for the third time. The stableman is played by Terry Wilson, better known as *Wagon Train's* Bill Hawks. Jonathan Harper's (billed now as John) ninth and final appearance as Dodge City undertaker Percy Crump.

#576: HOSTAGE!
(12-11-72)

WRITER: Paul F. Edwards
DIRECTOR: Gunnar Hellstrom
CAST: William Smith, Geoffrey Lewis,
Marco St. John, Nina Roman,
James Chandler, Hal Baylor, Sandra Kent,
Stafford Repp

To force the release of a condemned murderer, the man's psychotic brother vows to kill Kitty if the excecution takes place.

NOTES: Dramatic landmark episode. Matt at Kitty's bedside in Doc's office for a change. Matt: "I need you Kitty." Kitty: "I couldn't live without him, Doc." Matt takes off his badge once again. Matt to Festus and Newly: "Been a lot of good years." Climax shot at Vasquez Rocks.

#577: JUBILEE
(12-18-72)

STORY: Jack Freeman
TELEPLAY: Paul Savage
CAST: Tom Skerritt, Scott Brady, Alan Hale,
             Collin Wilcox-Horne, Lori Rutherford,
             Todd Cameron, Whitey Hughes

Believing he can finally better his station in life by racing his quarter horse, a destitute homesteader neglects his farm and his needy family.

NOTES: Partially filmed in Bronson Canyon. Billy Banner is played by the late stuntman Whitey Hughes.

#578: ARIZONA MIDNIGHT
(01-01-73)

WRITER: Dudley Bromley
DIRECTOR: Irving J. Moore
CAST: Billy Curtis, Stanley Clements,
             Mills Watson, Ken Mayer, Sandye Powell

A little person enters the Long Branch and offers $50 to anyone who will take care of him when he is transformed into an elephant.

NOTES: Kitty tells Arizona (Curtis) her actual name is Kathleen. Arizona says the name Festus "sounds like a cold sore." The producers wanted Billy Barty for the role of Arizona, but he was not available. Not one of the series' better moments.

#579: HOMECOMING
(01-08-73)

WRITER: Calvin Clements
DIRECTOR: Gunnar Hellstrom
CAST: Richard Kelton, Robert Pratt, Ivy Jones,
            Stuart Margolin, Lurene Tuttle, Lynn Marta,
            Claudia Bryar

Doc becomes a hostage when two outlaw brothers stop in Dodge City to look in on their ailing mother.

NOTES: Anna (Tuttle) to Doc: "Buffalo used to graze right where Dodge is today." Rare snowfall in Dodge at end of episode.

#580: SHADLER
(01-15-73)

WRITER: Jim Byrnes
DIRECTOR: Arnold Lathan
CAST: Earl Holliman, Diana Hyland, Denver Pyle,
            Linda Watkins, Alex Sharp, Pat Conway, Ken
            Lynch, John Davis Chandler, Donald Barry,
            James Jeter, John Carter, Bill Erwin, Meg Wyllie,
            Tom Pittman, Barry Cahill, Wallace Earl

Newly and an escaped convict pretending to be a priest join forces to prevent a town from being taken over by a band of outlaws.

NOTES: Matt shows up at the very end. The late Donald Barry is better known to Western enthusiasts as Donald "Red" Barry, star of dozens of B-Westerns. Filmed at the same locale near Vasquez Rocks as "McCabe" (#527).

#581: PATRICIA
(01-22-73)

WRITER: Calvin Clements
DIRECTOR: Alf Kjellin
CAST: Jess Walton, Ike Eisenmann,
             John Baer, Gail Bonney, Donald Elson,
             Richard Lundin

Doc discovers that the woman Newly plans to marry has leukemia.

NOTES: Newly is the only regular character to get married. Doc breaks his oath when he tells Matt and Kitty of Patricia's disease. Newly doubts his ability to be a doctor, but Doc says he has practiced medicine for 40 years and wants to pass his knowledge on to Newly. Dodge City pulls together in the wake of a tornado.

#582: A QUIET DAY IN DODGE
(01-29-73)

WRITER: Jack Miller
DIRECTOR: Alf Kjellin
CAST: Margaret Hamilton, Leo Gordon,
             Shug Fisher, Douglas V. Fowley, John Fiedler,
             Helen Page Camp, J. Pat O'Malley,
             Walker Edmiston, Herb Vigran, Willie Ames,
             Henry Wise, Michelle Breeze

After going two days without sleep, Matt faces another one when a series of calamities requiring his attention break out in Dodge.

NOTES: Rare humorous episode directly involving Matt. Kitty finally gets Matt alone, but he falls asleep. Margaret Hamilton, best remembered as the Wicked Witch of the West in *The Wizard of Oz*, curses and makes the cast burst out in laughter in a blooper from this episode.

#583: WHELAN'S MEN
(02-05-73)

WRITER: Ron Bishop
DIRECTOR: Paul Edwards
CAST: Robert Burr, William Bramley,
              Noble Willingham, Harrison Ford,
              Frank Ramirez, Gerald McRaney, Bobby Hall,
              Seamon Glass, Ed Craig, Richard Hale

Kitty literally bets Matt's life in a card game with outlaws who plan to kill the marshal and destroy Dodge City.

NOTES: Matt shot in left arm once again. Like "The Prisoner" (#488), Kitty's poker skills save the day. Second episode with Harrison Ford.

#584: KIMBRO
(02-12-73)

WRITER: Jim Byrnes
DIRECTOR: Gunnar Hellstrom
CAST: John Anderson, Doreen Long, Michael Strong,
              William DeVane, Rick Weaver, Tom Falk,
              Lisa Eilbacher, Wendell Baker

Matt deputizes a mentor who has fallen on hard times.

NOTES: Kimbro (Anderson) cleaned up Abilene and allowed and underage Matt to be his deputy. When Kimbro asks Matt how many times he has been shot, Matt replies, "A few." Kitty asks Matt what he is going to do when he is Kimbro's age. Dennis Weaver's son Rick plays Turkey Stratton. Final shootout filmed at Vasquez Rocks.

#585: Jesse
(02-19-73)

WRITER: Jim Byrnes
DIRECTOR: Bernard McEveety
CAST: Brock Peters, Don Stroud, Jim Davis,
Regis J. Cordic, Leonard Stone, Norman Bartold,
Lloyd Nelson, Robert Pine, Ted Gehring,
Larry Finley, Pete Kellett, Karen Welch

Festus and Newly have no choice but to arrest one of Festus' friends, much to the displeasure of the man's fellow cattle drovers.

NOTE: Matt shown briefly in Tribune, Kansas, along with Festus and Newly. Second solid guest appearance by the late Brock Peters.

#586: Talbot
(02-26-73)

WRITER: Jim Byrnes
DIRECTOR: Vincent McEveety
CAST: Anthony Zerbe, Salome Jens,
Peter Jason, Robert Totten

An outlaw planning to rob the Dodge bank comes to the aid of an abused woman and has a change of heart that does not sit well with his partners.

NOTES: The last of Anthony Zerbe's three *Gunsmoke* episodes. Another good performance by writer/director Robert Totten (Eli).

#587: This Golden Land
(03-05-73)

WRITER: Hal Sitowitz
DIRECTOR: Gunnar Hellstrom

CAST: Paul Stevens, Victor French, Richard Dreyfuss, Bettye Ackerman, Kevin Coughlin, Joseph Hindy, Wayne McLaren, Scott Selles, Robert Nichols

Matt is frustrated when Jewish immigrants refuse to cooperate in his investigation of who killed one of their family members.

NOTES: Richard Dreyfuss (Gearshon) went on to star in such memorable films as *Jaws*, *Close Encounters of the Third Kind* and *The Goodbye Girl*, for which he won an Oscar. This episode won the Mass Media Award from the National Conference of Christians and Jews.

EPISODE GUIDE

SEASON 19
September 10, 1973–April 1, 1974

Gene Evans & Arness in "The Iron Blood of Courage," 1974

#588: WOMEN FOR SALE, PART 1
(09-10-73)
#589: WOMEN FOR SALE, PART 2
(09-7-73)

WRITER: Jim Byrnes
DIRECTOR: Vincent McEveety
CAST: Gregory Sierra, Shani Wallis, James Whitmore,
            Kathleen Cody, Dawn Lyn, Nicholas Hammond,
            Lieux Dressler, Dan Ferrone, Sally Kemp

Matt comes to the rescue of captives being sold into slavery by Comancheros.

NOTES: Rare voice-over narration, spoken by William Conrad, radio's Matt Dillon. The year given is 1873. Charles Seel, normally cast as Dodge City telegrapher Barney Danches, plays "McCloud." Gregory Sierra portrayed Puerto Rican junkman Julio Fuentes on the sitcom *Sanford and Son*. More location shooting in Arizona.

#590: MATT'S LOVE STORY
(09-24-73)

WRITER: Ron Bishop
DIRECTOR: Gunnar Hellstrom
CAST: Michael Learned, Victor French, Keith Andes,
               Jonathan Lippe, William Schallert, Richard
               Lundin, S. Michael De France, Neil Summers

Matt, suffering from amnesia after being wounded by an outlaw's bullet, is nursed back to health by an attractive woman rancher.

NOTES: This episode was the basis for the second *Gunsmoke* telefilm "The Last Apache" (1990). Michael Learned was co-starring on *The Waltons* at the time. The Starcourt ranch house is the same structure at Old Tucson used as the Cannon homestead on *The High Chaparral*. Notation at the end of closing credits: "Portions of this picture were filmed in the Cornonado National Forest."

#591: THE BOY AND THE SINNER
(10-01-73)

WRITER: Hal Sitowitz
DIRECTOR: Bernard McEveety
CAST: Ron Moody, Vincent Van Patten,
               Warren Vanders, John Crawford, Ken Lynch,
               Read Morgan, Florida Friebus, Hal Baylor

An alcoholic old drifter is trapped between scheming gunmen and a farm boy who wants to help him reform.

NOTES: Florida Friebus (Mrs. Travers) played the ditzy Mrs. Bakerman on *The Bob Newhart Show*.

#592: THE WIDOWMAKER
(10-08-73)

WRITER:	Paul F. Edwards
DIRECTOR:	Bernard McEveety
CAST:	Steve Forrest, Barra Grant, David Huddleston, Randolph Roberts, Jerry Gatlin, James Chandler, Don Carter, Rand Bridges, J.R. Clark

When a former gunslinger trying to live a peaceful life continues to attract aspiring fast draw challengers to Dodge City, Matt reluctantly tells him he has to leave.

NOTES: Steve Forrest (Coltrane) in a rare sympathetic *Gunsmoke* role.

#593: KITTY'S LOVE AFFAIR
(10-22-73)

STORY:	Susan Kotar & Joan E. Gessler
TELEPLAY:	Paul Savage
DIRECTOR:	Vincent McEveety
CAST:	Richard Kiley, Leonard Stone, Christopher Connelly, Paul Picerni, Don Keefer, Jack Perkins, Gerald McRaney, Del Monroe, Virginia Baker, Richard D. Hurst, Ed Long, Rayford Barnes, James Almanzar, Pete Kellett, Ken Kenopka, Phil Chambers, Louis Elias, Jeff Parks

Kitty is torn between her affection for Matt and attraction to ex-gunfighter Will Stambridge, who is eventually accused of murder.

NOTES: Yet another spoiled vacation for Matt and Kitty, who is fed up after 18 years of disappointments.

#594: THE WIDOW AND THE ROGUE
(10-29-73)

STORY: Harvey Marlowe & Paul Savage
TELEPLAY: Paul Savage
DIRECTOR: Bernard McEveety
CAST: James Stacy, Beth Brickell, Clay O'Brien,
              Helen Page Camp, Monica Svensson,
              Walker Edmiston, Paul Sorensen,
              Richard Lundin

Festus and his prisoner, traveling through the desert on foot, stumble across a woman and her son being menaced by Comancheros.

NOTES: Location filming in Arizona. Beth Brickell co-starred with Dennis Weaver on the *Gentle Ben* series.

#595: A GAME OF DEATH...AN ACT OF LOVE, PART 1
(11-05-73)
#596: A GAME OF DEATH...AN ACT OF LOVE, PART 2
(11-12-73)

WRITER: Paul F. Edwards
DIRECTOR: Gunnar Hellstrom
CAST: Morgan Woodward, Michael Learned,
              Paul Stevens, Donna Mills, Whitney Blake,
              John Pickard, Geoffrey Horne, Garry Walberg,
              Owen Bush

Matt has a difficult time finding an attorney to defend some Indians accused of murdering the wife of one of Dodge City's leading ranchers.

NOTES: Sanderson (Woodward) makes a reference to Matt taking off to avenge Kitty's beating in "Hostage!" (#576). Exceptionally well-written episode later adapted by Jackson Flynn as the 1974 *Gunsmoke* paperback novel "The Renegades."

#597: LYNCH TOWN
(11-19-73)

STORY: Joann Carlino & Anne Snyder
TELEPLAY: Calvin Clements
DIRECTOR: Bernard McEveety
CAST: David Wayne, Mitch Vogel, Scott Brady,
               Warren Kemmerling, Ken Swofford,
               Norman Alden, Julie Cobb

Matt demands that an alcoholic judge hold an inquest into the hanging of a possibly innocent man, but the boss of the town objects.

NOTES: Julie Cobb is the daughter of *The Virginian*'s Lee J. Cobb

#598: THE HANGING OF NEWLY O'BRIEN
(11-26-73)

WRITER: Calvin Clements
DIRECTOR: Alf Kjellin
CAST: Billy Green Bush, Jimmy Van Patten,
               Jessamine Milner, Rusty Lane, Jan Burrell,
               Deborah Dozier, Walter Scott, Bobby Hall,
               Donald Elson, Billie Bird, Arthur Malet,
               Erica Hunton

Doc is shot when he and Festus attempt to rescue Newly from being hanged by backwoods settlers.

NOTES: Newly gets his first shot at doctoring solo. This episode is significant for being the last of Glenn Strange's 222 appearances as

Long Branch bartender Sam Noonan. Strange, suffering from cancer, is the last character shown, grinning and dispensing beers for the townsfolk.

#599: SUSAN WAS EVIL
(12-03-73)

WRITER: William Keys
DIRECTOR: Bernard McEveety
CAST: Kathleen Nolan, Art Lund, Kathy Cannon, George Di Cenzo, Henry Olek, Jim Gammon, Robert Brubaker

A woman who has sold her stagestop and plans to leave for St. Louis with her selfish neice falls in love with the wounded outlaw Matt is bringing back to Dodge City.

NOTES: James Arness and George Di Cenzo co-starred on the *McClain's Law* series. Robert Brubaker's last guest role before taking over as Sam's replacement at the Long Branch Saloon.

#600: THE DEADLY INNOCENT
(12-17-73)

WRITER: Calvin Clements
DIRECTOR: Bernard McEveety
CAST: Russell Wiggins, Charles Dierkop, Herb Vigran, Jack Garner, William Shriver, Erica Hunton, Denny Arnold

Festus has the unenviable job of delivering his mentally challenged young friend to a state asylum for the insane.

NOTES: Festus has known Billy (Wiggins) for five years. Episode won the Golden Spur Award from the Western Writers of America as well as an award from the President's Council on Mental Retardation.

#601: THE CHILD BETWEEN
(12-24-73)

WRITER: Harry Kronman
DIRECTOR: Irving Moore
CAST: Sam Groom, Alexandra Morgan,
            John Dierkes, Eddie Little Sky,
            Pete Kellett, Bill Hart, Alex Sharp

An Indian woman with a sick child does not trust Newly's medical opinion, so she takes the baby to a Comanche medicine man.

NOTES: Newly substituting for Doc. Alex Sharp, who also did some writing for television, appeared in seven episodes of *Gunsmoke*.

#602: A FAMILY OF KILLERS
(01-14-74)

WRITER: William Keys
DIRECTOR: Gunnar Hellstrom
CAST: Glenn Corbett, Anthony Caruso,
            Mills Watson, Morgan Paull,
            Zina Bethune, Stuart Margolin,
            George Keymas, Frank Corsentino

Matt joins the hunt for a clan of killers to prevent a fellow marshal from going outside the law to avenge a murdered deputy.

NOTES: Kitty mentions the Ronigers having an 18th baby. One of the best episodes of the season.

#603: LIKE OLD TIMES
(01-21-74)

WRITER: Richard Fielder
DIRECTOR: Irving Moore

CAST: Nehemiah Persoff, Gloria de Haven,
         Dan Travanty, Charles Haid, Victor Izay,
         Robert Brubaker, Rhodie Cogan, Hal Bokar,
         Richard Lundin

After serving a 12-year prison term, an infamous safecracker returns to Dodge in hopes of starting a new life, but a couple of thieves want to make use of his old skills.

NOTES: First of eight appearances by Robert Brubaker as Floyd, the new Long Branch bartender, who, in reference to Sam, says, "We lost him a while back. Everybody around here misses him a lot." Matt calls him Floyd, although billed simply as Bartender. Last episode with Tom Brown as Ed O'Connor and Roy Roberts as banker Harry Bodkin. Dan Travanty (later spelled Travanti) and Charles Haid were reunited as regulars on the series *Hill Street Blues*.

#604: THE TOWN TAMERS
(01-28-74)

WRITER: Paul Savage
DIRECTOR: Gunnar Hellstrom
CAST: Jim Davis, Jean Allison, Ike Eisenmann,
           Rex Holman, Leo Gordon, Sean McClory,
           James Jeter, Kay Kuter, James Chandler,
           Julie Bennett, Don Megowan, Clay Tanner,
           Ed Call, Mary Betten, Larry Randles

Matt and a fellow lawman Luke Rumbaugh clean up Hilt, Kansas, but Matt and Festus must return after Luke's domestic situation causes him to lose control of the town.

NOTES: Saloon in Hilt is the set of the Dodge House lobby.

#605: THE FOUNDLING
(02-11-74)

WRITER: Jim Byrnes
DIRECTOR: Bernard McEveety
CAST: Kay Lenz, Donald Moffat, Dran Hamilton,
               Bonnie Bartlett, Don Collier, Jerry Hardin,
               Ted Jordan, Woodrow Chambliss,
               Robert Brubaker

Distraught after being forced to shoot a drunken farmer, Matt goes off by himself and comes across a runaway young woman and her illegitimate baby.

NOTES: Kitty, who mentions Sam, wants to keep Lettie's (Lenz) baby. Doc calls Lathrop "Woody."

#606: THE IRON BLOOD OF COURAGE
(02-18-74)

WRITER: Ron Bishop
DIRECTOR: Gunnar Hellstrom
CAST: Lloyd Bochner, Eric Braeden, Mariette Hartley,
               Patti Cohoon, Miriam Colon, Gene Evans,
               John Milford, Bing Russell, Robert Karnes,
               John Baer, Lloyd Nelson, Jerry Gatlin,
               Elizabeth Harrower, Nick Ramus

The wives of a hired gunman and a stubborn rancher decide to take matters into their own hands to end a feud over water rights.

NOTES: Another solid script by Ron Bishop. Long Branch bartender not Robert Brubaker.

#607: THE SCHOOLMARM
(02-25-74)

WRITER: Dick Nelson
DIRECTOR: Bernard McEveety
CAST: Charlotte Stewart, Lin McCarthy,
              Scott Walker, Todd Lookinland,
              Howard Culver, Laura Nichols,
              Kevin C. McEveety

Carl Pruitt, a widower with a young son, is accused of killing the traveling salesman who raped the local school teacher.

NOTES: Second guest appearance by Charlotte Stewart as the title character, and who also played the school teacher on *Little House on the Prairie*.

#608: TRAIL OF BLOODSHED
(03-04-74)

STORY: Earl W. Wallace
TELEPLAY: Paul Savage
DIRECTOR: Bernard McEveety
CAST: Craig Stevens, Kurt Russell, Tom Simcox,
              Harry Carey, Jr., Janit Baldin, Larry Pennell,
              Woodrow Chambliss, Nina Roman,
              Read Morgan, Gloria Dixon

After an escaped convict beats and robs Dodge storekeeper Lathrop, he is pursued by Festus and his own nephew, whose father he has killed.

NOTES: Doc calls Lathrop "Woody" again. The late Craig Stevens will be familiar to fans of the *Peter Gunn* series. Episode largely a showcase for Kurt Russell, son of Bing Russell, who had just guest starred in "The Iron Blood of Courage" two weeks before.

#609: Cowtown Hustler
(03-11-74)

WRITER: Jim Byrnes
DIRECTOR: Gunnar Hellstrom
CAST: Jack Albertson, Jonathan Goldsmith Lippe, Nellie Bellflower, Dabbs Greer, Henry Beckman, Lew Brown, John Davis Chandler, Richard O'Brien, Robert Swan, Chuck Hicks

An aging billiard player hoping for one last big score takes a young hustler under his wing and heads for Dodge City.

NOTES: First scene in Dodge's billiard parlor in years. Dabbs Greer appears as a station manager, not Wilbur Jonas. Frequent guest star Jonathan Lippe now billed as Jonathan Goldsmith Lippe.

#610: To Ride a Yellow Horse
(03-18-74)

WRITER: Calvin Clements
DIRECTOR: Vincent McEveety
CAST: Louise Latham, Kathleen Cody, Thomas Leopold, John Reilly, Parker Stevenson, Herb Vigran, Simon Scott, Elizabeth Harrower

A bitter woman does not consider Newly good enough for her daughter.

NOTES: Festus once again does the calling at a barn dance. Last episode filmed for Amanda Blake's final season on the series, but not her last appearance.

#611: DISCIPLE
(04-01-74)

WRITER: Shimon Wincelberg
DIRECTOR: Gunnar Hellstrom
CAST: Dennis Redfield, Frank Marth,
             Marco St. John, Paul Picerni, Robert Phillips,
             R.L. Armstrong, David Huddleston,
             Claire Brennen, Ted Jordan, Robert Brubaker,
             Woodrow Chambliss, Charles Wagenheim,
             Charles Seel, Bobby E. Clark

Seriously wounded in his gun arm, Matt resigns as marshal and encounters an army deserter who is an expert marksman, but does not believe in violence.

NOTES: Matt wears both his familiar red shirt as well as a blue one. Although still not named in the closing credits, Burke calls the new Long Branch bartender Floyd. Amanda Blake's final appearance as Kitty. Also Charles Seel's last episode as Barney Danches.

EPISODE GUIDE

SEASON 20
September 9, 1974–March 31, 1975

#612: MATT DILLON MUST DIE
(09-09-74)

WRITER: Roy Goldrup
DIRECTOR: Victor French
CAST: Morgan Woodward, Joseph Hindy,
Bill Lucking, Henry Olek, Douglas Dirkson,
Frederick Herrick, Elaine Fulkerson

Matt kills a member of a mountain clan and must make his escape across snowy terrain on foot.

NOTES: New opening for the final season showing Front Street, Doc at his desk, Festus and Ruth outside the Long Branch, Newly in his gun shop, and Matt once more preparing for a showdown in the street. Episode a Western version of the classic *The Most Dangerous Game*, with Morgan Woodward in his 18th and last appearance on the series. Filmed on location in Kanab, Utah.

#613: TOWN IN CHAINS
(09-16-74)

WRITER: Ron Bishop
DIRECTOR: Bernard McEveety
CAST: Ramon Bieri, Gretchen Corbett, Lance Le Gault,
Ron Soble, Don Stroud, Russell Wiggins,
Med Flory, John Crawford, Thad Hall, Lloyd
Nelson, Neil Summers, Paul C. Thomas,

Francesca Jarvis, Bernice Smith, Mari Martin, Margaret L. Kingman

Outlaws disguised as soldiers tell a sheriff that Matt is a wanted man.

NOTES: Filmed in Arizona's Coronado National Forest and at Old Tucson.

#614: THE GUNS OF CIBOLA BLANCA, PART 1 (09-23-74)
#615: THE GUNS OF CIBOLA BLACA, PART 2 (09-30-74)

WRITER: Paul Savage
DIRECTOR: Gunnar Hellstrom
CAST: Harold Gould, Dorothy Tristan, Richard Anderson, Michael Christofer, James Luisi, Jackie Coogan, Henry Beckman, Gloria Le Roy, Shug Fisher

Matt, Festus and Newly ride out in search of Doc, who is a prisoner in a Comanchero leader's headquarters.

NOTES: Doc was returning to Dodge City from a medical convention. Character Lila Ross (Tristan) created to replace Amanda Blake's Kitty, originally included in the script.

#616: THIRTY A MONTH AND FOUND (10-07-74)

WRITER: Jim Byrnes
DIRECTOR: Bernard McEveety
CAST: Gene Evans, Nicholas Hammond, Van Williams, David Brian, Ford Rainey, Kim O'Brien, Victor Izay, Hal Baylor, Bonnie Jedell, Hank Kendrick

Matt and Festus chase after a trio of cowboys who are afraid the changing times will leave them with little of value and have taken money they feel is theirs.

NOTES: Matt, in a blue shirt rather than red, knew Will (Evans) in the old days. Victor Izay's ninth and final appearance as saloon owner Bull. Episode an elegy for the Old West, circa 1873, with closing narration: "Their names do not roll with the thunder of Jefferson or Paine, but between 1866 and 1882, for thirty dollars a month and found, these hard and lonely men pushed five million cattle into the heartland of a growing nation. They were the builders of this land."

#617: THE WIVING
(10-14-74)

WRITER: Earl Wallace
DIRECTOR: Victor French
CAST: Harry Morgan, John Reilly, Herman Poppe,
              Michele Marsh, Dennis Redfield, Karen Grassle,
              Linda Sublette, Fran Ryan, Robert Brubaker,
              Rod McGaughy, Bobby E. Clark

Warned by their father not to come home without wives, three farm boys go into Dodge City and resort to kidnapping their intended brides.

NOTES: Matt once again in blue shirt. First of five appearances by Fran Ryan as new Long Branch owner Hannah, who remarks that the saloon has been nothing but trouble ever since she took it over, but never says how she acquired it. No mention of Kitty. Robert Brubaker now billed as Floyd. Karen Grassle and director French were on *Little House on the Prairie* by the time this episode, the first filmed for the season, aired. A weak segment in the context of *Gunsmoke*.

#618: THE IRON MEN
(10-21-74)

WRITER: John Mantley
DIRECTOR: Gunnar Hellstrom
CAST: Cameron Mitchell, John Russell,
            Barbara Colby, George Murdock,
            William Bryant, Marc Alaimo, Paul Gehrman,
            Eric Olson, Alec Murdock

In the town of Brimstone, Matt recognizes a drunk as a former lawman he once knew when they were young deputies in Laredo.

NOTES: Rare script by executive producer Mantley. Cameron Mitchell portrayed Buck Cannon on *The High Chaparral.* John Russell was Marshal Dan Troop on *Lawman.*

#619: THE FOURTH VICTIM
(11-04-74)

WRITER: Jim Byrnes
DIRECTOR: Bernard McEveety
CAST: Biff McGuire, Leonard Stone,
            Woodrow Chambliss, Paul Sorensen,
            Howard Culver, Victor Killian,
            Lloyd Perryman, Frank K. Janson, Al Wyatt,
            Ben Bates, Alex Sharp

An unknown sniper has Dodge City on edge, and Matt has a hunch Doc is the killer's next target.

NOTES: One of the best episodes from the final season also contains one of the series' biggest blunders. Newly reads from an old trial record dating back to April 1859 and says the jury included Chester Goode, Quint Asper and Doc. The problem is, *Gunsmoke* took place *after* the Civil War (1861-65), in which Chester, Doc and Matt took part before coming to Dodge City, and Quint was a young boy living with the Comanches in 1859. Matt tells Newly that Chester "used to work for me here, before your time, left after the trial." As for Quint, Matt says he left for California about ten years ago. Howard Culver's 48th and final episode as Dodge House desk clerk Howie Uzzel.

#620: THE TARNISHED BADGE
(11-11-74)

WRITER: Robert Vincent Wright
DIRECTOR: Michael O'Herlihy
CAST: Victor French, Ruth McDevitt,
              Pamela McMyler, Nick Nolte, Ross Elliott,
              Steve Raines, Hank Worden

Matt is saddled with the unfortunate task of firing Sheriff Harker, an old friend who is abusing the power of his office in Ludlow, Kansas.

NOTES: The jail in Ludlow is the Dodge jail set stripped down and rearranged. Nick Nolte went on to fame in the mini-series *Rich Man, Poor Man* and such feature films as *48HRS*. Ross Elliot played Sheriff Abbott on *The Virginian*.

#621: IN PERFORMANCE OF DUTY
(11-18-74)

WRITER: William Keys
DIRECTOR: Gunnar Hellstrom
CAST: Eduard Franz, David Huddleston,
              Bonnie Bartlett, Rance Howard

Matt jails a pack of outlaws, but a judge tells him there is insufficient evidence to hold them.

NOTES: Judge Kendall (Franz) comes to Dodge because Judge Brooker is ill.

#622: Island in the Desert, Part 1
(12-02-74)
#623: Island in the Desert, Part 2
(12-09-74)

WRITER: Jim Byrnes
DIRECTOR: Gunnar Hellstrom
CAST: Strother Martin, William C. Watson,
             Regis J. Cordic, Hank Brandt

Festus, wounded and left to die, is rescued by a demented prospector who forces him to carry sacks of gold dust across the desert.

NOTES: Final two-part episode of the series, shot partially in California's Glen Canyon Recreation Area. Jail in Cottonwood is same as in "The Tarnished Badge."

#624: The Colonel
(12-16-74)

WRITER: Arthur Dales
DIRECTOR: Bernard McEveety
CAST: Lee J. Cobb, Julie Cobb, Richard Ely,
             Randolph Roberts, Roy Jenson,
             Robert Brubaker, Todd Lookinland,
             Dan Travanty, Pete Kellett

A former army officer, now Dodge City's resident drunk and banned from attending his daughter's wedding, runs into outlaws before he can leave town.

NOTES: Buck Taylor's 100th episode as Newly O'Brien. Brief reprise of Matt's wild ride from 1967's "Nitro!" Matt wears a blue shirt in one scene. Sign over the livery stable still reads Hank Patterson. Lee J. Cobb, star of such classic films as *On the Waterfront* and *12 Angry Men*, was the first owner of the Shiloh Ranch on *The Virginian*. Julie Cobb is his daughter.

#625: THE SQUAW
(01-06-75)

WRITER: Jim Byrnes
DIRECTOR: Gunnar Hellstrom
CAST: John Saxon, Arlene Martell,
             Tom Reese, Morgan Paull

An outlaw being tracked by Matt is aided by an Indian woman.

NOTES: Ken Curtis' 250th episode as Festus Haggen. Location filming at Vasquez Rocks. Tom Reese's 13th guest appearance.

#626: THE HIDERS
(01-13-75)

WRITER: Paul Savage
DIRECTOR: Victor French
CAST: Ned Beatty, Mitch Vogel,
             Lee de Broux

Festus tries to convince a young hide skinner to seek a better path, advice that does not sit well with the outfit's leader.

NOTES: Academy Award winner Ned Beatty co-starred in such films as *Network, All the President's Men, Superman* and *Deliverance*. Mitch Vogel's third and final appearance. Last of Woodrow Chambliss' 31 episodes as Lathrop.

#627: LARKIN
(01-20-75)

WRITER: Jim Byrnes
DIRECTOR: Gunnar Hellstrom
CAST: Richard Jaeckel, Anthony Caruso, Robert Gentry,
             Robert Sorrells, Kathleen Cody, Maggie Malooly,

Michael Le Clair, Jack Rader, Elliot Lindsay, Gilman W. Rankin

A badly wounded Newly and his prisoner are pursued by bounty hunters.

NOTES: Last of Anthony Caruso's 15 guest appearances.

#628: THE FIRES OF IGNORANCE
(01-27-75)

WRITER: Jim Byrnes
DIRECTOR: Victor French
CAST: Allen Garfield, John Vernon,
            Lance Kerwin, Diane Shalet, Herb Vigran,
            George DiCenzo, Karen Oberdiear,
            John Pickard, Charles Wagenheim,
            Robert Brubaker, Janet Nichols,
            Ted Jordan

Despite the fact that his son wants to attend school, a Dodge City farmer disagrees and goes to court insisting that a father's rights are more important than an education.

NOTES: Nearly 15 minutes before any of the regular cast (Matt and Doc) show up. Episode won a National Education Award. The last of Charles Wagenheim's 28 appearances as Charlie Halligan. Herb Vigran's tenth and final episode as Judge Brooker.

#629: THE ANGRY LAND
(02-03-75)

STORY: Herman Groves
TELEPLAY: Jim Byrnes
DIRECTOR: Bernard McEveety
CAST: Carol Vogel, Eileen McDonough,
            Dayton Lummis, Bruce M. Fischer

Matt discovers that a recently widowed woman wants nothing to do with her orphaned niece.

NOTES: A solo Matt episode. On the *Law of the Plainsman* series, Lummis portrayed lawman Andrew Morrison.

#630: BRIDES AND GROOMS
(02-10-75)

WRITER:	Earle W. Wallace
DIRECTOR:	Victor French
CAST:	Harry Morgan, David Soul, Amanda McBroom, Michele Marsh, Dennis Redfield, Spencer Milligan, Ray Girardin, Jim Backus, Fran Ryan

Farmer Jed Hockett's plans for finally getting his three sons to the altar do not go smoothly.

NOTES: Even more dismal sequel to this season's lame episode "The Wiving." David Soul began co-starring on the *Starsky and Hutch* series later in the year.

#631: HARD LABOR
(02-24-75)

STORY:	Hal Sitowitz
TELEPLAY:	Earl W. Wallace
DIRECTOR:	Bernard McEveety
CAST:	John Colicos, Hal Williams, William Smith, Kevin Coughlin, Ben Piazza, Gregory Sierra, Gerald McRaney, Don Megowan, Jackie Russell, Lloyd Nelson, Fred Lerner

After killing an escaped outlaw in the town of Bedrock, Matt is given a life sentence by a crooked judge and forced to work in a silver mine.

NOTES: Cast includes several veteran guest stars, and although they could not have known it at the time, this was the last episode of *Gunsmoke* to be filmed. Plot similar to segments on such series as *Bonanza, Cheyenne, Cimarron City, Wanted Dead or Alive* and others. Both Gregory Sierra and Hal Williams were semi-regular characters on the *Sanford and Son* sitcom at this time.

#632: I HAVE PROMISES TO KEEP
(03-03-75)

STORY: William Putnam
TELEPLAY: William Putnam & Earl W. Wallace
DIRECTOR: Vincent McEveety
CAST: David Wayne, Tom Lacy, Ken Swofford,
            Ken Renard, Trini Tellez, Fran Ryan,
            John Wheeler, Ed McCready

Festus encounters prejudice when he helps a preacher build a church that will be open to everyone, including Indians.

NOTES: Festus is in the town of Nescatunga after delivering a prisoner. Writer William Putnam is in reality an alias for veteran *Gunsmoke* scribe Paul Savage.

#633: THE BUSTERS
(03-10-75)

WRITER: Jim Byrnes
DIRECTOR: Bernard McEveety
CAST: Gary Busey, John Beck, Lynn Benesch,
            Randy Boone

A young bronc buster working to earn enough money for a ranch in Montana is critically injured when thrown by a particularly wild horse.

NOTES: The September 1, 1975 rerun of this episode was the last CBS network broadcast of *Gunsmoke*. Years later, Gary Busey proudly told late night host David Letterman, "I was the last guy to die on *Gunsmoke*." The 103rd and final appearance of Buck Taylor as Newly O'Brien. Randy Boone co-starred on *The Virginian* and *Cimarron Strip*. Jim Byrnes earned a Best Western Television Script award from the Western Writers of America.

#634: MANOLO
(03-17-75)

STORY:	Harriet Charles & Earl W. Wallace
TELEPLAY:	Earl W. Wallace
DIRECTOR:	Gunnar Hellstrom
CAST:	Robert Urich, Nehemiah Persoff,
	Mark Shera, Fran Ryan, Brian James

Fearing he might cause his father's death, a Basque shepherd is reluctant to follow his people's tradition of fighting the man.

NOTES: Fifth and final episode with Fran Ryan as Long Branch owner Hannah. The late Robert Urich appeared in the landmark mini-series *Lonesome Dove* and starred in several series, including *Vega$, Spencer: For Hire* and *S.W.A.T.*, which co-starred Mark Shera, best known for the *Barnaby Jones* series. Sixth *Gunsmoke* episode guest starring Nehemiah Persoff.

#635: THE SHARECROPPERS
(03-31-75)

WRITER:	Earle W. Wallace
DIRECTOR:	Leonard Katzman
CAST:	Terry Williams, Suzanne Benton,
	Victor French, Jacque Aubuchon,
	Bruce Boxleitner, Lisa Eilbacher,
	Graham Jarvis

Festus gets stuck walking behind a mule instead of riding one when he helps a lazy family of farmers plant a crop to keep from being evicted.

NOTES: Sadly, a weak final first-run episode. Ken Curtis' 256th appearance as Festus, Ted Jordan's 108th appearance as Nathan Burke, Robert Brubaker's eighth appearance as Long Branch bartender Floyd. Bruce Boxleitner later co-starred with James Arness on the series *How the West Was Won*.

THE GUNSMOKE TELEVISION MOVIES

GUNSMOKE: RETURN TO DODGE
September 26, 1987

WRITER: Jim Byrnes
DIRECTOR: Vincent McEveety
CAST: Earl Holliman, Ken Olandt, W. Morgan Sheppard,
Patrice Martinez, Tantoo Cardinal, Steve Forrest,
Mickey Jones, Frank M. Totino, Robert Koons,
Walter Kaasa, Georgie Collins, Tony Epper, Louie
Elias, Ken Kirzinger, Denny Arnold, Alex Green,
Paul Daniel Wood, Larry Muser, Robert Clinton,
Frank Huish, Jacob Rupp, Mary Jane Wildman

Matt is briefly reunited with Kitty when Newly tracks him down to report that his old foe, Will Mannon, has come to Dodge City seeking revenge.

NOTES: Matt is wounded and bedridden for three weeks. Kitty to Matt: "I've got you out from under my fingernails, and you're going to stay out." Flashback sequences include scenes from the episodes "The Badge" (#508, 1970) and "Mannon" #480, 1969). Film "affectionately dedicated to the memory of Milburn Stone, Glenn Strange, James Nusser, Woodrow Chambliss, Charles Wagenheim, Charles Seel, Roy Barcroft." Shot in Canada with "Special thanks to the people of Canmore and Calgary, and to Kananaskis County, Alberta."

Arness, Amy Stock-Poynton, Joe Lara in "The Last Apache"

GUNSMOKE: THE LAST APACHE
March 18, 1990

WRITER: Earle W. Wallace
DIRECTOR: Charles Correll
CAST: Richard Kiley, Amy Stock-Poynton, Geoffrey
            Lewis, Joe Lara, Joaquin Martinrez, Sam Vlahas,
            Hugh O'Brian, Michael Learned, Peter Murnik,
            Robert Covarrubias, Ned Bellamy, Dave Florek,
            Kevin Sifuentes, Robert Brian Wilson,
            Blake Boyd, James Milanesa

Matt learns he has a daughter, and that she has been kidnapped by Apaches.

NOTES: Story takes place in Arizona, circa 1886. Beth (Stock-Poynton) is already 21-years-old when Matt finds out about her. Film "is dedicated to the memory of our beloved friends and artists Miss Amanda Blake, Stan Hough, and writer emeritus Mr. Ron Bishop." Shot largely in Texas with thanks to "Department of Interior and National Park Service, Texas Parks and Wildlife Department, Big Bend Ranch, State Natural Area, Alamo Village (Bracketville, Texas), Bill Moody's Rancho Rio Grande.

GUNSMOKE: TO THE LAST MAN
January 10, 1992

WRITER: Earle W. Wallace
DIRECTOR: Jerry Jameson
CAST: Pat Hingle, Amy Stock-Poynton, Matt Mulhern,
             Jason Lively, Joseph Bottoms, Morgan Woodward,
             Mills Watson, James Booth, Amanda Wyss,
             Jim Beaver, Herman Poppe, Ken Swofford,
             Don Collier, Ed Adams, Kathleen Todd Erickson,
             Loy W. Burns, Andy Sherman, Clark A. Ray,
             Michael F. Woodson, Erol Landis, William J. Fisher,
             Stephen C. Foster, Ric San Nicholas,
             Jimmy Don Cox, Richard Glover

After his cattle are stolen, Matt finds himself embroiled in the Pleasant Valley range war of the 1880s.

NOTES: Begins with Mike Yardner's (Michael Learned) funeral. Sheriff Abel Rose (Woodward) last worked with Matt in 1871. Colonel Tucker played by Pat Hingle, briefly Dodge City's doctor during Season 17 (1971). Sheriff Tom portrayed by Don Collier, whose regular series work included *The Outlaws, The High Chaparral* and *The Young Riders*. Shot in Arizona during late 1990 and early 1991. "This film is dedicated to the memory of John Meston."

Ali MacGraw, Arness, James Brolin in "The Long Ride"

GUNSMOKE: THE LONG RIDE
May 8, 1993

WRITER: Bill Stratton
DIRECTOR: Jerry Jameson
CAST: James Brolin, Amy Stock-Poynton,
        Christopher Bradley, Patrick Dollaghan,
        Don McManus, Marco Sanchez, Ali MacGraw,

Tim Choate, Michael Greene, Stewart Moss,
Jim Beaver, Sharon Mahoney, Richard Dano,
Ed Adams, John David Garfield, Victor Izay,
Doug Katenay, Fred Lopez

Bounty hunters crash the wedding of Matt's daughter and say the former lawman is wanted for murder.

NOTES: Beth (Stock-Poynton) marries Josh (Bradley), not Will, her love interest in *The Last Apache*, as some sources have stated. The supposed eye witness to the murder Matt allegedly committed is a horse thief from Kansas whom Matt once arrested in Dodge. Pastor Zach played by Victor Izay, who ran the Bull's Head Saloon during the original series. James Brolin co-starred with Robert Young in the popular medical series *Marcus Welby, M.D.* and is the father of actor Josh Brolin. Ali MacGraw starred in such films as *Love Story*, *The Getaway* and *Convoy*.

GUNSMOKE: ONE MAN'S JUSTICE
February 10, 1994

WRITER: Harry & Renee Longstreet
DIRECTOR: Jerry Jameson
CAST: Bruce Boxleitner, Amy Stock-Poynton,
                 Alan Scarfe, Christopher Bradley, Mikey Lebeau,
                 Kelly Morgan, Six Eyes, Hallie Foote,
                 Clark Brolly, Don Collier, Ed Adams,
                 Wayne Anthony, Bing Blenman, Tom Brinson,
                 Dave Adams, Sandy Gibbons, Mike Kevil,
                 Richard Lundin, Kyle Marsh, Jonathan Mincks,
                 Billy Joe Patton, Ric San Nicholas,
                 Forrie J. Smith, Robin Wayne

Matt and a young stranger join forces to track down a gang of ruthless outlaws.

NOTES: Matt reveals that his father was a Texas Ranger who was shot in the back. Matt's badge shown in a frame on the fireplace mantel. For old time's sake, Matt shot in the left arm one last time. Third teaming of Boxleitner and Arness, following *How the West Was Won* and remake of *Red River*. Don Collier once again plays a sheriff.

INTERVIEWS

PEGGY REA

The late Peggy Rea was born in Los Angeles on March 31, 1921, and entered the world of show business as a secretary at the legendary Metro-Goldwyn Mayer studio in Culver City. Though recognized primarily as a character actress from the series *The Waltons*, *The Dukes of Hazzard* and *Grace Under Fire*, a guest star on more than fifty more (*I Love Lucy, Hazel, Dr. Kildare, Ben Casey, The Man from U.N.C.L.E.*, etc.), several television movies and mini-series (including *How the West Was Won*), and nearly twenty feature films (*7 Face of Dr. Lao, Walk Don't Run, Valley of the Dolls, In Country* among them), few viewers are aware that she was a production secretary for *Gunsmoke* and *Have Gun-Will Travel*. She also appeared in several episodes of both shows. In 2000 and 2001 I had the pleasure of speaking at length with Peggy for a project that, unfortunately, did not reach fruition. Ms. Rea died of congestive heart failure at her condominium in Toluca Lake, California, on February 5, 2011. Following are excerpts from those conversations that will be of interest to Western fans.

Q: Considering that you began as a secretary at M-G-M in the 1940s, Hollywood's Golden Age, I would guess you've no doubt seen a lot of changes in the entertainment industry, both in front of and behind the camera.

A: Yes, indeed. I'll be 80 in March, so your guess is pretty good.

Q: What strikes you in particular about changes in the industry?

A: Well, I was on an interview at Universal yesterday—about froze to death—and I noticed how many more women there are on the crew than there used to be.

Q: Now, you were a secretary on *Gunsmoke* its earliest days.

A: Yes, from the pilot on.

Q: Exactly what did you do there in the office?

A: Everything. There were two girls in the office, and we ran the whole show. Now it takes a whole office full of people.

Q: Were the interiors of those early episodes filmed at what's now known as Raleigh Studios?

A: Yes, they were.

Q: And then the production moved to Paramount.

A: Yes, we moved across the street to Paramount. I was on *Gunsmoke* for the pilot and the first two seasons, as a secretary. And then I switched to *Have Gun-Will Travel* in 1957. I was on it for six years, four years as a secretary and the last two in casting. We were at Paramount until the end.

Q: Going back to *Gunsmoke*, it's been said that Milburn Stone more or less ran the show. What does that mean?

A: Well, he and Amanda kind of tried to rewrite the scripts, from the second season on.

Q: Milburn was quite a character, wasn't he?

A: Yes, he was.

Q: But also very professional. He was the one who made that famous quote about acting being an honorable profession as long as no one caught you at it.

A: Oh, yes! I know that quote!

Q: I've always admired you because you're just so natural.

A: Well, I'm very pleased to hear that. Yes, acting is a great profession as long as you don't get caught acting! I love that!

Q: In a television interview, Burt Reynolds mentioned Milburn telling him that. Now, did you get to know Dennis Weaver and Arness pretty well?

A: Oh, God, yes! I'll say!

Q: Did you have a chance to get to know Burt Reynolds when he was on the show?

A: No, not at all. I don't remember him being on the set when I did my bits. I was probably on just two or three episodes when he was there.

Q: I hear that Mr. Arness is in the hospital now with bleeding ulcers.

A: He is? Oh, shoot—I didn't know that.

Q: I've also heard that David Dortort, who wrote the foreword for my book on *Bonanza*, isn't doing too well.

A: Yes, it seems I read something about that just the other day.

Q: Did you ever meet him when you did your *Bonanza* episodes?

A: He might have come down to the set, but I don't recall that we were ever introduced.

Q: Were there any differences between working on *Gunsmoke* and *Have Gun-Will Travel*?

A: Well, I only worked for *Gunsmoke* the first two years, and then later on as an actress, many times. Was there any difference between the two? Well, sure.

Q: For example, an actor once told me that *Bonanza* was a more professional set, but *Gunsmoke* was a lot more relaxed.

A: Well, yes, on *Gunsmoke* Jim was more relaxed. And Dennis. You know, they were just great. *Bonanza*, I did just one.

Q: Actually, you did two.

A: Oh, yes! Yes! Years later I did one when they were at Warners. I drove a wagon on stage, right into a wall. There was a wrangler on the floor, but I still managed to hit the wall.

Q: You were in the second episode of *Bonanza* ever filmed. You didn't have any lines, but you got to dance with all the Cartwrights.

A: I danced with Hoss, and we both lost three pounds. We were dancing for two days and almost fainted. We did that in color, and the lights were so hot that Jack Carter, who was the guest star, said if they didn't turn the air on, we can't do this.

Q: Did you have a good time working on *Bonanza*?

A: Oh, yeah, well, Michael Landon was just darling. I think I ran a dress shop in that second one, and I was only supposed to work for one day, but they realized they needed to do some more writing to explain who I was. At the time I had my car in the shop for some transmission work and had to rent a car to get to the studio. Well, Michael Landon heard about it and told me that since I was getting extra work I ought to forget about the transmission work and buy a new car.

Q: Did you?

A: I think I did. It turned into quite a profitable little part.

Q: I have a lot of your appearances on tape, including those two. Would you be interested in having copies of anything?

A: Well, there's a *Gunsmoke* I did that's quite famous called "Baker's Dozen." That one is a charmer.

Q: And you played the same character again in an episode called "The Lost."

A: I did? You're really up on this! Now, you know that the script for "Baker's Dozen" was written by Milburn Stone's brother. And they wouldn't do it. They thought it was too sentimental, too sugary sweet. And Milburn kept bugging Jim Arness about it, so Jim finally told the producer, "You've got to do this one and get Milburn off my back. I'm sick of hearing about it, so just work it out. Do it!"

Q: Evidently that script had been lying around a long time. At one point it was going to be a Chester story…

A: Yes, that's true. And Jim put his foot down and said, "I don't want to hear anymore about it, just do the damn script!" Well, they did it over Easter vacation. They did it in half the time it usually took, and because school was out they used all the staff's kids. Our yard looked like a kindergarten, and Dobe Carey was my husband. He was a sweetheart! He lives in Colorado now, and so does Andy McLaglen. Well, anyway, they shot that show in half the time, and Denver Pyle was just appalled. He was rushed out there—he was playing the judge—and I was on the set when they were changing lines as we shot. Denver said, "What the hell is going on!" And I said, "Denver, just jump in there and do it! They're doing this fast." He said, "My God, I'll say." Well, they shot it and put it all together. It was absolutely charming! And we were scheduled to be opposite the Oscars. Now, that's how much CBS didn't care. That's what's called trying to bury a show, right?

Q: Well, actually, it first aired on Christmas Day, 1967. You're thinking of the rerun, in April 1968.

A: Well, that's when Martin Luther King was assassinated, and the Oscars were canceled. The very first time the Oscars were canceled. And people who were all geared to watch the Oscars that night watched *Gunsmoke* instead. And we had a terrific audience, one of the highest rated shows. And ever since, it's one that's been rerun a lot.

Q: And Milburn Stone won an Emmy for it. Isn't that something?

A: And they didn't want to air it! So that's the story on that show.

Q: You played the same character, Mrs. Roniger, a few years later.

A: I guess I did.

Q: The one where Kitty finds the girl in the wilderness and brings her back to live with your family.

A: Oh, yes!

Q: Now, in between those two you did an episode called "O'Quillian," and caroused with Victor French. You played a saloon girl.

A: Yes, I loved that!

Q: What was Victor French like? Was he quite a character?

A: He was very charming, great fun.

Q: I almost went to see him in a play back when I lived in Los Angeles, at a little theater that I believe was on Sunset. It was Chekov's "The Seagull." And I thought, wow, this guy has quite a range.

A: Oh, yes, he was a good actor.

Q: You did an episode of *Gunsmoke* back in the Dennis
         Weaver days called "Chester's Indian." You were in it so
         briefly you might not remember it.

A: Well, they would give me little things to do now and then,
         and sometimes a really good part like "Baker's Dozen."

Q: "Chester's Indian" was in 1962.

A: Now, that's the first year I went back to acting. After *Have
         Gun*, and I've been acting ever since. I did a movie with
         Tony Randall right off the bat.

Q: Well, you're on here just about every morning of the week
         on *Grace Under Fire* reruns.

A: Absolutely! Well, that's the best news of the week because
         the residuals have been tapering off, and I know it's
         running somewhere. They've been keeping me going for
         the last three years.

Q: I know you've been asked dozens of questions about *Have
         Gun-Will Travel* for a couple of recent books, so I'm not
         going to repeat them, but what's your most vivid memory
         of working with Richard Boone? When somebody says his
         name, what's the first thing you flash on? You had roles in
         several episodes.

A: Oh, God, what a six years that was! After two years on
         Gunsmoke, I was the veteran production secretary of the
         company, so they put me on *Have Gun*, and I worked on
         it the whole six years. And they were six great years, with
         Dick Boone and Andy McLaglen. And Sam Rolfe.

Q: Was that the highlight of your career?

A: Well, it was a fun six years, I can tell you that. Any specific memories of Boone? Oh, lots—but I can't talk about them! Too many to mention. He was kind enough to make sure I was in at least one show each season, but I have to say I was really disappointed when he did *The Richard Boone Show* and didn't take me with him

Q: That was done at M-G-M, so it would have been a sort of homecoming for you.

A: Yes, it would! I was sick about it for a long time.

Q: I've read that Boone wasn't exactly crazy about horses.

A: No, he wasn't, and neither was Jim Arness. But they couldn't help but look good riding them.

Q: Do you have any memories of working on *The Wild, Wild West* or *Death Valley Days*?

A: *Wild, Wild West*, I did one. I was a squaw, and Anthony Caruso was a the chief. And for a couple of minutes I carried a dwarf guy on my back.

Q: Was that Michael Dunn?

A: Yes, and that was it. I did a couple of nice *Death Valley Days* for Bob Stabler, up in Northern California. It was a nice show.

Q: Do you have a favorite job, anything that stands out?

A: Oh, absolutely, a movie called *In Country*, with Bruce Willis. Now, that's it. That's my fifteen minutes of fame. We opened the Toronto Festival, we opened the Mill Valley Festival. Norman Jewison took me with him, and we went back to Kentucky for the opening there, in the

Warner Bros. plane. It started a whole lot of nice things for me, but that was the best.

Q: Do you have any memories of working on *Love Field*? That was also a pretty high profile film.

A: Oh, my, yes. I still hear from an insurance man I met there in Wilson, North Carolina. I'm known in the Midwest and South not for *Gunsmoke* or *Have Gun* or *The Waltons*, but for *The Dukes of Hazzard*! I'll probably always be remembered as Lulu Hogg!

JEREMY SLATE

The late Jeremy Slate was a versatile actor on screens big (*North by Northwest, The Devil's Brigade*) and small (*Perry Mason, Combat!, Bewitched, The Untouchables*), capable of playing heroes and villains, and equally as credible whether performing opposite John Wayne or Elvis Presley. Western enthusiasts no doubt remember him best from the features *The Sons of Katie Elder* and the original *True Grit,* as well as such series as *Bat Masterson, The Deputy, Have Gun-Will Travel, The Virginian* and particularly several episodes of *Bonanza* and *Gunsmoke.* I was fortunate to be introduced to Jeremy by Dan Turpin, a former bus driver for country singer Merle Haggard, and we soon became what Jeremy termed "talking buddies." We exchanged telephone calls, letters, Christmas cards, and, when his macular degeneration became a problem, he would send me correspondence recorded on cassettes. In return, I supplied him with as many of his television appearances as I could, several of which he had never seen, and Morgan Woodward and I made an unsuccessful attempt to honor him with a Golden Boot Award. He invited me to his home in California, and I was in the process of helping him find a publisher for his World War II memoirs (while in the Navy, which he joined at 16, the destroyer he was on participated in the D-Day invasion of Europe) when he passed away at the age of 80 on November 19, 2006, at the UCLA Medical Center, a victim of esophageal cancer. His last acting job was on an episode of the sitcom *My Name Is Earl.* Needless to say, he appreciated his fans and was an exceptionally friendly person. What follows is one of our first discussions of his Western credits.

Q: I was trying to determine the other night which episode of *Pony Express* you may have been on. I've got the plots and the airdates, but the information is real sketchy.

A: I think Robert Altman directed it. I could be wrong, but I think I was a deputy sheriff. You know, back then there were so many of those shows that I can't remember exactly which one it was. But I'll tell you something weird. My wife put on one of those tapes you sent, "The Raid" from *Gunsmoke,* and I'm watching it and see, wow, Gary Lockwood. And then, wait a minute, who's that character in the middle there? He looks just like me. Then I turned to my wife and said, "Wow! This is one that I'm in!" There have been several times this has happened to me. I'm sitting there watching and don't know anything about it. I couldn't remember anything about it! It's like watching someone else, but I love that to happen. I can't get over it! It happened to me with a couple of *Gunsmokes*, one I did with Denver Pyle that I didn't remember at all. And it's really weird because I remember most of my things. Almost all of them, you know? When I see them, I remember them, but I sure didn't remember that one you sent. And it was such a kick to find out it was "The Raid."

Q: I think I've sent you all seven of your *Gunsmokes*.

A: Oh, yeah, I think so. That's great.

Q: I know you did some acting in New York, but when did you first go out to California?

A: It was 1958, and, well, I guess within about six months I had a series, *The Aquanauts*.

Q: I used to watch it. I even had an *Aquanauts* comic book.

A: Yeah! I've seen that! I've got one!

Q: Is it kind of green? The cover?

A: Yeah! I'll be darned! That was the first job I had in Hollywood, and then I just went on from there, to guest star and stuff like that.

Q: Now, did you have any riding ability before coming to Hollywood?

A: Not much, but yeah, I was familiar with horses. That was an easy part of my existence. I could ride a horse, yeah.

Q: Was *Bat Masterson* the first Western series you were ever on?

A: Yes, it was the first Western.

Q: I used to live in Los Angeles, and I go out there every now and then to visit friends, but where in the heck was Ziv, where they did *Bat Masterson*?

A: Right on Santa Monica. It's now a supermarket. But it was an old, old studio. A lot of old wooden sets, great for syndication. They had *Highway Patrol*, *Bat Masterson*, our series, and they had *Men into Space* with William Lundigan. I got a two day job on *Men into Space;* that was my first job.

Q: What was your impression of Gene Barry? My wife had a chance to meet him a couple of times, and she said he was very different both times.

A: Well, he was obviously hung up on himself as an actor, you know what I mean? He gave the impression of, "Boy, I'm a good looking guy." That kind of thing. Except that he was very nice, but somewhat distant.

Q: And you did *The Deputy* with Henry Fonda.

A: Yes, I did, but I don't remember that series at all.

Q: Do you remember if it was intimidating working with him?

A: No, no. You know, I don't remember meeting him, but I guess I must have.

Q: And then you did seven *Gunsmokes*, two of them two-parters. You say "The Gallows" is your favorite?

A: Yeah, and I remember that one pretty well because most of it was just me and Jim Arness. At one time he told me it was his favorite episode, which I was happy to hear. I loved the whole cast. They were great, they were just plain great. Just like down home.

Q: I understand that Milburn Stone kind of called the shots, that they deferred to him, but with respect.

A: Yeah, that's true. And they were really nice to each other, nice to me, nice to everybody. A great show to be on.

Q: Where exactly was "The Raid" filmed? At the end it looks like they were out in Death Valley or Joshua Tree, maybe around Lancaster.

A: I don't really remember, but it seems to me most of it was in town, but they may have gone out to Thousand Oaks or somewhere like that. It's been so long. I did so many things between 1960 and 1970 that it's hard to remember everything.

Q: That was only the second two-part *Gunsmoke*.

A: Really? Wow...as I mentioned in one of my letters, that had an amazing cast. John Anderson and Jim Davis...oh, yeah!

Q: John Kellogg, Richard Jaeckel...

A: Oh, yeah, Richard Jaeckel. I saw him and I said, "Is that Richard Jaeckel?"

Q: He just passed away.

A: Yeah, I know. I thought he was never going to pass away. He looked the same way every time, through the years.

Q: Do you have any recollections of filming that episode?

A: No, I really don't. Was Jack Lambert in that?

Q: No, he wasn't.

A: Well, Jack Lambert was in one of the *Gunsmoke*s I did. I think another one you sent me, that "Abelia." Yeah, he seemed like he'd be a really mean guy, but one day he came up and showed me that he had this little kitten inside his coat. You wouldn't expect that from a guy who looked the way that he did!

Q: Now, where was "Waste" shot, the one with Ellen Burstyn? Kanab, Utah?

A: Yeah. They had a cowboy town out there.

Q: What was your impression of Ellen Burstyn?

A: Oh, Ellen Burstyn and I got along well, yeah. And Ruth Roman.

Q: And Shug Fisher!

A: Oh, yeah, Shug Fisher. He was a *Gunsmoke* regular, a real character, yeah.

Q: I've read your comments about working on *Have Gun-Will Travel*, but I have to ask you if Richard Boone was pretty intense?

A: Boone? Oh, yeah, he was pretty intense, all right. He definitely called the shots on that one, he sure did. I think it showed, too!

Q: That was filmed at Paramount, the place where *Bonanza* was done. What was your impression of that cast?

A: Oh, that was a lot of fun, too. I got along with Dan Blocker really well, we had a mutual friend, Ramblin' Jack.

Q: Ramblin' Jack Elliott?

A: Yeah, Ramblin' Jack. He was a mutual friend, so we got along real well together. I think I've mentioned this to you before, but one of the things I got a kick out of on *Bonanza* was Michael Landon comes in one day, wearing lifts, and Dan and Lorne and Pernell all know this. They stand beside him, and they've all got lifts on! They all got taller and taller, it was so funny, it was hysterical.

Q: Hopefully you remember those comments from David Dortort I sent along to you. He had a lot of nice things to say about you. He said that usually if they didn't like someone, they didn't ask them back, but you were on there three times.

A: Yeah, three times.

Q: Denver Pyle was nominated for an Emmy for that last episode you were in, "Passing of a King."

A: Really? I didn't know that.

Q: Now, at the end of that episode, you and Landon have this terrific fight. And I don't recall seeing any doubles. I know he did a lot of his own stunts, and I can't imagine you using one.

A: Yeah, I think we did all of that ourselves.

Q: You did the episode "A Man without Land" with Royal Dano. Didn't he have an acting school?

A: Yes, he did. Now, he was a very nice man. He seemed, to me, to be an actor who was in love with his voice. Like Lorne Greene.

Q: Were there any interesting differences between working on *Gunsmoke* and *Bonanza*?

A: You know, it seems to me that it was like day and night, and yet I couldn't put my finger on it. Except that production on *Bonanza*, on the Paramount lot, seemed to be more regimented, with everything moving right along. And on *Gunsmoke* it was much more casual. You know, you're on the set, and there's Jim Arness sitting over there relaxing.

Q: You worked with Robert J. Wilke in *Bat Masterson*.

A: Was it *Bat Masterson*? Yeah, I knew Robert really well. He was good, a good actor. You look at him and it was, boom! He was threatening, but not really.

Q: *The Sons of Katie Elder* had a heck of a cast, top to bottom. And the films seemed more realistically paced back then, not so frantic to conform to today's short attention spans. The need for immediate gratification.

A: Oh, yeah, right, right. Wayne was sort of winded on that set. That was the first thing he did after he lost a lung, and he had an oxygen thing with him all the time. And he got into some of the fighting, and some of that stuff, and he scared us. No one expected him to go in the water for that shootout by the lake, but he was pretty game. We shot the whole thing in Mexico.

Q: That looks like you, but a stunt double for Dean Martin, where he knocks you out of your saddle. You did your own stunts, didn't you?

A: Oh, yeah, and I directed that scene where I get shot by James Gregory. Henry Hathaway let me direct that. And I directed another of my death scenes, in *Born Losers*. But I hated Henry Hathaway. He was a son of a bitch, a psychotic.

Anyway, he said to me, "I understand you're a good die-er." I said, "Yeah, I've got a reputation for that." So he said, "Well, do you want to direct this? What do you want?" I said, "I want a wire pull. I've never had a wire pull before." So he let me and a stunt man set it up.

Q: How many takes did you have to do?

A: About four. But it was easy. I had the thing around my waist, and there were a couple guys behind a tree. All I had to do was leap in the air, and they pulled me back.

Q: Did Hathaway remember you from *Elder*? Is that how you got the role in *True Grit*?

A: No, the reason I got *True Grit* was because I was under contract to Hal Wallis. He wanted to get me in everything. You notice I got top billing over Dennis.

Q: Dennis Hopper, yeah. He was quite a character in those days, wasn't he?

A: Oh, yeah, we hung out a lot together. He's pretty intense, too.

Q: I talked to someone once who said *True Grit* would have been a better film if you and Glen Campbell had swapped parts.

A: Yeah, good point! I'll be darned!

Q: Unfortunately, you only had that one scene. Where was that filmed?

A: Up in Mammoth Lake. I think it might have been June Lake, one of those up there. State land, Federal land. Henry Hathaway had a way of getting great locations out of the government, leasing land that had never been used before.

Q: What's your opinion regarding the decline of the Western genre? There are so many theories out there.

A: Well, I don't know for sure, but it got too pat. The white hats and the black hats, you know, that kind of thing. It got to be too much for people. And then other films started to come in. You know, I call my motorcycle films Westerns on bikes, instead of horses. I guess it was just a matter of them getting tiresome. Once in a while something good comes along, like *Dances with Wolves* or *Unforgiven*.

MORGAN WOODWARD

He has a well-deserved reputation of being one of the most imposing and charismatic Western stars who ever strapped on a six-gun—usually opposing the forces of law and order—but Morgan Woodward is actually an actor of wide range. In 1968 he was nearly nominated for an Oscar for his role as the silent prison guard in the Paul Newman classic *Cool Hand Luke*. He has worked in nearly every genre imaginable, including comedy, science-fiction, drama, and of course, the Western. Fittingly, he was born in Fort Worth, Texas, in 1925, and his first career choice was singing opera. However, sinus trouble prevented him from pursuing that goal, and after military service—in World War II and Korea—he enrolled at the University of Texas. Despite his earning a degree in corporate finance, fate once again had other plans. Morgan's college roommate happened to be Fess "Davy Crockett" Parker, who later convinced Walt Disney to give his former fraternity brother a part in an upcoming production. And the rest, as the old adage goes, is history. Eventually, Morgan landed guest roles on more than thirty different television Westerns, including a long stint as Shotgun Gibbs on *The Life and Legend of Wyatt Earp*. He also appeared in eleven episodes of *Wagon Train,* but more significantly, eighteen episodes of *Gunsmoke*. (Some historians claim nineteen; technically Morgan's character died in the first installment of the two-part "Vengeance," with the second half erroneously considered an additional episode.) The late John Mantley's wife, Angela, said in a letter to me:

"John and I consider Morgan Woodward a consummate actor, investing all his roles with dead-on interpretations. Everyone, fan or friend alike, is struck first by his presence, which is imposing enough. The tall Texan with piercing blue eyes, strong physical physique and a sincerity that comes from within, has a face that could grace Mount Rushmore. His voice is mellifluous, his manner elegant. As an actor, he commands respect, but ever so gently; yet he can be a formidable 'heavy'—ususally with a few words. He has imbued his roles in film and television with that quiet strength and believability so reminiscent of Spencer Tracy. Morgan Woodward in custom-made Western duds can also make women swoon and men envy."

For more than a few years, Morgan and I have corresponded and spoken at length on many occasions in preparation for what will hopefully one day be the definitive autobiography of the man. He claims to have a poor memory, but the following excerpts from hours of conversations suggest otherwise.

Q: You first arrived in Hollywood in 1955, correct?

A: Well, I guess I started out with Disney. The second picture I did for Disney—I was under contract to Disney when I first came out here—was *The Great Locomotive Chase*, which was his first live action motion picture. Then I did *Westward Ho, the Wagons*, and then I did *Along the Oregon Trail*. I think that's what it was called. Then I went into *Wyatt Earp*; I was on *Wyatt Earp* for three years. And then I did more *Gunsmokes* and more *Wagon Trains* than anybody not under contract.

Q: I believe you were in 34 different television Westerns. Did you have a favorite?

A: Well, *Gunsmoke* was always my favorite.

Q: What about your theatrical Westerns?

A: I enjoyed doing *One Little Indian*, which was for Disney. I'd almost need a list in front of me to remember them all. *Westward Ho, the Wagons*; I did a couple with Audie Murphy.

Q: And *Firecreek* with Henry Fonda and Jimmy Stewart. That must have been quite an experience.

A: Well, it was quite an experience because it had the biggest cast of stars I'd ever worked with. Just a monumental cast, but it was not a very good picture. That one was done by the *Gunsmoke* people out in an area known as Conejo Ranch, which is all gone now.

Q: Now, I have your first television Western as being an episode of *Zane Grey* with Wendell Corey, in 1956. "A Quiet Sunday in San Ardo."

A: Yes, I guess that's probably right. Wendell Corey was in that.

Q: I know the episode "Lobo" was your favorite *Gunsmoke*.

A: Yes, that's right. But, now, there was another early TV Western with Rex Allen, *Frontier Doctor*. That was either 1956 or '57.

Q: Are there any other episodes from other shows that tend to stand out besides *Gunsmoke*? Anything that left an impression?

A: Again, I'd almost have to have a list in front of me.

Q: What always impressed me was your ability to play roles that appeared similar on the surface, but they developed into characters that were remarkably different as the stories progressed. You could portray a family patriarch three times, or a mountain man six times, yet each patriarch and each mountain man was different. I don't imagine that was an easy task, but you pulled it off every time, as though you looked inside yourself and turned yourself inside out with every part.

A: I'm glad you saw that. I haven't thought about it, but I'm glad it came off.

Q: You did seven episodes of *Bonanza*. Did you have any particular favorite?

A: Well, I can't remember them all. I know I did one with Pernell Roberts.

Q: "The Toy Soldier." What was it like to work with him? I get all different kinds of reactions when I ask about him.

A: I got along fine with Pernell. He was my neighbor up in Hollywood Hills here. Unfortunately, he made a mistake leaving *Bonanza*, thinking he was going to be doing Stratford-On-Avon. But he made the same mistake a lot of people make, thinking, 'Well, this is beneath me, and I'm going to do great things.' And they just don't seem to understand. It's amazing the number of people in these ensemble shows who don't realize that once they're no longer on the show, nobody cares, nobody hires them. Very few are able to go on and establish themselves as an individual performer. Not because they're not good; Pernell's a very good actor. Unfortunately, he made a mistake, and he paid dearly for it. He didn't work for a long time, until he got that doctor show. But you had Dennis Weaver leaving *Gunsmoke*, and Robert Horton leaving *Wagon Train*. It took them a while to reestablish themselves.

Q: Do you remember that episode "Four Sisters from Boston" with Vera Miles?

A: Yes, yes, I do. I did a picture later for Disney, *One Little Indian*, with Vera. She was a beautiful girl.

Q: Your last *Bonanza* was "The Prisoner."

A: Up in the mountains, yes. I remember that.

Q: David Dortort holds you in very high esteem. You did a lot of work for him.

A: Yes, I did. I hold him in very high esteem as well. I went over and spoke to him at the Golden Boot Awards, because I nominated him, I'd been fighting for him. I'm on the executive committee of the Golden Boot, and I told him if they didn't give it to him this time, the Bad Guy was coming out retirement!

Q: I know you did three *High Chaparrals* and three *Restless Guns*, which David produced. You were in an episode of *Restless Gun* with Dan Blocker.

A: That's right. And James Coburn was in that, too. I was the bar owner, all dressed to the nines, and Coburn was one of my henchmen, one of my gunsels, and I've got a picture from that. So when Coburn got the Golden Boot, I told him I had something I'd always wanted to give him. And he said, "It's a picture of you, isn't it?" And I said, "Well, take a look at this." And I'd had it autographed to say, "Jim, I could have been a big star, too, if you hadn't stolen all my parts." He got a big kick out of that.

Q: Backtracking a bit, are there any memories of working on *Bonanza* that stand out?

A: Well, you mentioned "Four Sisters." I remember that. And I remember "The Prisoner." I always liked working with Dan Blocker. He was from Texas, and so am I. We used to see each other all the time, we were fairly social, before he died. It was always a pleasure. Dan was a lot of fun, a hell raiser. The first time I worked with him was on *Tales of Wells Fargo*, and then *The Restless Gun*. I was concerned about his health because on *Bonanza* he spent most of his lunch break drinking martinis. And eating. He really abused himself. I don't know this for sure, but he probably had a lot of lousy medical advice, and a lot of lousy medical care.

Q: Did you get along all right with Lorne Greene and Michael Landon?

A: Lorne had a colossal ego, but oh, yeah, fine. I hated to see Lorne in his last days. I don't know if he was experiencing memory problems or what, but he was using cards with his lines printed on them. He had to rely on those a lot of the time. And Mike was a cocky, very arrogant young guy. Very bright, very clever, very quick. It was obvious when you met him that he was intelligent, a very ribald sense of humor. But very cocky. He was not a large man, but for his size he was a strong man. He liked to arm wrestle with people, and most of the time he would win. He wore those boots with lifts in them to make him look taller, which was fine. But I never worked with Michael on any of his shows, *Highway to Heaven* or *Little House on the Prairie*. Nothing. Victor French was a friend of mine, and he directed some, but I never heard anything. And there were certainly some shows I would have liked to have been in, but the biggest mistake I ever made with my agents was not being right on top of them all the time. That was a terrible mistake, but I didn't want to pester them constantly. I just assumed they were doing their job, but they were not. I didn't start calling them more until later in my career.

Q: Was he always that way throughout your association with *Bonanza*? You did episodes all the way from 1960 up to 1971. Did he always strike you as being like that?

A: Well, yes, but I got along with him okay.

Q: You worked with so many illustrious performers during your career, I'd like to ask you what your impressions were of some of them. Like Richard Boone.

A: I liked Boone, and he seemed to like me. He and I were about the same type, big nose and bad skin. He had a drinking problem, and the last time I worked with him on that detective series at Universal, *Hec Ramsey*, well, you had to shoot Dick's scenes early in the morning, because by the time lunch was over, he was pretty well done in. I think that's one reason the show didn't go on.

Q: Do you have any memories of working with Ann Sheridan? She was on that show *Pistols 'n' Petticoats*.

A: I sure do. Ann was dying when I worked with her. She had lung cancer and was very, very thin, but she was still a nice gal. Ann was a Texan and a beautiful lady. Even though she had cancer, she was smoking, using those aqua filters.

Q: They used to shoot those half-hour shows in about three days, didn't they?

A: Well, no, five days. And about six or seven days for the hours.

Q: How about Chuck Connors?

A: Chuck and I got along great, although he was not that popular with most people. I was on that show he did after *The Rifleman, Branded.* That one was with Bruce Dern.

Q: Yes, "The Wolfers." How was Bruce to work with?

A: He was a little eccentric. We'd be ready to shoot, and he'd be off running track. That didn't make him too popular with the director. We were going to do a scene where they were going to use squibs, that fake blood, and he refused to do it. Wanted to use his double.

Q: How about Robert Duvall, who you worked with on *Cimarron Strip?*

A: I don't think I had any scenes with him. I just don't remember, except that in that one I remember they cast me against type, sort of a scaredy-cat. I believe I did two episodes of *Cimarron Strip.*

Q: Actually, you did three. The one with Robert Duvall and Richard Boone, and then one with Albert Salmi and Denver Pyle, and one with Tuesday Weld. In the one you did with Boone, he kills you.

A: Well, I'm not surprised to hear that, because I usually wound up dead. I do remember Tuesday. And I did a *Rawhide* with Eddie Albert and, of course, Clint. We shot that on the back lot at CBS Studio City.

Q: What was it like to work with a young Clint Eastwood?

A: I just did that one show with him, and that could have been the last year of *Rawhide*. I don't even remember how long that ran.

Q: You were in the seventh season, and it was on for eight.

A: Eight? I'm surprised I didn't do more.

Q: And you did a *Kung Fu* with John Carradine.

A: I did a couple of *Kung Fu*s. On that one I think they boiled me in soap. I'd been hanged, and then somebody did me in and I fell into a vat of boiling soap in that thing.

Q: Do you recall working with Harrison Ford on *Gunsmoke*?

A: I sure do, and when I met him on that show we talked quite a bit, and I thought, "You know, I'll bet this guy's got a good future in pictures." There was just something about him. Plus, he was making his living as a carpenter at that time, and I asked him if he could come over to my house and do some cabinet work for me. But he was doing an office for some producer or director, so he said it would be a few weeks. Well, I never heard from him again, and I didn't call him, so we just sort of dropped it. You know, he got hurt on that *Gunsmoke* I did with him, "The Sodbusters." He got hurt during the shootout, cut his chin or broke a tooth or something.

Q: You had quite a long monologue in "The Sodbusters" that was very impressive.

A: I did that in one take, and John Mantley tried to get me an Emmy nomination, but unfortunately, that did not happen.

Q: Do you remember working with Peter Lorre on *Wagon Train?*

A: Oh, sure. He was a nice guy. Actually, I went to his home there in Beverly Hills with Fess Parker one day. Had a glass of wine. A very nice man.

Q: James Arness went to college about twenty minutes from where I live, and I heard that back in the late '50s or early '60s he came back for a reunion at some kind of resort and he and his buddies supposedly tore the place up. By all accounts he's a real fun loving guy.

A: Oh, yes, he's a great guy, I'll tell you. Very private, but he loves to have a good time, with a great sense of humor.

Q: Now, you did eleven episodes of *Wagon Train*. Are you aware that you were in the very last episode?

A: No, I'm not. You've been able to keep track of things I have no idea about.

Q: That was with Rory Calhoun, Arthur Hunnicutt and Mort Mills. May of '65.

A: I'd worked with Rory before, on *The Texan*, and I did a movie with him at Universal with Rod Cameron and Ruta Lee. I think it was called *Gun Hawk*, and if you ever come across it, I hope you don't watch it! It's not very good at all. It was directed by a guy named Edward Ludwig, who liked me very much. He told me, "You know, I like to watch you when you get mad because you get really excited, you open your eyes and get a kind of crazed look." I remember during that picture he kept saying, "I want to see those eyes really pop open!" Unfortunately, I paid attention to him! And the screenplay was one of the worst I'd ever seen in my life. It was just awful, the director was terrible. It was an Allied Artists production, made for about thirty-five cents.

Q: And you did a *Hec Ramsey* with Rory. You worked with quite a number of people. Jay Silverheels, Victor French…

A: Yeah, I worked with Jay quite a bit. And I worked with Victor both as an actor and director. He directed me in *Gunsmoke* and on *Dallas*. And I worked with John Anderson on *Wyatt Earp* and, I think, *Death Valley Days*. And, let's see, James Stacy on *Lancer* and *Have Gun-Will Travel*. Just so many people…

Q: Henry Darrow is supposed to be a pretty friendly guy.

A: Yes, Henry is a good friend of mine. And old Denver Pyle, who we just lost. And Sam Elliott is a good friend. I've probably forgotten half the people I worked with!

Q: Getting back to *Wagon Train*, was there much difference between the years Ward Bond was on the show and later, when John McIntire took over the lead? I know Howard Christie was still producing it.

A: Yes, "Red" Christie. Very nice guy. Of course he was nice to me because I did so many of them. Anyway, Ward Bond was a very loud, volatile, kind of violent, profane guy. As a matter of fact, he couldn't speak without using profanity. I don't think he meant anything by it. That was just the way he was. He was not a mean man, as far as I could see. I never saw him abuse anybody. I never had any conflict with Bond. Back in those early days, I went in, did my part, kept my mouth shut most of the time, and did what I thought I did best. John McIntire was a great guy, and I liked his wife, Jeanette Nolan. *Wagon Train* had a more pleasant atmosphere after John came on.

Q: How about Frank McGrath? He was on the show all eight years.

A: Oh, he was just incredible! He was just exactly off-screen the same way he was on-screen. Christie was down on the set one day, and right in front of me, Frank said, "Hey, Red! Morgan's on the show again. Goddamn it, why don't you just sign him to a contract? He's doing more shows than the rest of us." He was a real character.

Q: I've actually run into people who, in their hazy memories, actually remember you as being a regular on *Wagon Train* or *Gunsmoke* because you did so many.

A: Well, that's true. I know that some people thought that I was, even though I never did any two characters that were the same.

Q: You were in 34 different Western series, including most of the major ones, and you probably would have been in even more if you hadn't been a regular on *Wyatt Earp*.

A: Yeah, I was on there with Hugh O'Brian for three years, 1958 to '61, and we did more shows per year than they do now. We did two a week, a thirty-minute segment in about two-and-a-half days, mostly at Melody Ranch.

Q: How did you come to be hired for *Earp*?

A: I did two episodes in '57, a bare knuckle fighter in one, and a Texas Ranger named Captain Langly in another. He was almost like Shotgun Gibbs, so they just turned Langly into Shotgun Gibbs. And fired Mason Alan Dinehart, who was playing Bat Masterson. Replaced him with me.

Q: You did a *Bat Masterson* with Gene Barry, in 1960. "The Big Gamble."

A: I guess it was about that time.

Q: Now, why did you leave *Earp*? If your character died, I must apologize for not remembering.

A: Hugh didn't want to do it any more. He was giving the company such a bad time because they weren't paying him anything, paying him peanuts. And he was going out on weekends, doing these personal appearance things, and he was just not real happy. He'd been doing it six years, and I think he wanted to move on. Hugh was not the easiest guy to get along with, but he was not treated well. He didn't make a lot of money. He was very upset because Chuck Connors was making two or three times the money for *The Rifleman*. I didn't make any money from it either. I think the most money I ever got was just $350 a show. I was just the second banana, but it certainly didn't make me happy that they weren't going to do it any longer because it was popular enough that it would have gone on. It was a very highly rated show, and I would have continued riding that mule into the sunset. I liked getting that check every week! And I had kind of a hard time getting started again after being on that show for three years because every time my agent tried to get me something, they'd say, "Oh, that old guy that rides a mule?" I was thirty-one! But I was sort of typecast as a Western actor. So it took a while to get established.

Q: I believe the last Western you did before retiring was *The Adventures of Brisco County, Jr.*, in 1994.

A: That was one I'd kind of like to forget because on the very last day of shooting, the sun was going down and we had a long shot to do, and they'd given me the wrong pages. I didn't know my dialogue, and I was just really upset with what happened there. I never did see the program, and I hope it wasn't as bad as I thought. The industry has changed so much in so many ways that I really can't say I miss it. It's very impersonal, very commercial. Get it shot, get it done. It's all about money and ratings.

Q: I was always waiting for you to pop up on *Paradise* or *The Young Riders*.

A: Well, I'll tell you, I was very disappointed. I don't know what happened there. Either the producers of those shows weren't enamored of my work, or it could have been that when that new breed of people came in, they didn't know one actor from another. But back in those days I was sort of looking forward to retiring.

Q: One of the last things you did was the third *Gunsmoke* movie, "To the Last Man," in 1992. That was shot in Arizona, wasn't it?

A: Yeah, with Pat Hingle, down near the Mexican border.

Q: I think one your most interesting *Gunsmoke* episodes was "Hackett," with Earl Holliman where you play the timid farmer instead of the outlaw, which would have been what most people would have expected.

A: They reversed those roles. I was originally supposed to play Earl's role, and John Mantley said, "Hey, I don't want you to play any more bad guys, I want you to play this farmer." And this was right at the last minute! But I said, "Well, okay, let's try it."

Q: But you pulled it off. Very different from, say, "Death Train," where you played this sort of aristocrat on that train with the disease. All people have to do is take a look at that episode and compare it with "Hackett" or "Lobo," and they'll see what a range you had. It's to Mantley's credit that he did.

A: "Lobo" was the first time I ever watched myself on screen and forgot it was me! *Gunsmoke* was a lot of fun, and certainly my favorite of all the shows I did, by far. It was just like a family, and everyone did just a super job. They had the best costumer I ever had, and everybody worked together just really well. John Mantley even used to come down to set to welcome the new actors.

Q: Was that the easiest one to work on, too?

A: It was because the producers, John Mantley and Leonard Katzman and all those people, left me alone. They had faith in what I could do. And they had a great, great cast. And they had good directors. It was just a great company to work for. And I didn't start working on *Gunsmoke* regularly until 1965. I couldn't get on there before that because I'd had a run-in with a casting director who had a slightly different lifestyle than I did, and he wouldn't hire me. Back when it was a thirty-minute show, I only did one, and you'd have to look very quickly to see me because I only had a day's work. I'd just come to California, and Lynn Stalmaster's partner, Jim Lister, didn't hire me for any more. He was the guy I had the problem with. But when Pam Polifroni took over, well, I worked on there pretty steady after that. I did three shows practically back-to-back, and you weren't supposed to do but one a year, so CBS in New York wired the company in Hollywood and said, "For God's sake, there must be somebody else out there other than Morgan Woodward who can do *Gunsmoke!*" Now, you mentioned that episode "Death Train." I remember that the director, Gunnar Hellstrom, took me aside one day and asked who my agent was. I told him it was Meyer Mishkin and asked him why. And he said, "I was just stunned in our production meeting when I found out what you were working for. Do you realize you're the star of half these shows, and you're working for half of what other people are getting?" I was dumbfounded, too. He said, "Well, you should either have a talk with your agent, or get rid of him, and if you ever tell anyone we've had this talk, I'll deny it."

Q: Well, what happened then?

A: I got more money. I went to my agent, and we negotiated for a better salary. I don't mean to sound immodest, but at that time I was the hottest guest star on *Gunsmoke*.

Q: I believe you shot that "Death Train" episode in the summer of 1967.

A: Yes, as a matter of fact we did. And I can tell you it was the hottest summer I've ever experienced, and in those clothes and setting the train on fire, it was just unbearable. Dana Wynter said she wasn't perspiring, she used the old cliché that ladies do not perspire, they glow.

Q: I've heard that James Arness is not feeling very well these days.

A: No, he's not. As a matter of fact, when we did that *Gunsmoke* picture, "To the Last Man," I wasn't sure he was going to be able to finish, but then he amazed everybody by doing two more! Those operations he had back when he was shot at Anzio didn't seem to help. In fact, he seemed to get worse all the time. I don't know what other problems may have been bothering him, but he never complained. Back when we were doing *Gunsmoke* as a series, we were both so tall they couldn't shoot up at us, they had to shoot down! But now we've both shrunk with age.

Q: As you said, your old friend Pat Hingle was in "To the Last Man." What was it like to work with him?

A: Well, Pat's a terrific actor, he's had an absolutely marvelous career, but the only thing I ever saw him do that I thought he was not good in was "To the Last Man." I was just very disappointed when I saw it. I know that he couldn't stand the director, disagreed with practically everything the director wanted to do, and he just walked through it. I was surprised. I don't think he intended to walk through it, but it could have been that he wasn't feeling well, though he seemed to be fine. Now, I was supposed to play his part, but later I thought, "Boy, am I glad I didn't have to play that part." When I saw the picture I was just very, very pleased that I got to play the part of the sheriff. But we had very bad luck with that picture because it was supposed to follow the World Series, and that would have really been a big boost. Unfortunately, the World Series went overtime, so it played two or three weeks later. When it eventually did play, the minute it was over, the phone rang, and it was Fess Parker. He told me, "I think that's the best thing I've ever seen you do." And I said, "Really?" I was pleased at how it turned out, but I'm not sure it's the best thing I ever did. I think Fess probably said that because he always saw me as a heavy, and he was especially impressed by the scene where Arness is chastising me for selling out. At any rate, Fess is my best friend, and it was nice to have a best friend call and say it was good.

Q: I've also heard that Dennis Weaver's come up with an idea for him and Arness to do a special about Matt and Chester in their twilight years, sitting down and reminiscing at the turn of the century.

A: I think it would be great. I hope they will. But, you know, you've got these thirty-something producers and directors who are only interested in putting out this crap that they do today. At any rate, I'm going to try to check up on Jim, but he's very hard to get in touch with. He's very, very private. But he's also a very nice man, never rude but always kept to himself. He's almost never seen in public. But I think Jim is just a terrific guy. We had a lot of fun working together, and I started him on his flying career. It was a very pleasant ten years together. We had sort of a mutual admiration thing going.

BIBLIOGRAPHY

BOOKS

Arness, James, with James E. Wise, Jr. *James Arness: An Autobiography*. Jefferson, NC: McFarland & Co., 2001.

Barabas, SuZanne and Gabor Barabas. *Gunsmoke: A Complete History*. Jefferson, NC: McFarland & Co., 1990.

Brooks, Tim and Earle Marsh. *The Complete Directory to Prime Time Network and Cable TV Shows 1946—Present: 20th Anniversary Edition*. New York: Ballantine Books, 1999.

Burgoyne, Beckey. *Perfectly Amanda: Gunsmoke's "Miss Kitty" To Dodge and Beyond*. Chandler, AZ: Five Star Publications, 2010.

Burlingame, Jon. *TV's Biggest Hits: The Story of Television Themes From "Dragnet" to "Friends."* New York: Shirmer Books, 1996.

Carey, Harry, Jr. *Company of Heroes: My Life as an Actor in the John Ford Stock Company*. Lanham, MD: Madison Books, 1996.

Carne, Judy and Bob Merrill. *Laughing on the Outside, Crying on the Inside*. New York: PaperJacks, Ltd., 1986.

Costello, Ben. *Gunsmoke: An American Institution*. Chandler, AZ: Five Star Publications, 2006.

Goldstein, Stan and Fred Goldstein. *The TV Guide Quiz Book*. New York: Bantam, 1978.

Hake, Ted. *Hake's Guide to TV Collectibles*. Radnor, PA: Wallace-Homestead Book Company, 1990.

Hake, Ted. *Hake's Guide to Cowboy Collectibles*. Radnor, PA: Wallace-Homestead Book Company, 1994.

Magers, Boyd, Bob Nareau, Bobby Copeland. *Best of the Badmen*. Madison, NC: Empire Publishing, Inc., 2008.

Maltin, Leonard. *Movie and Video Guide 1994*. New York: Signet, 1993.

Metz, Robert. *CBS: Reflections in a Bloodshot Eye*. Chicago: Playboy Press, 1975.

Miller, Lee O. *The Great Cowboy Stars of Movies & Television*. Westport, CN: Arlington House Publishers, 1979.

O'Neil, Thomas. *The Emmys*. New York: Penguin Books, 1992.

Paper, Lewis J. *Empire: William S. Paley and the Making of CBS*. New York: St. Martin's Press, 1987.

Peel, John. *Gunsmoke Years*. Las Vegas, NV: Pioneer Books, Inc., 1989.

Reynolds, Burt. *My Life*. New York: Hyperion, 1994.

Stine, Whitney, with Bette Davis. *Mother Goddam*. New York: Berkley Publishing Corporation, 1975.

Weaver, Dennis. *All the World's a Stage*. Charlottesville, VA: Hampton Roads Publishing Company, Inc., 2001.

ARTICLES

"Actors Name Arness 'Man of the Year'," United Press, March 21, 1973.

"Actors Vie to be Marshal Dillon in Upcoming *Gunsmoke* Film," *The Los Angeles Times*, February 6, 2010.

Alban, Joyce. "The Public Eye: Gunsmoke," *TV-Radio Mirror*, 1965.

Amory, Cleveland. "*Gunsmoke*," *TV Guide*, March 14, 1964.

"Arness is Mayor for a Day," United Press, August 20, 1986.

Baker, Joe. "Doc Remembered His Friends," Associated Press, June 13, 1980.

Beck, Marilyn. "On Entertainment," Associated Press, May 27, 1985.

"Blake Cause of Death Revealed," *The Los Angeles Times*, November 6, 1989.

Brady, James. "In Step with Peter Graves," *Parade Magazine*, June 28, 1998.

Buck, Jerry. "Buck Rogers is Responding to Treatment of the Doctor," *TV View*, April 19, 1981.

"Buck Taylor," *Biography Magazine*, January 2000.

Burns, Bob and Tom Weaver. "Glenn Strange: One of a Kind," *Films of the Golden Age*, Number 34, Fall 2003.

"Busy Day at the Office," *TV Guide*, January 30, 1971.

Chapman, Art. "A Whiff of *Gunsmoke*," *The Chicago Tribune*, March 11, 1990.

"Chester, Kitty and Doc: Dances, Songs and Snappy Patter," *TV Guide*, January 2, 1960.

Cohn, Paulette. "Remembering *Gunsmoke*," *American Profile*, October 26, 2008.

Cox, Stephen. "When Viewers Stayed the Heck in Dodge City," *The Los Angeles Times*, September 3, 1995.

De Roos, Robert. "The Greta Garbo of Dodge City," *TV Guide*, December 10, 1966.

Doan, Richard K. "The Doan Report," *TV Guide*, May 13, 1972.

Doan, Richard K. "The Doan Report," *TV Guide*, July 12, 1975.

Finnigan, Joseph. "TV Teletype," *TV Guide*, May 25, 1974.

Finnigan, Joseph. "TV Teletype," *TV Guide*, May 24, 1975.

Folkart, Burt A. "Ken Curtis; Played Festus on *Gunsmoke*," *The Los Angeles Times*, April 30, 1991.

Freeman, Don. "Back in the Saddle Again," *TV Guide*, February 5, 1977.

Harding, Henry. "For the Record: Farewell to Dodge," *TV Guide*, December 2, 1961.

Harding, Henry. "For the Record: Autry's Loss," *TV Guide*, September 8, 1962.

Hughes, Mike. "Blake Remains TV's First Liberated Woman," Gannett News Service, September 26, 1987.

"I Can't Live Up to What People Think I Am," *TV Guide*, February 24, 1979.

Jenkins, Dan. "TV Teletype," *TV Guide*, June 23, 1962.

Johnson, Ted. "Western Reserve," *TV Guide*, January 8, 2000.

Klasne, William. "Why *Gunsmoke* is Still Going Strong After 18 Years," Associated Press, July 20, 1973.

Laurent, Lawrence. "*Gunsmoke* Aiming for Even 20 Years," Gannett News Service, March 9, 1973.

Lloyd, Robert. "Appreciation: James Arness, 1923-2011," *The Los Angeles Times*, June 3, 2011.

Lovell, Glenn. "Gunsmoke Still Riding Tall in the Saddle," *The Chicago Tribune*, September 2005.

MacKenzie, Robert. "McClain's Law," *TV Guide*, January 16, 1982.

Magers, Boyd. *Western Clippings*, 1998–2011.

Mark, Norman. "*Gunsmoke*: Togetherness on the Long Trail," *The Chicago Daily News*, May 29, 1971.

Mark, Norman. "Goodbye, *Gunsmoke*, We Knew You When," *The Chicago Daily News*, May 2, 1975.

"Marshal from Minneapolis," *TV Guide*, May 11, 1957.

"Matt Dillon Hanging Up Guns," Associated Press, April 30, 1975.

"Milburn Stone of *Gunsmoke* Dies," *The Chicago Sun-Times*, June 13, 1980.

"Miss Kitty Feels Right at Home," Associated Press, May 27, 1985.

"Mona Lisa of the Long Branch," *TV Guide*, December 10, 1960.

Morhaim, Joe. "She Who Never Gets Kissed," *TV Guide*, March 15, 1958.

O'Hallaren, Bill. "When Chester Forgot to Limp," *TV Guide*, August 23, 1975.

O'Hallaren, Bill. "Holy Gunsmoke, It's Matt Dillon and Miss Kitty Back at the Long Branch!," *TV Guide*, September 26, 1987.

Oliver, Myrna. "Rites for Amanda Blake of Gunsmoke Planned," *The Los Angeles Times*, August 18, 1989.

Phillips, Dee and Bev Copeland. "Riding High on the Waves of Indignation," *TV Guide*, June 12, 1965.

Raddatz, Leslie. "Home, Home in the Clink," *TV Guide*, July 20, 1963.

Raddatz, Leslie. "I Love Amanda," *TV Guide*, June 6, 1964.

Raddatz, Leslie. "Look What's Happened to These Dodge City Citizens," *TV Guide*, August 17, 1968.

Raddatz, Leslie. "The Dodge City Gang," *TV Guide*, March 18, 1972.

Raddatz, Leslie. "Dodge City's Designated Hitter," *TV Guide*, December 8, 1973.

Rosenberg, Howard. "When James Arness Talks, People Listen," *The Los Angeles Times*, November 18, 1981.

Salisbury, Ann. "Physician, Heal Thy Show," *TV Guide*, March 19, 1988.

Scott, Vernon. "Doc Restless in Retirement," United Press International, January 1978.

Seiler, Michael. "Guess What *Gunsmoke*'s Got," Gannett News Service, December 1, 1973.

"Spare Your Sympathy," *TV Guide*, January 25, 1958.

Stahl, Robert. "Gunsmoke," *TV Guide*, November 26, 1955.

"Tall in the Saddle—and On the Ground Too—Part 1," *TV Guide*, November 25, 1961.

"Tall in the Saddle—and On the Ground Too—Part 2," *TV Guide*, December 2, 1961.

"Television's Tight Little Band," *TV Guide*, January 11, 1964.

Thomas, Bob. "*Gunsmoke* Actor Weaver Dies at 81," *The Los Angeles Times*, February 27, 2006.

"Where Westerns Are Filmed," *TV Guide*, April 5, 1958.

Whitney, Dwight. "Why *Gunsmoke* Keeps Blazing Away," *TV Guide*, December 6, 1958.

Whitney, Dwight. "It Looked Like Ol' Matt Was Through," *TV Guide*, August 22, 1970.

EPISODE INDEX

INDEX OF TELEVISION SHOWS, FILMS & PLAYS

Index of Names

Rothwell, Robert: 364, 400, 408

Rowe, Arthur: 373, 383, 386, 391

Rowland, Henry: 310

Rubin, Benny: 401

Rudley, Herbert: 163, 175

Ruffino, Val: 264

Rumsey, Burt: 153, 161, 163, 164, 165, 206

Rupp, Jack: 467

Ruskin, Joseph: 264, 354

Russell, Bing: 144, 157, 200, 236, 252, 359, 451, 452

Russell, Jackie: 372, 463

Russell, John: 458

Russell, Kurt: 127, 313, 452

Russell, William D.: 166, 171, 173, 175

Rust, Richard: 205, 217, 235

Rutherford, Gene: 365

Rutherford, Lori: 437

Ryan, Fran: 60, 123, 135, 429, 457, 463, 464, 465

Rydell, Mark: 317, 323, 327, 328, 335, 339, 340, 349, 351, 352

Ryder, Alfred: 203

Ryder, Eddie: 436

Saber, David: 168

Sage, Willard: 186, 316, 334, 341

St. John, Marco: 436, 454

Salmi, Albert: 341, 363, 414, 500

Sampson, Robert: 366

Sanchez, Marco: 470

Sande, Walter: 250, 327, 394, 397, 424

Sanders, Hugh: 262

Sanders, Steve: 361

Sandor, Steve: 381

Sanford, Donald S.: 408, 411, 417

Sarafian, Richard C.: 324, 367, 377

Sargent, Dick: 263

Sargent, Joseph: 168-69, 210, 269, 280, 291, 292, 320, 331, 334

Sarracino, Ernest: 413

Savage, Paul: 6, 94, 102, 106, 125, 130, 133, 136, 292, 293, 296, 300, 307, 308, 334, 336, 337, 343, 356, 363, 380, 386, 389, 390, 434, 437, 445, 446, 450, 452, 456, 461

Saxon, Aaron: 191

Saxon, John: 327, 340, 353, 369, 461

Scarfe, Alan: 471

Schallert, William: 184, 202, 292, 385, 402, 444

Scharf, Sabrina: 393

Schiller, Norbert: 150

Schneider, Joseph: 369

Schuck, John: 394, 404

Schultz, Keith: 372

Schuyler, Dorothy: 145, 149, 157, 171

Schwartz, Sam: 160

Scollay, Fred J.: 337, 363

Scott, Brenda: 287

Scott, Evelyn: 149, 150

Scott, Jacqueline: 60, 104, 109, 116, 204, 275, 309, 353, 370, 382-83, 395-96, 427

Scott, Ken: 323

Scott, Pippa: 257-58, 423

Scott, Richard D.: 417

Scott, Simon: 453

Scott, Walter: 447

Scotti, Vito: 339, 369, 394, 414

ABOUT THE AUTHOR

David R. Greenland has been writing professionally for nearly forty years. His work has appeared in numerous newspapers and magazines, including *Classic Images*, to which he contributes the monthly "What's Out There" column. He is the author of *Bonanza: A Viewer's Guide to the TV Legend*, *Rawhide: A History of Television's Longest Cattle Drive* (both available from BearManor Media) and co-author of *Inside the Fire: My Strange Days with the Doors* by B. Douglas Cameron. He first visited Dodge City during the summer of 1968.